World Literature:

1800 TO THE PRESENT
Second Edition

Arthur H. Bell, Vincent F. Hopper, and Bernard D.N. Grebanier

BARRON'S

All inquiries should be addressed to:
Barron's Educational Series, Inc.
250 Wireless Boulevard
Hauppauge, New York 11788

Library of Congress Catalog Card No.: 94-6600
International Standard Book No. 0-8120-1812-5

Library of Congress Cataloging-in-Publication Data

Bell, Arthur, H., 1946–
    World literature / by Arthur H. Bell, Vincent F. Hopper, and Bernard
D.N. Grebanier. — 2nd [rev.] ed.
        p.   cm. — (College review series)
    Rev. ed of: Essentials of European literature. 1952.
    Includes bibliographical references and indexes.
    Contents: 1. Early origins to 1800 — 2. 1800 to the present.
    ISBN 0-8120-1811-7 (v. 1). — ISBN 0-8120-1812-5 (v. 2)
    1. Literature—History and criticism. I. Hopper, Vincent Foster, 1906– .
II. Grebanier, Bernard D.N., 1903– . III. Bell, Arthur H. (Arthur Henry), 1946– .
Essentials of European literature. IV. Title. V. Series.
PN524.H6   1994
809—dc20   94-6600
                                                                            CIP

PRINTED IN THE UNITED STATES OF AMERICA
4567 9770 987654321

PREFACE

Beginning with the early waves of Romanticism that swept across borders and cultures, the world literature of the past two centuries has witnessed an opening of the floodgates to many new themes, forms, approaches, and readers. Particularly of note is the shift toward politicization of literary texts, a movement comparable in many ways to the religious influence on texts, authors, and readers in the Middle Ages and early Renaissance. Also apparent is a new freedom on the part of the writer to express aspects of human experience judged in earlier times to be too peculiar, individual, precious, or distasteful for public view. That freedom extends as well to the lives of writers, whose wandering paths have ushered in a fascination with biography and autobiography as literary genre.

In short, the story of modern world literature is rich in surprise, detail, and implication. This updated and expanded edition seeks to add to that richness by including new discussions of Proust, Gide, Beauvoir, Camus, Genet, Duras, Böll, Grass, Mauriac, Gorky, Pasternak, Solzhenitsyn, Kafka, Pessoa, Garcia Lorca, and many others. This edition also looks beyond European literatures to consider the substantial achievements of African, Chinese, Japanese, Indian, and Latin American literatures. New features such as the "Works at a Glance" summaries, review questions, bibliographies, and glossary are intended to make this edition even more useful for both the student and general reader. As in previous editions, it has been our goal to tell the story of world literature clearly, but without refuge in oversimplification. World literature in the past two centuries contains a glorious mixture of puzzlement and contradictions. This general guide is best used not as a way around the challenges and difficulties of texts and literary movements but as a bridge directly to them.

Arthur H. Bell
University of San Francisco
April 1994

PREFACE
TO THE FIRST EDITION

This book was written with the express intention of filling the long-felt need for a dependable and comprehensive guide to Continental European Literature. It is hoped that herein will be found the answers to the many questions that inevitably plague the reader who adventures into an unfamiliar literary realm.

There was a time when our teaching of literature was confined exclusively to the study of English and American authors, because it was then believed that advanced study of a foreign language was necessary for the reading of non-English men of letters. But, gradually, educators have come to realize the absurdity of turning out college graduates who had studied works of minor English writers but who had never even read such masterpieces as Dante's *Divine Comedy* or Goethe's *Faust*. Even in the traditional survey course in English literature, the relationship of English to continental literatures soon became apparent; the English Renaissance, for example, must be understood as much more an outgrowth of continental literary trends than a development of its Anglo-Saxon and Middle English predecessors.

Considerations such as these prompted the gradual introduction into college curricula of literature courses which would more nearly than in the past approximate Matthew Arnold's conception of literature as "the best that has been thought and said in the world." Under such titles as "Comparative Literature," "General Literature," "Humanities," and "Great Books," many new courses have accordingly been devised in which translations of foreign books are studied as texts either exclusively or in conjunction with English works.

Concurrently, several excellent new anthologies and many new translations and inexpensive reprints of good earlier translations have been published or are in the process of being prepared. The attractiveness of these translations, together with the popularity of a few excellent radio programs which range far and wide in their discussions of great books, has disclosed to many literate adults the hitherto-unsuspected treasures which exist outside of the strictly "Anglo-Saxon" world.

Having all these things in mind, the authors have tried to put together a book which will be as readily available as the translations themselves, which will acquaint the reader with the outstanding European authors, which will relate these authors to the cultural patterns of their respective milieux, and which will heighten the reader's understanding and enjoyment of the books themselves. In order to bring into focus the many historical trends, aesthetic developments, national tendencies, and highly individualized artistic talents, the authors have adopted what they believe to be a sensible plan of organization. A total view of the history of European literature is conveyed by the chapter divisions, beginning with the early Middle Ages. The guide to the different national literatures will be of assistance to those who are interested particularly in the literary history of a single country.

Since the general aim of these volumes has been to examine European literature as a whole, each chapter is concerned with a single phase of continental literature, opening with a comprehensive description of the period in question. The ensuing subdivisions of most of the chapters then concentrate on the national literatures which were outstanding during that period, beginning with general discussion and then turning to the examination of individual authors. Major authors are given extended treatment; lesser authors are touched on briefly. The first volume covers the Christian era up to the end of the neoclassic period. The second volume opens with the Romantic Movement and carries the literary history well through the end of the nineteenth century. An index is added at the end of each volume to provide ready reference for those seeking information on a specific author, book, literary trend, or historical period.

A third volume provides an extensive bibliography which will serve as a guide for readers who require English translations of foreign works. It also provides a well-arranged compilation of reference books in English on authors, national literatures, and periods for those seeking more extensive information on a particular phase or section of the broad field surveyed in the first two volumes. We believe that this bibliography alone would justify these volumes, since no comparable bibliography for the needs of the general English-reading student is now in existence.

Although the hobgoblin of consistency has been perpetually tugging at our elbows, this grim spectre has been often deliberately warded off for the sake of holding to the criterion of inclusion of what will be most valuable to English-speaking readers. For example, Dante's religious epic is usually described as "The Divine Comedy" (not *La Divina Commedia*), but Dante's "Hell" is customarily referred to by its Italian title, *Inferno*. Because of such charming inconsistencies among English readers, the authors have listed both the original titles and their translated titles, but have given prior position to whichever version has become habitual in the English-speaking world. The same criterion, usefulness to English readers, has guided the authors in their selection of material, the placing of emphasis, and the kind and extent of treatment accorded individual authors and titles.

In a number of colleges, masterpieces of English literature are also included in the courses for which this work is intended. To supplement these pages on Continental literature, we call attention to Prof. Grebanier's *The Essentials of English Literature* issued by the same publishers in two volumes, to which our own volumes are companions in the series. If we may quote from the preface to that book, we too feel that "a history of literature can justify itself only to the extent that it succeeds in inviting its reader to study and enjoy the literature described." We too hope that the student "will find in this book much of the assistance required for sound reading, as well as enough pregnant suggestion to encourage the formation of individual judgment and opinion." ... "With little sympathy with that company of 'scholars' which is familiar with literature by date and title only," the authors have provided summaries, commentaries, and background materials connected with major works to "smooth the road for the reader who goes directly to the work itself."

In the preparation of this comprehensive survey, the authors are keenly aware of their indebtedness to generations of scholars, translators, and literary historians. We are also indebted to the many instructors throughout the nation who in their enthusiasm for this book when projected have been extremely generous in supplying valuable information concerning European Literature courses given at their respective colleges, and, less obviously, we are indebted to the many students, past and present, whose questions and perceptions alike have indicated the kind of material which a book of this kind should contain. A special acknowledgment of gratitude is owed to Prof. Rod W. Horton of New York University for his contributions on several scholarly matters and to Miss Catherine Grace for her expert assistance in the preparation of large portions of the manuscript.

Vincent F. Hopper
New York University
Bernard D. N. Grebanier
Brooklyn College
June 15, 1952

CONTENTS

Part 2
THE GOLDEN AGE OF
GERMAN LITERATURE

Part 3
THE RISE OF REALISM AND NATURALISM

Part 4
THE RISE OF RUSSIAN LITERATURE

Part 5
EXPERIMENTATION AND REVOLT

Part 6
RECENT DIRECTIONS FOR MAJOR WORLD LITERATURES

CHRONOLOGY OF HISTORICAL AND

HISTORICAL EVENTS

Maratha Wars in India
extend British rule
1803

Britain annexes
Australia
1820

Livingstone
in Africa
1840

Coronation of
Napoleon as
Emperor
1804

Death of
Napoleon
1821

Battle of
Trafalgar
1805

Battle of
Leipzig
1813

Iturbide
crowned
Emperor
of Mexico
1822

Greek
Independence
1829

Peninsular
War in
Spain and
Portugal
1807

Battle of
Waterloo
1815

Monroe
Doctrine
1823

Abolition of
slavery in the
Commonwealth
1833

Shaka
Zulu
begins
reign
1819

First Opium War
1839

War
of 1812

Revolutions
in France,
Austria,
Germany,
and Italy
1848

Grimm
brothers,
Fairy Tales
1812

Stendhal,
*Le Rouge
et le Noir*
1830

Goethe,
*The Elective
Affinities*
1809

Dumas,
*The Three
Muskateers*
1828

Mme. de Staël,
Corinne
1807

Leopardi,
Canzoni e Versi
1824

Gogol,
Dead Souls
1842

Novalis,
Hymn to the night
1800

Hugo,
Odes
1819

Andersen,
Fairy Tales
1835

LITERARY EVENTS

LITERARY EVENTS

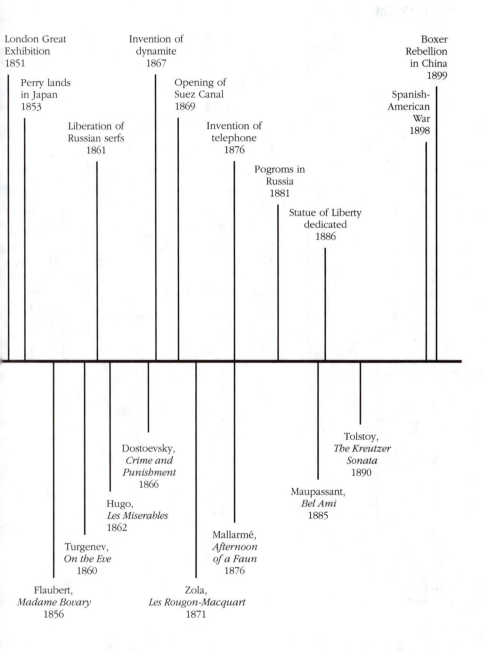

London Great
Exhibition
1851

Perry lands
in Japan
1853

Liberation of
Russian serfs
1861

Invention of
dynamite
1867

Opening of
Suez Canal
1869

Invention of
telephone
1876

Pogroms in
Russia
1881

Statue of Liberty
dedicated
1886

Boxer
Rebellion
in China
1899

Spanish-
American
War
1898

Dostoevsky,
*Crime and
Punishment*
1866

Hugo,
Les Miserables
1862

Turgenev,
On the Eve
1860

Flaubert,
Madame Bovary
1856

Mallarmé,
*Afternoon
of a Faun*
1876

Zola,
Les Rougon-Macquart
1871

Maupassant,
Bel Ami
1885

Tolstoy,
*The Kreutzer
Sonata*
1890

CHRONOLOGY OF HISTORICAL AND

HISTORICAL EVENTS

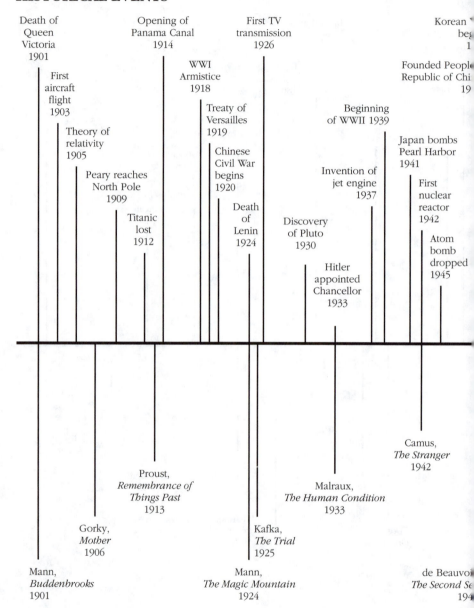

Death of
Queen
Victoria
1901

First
aircraft
flight
1903

Theory of
relativity
1905

Peary reaches
North Pole
1909

Titanic
lost
1912

Opening of
Panama Canal
1914

WWI
Armistice
1918

Treaty of
Versailles
1919

Chinese
Civil War
begins
1920

Death
of
Lenin
1924

First TV
transmission
1926

Discovery
of Pluto
1930

Hitler
appointed
Chancellor
1933

Beginning
of WWII 1939

Invention of
jet engine
1937

Korean
be
1

Founded People
Republic of Chi
19

Japan bombs
Pearl Harbor
1941

First
nuclear
reactor
1942

Atom
bomb
dropped
1945

Mann,
Buddenbrooks
1901

Gorky,
Mother
1906

Proust,
*Remembrance of
Things Past*
1913

Mann,
The Magic Mountain
1924

Kafka,
The Trial
1925

Malraux,
The Human Condition
1933

Camus,
The Stranger
1942

de Beauvo
The Second Se
194

LITERARY EVENTS

LITERARY EVENTS

Above the timeline (world events):

Independence of Ghana 1957

Warsaw Pact 1955

Death of Stalin 1953

Cuban missile crisis 1962

Gagarin first man in space 1961

Castro takes Cuba 1959

Assassination of John F. Kennedy 1963

Chinese Cultural Revolution 1966

Resignation of De Gaulle 1968

Britain, Ireland, and Denmark join EEC 1973

Man on the moon 1969

End of Vietnam War 1975

SALT II Treaty USSR invades Afghanistan 1979

Assassination of Sadat 1981

Gorbachev becomes USSR leader 1985

Chernobyl nuclear accident 1986

Seoul Olympics 1988

Dissolution of the U.S.S.R. 1991

Completion of Channel Tunnel 1993

Below the timeline (literary events):

Frank, *The Diary of Anne Frank* 1955

Grass, *The Tin Drum* 1959

Pasternak, *Doctor Zhivago* 1957

Márquez, *One Hundred Years of Solitude* 1967

Solzhenitsyn, *One Day in the Life of Ivan Denisovich* 1962

Böll, *Group Portrait* 1973

Naipaul, *A Bend in the River* 1979

Calvino, *Polomar* 1984

Kundera, *The Unbearable Lightness of Being* 1985

Gordimer, *My Son's Story* 1991

Walcott, *Omeros* 1992

Boll and Vennewitz, *Irish Journal* 1993

Part *1*

THE ROMANTIC MOVEMENT IN FRANCE AND ITALY

WORKS AT A GLANCE

Jean-Jacques Rousseau

1750	*Discourse on the Sciences and the Arts*		1762	*Émile; The Social Contract*
1752	*The Village Soothsayer*		1763	*Letters from the Mountain*
1755	*Discourse on the Origin of Inequality*		1764–1770	*The Confessions*
1758	*Letter to d'Alembert*		1782	*Reveries of a Solitary*
1761	*The New Héloïse*			

Abbé Bonnot de Condillac

1754	*Treatise on the Sensations*

Claude Adrien Helvétius

1758	*Concerning the Spirit*	1771	*Concerning Man*

Paul-Henri Thiry d'Holbach

1770	*The System of Nature*

Julien Offray de la Mettrie

1748	*The Man-Machine*

Constantin François de Chasseboeuf, Count Volney

1787	*Travels in Egypt and Syria*	1791	*The Ruins of Empires*

Jacques Turgot

1761	*On the Progress of the Human Spirit*	1767	*Letter on Tolerance*

Marie Jean Antoine Nicolas Caritat, Marquis of Condorcet

1776	*Reflections on the Corn Trade*	1794	*Sketch for an Historical Picture of the Progress of the Human Soul*

André Marie Chénier

1784	*Elegies*	1795	*Idylls*
1786	*Bucolics*	1795	*Iambs*

Jacques Henri Bernardin de Saint-Pierre

1773	*Voyage a l'Ile de France*	1788	*Paul and Virginia*
1784	*Studies of Nature*		

François-René de Chateaubriand

1797	*Essay on Revolutions*	1831	*Historical Studies*
1801	*Atala*	1834	*Voyage to America*
1802	*The Genius of Christianity*	1836	*Essay on English Literature*
1807	*René*		
1809	*The Martyrs*	1844	*Life of Rancé*
1811	*Journey from Paris to Jerusalem*	1848–1850*	*Memoirs from Beyond the Tomb*
1815	*On Bonaparte and the Bourbons*		
1826	*The Natchez; The Adventures of the Last of the Abencérages*		

Mme. de Staël

1796	*On the Influence of the Passions on Happiness*	1806	*Corinne*
		1810, 1812	*Concerning Germany*
1800	*On Literature*	1818	*Considerations on the French Revolution*
1802	*Delphine*		
1804	*On the Character of M. Necker and of His Private Life*	1821	*Ten Years of Exile*

Benjamin Constant

1816	*Adolphe*

Joseph de Maistre

1819	*On the Pope*	1821	*On the Gallic Church; Saint Petersburg Soirées*

Xavier de Maistre

1794	*Journey around My Room*

Étienne Pivert de Senancour

1804	*Obermann*

Alphonse Prat de Lamartine

1820	*Meditations*	1825	"The Last Song of Childe Harold's Pilgrimage"
1823	*New Meditations*		

*Date of Composition

Alphonse Prat de Lamartine (continued)

1835	Travels in the Orient	1830	Poetical and Religious
1836	"Jocelyn"		Harmonies
1838	"The Fall of an Angel"	1849	Les Confidences; Graziella;
1847	History of the Girondins		Raphael

Victor-Marie Hugo

1822	Odes et Poésis Diverses	1859, 1877,	The Legend of
1826	Odes and Ballads	1883	Centuries
1827	Cromwell	1862	Les Misérables
1829	Les Orientales	1866	The Free Theater;
1830	Hernani		Toilers of the Sea
1831	The Hunchback of Notre	1869	The Man Who Laughs
	Dame; Autumn	1872	The Terrible Year
	Leaves	1874	Ninety-three
1832	The King Amuses	1877	The Art of Being a
	Himself		Grandfather
1835	Songs of Twilight	1878	The Pope
1837	Inner Voices	1879	The Supreme Pity
1838	Ruy Blas	1881	Religions and
1840	Rays and Shadows		Religion; The Ass
1843	The Burgraves	1882	The Four Winds of the
			Spirit; Torquemada

Alfred de Musset

1830	Tales of Spain and Italy; The	1835–1837	Nights
	Venetian Night	1836	Don't Swear About
1833	André del Sarto; The Whims		Anything
	of Marianne	1836	Letter to Lamartine
1834	Lorenzaccio; You Don't	1836	Confessions of a Child
	Trifle with Love		of the Age
1835	Rolla	1836	Tales

Alfred de Vigny

1826	Poems Ancient and Modern;	1835	Tales of Military Servitude
	Cinq-Mars		and Grandeur; Chatterton
1831	The Marshall of Ancre	1864	The Fates
1832	Stello		

Alexander Dumas *père*

1829	Henry III and His Court	1841	A Marriage under Louis XV
1830	Christine	1843	The Ladies at Saint-Cyr
1831	Charles VII; Richard of	1844	The Three Musketeers; The
	Arlington		Count of Monte Cristo
1832	The Tower of Nesle	1845	The Black Tulip
1839	Mlle. de Belle-Isle		

Théophile Gautier

1830	*Poésies*	1852	*Enamels and Cameos*
1833	*Albertus; The Comedy of Death*	1856	*"The Romance of a Mummy"*
1835	*Mademoiselle de Maupin*	1861–1863	*Captain Fracasse*

Charles-Augustin de Sainte-Beuve

1828	*Historical and Critical Sketch of French Poetry in the Sixteenth Century*	1840–1860	*History of Port-Royal*
		1844	*Literary Portraits; Portraits of Women*
1829	*The Life, Poetry, and Thoughts of Joseph Delorme*	1846	*Contemporary Portraits*
		1857–1862	*Monday Chats*
1830	*Consolations*	1860	*Chateaubriand and His Literary Circle*
1834	*Pleasure*	1863–1870	*New Mondays*
1837	*August Thoughts*	1875	*First Mondays*

Pierre Jean de Béranger

1815	"The Garret"	1825	"Memories of the People"
1815	"The King of Yvetot"	1825	"The Good Old Woman"
1825	"Roger Bontemps"	1833	"The Beggars"

Charles Nodier

1802	*The Outlaws*	1822	*Trilby*
1803	*The Painter of Salzburg*	1839	*The Novena of Candlemas*
1818	Jean Sbogar	1844	*Brisquet's Dog*

Alexander Soumet

1822	*Clytemnestra; Saul*	1827	*The Maccabees; Joan of Arc*
1824	*Cleopatra*		

August Barbier

1832	*Iambes*

Gérard de Nerval

1851	*Travels to the East*	1855	*The Gallant Gypsy*
1854	*Daughters of Fire*		

Casimir Delavigne

1815, 1827	*The Messenians*	1829	*Marino Faliero*
1819	*The Sicilian Vespers*	1832	*Louis XI*
1821	*The Pariah*	1833	*The Children of Edward*

Count Vittorio Alfieri

1775	*Cleopatra*	1784	*Orestes*
1777	*Philip II*	1787	*Mary Stuart*
1779	*Polynices*	1786	*Saul*
1781	*Antigone*	1804	*Autobiography*

Alexander Manzoni

1815	*Sacred Hymns*	1822	*Adelchi*
1820	*The Count of Carmagnola*	1825	*The Betrothed Lovers*
1821	"The Fifth of May"		

Giacomo Leopardi

1826	*Verses*	1846–1880	*Collected Works*

1
THE EARLY FRENCH ROMANTICS

THE GEOGRAPHY OF ROMANTICISM

That powerful reaction against Neoclassicism in liberation of the imagination and rediscovery of Nature, which literary history calls the Romantic movement, in its beginnings eddied back and forth among England, France, and Germany. Its first faint ripples were in mid-eighteenth-century Britain among a group of poets who, in one way or another, deliberately violated neoclassical precept: Thomson, Gray, Collins, Macpherson, Chatterton, and Cowper. These men, and certain of their English contemporaries, though in most respects typical sons of the Age of Reason, tended to turn their backs upon cities and centers of culture for their inspiration, and to seek subjects and settings for their poems in mountains and valleys, forests and meadows, brooks and roaring cataracts. None of these poets was a great genius, and none of them wrote of these subjects with much excellence; all of them employed a vocabulary either too elaborate or too recondite to give conviction to their effusions on Nature. But what they wrote was sufficiently original, appearing as it did when Neoclassical authorship was at its height—sufficiently original to seem startlingly fresh at the time, and certainly attractively unorthodox to their admirers in France and Germany, as well as in England. It would be impossible to exaggerate the vogue, for instance, of Macpherson's *Ossian*, which today strikes us as being more silly than inspired: a great poet like William Blake never outgrew its influence; it was the favorite book of Napoleon, Chateaubriand, and Lamartine; and it exercised an overwhelming effect on Goethe when he was young.

The next great impetus to the Romantic movement originated in France, where it took on a political cast. No single author did more to accelerate the philosophy of Romanticism in Western Europe than did Rousseau; but a number of the French Neoclassical writers contributed their share. Voltaire, Diderot, and the Encyclopedists were indeed rationalists, but to the extent that they helped formulate the concept of "the Rights of Man," opposed the philosophy of the Old Regime, and paved the way for the French Revolution—to that extent they too influenced the Romantic movement. The comedies of Beaumarchais, with their satire at the expense of the upper orders, also fell in with the new spirit of political independence associated with the Romantic movement, despite the classicism of their style.

There were other writers in eighteenth-century France with whom we have presently to deal who strengthened Romanticism in France: Chateaubriand, Mme. de Staël, and Bernardin de Saint-Pierre, to mention the leaders.

Soon after these French beginnings, the younger contemporaries of Lessing in Germany began to develop other aspects of the Romantic movement, very often under the direct influence of Shakespeare and the English pre-Romantic writers (like Thomson and Macpherson): young Goethe, young Schiller, and others of their generation.

The first full-fledged Romantic movement, stimulated by the earlier English and French beginnings and somewhat by German literature and philosophy, arose in England in the poetry of Blake, Burns, Wordsworth, Coleridge, and Southey. Rousseauistic influences are strong in the work of all these men (with the possible exception of Coleridge, who was more deeply immersed in German transcendental philosophy). It is common to date the Romantic movement in England as officially opening in 1798 with the publication of the *Lyrical Ballads*, containing poems by both Wordsworth and Coleridge. (Burns, in fact, was dead by then, and Blake had written and published, without a public, the works by which he will be best remembered. But the prestige of the *Lyrical Ballads* somewhat justifies its claim to usher in the Romantic movement.) A second generation of English Romantics, by then profoundly stirred by the tendencies emanating from Germany as well as France, gave English literature some of its best-loved poetry in the works of Byron, Shelley, and Keats. To this period also belong the enormously popular novels of Sir Walter Scott, and the essays of Lamb and Hazlitt. With the death of Byron in 1824, the great period of Romantic poetry in England was over.

This imposing body of English Romantic creativeness for a second time made English literature a great influence on the continent, particularly among French authors. French literary historians account the height of the French Romantic movement as lying between the first of Lamartine's *Meditations* in 1820 and the last of Hugo's important tragedies, *The Burgraves*, in 1843. The great French writers of this period were Lamartine, Hugo, Musset, Vigny, Gautier, George Sand, Sainte-Beuve, Dumas *père*, Stendhal, and Merimée.

THE NATURE OF ROMANTICISM

We have said of Classicism that it aims above all at clarity, lucidity, and simplicity. Neoclassicism preferred dignity to passion, cleverness to fervor, and cold good sense to exalted inspiration. Because of the Neoclassical desire for clarity, form was of great consideration to the practicing Neoclassicists. Correctness in style, conduct, ideas, and social values became of paramount importance. Purely personal enthusiasms and dissatisfactions were not their concern; they sought the common denominator in human experience and emotional reaction. Alert to deviations from the norm, they were typically satirists, their intelligence critical more often than creative. This avoidance of the particular caused them to use a formalized diction to avoid vulgarity, and a generalized vocabulary to avoid overtones of singularity. Elegance, polish, wit—these were the attractions of Neoclassicism. It prided itself on keeping the emotions well subjugated to the dictates of logic.

The Romantic movement was primarily a reaction against Neoclassicism, a rebellion in behalf of aspects of human nature and experience that Neoclassicism tended to thwart. George Saintsbury has said, with considerable insight, "Classicism might be said to be method and Romanticism energy." If Neoclassicism made much of order and lucidity, Romanticism made much of freedom and imagination. We find Romantic writers in revolt against the authority of reason; they accorded a higher place to the productions of the imagination. Also, far from seeking to avoid the personal and isolated experience, they gloried in their individualism. It was with them that the first person singular began to stud the pages of books. They treasured the traits that distinguished each of themselves from other human beings. They often demonstrated a lively interest in the welfare of humanity, but they sought to understand the problems of the world only through the prisms of their own personalities. If the Neoclassicists were conformists, the Romantics were—often violently—individualists.

The Romantics were also, as we have said, rediscoverers of Nature. Wild countrysides bored the typical Neoclassicist, who could tolerate Nature only when tamed into geometric patterns or graceful vistas. Neoclassical writers spoke of "nature" often enough, but they always used the word to mean *human* nature. The Romantics, more concerned with their own personalities than with anyone else's, became enamored of untamed Nature—towering mountains, overhanging rocks, thick forests, dim caves, tempestuous seas. They also discovered the charm of country people, simple folk who had never been exposed, as they saw the situation, to the baleful influence of urban culture—innocent men and women who grew up under the beneficent tutelage of Nature alone.

The elegance of Western culture, of which the Neoclassicists had been most proud, became the bane of the Romantics. Their imagination longed to dwell on far-off, exotic lands. And whereas the Neoclassicists had been interested exclusively in their own times and contemporary society, the Romantics' thoughts were most at home in a romantic past—the Middle Ages or even primitive eras.

Finally, it may be said of the Romantics that they were extraordinarily fond of suffering. They considered it a badge of superiority to go about with blighted, melancholy feelings, to be deeply affected by everything they saw or experienced; to find the tragic implication in the most trifling occurrence was a proof to them that they were sensitive.

Any discussion of the origins of Romanticism is likely to consider at the outset the writings of Jean-Jacques Rousseau. Of him it has been said that no man, with the exception of Jesus, has exerted a greater influence on the thoughts of mankind.

JEAN-JACQUES ROUSSEAU (1712–1778)

Considering the vast influence of Rousseau upon the thought of the Western world, we are all the more astonished to find how little of the thinker there is in his writings. He deemed himself, and is invariably presented as, a philosopher; but he had nothing resembling a philosophic system, and he is often illogical and inconsistent. Second to none in charging the atmosphere with the kind of thought that turned men's minds to revolution, Rousseau is actually reactionary in his fundamental ideas. In this respect Rousseau was almost alone among the prominent philosophes of his century. Men like Voltaire, Montesquieu, and Diderot were convinced that society is capable of improvement through the amelioration of social institutions. Fundamentally their teachings imply the axiom that the conditions of life are subject to almost indefinite betterment; humanity can learn to apply more and more intelligence to the solution of its problems, and society thereby will become better than it has been. Some of the rationalists went much further; Condorcet, for example, insisted (as did the English rationalist, Godwin) that society was actually improving all the time, and that the exercise of reason would someday make people virtually perfectly happy. But Rousseau, to begin with, distrusted the exercise of reason altogether; moreover, he found his golden age in the past, not the future. Humanity, he taught, had foolishly surrendered the felicity it once had had; to recapture it, people must turn back the clock, and pattern life according to the model furnished by the days of the patriarchs Abraham and Isaac. Today it is little short of amazing to consider the paradox that such being the basis of his thinking, Rousseau could still have been the most revolutionary influence of his time.

Rousseau's writings are peppered with ideological assertions, all of them beyond possibility of proof or historical demonstration. Rationalists like Voltaire and the Encyclopedists held Hobbes's view that people are by nature selfish; but they also believed that the logic of self-interest would teach people to improve social institutions and to evolve better government through clear-headed criticism. Rousseau, however, believed that people are by nature "benevolent." It is society that has corrupted them. All that people call civilization has really operated to destroy their happiness; society has distorted their intrinsic goodness and is responsible for the development of evil.

The villain in the human make-up, according to Rousseau, is the reasoning faculty. "Cold reason has never accomplished anything," he declared. Only emotion is worthy of reliance. Reason usually leads one to error; only the emotions know the pathway to truth. Rousseau went so far as to affirm that whenever he *thought*, he was likely to be wrong, and that it was only when he *felt* that he was bound to be right. It is perhaps his complete rejection of the values of the Age of Reason that accounts for his prestige. To eighteenth-century readers hungering for an emancipation of the feelings, he seemed to be giving a philosophic basis for emotional indulgence.

Certainly the vogue of Rousseau demonstrates the power of mere rhetoric over quietly reasoned thought. The emotional energy of his prose was as responsible as anything for his ability to win over the public. Colored by his emotional outbursts, the moving periods of his style could persuade where the sharp shafts of Voltaire's wit struck in vain. A Swiss by birth, Rousseau came as a stranger to French literature, which already had a long tradition of rationality. No Frenchman would have thought of opening a discussion, as does Rousseau, with the bland remark: "Let us begin by laying aside the facts, since they have nothing to do with the matter."

The Confessions

In his fifties Rousseau spent several years (1764–1770) writing his autobiography, *The Confessions,* one of the most amazing books ever written. It is a strange mixture of unblushing (and unflattering) self-revelation and pretentious self-justification; in many details the narrative is highly suspect, particularly when there are no facts against which to check. However, our knowledge of Rousseau's earlier life is almost entirely dependent upon the account in *The Confessions.*

Although *The Confessions* is one of his last works, it nevertheless seems advisable to begin our discussion of Rousseau with it since it is the authority for any account of the years before he became a celebrity.

Jean-Jacques Rousseau was the offspring of a line that originated in France but had, as Protestants, found refuge in Switzerland during the sixteenth century. Rousseau's mother died giving birth to him. His father, a clockmaker of Geneva, was a man of little principle and undisciplined habits, who made a disordered attempt to begin his son's education. At the age of ten the boy was committed for two years to the tuition of a clergyman. After that Jean-Jacques was apprenticed to an engraver, for whom he did little work. Overstaying his hours of freedom one night, the boy decided to run away to Confignon, a Catholic hamlet near Geneva, and presented himself to the curate as an intended convert to Catholicism. That worthy sent him on to Mme. de Warens at Annecy, an ardent Catholic; she shipped him off to Turin for his conversion. In a few months the youth again ran away, and entered service as a lackey. Leaving that employment, he wandered about for a year, and moved from Lyons to Fribourg, to Geneva, to Berne, to Paris—to mention only a few of his stops. Penniless in the French capital, he returned at the age of twenty-one to the protection of Mme. de Warens. He was both a retainer and a lover of his mistress, a good-natured woman whose religion, despite her zeal for converting Protestants, owned more than a touch of deism. She was easy in her morals, kind in intention, and a better friend to Rousseau than he ever seemed to understand. She interested herself in his education, and sent him to St. Lazare for training in the classics, and appointed a music master for him. A vagabond by temperament, he suddenly set out for Lyons, and on returning once more to Annecy found Mme. de Warens not there. With scant knowledge of music, he set himself up as a teacher of music at Neuchâtel and gave a recital at Lausanne. Soon he was acting as secretary to a visiting Greek in Switzerland. Inveterately the vagabond, he wandered off to Paris. Learning that Mme. de Warens was now living at Chambéry, he traveled there on foot, and was affectionately welcomed by her. In 1736 to please Rousseau, whose health was impaired, she took a country house near Chambéry, *Les Charmettes*. Here he read much and dreamt more, indulging his fantasies to the limit. In 1738 ill-health gave him a new excuse for going off to Montpellier with a Mme. de Larnage. Naturally enough, when he returned once more to the establishment of Mme. de Warens he found another man installed as favorite. In 1740, therefore, feeling himself in too menial a position now, he accepted the post of tutor in the de Mably family at Lyons. At the end of a year he had thrown that employment up, and returned to *Les Charmettes* for a brief time. But in 1741 he quit the home of Mme. de Warens forever. He was determined now to cut a figure in the world of music at Paris through a new system of musical notation that he had invented.

These expectations proved vain. But he came to know at Paris Diderot, Fontenelle, and the Marquise de Broglie. The last-named procured him a position with the French Embassy at Venice in 1743, but at the end of the year he quarrelled with the ambassador and was back in Paris.

Rousseau now turned to writing music, and his opera *The Gallant Muses* attracted the attention of the Duke de Richelieu. Now began the period of his greatest social success. He was presented at the salon of Mme. d'Épinay. Although he was later to attack the manners of the upper classes, he had no objection to them at this time, and thoroughly enjoyed basking in the company of celebrated people. It was at this time too that he contracted a relationship that was to be life-long with a servant in a tavern, Thérèse Levasseur. She was an unattractive, illiterate woman, but deeply devoted to him. She also possessed a mother who proved the chief plague of Rousseau's life. According to Rousseau's own account, Thérèse bore him five children, illegitimately; these, despite the high-minded concern over the rearing of children he expressed in his epochal *Émile*, he abandoned to the mercies of a foundling asylum, almost as soon as each was born. Despite the many attacks of his enemies upon Rousseau for his acknowledged treatment of his offspring, there seems good enough reason to doubt that any of these children ever existed. Rousseau never saw any of them, and some scholars have shown evidence that they were the invention of Thérèse and her mother to assure the permanency of Rousseau's interest in his mistress. Towards the end of his life, Rousseau indeed did go through a marriage ceremony of sorts to "legalize" his relationship with Thérèse.

By Diderot Rousseau was entrusted with the commission of writing the articles on music for *The Encyclopedia*. His circle of acquaintance among the great increased rapidly.

It was in 1749 that he came into his own in the field of authorship, the field in which at last he was to achieve fame. He learned in that year of a prize to be offered by the Academy of Dijon for an essay on the topic: "Have the sciences and the arts contributed to the purifying of morals?" In 1750 Rousseau's prize-winning essay was published as the *Discourse on the Arts and Sciences*, and he became immediately famous. His enemies insisted later that he owed his ideas to Diderot's suggestion.

For reasons hard to fathom Rousseau now gave up a lucrative post offered him at the receiver-general's office, and went to live in garret lodgings, where he supported himself, as he did for most of the rest of his life, by the unprofitable drudgery of copying music. He was still, however, a frequenter of the salons. At the court he presented an opera of his composition, *The Village Soothsayer* (1752), and it was well received. He was slated for a pension, but with inexplicable indifference in a man so hungry for success, he did not obey a summons to appear at Court. Instead, deciding that he wished to make peace with his fellow Genevans, he returned to his native city for a visit in 1754, and once more embraced the Calvinistic faith.

In 1755 there appeared a new *Discourse* by him, also written on a question proposed by the Academy at Dijon: the origin of inequality among mankind. Rousseau's *Discourse on the Origin of Inequality* did not win the prize this time, but was eminently popular. It was on a subject of great interest to its author, and has ever been one of his most widely read works.

Mme. d'Épinay now bestowed upon Rousseau and his Thérèse a cottage, celebrated as the *Hermitage*, and for a year (1756) Rousseau lived there working on his lengthy novel *La Nouvelle Héloïse* (*The New Eloisa*, as it was soon called in its English translation). The novel was partly inspired by his infatuation for Mme. d'Épinay's sister-in-law, Mme. d'Houdetot, who was already equipped with a husband and a lover, and therefore not prepared to indulge his passion. Rousseau's worst traits were thereby encouraged; he became suspicious of everyone, and was convinced that his friends Diderot, Grimm, and Duclos were treacherously misrepresenting him to Mme. d'Épinay. Many quarrels ensued, which Thérèse and her mother did their best to augment, and Rousseau began to be considered too much of a liability to his benefactors. Mme. d'Épinay invited him to accompany her on a visit to Geneva; Rousseau chose to interpret this graciousness as a command given to an inferior, and his refusal was most offensive. In consequence he was asked to leave the *Hermitage* in December 1757.

The break with Mme. d'Épinay's circle proved a turning point in his life. Thereafter he was at open enmity with Diderot, the Encyclopedists, and their friends. At his little house in Montmorency he composed his *Letter to d'Alembert* (1758), an attack on the stage in general and on Voltaire and d'Alembert in particular. D'Alembert had suggested the establishment of a theater in Geneva, where public plays had been forbidden since the days of Calvin. Rousseau, in answer, attacked tragedies for encouraging our passions, and comedies for making us too cruelly conscious of the ridiculous. He even went so far as to accuse Molière of encouraging vice in his masterpieces by making us laugh at virtuous men. Voltaire's plays also came in for a drubbing.

Considering, in addition, Voltaire's passion for the theater, it is hardly to be wondered at that Rousseau became *persona non grata* to Voltaire's circle of friends.

Rousseau's neighbors at Montmorency, the Marshal of Luxembourg and his lady, became his patrons now. He was often at their château and met there men and women in the highest ranks of French society; and in 1759 they turned over a wing of their house for his living quarters. These were the years in which his most important work was finished and saw publication. In 1761 *La Nouvelle Héloïse* was published, and achieved great popularity. In 1762 *Émile* was published both in Paris and the Netherlands; in the same year the *Social Contract* also appeared at Amsterdam. While this important creative activity was proceeding, Rousseau's noble patrons were called upon to exercise the utmost tact and forbearance, for their captive genius was often rude and always egocentric. Their patience and goodness to him were uniformly exemplary.

But his days of prosperity were over, even as his fame was at its height. The parliament at Paris condemned *Émile* in June 1762, and asked for the arrest of the author. Warned by Mme. de Luxembourg, Rousseau escaped arrest in the Marshal's own carriage and fled to Switzerland. The governor of Neuchâtel proved a good friend to the author. But turbulence had become Rousseau's native element, and when the Genevan Council also condemned *Émile*, Rousseau renounced the Swiss citizenship of which he had been so proud, and in his *Letters from the Mountain* (1763) bitterly attacked the constitution of Geneva. This behavior did nothing to increase his popularity in the vicinity, and believing himself threatened, he quit the neighborhood for the Île St. Pierre on Lake Bienne. Here he was able to enjoy for the last time a short period of peace and tranquillity in rural surroundings. The government, however, ordered him to leave its territory, and, after some hesitation as to where to go next, Rousseau accepted the generous offer (1765) of the great Scottish philosopher, David Hume, to come to him in England and make his home there. He traveled via Paris to England, where he arrived in January, 1766. It is up to this point of his life that *The Confessions* takes us.

Rousseau had made the acquaintance of James Boswell, Samuel Johnson's great biographer, and it was into Boswell's hands that Rousseau confided the task of managing Thérèse's transportation to England. London society began to lionize the great exile, though he professed to find all those attentions noxious. To placate him, Hume was able to negotiate with a Mr. Davenport of Derbyshire an arrangement for Rousseau's dwelling with the latter, so that he could be in the country, as he loved to be. It was there that Rousseau composed most of *The Confessions*. His own bad temper delayed the granting of a pension by George III to him, though he blamed his benefactor Hume for that. Finally, unreasonable in his accusations and suspicions, he wearied even patient Hume, whom Rousseau expected to quarrel with his own best friends for no reasons. In May 1767 Rousseau fled to France, not without writing letters libeling those who had been kindest to him. He was briefly entertained by the father of Mirabeau and by the Prince de Conti—but could not tolerate either long. He wandered about again, helped everywhere, and everywhere turning on his benefactors. In 1770 he was back in Paris again, earning his living by copying music once more. He finished his *Confessions*, and composed his *Rêveries du Promeneur Solitaire* (*Reveries of a Solitary*), a sequel to the *Confessions*. His imaginary enemies were ever on the increase, however, and at last, the tired victim of a persecution complex, he accepted the kind offer of hospitality extended by a wealthy man, de Girardin; Rousseau was installed by him at a little house in Ermenonville. He had only a few months of joy in the country there, poisoned by his suspicions of Thérèse's faithfulness. When he died, apparently of apoplexy, on July 2, 1778, rumors began to circulate that he had commited suicide.

IMPORTANCE

Despite his capacity for making enemies of the best-intentioned of friends, Rousseau's reputation increased by leaps and bounds after his death. He became a great hero to the French Revolution, and the principles of the *Social Contract* inspired much of theory of the Jacobin party. The fact that his appeal was unreasoned and emotional made him much more influential on the republicans than the logical Montesquieu or the critical Voltaire.

His influence has been even more lasting in fields beyond politics. In education the tendency known as "progressive" can be traced right back to *Émile* with its basic idea that teaching should never outstrip the interest or desire to learn on the part of the pupil. In religion, Rousseau's break with the atheistical implications of the rationalists had not a little to do with a revival of religious enthusiasm. In literature, particularly through *La Nouvelle Héloïse* and the *Confessions*, Rousseau did more than anyone else to spread through Europe the vogue of sentimentalism that had had its timid beginnings earlier in the century in England. And, perhaps most important of all, it is to Rousseau that we can particularly trace that sensitiveness to the beauties of nature that we associate with the Romantic movement. The power that Wordsworth was to find in the meanest flower to stir the deepest thoughts in him he must have learned, consciously or unconsciously, from Rousseau; it is just such reflections in the presence of nature that make Rousseau the most original man of his generation. There is much point in Goethe's observation: "In Voltaire we see the end of a world; in Rousseau the beginning of a new one."

Before taking leave of the man himself, we should say a few words about the *Confessions* as a work of literature. Despite the questionableness of some of the details of his life as related by the author, the *Confessions* is amazing for the candor with which he tells of acts that most men would be at the greatest pains to conceal. If Rousseau is remembered as one of the world's most ungrateful and ungracious men, it is because he himself has broadcast the fact to the world. Nothing is more characteristic of the Romantic movement than its passionate devotion to self-revelation. The *Confessions* of Rousseau set the vogue for that.

Discourse on the Sciences and the Arts

Rousseau was thirty-seven when he published his first work, *Discours sur les Sciences et les Arts*. Nevertheless, though he commenced his career as a writer this late, the fundamental bias of his teaching is here completely revealed: In his review of the old heroic virtues of the ancient Romans, he upholds the superiority of the simple life to the manners of an artificial society like that of Paris in his own day. The *Discourse* (1750) is made up of two parts. The first, written with scant knowledge, is an historical survey of society, and deals with the examples of Egypt, Sparta, Athens, Rome, and contemporary Europe. He concludes:

> Men ought to learn from Nature that like a mother snatching a dangerous weapon from the hands of her child, she would have preserved us from science…. All the secrets she conceals are just so many evils from which she would protect us…. Men are perverse; but they would have been far more unhappy had they had the misfortune of being born learned.

The second part of the *Discourse* is "philosophical" and attempts to explain how the arts and sciences have managed to corrupt humanity. He concludes that the only knowledge worth acquiring is the knowledge of virtue—and for that we do not need the arts and sciences. "The principles (of virtue) are engraved on every heart."

The piece is written in a style more suitable to oratory than to formal prose, and is full of inconsistencies in argument. But it caught the public's imagination.

Discourse on Inequality

This *Discourse* (*Discours sur l'Origine de l'Inégalité parmi les Hommes*) (1755) begins with a long and flattering dedication to the Republic of Geneva, of which Rousseau constantly reminded the world he was a citizen. After the preface, Rousseau plunges into a description of primitive man, living in felicity in the happy ignorance that constitutes a state of nature. Primitive man was in perpetual good health just because he did not know how to think. "A state of reflection is a state contrary to Nature…. A thinking man is a depraved animal." Clothes were a superfluity, and man lived long without them. Man's senses were then more powerful than now; they protected him from danger when it was imminent. Rousseau next indulges in a long and fanciful history of the origin and development of language. After this digression, he turns to a refutation of Hobbes' axiom that man in a state of nature was a vicious creature, perpetually at war against his fellows. On the contrary, our author insists that intrinsic in human beings is the great virtue of compassion. And from compassion stem the equally valuable virtues of benevolence and friendship—and by these the natural man lived. The primitive man, knowing love only on the physical level, was not subject to the violence that civilized refinements have introduced into the relationship of the sexes.

Part Two of the *Discourse* opens with one of those dramatic unprovable assertions for which Rousseau's writings are notorious: "The first man who enclosed a piece of ground, and said 'This is mine!' and found people foolish enough to believe him, was the real founder of civil society." This remark begins Rousseau's attack on private property—a revolutionary point of view that in itself was enough to make him the most original radical of his day. The work then proceeds to trace the development of human society until men lost their felicity. Man first ceased living as an individual and took to group existence. With the growth of families, homes were built, and men claimed ownership of the ground they cultivated. From this practice enmities began to develop. The next step found the most powerful men making alliances among themselves against the weak, and thus inequality came into existence. "Usurpations by the wealthy, theft by the poor, and the unrestrained passions of both, stifled the cries of natural compassion and the feeble voice of justice, and men were of a piece with greed, ambition, and evil." It was in this fashion that war first arose. Time and custom have perpetuated inequality in defense of those who own property and position. As for government, in the days of the patriarchs there was a just balance maintained between the need of protection and mutual restraint. Since then government has become increasingly evil. Oppression has steadily gained "ground without the oppressed's being able to know where it must end." The logical conclusion of the tendency of government will be a society in which no individual has anything, and there will be no law but the will of the ruling despots.

In the Appendix, Rousseau reaffirms his conviction that man is naturally good. "What has made him depraved to such an extent if not...the advances he has made and the knowledge he has gained?" Compare civilized man with the savage. "Savage man, when he has dined, is at peace with all of nature, the friend of all his fellows." Civilized man, on the other hand, "after having swallowed up treasures and ruined multitudes of people, ... ends by cutting every one else's throat until he makes himself master of the world."

La Nouvelle Héloïse

Julie ou la Nouvelle Héloïse (*The New Eloisa*) appeared in 1761. The title of this novel was inspired by the fact that its hero is the tutor of the heroine, in love with her, at one time her lover, and unable, because of circumstances, to marry her—a series of relationships that was true of the historic medieval lovers, Eloise and Abelard. There, of course, the similarity ends, for nothing could be further from the intense religious scruples of the scholar Abelard than the Rousseauistic egocentricity of the novel's St. Preux, unless it be the disparity between the high-principled Eloise and the sentimental Julie.

Julie d'Étanges is in love with her tutor St. Preux but is compelled to marry the noble Volmar. She does her best to remain a devoted wife to him and a loving mother to her children, but she is tortured by her frustrated passion for her old tutor. Volmar, the perfect rationalist-unbeliever, is a man of high principles, though cold in temperament. When his wife confesses her passion for St. Preux, he decides to prove his confidence in her ability to behave rationally. St. Preux, who has been wandering inconsolable among wild mountainous regions to forget his blighted love affair, is invited to come to the Volmars' and live with them. St. Preux accepts, but finds that living under the same roof with Julie is a constant torment and temptation to both of them. The impossible situation is terminated only by the death of Julie.

The novel is written in epistolary form, the correspondents being St. Preux; Julie; Julie's cousin Claire; an English philanthropist, Lord B—; and Volmar. St. Preux became the type of the unhappy, sensitive lover of nature, so dear to the Romantic movement, particularly after Byron accorded him so much worship. Rousseau's model was the English novelist Richardson's *Clarissa Harlowe*, but far exceeds its lachrymose original in the excess of its sentimentality. The long rambling novel is a fanciful confusion of social criticism, rhapsody, egotism, morbidity, and preaching. Its hostility to the nobility and its warm sympathy for the peasant are new and important notes contributive towards Romanticism. Also, as everywhere in Rousseau, there are endless raptures over the beauties of the countryside and mountains especially, and a reveling in emotion for emotion's own sake.

Though the novel as a whole is interesting now only for its great historical importance, it contains passages of lasting interest: St. Preux's critical picture of Parisian society, theaters, salons; the disquisition on suicide; the tributes to the mountain district of the Valais and Lake Geneva. It is from these pages that the romanticism of much of the poetry of Lamartine and the prose of Chateaubriand, Mme. de Staël, and George Sand stems.

The Social Contract

The Social Contract (*Le Contrat Social*) appeared in 1762. It is Rousseau's most important piece of political writing, and has been called "the catechism of the French Revolution." There are not any new ideas in this treatise, but Rousseau's impassioned prose found readers where his predecessors found none.

The First Book discusses the origin of the contract by which society has organized itself; the Second Book examines the concept of the "general will"; the Third Book deals with the problem of government; and the Fourth Book deals with civil religion.

According to Rousseau, government exists to carry out the will of the people. When the people set up a government to execute their will, they do not surrender their supreme authority. The government is therefore subject to recall or change at the sovereign will of the governed. It is not true, as has been often carelessly stated, that Rousseau espoused representative government such as we know it. Considering the will of the people supreme, Rousseau rejects the right of representatives to think for the people.

The basis for Rousseau's ideas in the *Social Contract* is the concept of the General Will. He distinguished between "the will of all" and the "general will." The will of all "takes account of private interests"; the general will "takes account of only the common interest." Without pretending that the will of the majority is always on the side of justice, he does maintain that under ideal conditions it is likely to be so. The government of despotism never can express the general will; a popular government alone can do that. In the latter, the individual surrenders willingly some of his private rights for the good of the rest of the community. Such rights are willingly surrendered to a good government. When a despot requires the surrender of private rights, he is only voiding the contract between the people and the government.

Émile

It is possible that *Émile* (1762) contains more of Rousseauistic teaching than any other of his works. As has been said, its publication brought denunciation on Rousseau's head from the authorities of Paris and was responsible for his long exile from the capital. Nevertheless, it remains the most fundamental of all books in the history of modern educational theory.

To call it a novel, as is common practice, is absurd. It does not even pretend to have a plot: the children Émile and Sophie are destined to marry each other and eventually do; the book is simply a tract showing how each is prepared by an ideal education for that event.

In a sense all that Rousseau had written was a preparation for *Émile*. Rousseau had established his conviction that man is by nature benevolent, and that it is society that corrupts that goodness into evil. To undo the malevolent effects of civilization, we must revise our ideas of education. *Émile* undertakes to show by practical example what that ideal education is.

Book One deals with the infancy of the child. Rousseau inveighs against the custom of well-to-do women sending out their babies to be nursed. He insists that a mother should suckle her own child. The swaddling of children also comes in for objections. The tutor appointed for Émile merely watches the child during these years to see that he does not acquire bad habits.

Book Two shows the tutor taking over Émile's education in earnest, his objective not being, however, as was habitual, to prepare his young charge for the institutions of contemporary society. Rather is the tutor's function the preserving of the boy from those baleful influences. Hence Émile is raised in the country. With his tutor ever by his side, little Émile is encouraged to learn by himself. He must never be urged or coerced into studying any subject. The time will come, Rousseau feels, when the boy will understand the need of acquiring various kinds of learning; and that is the time when each may best be acquired. Thus, little Sophie writes letters to her friend, and Émile, not knowing how to read or write as yet, is forced to rely upon his tutor. Finding this dependence an invasion of his privacy, the boy is now ripe for learning how to read and write and asks to be taught those skills. There is to be no reliance on books. Émile's mind is developed through conversations, object lessons, and artfully contrived experiments worked out with his teacher. There is to be no punishment for misdemeanors on Émile's part. If in a bad mood he smashes the windowpane in his room, he will be chilly at night, and thus learn more effectively the error of what he has done. When children are "disobedient, wicked, lying, greedy," it is only because they have learned those traits from their elders. Émile is to have plenty of physical training—swimming, racing, games. His regime is fairly Spartan; there are to be no soft beds for him to sleep on, and no shoes to guard his feet; his diet is to be chiefly vegetarian and sparse.

Book Three finds Émile already the "excellent animal" his preceptor planned. It is now time for him to develop his mind. Literature is still largely avoided. Émile is trusted with *Robinson Crusoe*, which has the advantages of being laid in a natural setting and of showing the resources of human ingenuity when deprived of the aid of civilized implements (and—also—the advantage of being English!). The materials upon which Émile's tutor continues to draw are still mostly aspects of nature. The lad is taught some astronomy by watching the motion of the sun, and some physics and biology by what he perceives in the garden. To prepare him for the necessities of life, he is also taught a trade—that of carpenter.

Book Four finds our pupil at the age of sixteen, when the awakening of the life of the senses brings the challenge of moral values. Émile is now allowed to mingle with human society, but particularly with an eye to cultivating in him the emotions of pity, self-respect, and generosity. It is now time too that he acquire a religion. The passage dealing with this matter constitutes the most celebrated pages of Émile, and has been known as the *Confession of Faith of the Savoyard Vicar*. Émile is taken by the vicar up a mountain below which the valley of the Po is unfolded in all its splendor. While the boy is deeply moved by that beauty, the vicar explains his own "natural religion," a kind of sentimental deism. For him the basis of religion is his belief in the existence of God and in the immortality of the soul. All matter is directed by the laws of God. One has no need of religious dogmas, for the heart tells us that there is a God, and that the world operates according to His wishes. To understand God one should shun books and study Him in Nature. Christ he admires as the gentlest and wisest of men; he does not commit himself as to Christ's divinity. This kind of faith, while obnoxious to the orthodox of Rousseau's own time, as the condemnation at Paris proves, is still a long distance from the cold rationalism of Voltaire and his circle whose opinions (whether consciously or unconsciously so) imply atheism, or certainly skepticism of Deity. *The Confession of Faith of the Savoyard Vicar* is written in Rousseau's most impassioned style, and shows his prose at its most powerful.

Émile is now ready for the business of living. Physically and morally he is safe from the contagions of the society in which he must mingle. But he is to remember that he will be safest in the country, nearest his best friend, Nature.

Since Émile ought now to marry, we turn our attention to the rearing of Sophie, whose whole education has been framed to make her Émile's ideal mate. Her training has been along the natural lines taken by Émile, but it never occurs to Rousseau that she too has a soul that ought to be cultivated for its own sake. The only point of view in the mind of her educator is that she must be prepared to make Émile happy. The function of women is to please men, "to be useful to them, to be loved and honored by them, to bring them up when young, to take care of them when old, to advise and console them." It is to those ends that Sophie's education is pointed. Few women today would be satisfied with such a program, as revolutionary as Rousseau's ideas were for his own time!

Émile concludes with the marriage of Sophie and Émile; Émile's tutor comes to live with them to educate their children.

Agreement or disagreement with Rousseau's precepts depends chiefly on whether one believes that the conduct of goodness is the product of nature or civilization. Adverse critics could point out that Nature can be cruel and is often indifferent to mankind's well-being; are not kindness and considerateness of other human beings lessons that civilization teaches? But whether basically right or wrong, Rousseau taught the world that children ought to be encouraged to make the best of their abilities instead of having learning imposed upon them, and beyond question *Émile* is responsible for the humanizing of educational methods. The educational theories of Pestalozzi, Froebel, and Richter were inspired by the book. In the realm of philosophy, Rousseau's reaction against the cold rationalism of his contemporaries made its mark on Kant, Fichte, Herbart, Goethe, Schiller, and Herder. "Progressive education" in our own time began with *Émile.*

OTHER PRE-REVOLUTIONARY PHILOSOPHES

In addition to Rousseau, there are a number of other philosophes who should be considered here because of their closer relation to the Romantic movement. The philosophes were not, technically speaking, really philosophers but rather literary men. For that reason histories of philosophy tend to ignore them. On the other hand, they were readable—and, moreover, widely read—to the degree that few professional philosophers have been, and for that very reason have been influential when the latter have been almost unknown to the general public. The philosophes aired their views in salons and, after exchanging views with their confrères, wrote their opinions in volumes uncluttered with the technical terms of professional philosophy.

Abbé Bonnot de Condillac (1715–1780)

The Abbé Bonnot de Condillac wrote copiously on many subjects, partly as a result of his being tutor to the grandson of Queen Marie Leczinska. But his best-remembered work is his *Traité des Sensations* (*Treatise on the Sensations*), published in 1754. A disciple of Locke, Condillac undertook to prove that all our ideas are merely "sensations transformed." He reduced the human understanding to the basic principle of perception. Man, he said, is like a statue in whom sensations have been aroused by the five senses. Condillac's prose is polished and clear, and succeeds in making the presentation of abstract ideas highly attractive.

Though a clergyman himself, Condillac influenced a whole school of antireligious thinkers, for this account of the origin of human ideas leaves deity out. The school itself, in reaction against the rationalists, was an influence upon the Romantic movement, with its stress upon intuitive processes of thought.

Claude Adrien Helvétius (1715–1771)

Claude Adrien Helvétius was a wealthy man of Swiss family. When still very young, he was appointed to the lucrative post of Farmer-General of Taxes, but soon gave that up to become Chamberlain to the Queen. A great frequenter of the *salons*, thirsty for a name in the world of letters, he was well-liked for his kindliness and many philanthropies. He married (1751) a noted beauty of the nobility, Mlle. de Ligneville, who made her home a celebrated attraction for literary men and women.

When Helvétius's *De l'Esprit* (*Concerning the Spirit*) appeared in 1758, it became notorious in religious circles, and was ordered burned for its immorality. After his death (1771) his *De l'Homme* (*Concerning Man*), a work of inferior quality, was published, and was bitterly attacked; Diderot himself wrote against it.

De l'Esprit is highly characteristic of the work of the *philosophes* from a stylistic point of view. It moves charmingly on the surface of ideas, is full of anecdote, and makes no pretense to heavy profundity. It is an attempt to base morality on a theory of selfishness, completely omitting any connection of moral codes with organized religion. There are brilliant passages in the book and some well-taken criticism of social corruption. Like Condillac, Helvétius traces ideas to sensation.

Some critics have recently shown that the materialism of Helvétius, with its insistence that people curb their selfishness out of consideration for the general good, predicts nineteenth century Utilitarianism. The most altruistic of men, Helvétius accounted for benevolence as proceeding from selfish motives; it was this point of view that authorities and Rousseauists alike found shocking.

Paul Henri Thiry d'Holbach (1723–1789)

Of all the antireligious philosophes, none went further than the Baron Paul-Henri Thiry d'Holbach, a German by birth and a Parisian by preference. His *Système de la Nature* (*The System of Nature*), which was published in 1770, was one of the major scandals in the literature of his day. Unabashedly materialistic in philosophy, d'Holbach described deity as a human invention to explain away the injustices of the world. There is a world mechanism of which humanity is but a part, and in which people serve without any freedom of action. Matter is eternal and in eternal motion; what we call Accident is a disguise for our ignorance of the laws by which matter acts. When human beings die, the soul no more exists than a clock can strike once it is broken.

The book was extreme enough to cause both Voltaire and Frederick the Great to object to it. Diderot, however, approved of it. The book's blistering assault upon government as in opposition to nature, and upon the injustices and cruelties of political institutions made it a great favorite of young radicals. It is written in a style that varies between real energy and dull oratory.

Julien Offray de la Mettrie (1709–1751)

Julien Offray de la Mettrie was a physician who is remembered for his *L'Homme-Machine* (*The Man-Machine*) (1748), a work that attempts to deny the existence of spiritual processes in people, and reduces all thoughts and acts to automatic responses of the human body. Voltaire, who did not agree with him, thought him a writer of some talent.

Constantin François de Chasseboeuf, Count Volney (1757–1820)

Volney spent four years of his earlier manhood traveling through Egypt and Syria. In 1787 he published his account of those travels in *Voyage en Egypte et en Syrie*. During the French Revolution he became a member both of the States-General and of the Constituent Assembly. His most important book, *Les Ruines, ou Méditations sur les Révolutions des Empires* (*The Ruins of Empires*, as it became known in England), was published in 1791. It is a contribution to the philosophy of history, and predicts the unification of all religious faiths through the apprehension that they all contain truth in common with one another. The book contemplates the decay of past kingdoms, once glorious, through wicked laws and corrupt governments. The despotic limitation of liberty and the lies of the priestcraft against natural law have always meant the death of any given civilization.

Les Ruines is Rousseauistic in the extent to which it glories in melancholy and sentimental reverie. It sounded many notes enchanting to the ear of the Romantics. With the English poet Shelley it was a powerful influence on his work.

Volney, who objected to the excesses of the Terror, was imprisoned but luckily escaped execution. In 1795 he came to the United States for a three-year visit. On his return he was appointed senator during the Consulate. He had known Napoleon earlier, attempted to resign when Napoleon became emperor, but was made a nobleman by the latter.

Les Ruines is no longer read, but it was highly esteemed in its own time, for Volney embodied all the most appealing qualities of the philosophes: their humanitarianism, their dislike of injustice, their hostility to organized religion, and their belief in the ultimate triumph of libertarian principles.

Jacques Turgot (1727–1781) and the Physiocrats

Jacques Turgot was so much a man of principle that unlike some of his fellow-philosophes he refused to enter the Church, for which he had been destined, because of his own distrust of religion. Through his family's influence he was given a post of great power at Limoges when he was in his early twenties. It is said that if his reforms had been followed generally throughout France, the century might have ended by taking far different paths from those upon which the Revolution hurled it. Under Louis XVI he was appointed Minister of Finance for the country (1774) and tried valiantly to curb the expenses of the Court and its entourage. Naturally, such conduct won him many enemies—among whom figured prominently Marie Antoinette. After two years, therefore, he was forced to resign. Luckily, he died before his opponents reaped the whirlwind they had sown.

Turgot's chief contribution to his country was not literary. By his abolition of forced manual labor, the corn laws, and the closed guilds, he gave Frenchmen freedom to work. His writings include several articles for the *Encyclopedia*, some memoirs, and a number of Latin discourses delivered at the Sorbonne. One of these discourses, *On the Progress of the Human Spirit* (1761), clearly enunciates the theory of a philosophy of history—one of the earliest of its statements—and shows the evolution of one age from the preceding. *His Letter on Tolerance* (*Lettre sur Tolerance*) (1767) is also worthy of note.

Turgot was the leading economist of a group known as the "Physiocrats." The name was invented by Pierre Samuel Dupont de Nemours (1739–1817), who ended his days in the United States near Wilmington, Delaware. Assistant to Turgot, he was the author of *Physiocratie, ou Constitution Naturelle du Gouvernment le Plus Avantageux au Genre Humain* (*Physiocracy, or the Natural Constitution of that Government Which Would Be Most Beneficial to the Human Race*), published in 1768.

The Physiocrats argued that all individuals comprising society have the same rights, no matter how their abilities may vary. Every man is taught by nature how to pursue his own best interests. Society is so organized as to limit, as it were by contractual arrangement, the rights of each individual only at the point where such rights interfere with the rights of others. Governments as such are evil, but necessary; hence governments should be limited to interfering with the natural rights of others only to the degree that they are safeguarding the natural rights of everyone. The right to work and to enjoy the fruits of work must not be molested. (We have seen how Turgot carried these theories into practice.) Freedom of exchange must be allowed full play; no monopolies should be tolerated; and no limits must be set to free competition. Among the Physiocrats, it was Jean Claude Marie Vincent, the Sieur de Gournay (1712–1759) who coined the famous phrase "laissez faire."

The Physiocrats (whose name comes from two Greek roots meaning *nature* and *to rule*) then went on to reason that the only productive labor is that which adds to the sum of raw materials available. The wealth of a nation consists in the excess of products from the land over production costs. The state should give every aid to agriculture, but should also impose the burden of the nation's taxes upon it.

Their doctrine of the natural rights of buying and selling was an important factor in the development of the French Revolution.

These ideas were first promulgated by a French merchant, Robert Cantillon in 1755 in an essay on *The Nature of Commerce* (*Essai sur la Nature du Commerce*), but it was François Quesnay (1694–1774) who was largely responsible for their attracting notice. Quesnay was physician to Louis XV and his Queen, and contributed copiously to the *Encyclopedia*; his chief work is the *Tableau Économique* (1758). He was deeply stirred by the extreme poverty of the lower classes, and his work was inspired by a desire to find the cause and cure for periodic depressions. He was a man universally admired for maintaining high principles in the midst of court life.

It cannot be said that the Physiocrats ever achieved any wide popularity. In a period remarkable for the gaiety and wit of its prose, the Physiocrats were concerned with a subject too abstruse and themselves too much lacked stylistic charm to interest a public that would read only if entertained. (It is hard to see how any period could have a better stipulation!) Voltaire pilloried them in his *L'Homme aux Quarante Écus* (*The Man with Forty Crowns*); nevertheless the theories of the Physiocrats were very important to Adam Smith in his formulation of the science of economics.

Marquis of Condorcet (1743–1794)

Because of his closeness to Turgot, the name of Condorcet is often linked with that of the Physiocrats. He was one of the noblest and most high-minded men who ever lived. Marie Jean Antoine Nicolas Caritat, Marquis of Condorcet, came of an ancient family and was still a boy when he made a reputation for himself as a mathematician. He was equally interested in philosophy and literature, and eventually became a very good friend of Voltaire, Turgot, and d'Alembert. In 1769 he was elected to the Academy of Sciences, for whose publications he wrote a great deal, often on complicated mathematical topics.

Although his writings include a very wide range of subjects, he was less an original thinker in philosophy than a sound and graceful exponent of the ideas of his time. Under Turgot's influence he wrote several pieces, particularly worthy of note being his *Réflexions sur le Commerce des Blés* (*Reflections on the Corn Trade)*, published in 1776 in behalf of free trade in grain. As a result of the charm of a number of eulogies he composed, he was elected to the French Academy in 1782; indeed, his fame became international, and the Academies at Turin, Philadelphia, and St. Petersburg also made him a member. He wrote a biograph of Turgot (1787) and also one of Voltaire (1787), both of which are admirably written and were widely read. In 1786 he married the extremely beautiful Sophie de Grouchy, who soon had one of the most famous salons of the period.

But Condorcet was to become one of the most pathetic victims of the maelstrom of the Revolution. A sworn democrat, he was one of the most enthusiastic supporters of the French Revolution, despite his rank, and composed voluminous plans for social reforms and suggested any number of ideal constitutions. He was chosen to represent Paris in the Legislative Assembly, was appointed secretary to the Assembly, and was the author of many of the addresses issued in its name, though he rarely spoke himself. Profoundly interested in education, he drew up a plan for a state educational system that was essentially the one adopted later by the Convention. He may thus be said to have laid the groundwork for the educational system as it has functioned in the France of our own time. He was one of the first to declare for a republic—quite in advance of the Jacobins; but he was against the death penalty for Louis. A member of no party, he naturally found himself with many enemies, particularly when he continued to launch courageous criticism at the head of the Convention as the Terror set in. He was condemned at last by that body, and for a while was kept in concealment by the brave Mme. Vernet. In order to spare her the consequences of befriending him, however, he escaped from her home, wandered around for days shelterless and starving, and was recognized as "probably a noble" by the copy of Horace in his pocket. He died in prison a day after his capture, possibly a suicide.

It was while he was living in the shadow of the guillotine that he wrote at Mme. Vernet's his most celebrated work, *Esquisse d'un Tableau Historique des Progrès de l'Esprit Humain* (*Sketch for an Historical Picture of the Progress of the Human Soul*) (1794). Despite his own victimization by the Revolution, Condorcet here could pen one of the most glowingly optimistic pictures ever conceived of the destiny of human society. In this *Sketch* he proves to his own satisfaction that all the evils of the time are a product of the machinations of kings and priests, wicked laws and cruel social institutions invented by the former. Mankind will, however, free itself of its shackles, for it is capable of illimitable progress in the future. The history of the human race is a history of gradual but definite progress, each age being superior to the preceding. Condorcet found three tendencies in this progress: the annihilation of inequality between nations; the annihilation of inequality between classes of society; and the gradual perfection of the nature of individuals in society. The terrible injustices of the Revolution, of which he was so conspicuous a victim himself, did not taint in the least his conviction that all would someday be perfectly happy.

EIGHTEENTH CENTURY PRE-ROMANTIC POETS IN FRANCE

However one may admire French prose of the eighteenth century, little can be said in praise of the French poetry of the same period. The low ebb of poetic taste is sufficiently demonstrated when we recall that Voltaire— whom we hardly ever think of as a poet at all—was recognized as the greatest poet of his time.

Most of the poets were content to imitate without inspiration the masters of the seventeenth century. Jean-Baptiste Rousseau (1669–1741), an imitator of Boileau, burdened his lines with pretentious mythological references; although clever enough, he never rises above artificiality. La Motte-Houdard (1672–1731), dramatist and critic, was best known for his fables in the style of La Fontaine. Louis Racine (1692–1763), son of the great dramatist, proved his Jansenist upbringing by two long poems, *La Grace* (*Grace*) and *La Religion* (*Religion*), both written with a ceremonious elegance.

A slight trend toward Romanticism began with imitation of the English Pre-Romantic poets. The Marquis of Saint-Lambert (1716–1803), a famous figure at the salons, a rival in love to Voltaire, wrote *Les Saisons* (*The Seasons*), published in 1769, a close imitation of Thomson's poem of the same name; this work made the description of natural scenery the fashion—a tendency that distinctly paved the way for the Romantic movement. J. F. Roucher (1745–1794), in his footsteps, composed *Les Mois* (*The Months*), a poem describing he aspects of nature during each month, and published in 1779. The most popular of these descriptive poets, and the man who deserved his success least, was Jacques Delille (1738–1813), whose translation of Virgil's *Georgics* was acclaimed as equal to the original. His best-known poem is *Les Jardins* (*The Gardens*), published in 1782; like his other works it is utterly destitute of real poetic quality. Evariste de Parny (1753–1814), a composer of frivolous and sometimes indecent verses, was nevertheless more gifted than any of these men as he proved in his elegiac poetry, where the melancholy is unaffected and sweet. But the only real poet in France of the eighteenth century was Chénier.

André Marie Chénier (1762–1794)

André Marie Chénier was the son of a Greek mother and a man who lived for a while in Constantinople and then became a French consul at Morocco. Chénier was born at the Turkish capital and was brought to France as a boy, receiving a good education there. At first, in consequence of his mixing as a young man in *salon* society, he wrote some quite insipid mythological verses. For six months in 1782 he served as a cadet in the army but resigned. Back in Paris he came to know a number of literary men, including Beaumarchais and the celebrated painter David. In 1787 he was appointed secretary to the French embassy at London and spent almost four years there. It was during these years that he wrote most of his important poetry. Indeed, after 1790, when he returned to France, he wrote almost no verse at all. His sympathies were with the Revolution, but he was not an extremist. Hostile to the republicanism of the Jacobins, Chénier desired to see France governed by a constitutional monarchy and was active in the defense of Louis XVI's life. Accused falsely of being a royalist, he escaped Paris in August of 1792, and lay in hiding for a while. When he was arrested, it was through the accident of mistaken identity. He was executed July 20,1794, on the same day as his fellow poet Roucher.

Only two of Chénier's poems were published during his lifetime. The rest of his poetry was published long after his death, and then in a sadly garbled condition. The first attempt at an edition of his works (1819) made a great sensation; but no satisfactory edition was published until the end of the nineteenth century.

It is common to consider Chénier a forerunner of the Romantics, but this view is justified only to a limited degree. It is true that his lines have a concreteness of imagery, a color, and a picturesqueness not to be found in the eighteenth century Neoclassicists. And he does, in some respects, seem like a precursor of nineteenth century poets like Gautier, Leconte de Lisle, and Prud'homme. But his ideas are those of his time. His thinking was influenced by the *Encyclopedia*; his artistic tastes were all classical: the ancient Greeks and Latins and the Renaissance humanists. But it is also true that there are a vivacity and fire in his poetry that bespeak genius, and a nobility which French poetry had not known since Racine.

His works have chiefly titles that remind one of his Greek origin. There are forty *Elegies*, written with grace and sensitiveness. The *Bucolics* and the *Idylls* show Chénier at his best. In this collection particularly worthy of note are the pieces: "L'Aveugle" (The Blind One), in which Homer is made to sing about the various themes of Greek poetry; "Le Mendiant" (The Beggar), in which Lycus's daughter wins hospitality for a beggar, who relates his adventures; and "La Liberté" (Liberty), a dialogue between a slave and a goatherd on the evil effects of slavery. While awaiting execution, Chénier wrote his most original work, the *Iambs*, an ironical satire on liberty and justice, which lashes out at the cowardice of his friends; these lines prove how fine a poet France lost at the guillotine.

Jacques Henri Bernardin de Saint-Pierre (1734–1814)

Of all of Rousseau's immediate disciples, none had a greater vogue among novelists than the author of *Paul and Virginia* (*Paul et Virginie*). Jacques Henri Bernardin de Saint-Pierre was a man of caprice, whose moods led him to wander over a considerable portion of the earth—though sometimes his travels were part of his profession of engineer. He visited Germany and Russia, Malta and Mauritius (an island in the Indian Ocean, east of Madagascar). An admirer of Rousseau, he met him in 1771, and from the master he developed a strongly Rousseauistic bent towards sentimentality. Unlike Rousseau's, however, his career is a record of unceasing success. During the French

Revolution, he was made superintendent of the Botanical Gardens in Paris, and Napoleon when Emperor granted him a number of profitable pensions.

In Bernardin de Saint-Pierre's narratives we find the cult of Nature exploited to the full. Nature, according to our author, has only the most beneficent intentions towards humanity; if people will only observe her and learn to understand her, they will know the beautiful and the good. Saint-Pierre's account of his three years' stay in Mauritius was published in 1773 as a series of letters, *Voyage à l'Ile de France* ("Ile de France" was the former name of Mauritius). His *Études de la Nature* (*Studies of Nature*), published in 1784, attempts to demonstrate the existence of God by his observations of Nature. In this work, though the argument is not very conclusive, the descriptions are rather remarkable, often glowing with color.

It is here that the historical importance of Saint-Pierre lies. Rousseau had popularized the kind of landscape to be found in Western Europe. It remained for Saint-Pierre to introduce to the general public the exotic landscape of the tropics. Rousseau had set the stage for Saint-Pierre's lush romanticism, and the latter's *Paul et Virginie* (1788) was greeted with acclaim.

Paul and Virginia: The novel is laid in Mauritius, then called Ile de France, and has a simple plot, which is unfolded by a friend of the families involved in the story. The widow de la Tour, mother of little Virginia, has been disowned by her family in France for her marriage to a social inferior; their child was born after M. de la Tour's death. Marie, who completes this little household, is their black slave, and is married to Domingo, slave to Marguerite, the de la Tours' neighbor. Marguerite was a peasant lass in Brittany until she fled to this tropic island after her lover had betrayed her; the child of this union is Paul.

Paul and Virginia, as might have been expected from the author, are raised according to the ideas in *Émile*; they learn from Nature, are not taught the lore of books, but become (like their elders) highly proficient in the practical arts; their sentimental code of morals also comes from *Émile*, and they mature in an environment of natural beauty and affection from their parents and the slaves. As the children grow up, the comradely feelings they have entertained for each other begin to give way to stronger emotions. Their mothers are not unaware of the change, and plan their marriage—which Virginia's mother is anxious to postpone for a while.

Circumstances now intervene to terminate this happy pastoral life. The aunt of Mme. de la Tour, until now appealed to in vain, agrees to a reconciliation and announces that she intends making Virginia her heir in France. The Governor of the island advises the acceptance of the offer, and Virginia leaves for Europe, vowing eternal love for Paul.

About a year later we discover Virginia in a convent, sent there by her aunt for an education; she finds the rigors of discipline there unendurable. Two years after that a ship is sighted off the coast of Paul's island. The pilot-boat brings joyful tidings: Virginia is aboard the ship, disinherited by her aunt for refusing a marriage arranged for her in Europe; the girl is returning to her true love.

But a terrific storm arises. Virginia out of modesty refuses the aid of a naked sailor, is washed overboard, and drowns. Paul valiantly tries to swim out to the boat, is beaten back by the waves, and loses consciousness. When he recovers he is inconsolable for the loss of Virginia. Two months later he dies of a broken heart, and is soon followed by Marguerite and Mme. de la Tour. Marie and Domingo eventually die, and then only the narrator of the story is left to tell their collective misfortunes.

Time has inevitably tarnished the charm of this sentimental tale. Nevertheless, the vividness of its descriptions of natural scenery is still affecting; they are likely to keep the book alive. Also, the importance of *Paul and Virginia* in hastening the Romantic movement by exploiting the interest of the exotic will insure its being remembered in literary history.

THE FRENCH REVOLUTION (1789–1796)

The cataclysm that we entitle the French Revolution is well enough known in its general significance. To study the philosophes is to study the leading ideas that the Revolution caused to be reduced to practice in the modern world. But the events of the Revolution and of the Napoleonic Era that followed have so often been present to the minds of writers that some outline of the leading incidents—if it be possible to make order out of that chaos—is justified, and even necessary in a history of literature.

The history of the eighteenth century is a history of preparation for the French Revolution. Voltaire, the Encyclopedists, Montesquieu, and Rousseau were the men who above all others paved the way for it on its theoretical side. Voltaire had sponsored the spirit of free criticism of the existing order, and had attacked injustice wherever he perceived it. The *Encyclopedia* had attacked religious intolerance, slavery, excessive taxation, and the penal code; it also turned men's minds to a respect for the natural sciences rather than for theology. Montesquieu had revealed to Frenchmen the superiority of England's limited monarchy to their own despotic government. Rousseau had launched the most powerful attack of all against things as they are; he had pictured modern civilization as enslaving people all their lives, and had everywhere stressed the right to be free and equal with all others.

It has often been remarked that France was the first great European country to sweep away the remnants of feudalism only because Frenchmen were among the least oppressed of Europeans. The philosophes had produced an intellectual atmosphere of enlightenment; the nation was prosperous on the whole; and the peasantry was much better off than elsewhere on the continent. The French agricultural classes looked upon their overlords as robbers whose depredations the law protected, and whose interference with freedom to sell and protect crops was becoming increasingly insufferable. The Court alone continued unenlightened.

On the eve of revolution, Louis XVI was still reasserting his forebears' position: "To me solely belongs the power of making the laws." He levied taxes according to his pleasure, and in one year spent $70,000,000 at his own discretion. He felt free to imprison anyone he wished by issuing sealed letters of arrest (*lettres de cachet*); anyone with influence at Court could jeopardize the personal safety of anyone against whom he held a grudge. Nevertheless, although no constitution or legislative body existed to represent the people, the King was to some degree limited by the parlements, the high courts of law. They claimed the right to protest against new laws to the King, urging that the ministers were not serving the King truthfully, and also could publish their protests. The King could, of course, compel the parlements to accept a law, but after the parlements' adverse publicity he did so at the price of personal prestige. These struggles between the parlements and the King were frequent during the eighteenth century; they did much, of course, to crystallize public opinion against the despotism.

Louis XVI himself, though he had few of the vices of his grandfather Louis XV, was a well-meaning king, but too indolent and badly educated to understand the forces in the midst of which he found himself when he came to the throne at the age of twenty (1774). His young queen, Marie Antoinette, first won the affection of the people by her light-heartedness and gaiety; later the serious scandals in which she became involved turned the public against her.

At first Louis XVI's reign promised well. The monarch appointed the great economist Turgot, whose theories we have already discussed, to the all-important post of Controller-General. But Turgot's wise economies evoked the enemies of the King's favorites, and in 1776 Turgot was dismissed. His successors Necker and Calonne spent recklessly until the latter was forced to report the country on the verge of bankruptcy. To avoid catastrophe Calonne informed the King that "everything vicious" in the State must be reformed.

The first step in the Revolution was the summoning of the Notables (prominent nobles and churchmen) in 1786. The King on that occasion was forced to admit that he needed the aid of his people. Calonne reported on the financial crisis and stressed the need of abolishing special privilege. The Notables would not back Calonne, and so the King dismissed him. The Parlement of Paris now assumed an historic role; it intervened by not only refusing to register new taxes but also by demanding that the only previously existing representative body of the nation as a whole, the Estates General, be called. This body had not been called since 1614, at which time it still maintained the feudal arrangement that gave equal voting power to representatives of the clergy, the nobility, and the people. By 1789, when the Estates General were summoned after a lapse of one hundred and seventy-five years, such a distribution was laughably inadequate to the emergency. Necker, who had been called to office again, agreed that the Third Estate, the representative of the people, should have twice as many votes as nobility and clergy combined.

By ancient custom each town and village had the opportunity to make a list of its grievances (the well-known *cahiers*). These cahiers, "the last will and testament of the Old Regime," prove how anxious the country was for a change in the government. From them emerges clearly the fact that Frenchmen were nearly all desirous of a national constitution to limit the power of the Court. When the Estates General met in May 1789, the Third Estate refused to be considered (as in feudal times) a separate body; it requested nobles and clergy to meet with it. When the two other "Estates" refused, the Third Estate declared itself to be the "National Assembly." This was the first national representative assembly on the continent in modern times. In the famous Tennis Court Oath, the Third Estate vowed to meet thereafter whenever necessary until the kingdom possessed a constitution. When Count Mirabeau urged his fellows not to disband at the King's order, at the end of a joint session of the three Estates, the King was forced to capitulate, and the three Estates met as one.

The King, now alarmed, was advised to dismiss Necker and gather the royal guards about him. The people now likewise determined to procure arms for their own protection, and in a frenzy of patriotism stormed the old fortress of the Bastille (July 14, 1789), where prisoners of state were confined. (This uprising of the people is still celebrated in France as equivalent to our Independence Day.) Volunteers under the enlightened Lafayette organized leading citizens to maintain order against rioting. Following the fall of the Bastille, cities all over France emulated the example of Paris in establishing a municipal government to displace the old aristocratic rulers.

In August 1789, the National Assembly abolished serfdom and other feudal institutions still surviving. Representatives of clergy and nobility surrendered their ancient rights to tithes and hunting privileges. In the same month the all-important Declaration of the Rights of Man was drawn up, a model followed by governments thereafter all over Europe.

The Declaration of the Rights of Man asserted the equality of all men, and the right of all men to participate in the formulation of the laws. It denied the right of governments to arrest and imprison without due process of law. It affirmed the right of every man to remain unmolested because of any of his opinions "provided that their manifestation does not disturb the public order." It described the rights of freedom of speech and the press as among the "most precious rights of man." It insisted on the rights of all men to participate in the fixing of taxes and to require an accounting by the people's representatives in the government.

The student will perceive at once the bearings of the teaching of the philosophes, particularly of Rousseau, upon this historic pronouncement.

When the King delayed ratifying the Declaration of the Rights of Man, rumors of the counterrevolutionary intentions of the Court began to multiply. A mob attacked Versailles in October 1789, and carried off the King to Paris, though protesting that their loyalty to his Majesty was greater than ever. The King, established at his Parisian residence, now became virtually a prisoner of the National Assembly. In November 1789 all the property of the Church was declared national property. Thus far the Revolution had accomplished great reforms without great social upheaval.

In 1790, however, changes began to be more violent. June of that year found the hereditary nobility abolished. Soon large numbers of noblemen began to leave the country, and these émigrés soon began to foment resentment against the nobility by entering into negotiations against France with foreign powers, and actually preparing an invasion of their native country. Louis XVI made matters worse for men of rank by attempting to flee to the border to join the royalists in June, 1791. He and Marie Antoinette were captured and brought back to Paris. Still anxious to maintain a limited monarchy, the National Convention preferred so to interpret the situation as to make it appear that the French people had rescued the King from abductors.

Nevertheless, the incident began to inspire republican sentiments in Paris. One of the numerous political clubs which had sprung up all over Paris, the Jacobins (so-called from the monastery where they first met), acted as a caucus to insure a solid vote against the aristocratic elements in the National Assembly. The Jacobins grew so strong that they felt safe in inviting the public to their meetings, and encouraged the formation of Jacobin clubs throughout France. Thus, in a short time, the Jacobins were able to control public opinion in the country. But at first, when the National Assembly disbanded to make place for the Legislative Assembly provided by the new constitution (October 1791), even the Jacobins were ready to agree to a limited monarchy.

The new Legislative Assembly declared all émigrés conspiring against France as convicted traitors if they failed to return to the country by the end of 1791. It took severe measures against all members of the clergy who would not swear to support the civil control of the church; and it started a war against Austria, which had been too sympathetic to the pleas of the émigrés. The declaration of war in April, 1792 commenced twenty years of war between France and the rest of Europe. Prussia became an ally of Austria immediately. When the Duke of Brunswick threatened to destroy Paris if the King were harmed in any way, the leaders of the Parisian civil government (the Paris Commune), republicans at heart, instigated an attack on the royal palace (August 1792). The Legislative Assembly was now determined to make France a republic. A new Constitutional Convention was summoned in September 1792, and it immediately abolished the monarchy. September 22, 1792 became the first day of the Year One of the Republic.

The radical Paris Commune by this time had rounded up thousands of suspects and executed many of them without much pretense of legal procedure. Encouraged by the successes of the French army, a small majority voted the virtually imprisoned King as guilty of treason, and he was put to death in January 1793. Riding high on the wave of their enthusiasm, the National Convention now offered to help the English achieve a republic too, and declared war on England in February 1793. Spain and the Holy Roman Empire joined the enemies of France, and the republic stood alone against all her neighbors. The French armies began to lose.

To meet the emergency, since the new constitution had not yet been drawn up, the Convention entrusted the government to a committee of nine (later, twelve) men, the Committee of Public Safety (April 1793), with boundless power. In the Convention proper a bitter conflict arose between the moderate republicans (the Girondists) and the radical Jacobins (the "Mountain"). The Jacobins wished to exterminate all vestiges of the monarchical system in France and declared all who sympathized to any degree with the clergy and the nobles to be enemies of the republic; their strongest dependence was upon the extremist Paris Commune. The Girondists, whose roots lay outside the capital, wished to dissolve the Paris Commune and to remove the Convention to some city where the legislative body could be free of the threat of mob violence. Craftily, the Jacobins thereupon accused the Girondists of trying to destroy unity in the republic and encouraged the Paris mob to demand the expulsion of the Girondist party. In June 1793 the Commune forced the arrest of the Girondist leaders. This act was the signal for a revolt all over France against the Jacobin leadership. An army was sent against the disaffected city of Lyon, and the dire punishment visited upon that town by the Convention's troops terrified the rest of the country into submission. Against foreign attempts at invasion the Convention's army had also several important successes.

Emboldened by triumphs, the Committee of Public Safety set up a Revolutionary Tribunal to try all who, even by their remarks, seemed guilty of disloyalty to the republic. The Terror was now at its height. Marie Antoinette was executed in October, 1793, countless nobles were sent to their death, many others were imprisoned, and thousands of people were killed in the provinces.

Among the Jacobins themselves division began. Danton, who had believed that the situation had necessitated the Terror, now felt that enough blood had been shed and thought it time the Terror ceased. Hébert, of the Paris Commune, on the other hand, felt that it had hardly begun. Under his influence, for example, a ceremony was held in the cathedral of Notre Dame to dethrone God and set up Reason as the new deity. Robespierre, who disliked both Danton's and Hébert's faction, was now the most powerful member of the Committee of Public Safety. In the spring of 1794 he caused Danton and Hébert to be executed. When the Convention began to observe the acceleration of executions by Robespierre's orders, the members began to fear for their own lives; the Convention ordered his arrest (July, 1794) and he was put to death. Shortly thereafter the Jacobin Club was disbanded and the Paris Commune abolished. The Reign of Terror was over; the country was crying for stability.

The Convention now at last drew up the long-awaited constitution, which called for a legislature of two houses and a Directory of five men. In October 1795 the Convention disbanded.

THE NAPOLEONIC PERIOD (1796–1815)

In 1796 the Directory appointed Napoleon Bonaparte (1769–1821), a Corsican of Italian descent, commander of the army in Italy. His military achievements there proved so brilliant that the Austrian government was glad to sign a peace treaty (1797). Returning to Paris, he persuaded the Directory to place him at the head of an expedition against Egypt, where he won some victories over the Turks. Hearing that the Directory in Paris was in confusion over a new threat of invasion, Bonaparte secretly left his army, and made his way back to France with a few trusted officers. The Directory was so completely corrupt a body that a conspiracy was easily hatched by Napoleon to form a new government. By the coup d'état of November 9, 1799, when Napoleon's men invaded the Legislature, a consulate of three was established to help draw up a new constitution, Napoleon being the First Consul. When the document was ready it resembled in many ways the government under Louis XIV; the people were allowed to vote for or against it. It was adopted, perhaps by necessity, by an overwhelming majority.

Having to prosecute the war against England, Russia, Turkey, Austria, and the Kingdom of Naples, Napoleon fought so well that by 1802 peace treaties had been signed by all the hostile powers. He now set about solving France's internal problems. He made peace with the Pope (1801) by restoring the Papacy's authority over the Church. He declared the enmity of the government toward the émigrés to be at an end (1802), and many thousands of exiled noblemen returned to France. The old titles were restored to many. By degrees he accustomed the country to the idea of accepting a monarch again. In 1802 he was made Consul for life, and in 1804 declared Emperor. He began at once to create a new nobility loyal to him, and increased the censorship of the press.

A part of his great ambition thus satisfied, Napoleon proceeded to encompass the rest. "There will be no peace in Europe," he said in 1804, "until it is under a single chief." The allies against France once more renewed war, gaining a new adherent in Sweden. Napoleon put an end to the Holy Roman Empire by the Treaty of Pressburg, after delivering a crushing defeat to Austria and Russia (1806). In March of 1806 he made his brother Joseph King of Naples and Sicily, and his brother Louis King of Holland. When Prussia joined the allies, one battle (Jena in October 1806) sufficed to establish Napoleon's supremacy over that country. In 1807 he made his friend, the Duke of Saxony, head of the new Grand Duchy of Warsaw. He created the Kingdom of Westphalia for his brother Jerome to rule. In 1808 he made his brother Joseph King of Spain, after forcing the royal family to abdicate; he followed this move with a personal conquest of Spain, after which he abolished the Inquisition and most of the monasteries. But the Spanish victory was never a secure one; guerrilla warfare continued to annoy the French throughout their stay on the peninsula. In 1809 Austria went to war with France again, but was soon defeated.

Josephine, his Empress, had proved childless during their marriage. Napoleon was anxious for an heir and so fell in with the scheme of Metternich, the Austrian minister, to cement peace between the inveterately hostile countries; Napoleon divorced Josephine and married the Austrian princess, Maria Louisa (1810). He was now at the height of his power; all of western Europe, with the exception of England, was at his command. There was indeed no continental state except Russia that Napoleon did not control.

In 1812 the Emperor began his fatal campaign against Russia. By the end of the year he was in retreat to Poland with only a fragment of the large army with which he had started. In October 1813 he suffered a crushing defeat at Leipzig at the hands of the combined Prussians, Austrians, and Russians. After that disaster the new autonomies established by Napoleon collapsed. During the year of his reverses (1813) the Spaniards also succeeded in ridding themselves of the French, with the help of Wellington. By March 1814 the allies had occupied Paris. Napoleon was compelled to resign his throne, and was succeeded by the Bourbon Louis XVIII. On the little island of Elba he was allowed to retain his title of Emperor while he remained a prisoner (1814).

The unpopularity of Louis XVIII and the disputes arising among the victorious allies emboldened Napoleon to make one more desperate attempt. He escaped from Elba, reached France in March 1815, and was greeted with enthusiasm by some of his old soldiers; but the French nation no longer trusted him. With such troops as he could muster Napoleon attacked the Prussians in the Netherlands successfully. But when he turned his army against Wellington at Waterloo (outside Brussels) in June 1815 he fought without avail; General Blücher's Prussian army put an end to Napoleon's career by coming to Wellington's aid. Now Napoleon was banished to the distant island of Saint Helena, where he was abandoned to his bitter memories.

The sovereigns and ministers of Europe felt that they had at last crushed the French Revolution. But though they proceeded to split up the continent according to their wishes, the principles established by the French Revolution were not to perish. The feudal system had been dealt its deathblow and serfdom disappeared from most parts of Europe.

While he was Emperor, Napoleon had kept most of the reforms accomplished in 1789. It was he who made Paris the most gracious of modern cities with its beautiful bridges and arches. He sponsored many public improvements, and his phenomenal success as a conqueror evoked a fierce national pride in Frenchmen.

From the years of the outbreak of the French Revolution to the end of the Napoleonic Empire, only three writers stand out as preeminent. One of them, Chénier, we have already discussed. It now remains for us to consider the other two, Chateaubriand and Mme. de Staël, as well as their lesser contemporaries.

FRANÇOIS-RENÉ DE CHATEAUBRIAND (1768–1848)

IMPORTANCE

For the first four decades of the nineteenth century François-René-Auguste, Viscount of Chateaubriand, dominated the French literary horizon. He was unmistakably the first thoroughgoing Romantic in the world of French letters. He carried further the exoticism of Bernardin de Saint-Pierre in his descriptions of nature; he made an interest in the medieval the new vogue; and he outdid Rousseau in his passionate preoccupation with himself, stressing particularly the melancholy of his temperament. He is Byron's most important forerunner as exponent of the *mal du siècle* ("the malady of the [nineteenth] century")—that melancholy which goes beyond the sentimental reflections of his predecessors into the realm of pessimism.

With him, as with Byron, this melancholy is something of a pose. But the Romantics became mighty fond of heroes who walked about feeling doomed and under the blight of a mysterious curse. It was Chateaubriand who set the style. After his death his reputation rapidly declined, somewhat because of the attacks of Sainte-Beuve, but during his lifetime he had no rival in France.

Early Life

François-René de Chateaubriand was born of an old Breton family at Saint-Malo, where he caught a love of the sea. Shut up in his father's château at Combourg with his parents and his sister Lucille for several years, he read through a wide range of books. There the rather morbid Lucille was the confidante of his own moody dreams. For a time (1786) he served in the army, and then obtained a commission in the cavalry. At Paris, while still a youth, he was presented at Court, but professed himself bored with any but the society of literary people. His first published verses (1790) exhibit the influence of uninspired neoclassical models.

Always haunted by a desire to travel, he set out from Saint-Malo in April, 1791 to discover America. He remained there little more than half a year, but his experiences were to be exploited constantly in his future writings. Actually he seems to have visited only the environs of the Great Lakes; something of a plagiarist, he did not scruple to draw upon the materials of English and French voyagers who had seen more of America and to imply that what he wrote was the fruit of his own observation. Nevertheless, he returned from the new continent with his imagination stored with the colors and impressions that were to supply materials for the rest of his literary career.

His return to France found the King a prisoner and the nobility hastily emigrating from the country. Like many of his rank, he escaped to England, where he received employment from a London bookseller. It was here that he published his *Essai sur les Révolutions* (*Essay on Revolutions*) in 1797, an attempt to compare the French Revolution with earlier revolutions. The study was never finished, and reached no further than Alexander the Great. The only significant thing about this book is that in it Chateaubriand, who was to become the most celebrated apologist for Christianity of his times, is revealed as thoroughly unsympathetic to that religion. His last chapter is entitled, "What Will Be the Religion Which Will Replace Christianity?" The book affords no answer.

When Napoleon was First Consul, Chateaubriand's friend Fontanes induced Napoleon to remove the name of the Chateaubriand family from the list of condemned émigrés, and the writer returned to France (1800). In 1801 Chateaubriand published *Atala*.

Atala

This romance was originally intended as an illustrative passage in Chateaubriand's major work, *The Genius of Christianity*, to demonstrate the "harmony of the Christian religion with scenes of nature and the passions of the human heart." However, it was issued before the larger opus independently.

The scene is in the wilderness of America near the banks of the Mississippi. The story is the romance of a young Indian warrior Chactas and his love, the Indian maid Atala. The story is told by the hero, a member of the Natchez tribe, in his old age on a moonlit night to his French friend, René. Chactas has visited France and knows Louis XIV's court. In his youth Chactas, after his tribe has been defeated, decides to leave his place of refuge in Saint Augustine to visit his native territory. But his old enemies, the Muscogulges, capture him again and condemn him to the stake.

Atala, a girl of the hostile tribe, who has been converted to Christianity and who has promised her dying mother to remain a virgin, has fallen in love with Chactas. She frees him, and together they wander through the untamed forests heavily overgrown with tropical luxuriance. A child of nature, Chactas would gratify his love for Atala, but she represses her passion in obedience to her oath. A terrible storm accompanied by shafts of lightning causes them to accept refuge when they are offered it by a pious hermit, Father Aubry.

In the hermit's cave Chactas asks to be made a Christian and to be married to Atala. She tells of her oath, but despite the kind assurances of the hermit, happiness is not for the lovers. In dread of her passion for Chactas, Atala has taken poison so that she may be not tempted to give herself to her lover. The good hermit manages to comfort Atala as she is dying. Chactas carries her to her grave as the wild wind blows.

Although, as has been said, Chateaubriand had never visited Louisiana, his descriptions of its wild life have continued to charm many readers, who look upon *Atala* as his most perfect performance. The characters of the lovers are winning in their innocence, and the scenes of their passion are written with much force. The work was enormously popular.

The Genius of Christianity

In 1802, just a few days before Napoleon made his peace with Rome, Chateaubriand issued his *Génie du Christianisme* (*The Genius of Christianity*). It impressed Napoleon so much that he appointed the author secretary to the Embassy at Rome in 1803, and the year after Ambassador to the Valais.

The Genius of Christianity is divided into four parts. Part One is an examination of the doctrines and dogmas of Christianity: the Bible, the sacraments, the existence of Deity, and the immortality of the soul. Part Two deals with the "Poetics of Christianity," in which the author examines the epic poems of Dante, Tasso, Milton, and Voltaire; the characters in the tragedies and epics of Racine, Tasso, and Voltaire; and the emotions represented in these works. It is in this section that the episode of *René*, later issued as a separate work (and which we shall presently discuss), appears. Then the author proceeds to a defense of the "marvelous" in medieval and Gothic literature against the "common sense" of Boileau and the Neoclassicists. Part Three, on the arts and belles-lettres, opens with a celebrated passage in praise of Gothic architecture, as revealed in Christian churches. Then follows a discourse on Christian philosophy, history, and oratory. The section concludes with an examination of the harmony between Christianity, nature, and the passions— for which the *Atala* episode was originally written as an illustration. The Fourth Part is a study of ceremonies—vestments, hymns, prayers, bells, the clergy. There follows an attack on the *Encyclopedia* by a proof of the usefulness of the clergy and Christianity to society. The last section of the work indicates the intention of the whole by showing how abysmal human society would be without Christianity.

The importance of *The Genius of Christianity* lies in the fact that it overturned completely the esthetic values of the Neoclassical school, and demolished the skeptical anti-Christian attitude of Voltaire and the Encyclopedists. Chateaubriand, because of the great success of the book, established the authentic poetic values of the Middle Ages and thereby afforded fresh sources of inspiration to his Romantic successors. He also was responsible for a new wave of religious exaltation and fervor, which was more than welcome after more than a century of Reason deified.

René

As has been remarked, *René*, like *Atala*, was originally part of *The Genius of Christianity*, but it was published by itself in 1807. The tale is a continuation of *Atala*, and is the account told this time by the young Frenchman, René, to his adopted father, the aged Indian Chactas, and Father Souël, the French missionary. René tells of his boyhood, his unhappy wanderings from country to country in search of peace of soul. He has seen the most ancient and the most modern monuments of civilization, but none of them has brought him contenting thoughts. Finally, he has sought the silence of the forests, but they too only suggested ideas of self-destruction. He was prevented from committing suicide by his sister Amélie, who sought him out to comfort him, and make him desire life again. Suddenly, however, Amélie disappeared and entered a convent. The poor girl had become the victim of feelings more than natural for her brother, and chose that method of thwarting them. Learning of these matters, René has fled to the wildernesses of the Louisiana forests.

The influence of *René* upon the Romantic movement proved very great. René, himself, finding happiness nowhere in the world, civilized or uncivilized, was accepted as a portrait of the author thinly disguised, and such parading of one's private griefs became a frequent aspect of Romanticism. The *mal de René*, in short, became the *mal du siècle*: the cultivation of perpetual frustration of desire and hope. Goethe's *Werther* was indeed an earlier model of the same, but *René* is written with much more poignancy and force, and had the added attraction of a style loaded with imagery and color of the exotic. Nature, in Chateaubriand as in Byron, constantly echoes the passions of the hero. René feels the kisses of his loved one in the motions of the wind, hears her voice in the whisperings of the stream; the stars in the sky and "the very principle of life itself" seem to be part of her he loves.

The note of incest, too, was not to be without its charms for the Romantics—the pleasurable shock of dreadful sins that, according to them, only the most sensitive are exposed to.

Chateaubriand's Later Works

The execution of the Duke d'Enghien caused Chateaubriand to turn against Napoleon, and he at once resigned his office. Thereafter he became an uncompromising foe of Bonaparte. He started once more on his travels, visiting Trieste, Venice, Greece, Constantinople, Palestine, Tunis, Carthage, and Spain (1806–1807). Returning to France, he bought a country home near Aulnay, and there completed *Les Martyrs* (*The Martyrs*) and his *Itinéraire de Paris à Jérusalem* (*Journey from Paris to Jerusalem*), which appeared respectively in 1809 and 1811. *The Martyrs* is a study in contrasts of the pagan and Christian religions, and includes a story of the time of the Emperor Diocletian during the persecution of Christians. *The Journey from Paris* contains some of its author's best writing in the lively descriptions of Greece and the Orient.

Chateaubriand continued his belligerence against Napoleon I, but was elected to the French Academy, although the authorities refused to permit him to deliver a lecture there. After Napoleon's downfall, he issued the most important argument in behalf of the Bourbon line of succession, *On Bonaparte and the Bourbons* (1815). Now a peer of the realm, he was first appointed Ambassador to Berlin (1820) and then Ambassador to London (1822). He soon was made Minister of Foreign Affairs in the French Cabinet, but proving unpopular with the King, he was asked to resign. After a brief period as Ambassador to Rome, he retired to private life. His *Historical Studies* (*Les Études Historiques*) (1831) and his *Essay on English Literature* (*Essai sur la Littérature Anglaise*) (1836) were followed by his *Life of Rancé* (*Vie de Rancé*) (1844). The *Essay* is particularly interesting for its commentary on Milton, which is a kind of preface to Chateaubriand's translation of *Paradise Lost*. The *Life of Rancé* is an uninteresting exercise in biography; the *Historical Studies* is a study in the philosophical and historical aspects of Christianity.

During this period Chateaubriand also published a series of pieces he had composed in youth: *Les Natchez* (1826), a prose epic written in his early London days, in which the Natchez Indians are represented as the type of primitive man, and as part of which *Atala* and *René* were first sketched; *Voyage to America* (1834), a series of his impressions during his American trip, describing vividly the wild country of the New World; *Les Aventures du Dernier Abencérage* (*The Adventures of the Last of the Abencérages*) (1826), an Oriental tale laid in Spain.

In his last years Chateaubriand worked intermittently at his autobiography, *Mémoires d'Outre-tombe* (*Memoirs from Beyond the Tomb*), which were intended to be published only after his death, but actually began to appear in *La Presse* several months before his death in 1848.

Memoirs from Beyond the Tomb

The *Mémoires d'Outre-tombe* (1848–1850) is a vast collection of personal reminiscences, experiences and impressions, and shows Chateaubriand's style at its most brilliant. It affords a complete picture of the author in his most attractive side—thereby differing strikingly from Rousseau's *Confessions*. It contains in something like totality the material from which he drew to write his best-known books, for Chateaubriand was ever one of the world's most personal writers. His childhood, travels, friends, family, acquaintances are all revealed to us as Chateaubriand would have us see the stream of his life. His self-absorption throughout all his experiences, his extreme self-consciousness about the fineness of his melancholy feelings strike us as a little ludicrous today. But there is no denying the charm and wistfulness of many pages, particularly those dealing with his youth at Combourg, where, he reflects sadly, "the cradle of my dreams (the forests) has disappeared like the dreams themselves." The autobiography has been much admired for its unique combination of poetry and realism throughout. The reason behind this fusion Chateaubriand makes clear: "It was in the forests that I made my songs about the forests—on board the ship that I depicted the sea—in camps that I spoke of battle—and in exile that I learned what exile means."

If we except Rousseau, who was not, properly speaking, a creator of belles-lettres, no writer exercised a greater influence on the Romantic movement than Chateaubriand. Lamartine, Hugo, George Sand, and Flaubert (in his romantic mood) wrote under his spell.

CHATEAUBRIAND'S CONTEMPORARIES

Mme. de Staël (1766–1817)

Chateaubriand's most prominent contemporary was the daughter of Louis XVI's minister Necker, Anne Louise Germaine Necker, who married a Swedish diplomat, Baron de Staël Holstein, and has been known to letters as Mme. de Staël. If Chateaubriand was an exile from the Republic, she became an exile from the Napoleonic Empire. Precocious as a child, she was early introduced into salon life at her mother's home. After her father's fall from grace in the early years of the Revolution, the family lived in retirement at Coppet, near Geneva (1792–1795) for three years. She was already the author of a book on Rousseau, and in 1796 published a treatise *On the Influence of the Passions on Happiness*. Next year she was back in Paris, and her salon began to be very influential in intellectual circles. In 1800 appeared her study of literature, *De la Littérature*, and in 1802 her first novel, *Delphine*. In the latter year her husband died.

Napoleon had by this time decided that she was a person inimical to his interests, and she was ordered to leave Paris in 1803. With her children she started on a tour of Germany, visiting Frankfort, Weimar, and Berlin. She met Goethe, Schiller, Fichte, and Schlegel. In 1804 the death of her father brought her back to Coppet, where she wrote his eulogy, *Du Caractère de M. Necker et de Sa Vie Privée* (*On the Character of M. Necker and of His Private Life*). Next year she went to spend more than a half year in Italy, and on her return in 1806 published her second novel, *Corinne*.

Finding it impossible to obtain the right to return to Paris, she invited to her home at Coppet, Switzerland, all who were foes of Napoleon. In 1807 she traveled again to Weimar, and then went on to Munich and Vienna. The fruit of her Germanic visits was *De l'Allemagne* (*Concerning Germany*), printed in Paris in 1810; but before the book could be sold, all copies were seized and destroyed by the police. She now married a young Swiss officer, de Rocca (1811). She was traveling again in 1812, to Vienna, St. Petersburg, Sweden, and England, where she saw *De l'Allemagne* at last in print. After a trip once more to Italy, she came to Paris on Napoleon's downfall, and began an exciting social whirl, and wrote her *Considerations on the French Revolution* (*Considérations sur la Révolution Française*), and her memoirs, *Ten Years of Exile* (*Dix Années d'Exil*). She died in 1817.

It would appear that Mme. de Staël was the most brilliant conversationalist of her time—"a thunderstorm," as her lover Benjamin Constant said of her. She was arrogant about her attainments and delighted in winning an edge over all the people of talent she knew—she gave Fichte exactly a quarter of an hour to expound his life's philosophy.

IMPORTANCE

Mme. de Staël's influence on French literature has been deep and enduring. With Chateaubriand she completed the discrediting in literature of the values of the Age of Reason—although she endorsed the doctrine of the perfectibility of humanity. Her belief in progress—so unlike Chateaubriand's pessimism—was based upon considerations of emotional enthusiasm and idealized morality, not the cold logic so dear to Voltaire and his friends. In belles-lettres she helped destroy the authority of Neoclassical dogma by insisting that the judgment of a literary work requires historical perspective and understanding of the social conditions that helped produce it. Most of all, she introduced into France an interest and sympathy for the literature of Germany, heretofore neglected, and thus proved one of the most effective forces for bringing about a cosmopolitan attitude towards literature.

Mme. de Staël's style is full of verve but is so near conversation that it seems often more like superior journalism than serious prose. But she abounds in felicitous phrasing and many brilliant judgments. Her best books are *Corinne* and *De l'Allemagne.*

In both her novels the heroines, Delphine and Corinne, are idealizations of herself; as with Chateaubriand's romances, the reading public was well aware of their autobiographical intent.

Delphine: This story of a blighted love affair has the distinction of having introduced *la femme incomprise* ("the misunderstood woman") into literature; the author herself, her lover Benjamin Constant, her mother, and Talleyrand were the originals of some of the character portraits. The book is sprinkled with the liberal ideas that so much provoked the wrath of Napoleon.

Corinne: Still read with some pleasure because of its author's lively apprehension of the beauties of Italy, it annoyed Napoleon enough with its great success to cause him to write an attack on it in the *Moniteur.* The story deals with the sentimental love affair between Corinne, a musician, poet, and artist, a woman of a glamorous past, and Oswald, a noble Englishman, who meet in Italy. He is already pledged to marry an English girl, Lucille, who turns out to be Corinne's half-sister. Corinne, a woman of the most exalted sentiments, releases Oswald so he can marry Lucille, and dies of a broken heart. Passages in this novel will strike the reader today as belonging more to an inspired guidebook to Italy than to a novel. Indeed, generations of tourists have so used *Corinne* to their great satisfaction, for Mme. de Staël was nothing if not proud of her eye for the beauties of Italy's past.

De l'Allemagne (On Germany): This has been pronounced the best book ever written about any country by a foreigner. It is divided into four parts: "On the Manners of the Germans," "On German Literature and Art," "On German Philosophy and Morals," and "On Religion in Germany." The literary section is the most interesting. Because of her own Romantic temperament, Mme. de Staël was particularly sensitive to the appeal of the poetry of Goethe, Schiller, and Klopstock, and to the criticism of Lessing and Schlegel (with whom she shared a vast enthusiasm for Shakespeare). Her judgment on German philosophy, though less competent, did it the service of introducing Kant and Fichte to Frenchmen. The romantic attachment she developed for things German went so far that she openly described the Germanic world as being victim of Napoleonic ambition.

De la Littérature (On Literature): This book is important for its attempt to discover "the influence of religion, manners, and laws upon literature" as well as the influence that literature exerts on them. Though inadequate in execution, particularly in her desire to prove the gradual progress of humanity over the centuries, nevertheless the attempt was historically important. She is weak on the classic schools, for which she had little sympathy, but very interesting on Shakespeare.

Benjamin Constant (1767–1830)

Benjamin Constant is remembered for the one novel he wrote: *Adolphe* (1816), inspired by his love affair with Mme. de Staël. In her novels the men are drawn without much interest, since everything is sacrificed to the portraiture of the heroine; in *Adolphe* the reverse is true. Here again we have a highly autobiographical work, this time centering about the hero alone. The story element is very slender: Adolphe has been in love with Ellénore, is tired of their affair, but has not the strength of character to terminate it. Constant's novel is astonishingly modern in its analysis of the moods of the hero, and even more so in its indifference to plot or incident. As such, it belongs more to the school of Stendhal, which was yet to be, than to its own age.

Constant was better known in his own day as an excellent orator. He was exiled by Napoleon, yet joined his cause during Napoleon's abortive attempt to regain power after his fall in 1814. Louis XVIII therefore banished him for a while in 1815, but he was recalled next year and elected deputy, in which office he was prominent among the liberals.

Joseph de Maistre (1754–1821)

Joseph de Maistre has been called the "chief religious medievalist of modern times." He was wholly unsympathetic to the modern temper, and wrote of the new science with abuse. His chief works are *Du Pape* (*On the Pope*) of 1819, *De l'Église Gallicane* (*On the Gallic Church*) of 1821, and *Soirées de Saint-Pétersbourg* (*Saint Petersburg Soirées*) of the same year. In the first two named, the author takes the most extreme position possible on the primacy of the pope. The pope is the source of every kind of authority, temporal as well as spiritual, and the kings of the earth are only his representatives. Joseph de Maistre's reaction against the rationalists of the eighteenth century and the consequent French Revolution was complete, and it co-operated with Chateaubriand to overthrow the influence of the Age of Reason. He argues in all his books from the premise that all that occurs in the world does so by the will of God. In *Saint Petersburg Soirées* he attempts to prove that war and capital punishment are demanded by the will of Providence; they are part of man's expiation for original sin.

Joseph de Maistre's skill in polemics reminds one of the great theologians of the Middle Ages. Unlike them, however, he was master of a brilliant rhetoric, a bold, sharp style that has rarely been equalled in French prose.

Xavier de Maistre (1773–1852)

Xavier de Maistre, Joseph's brother, who served as a general in the Russian army, was the author of several sentimental novels, written under the influence of the Englishman Sterne. His style is admirable for its naturalness and ease, as well as for the wit which balances the excess of sentiment. *His Voyage autour de Ma Chambre* (*Journey around My Room*), which was published in 1794, is based upon the delightful situation of a convalescing military officer regarding all the objects in his room and allowing them to yield up their associations. *Le Lépreux de la Cité d'Aoste* (*The Leper of Aoste*) is a charming, and high-principled dialogue between the soldier-author and a confined leper.

Étienne Pivert de Senancour (1770–1846)

Étienne Pivert de Senancour was a kind of latter-day Rousseau, whose melancholy is somewhat akin to Chateaubriand's. His *Obermann* (1804) is a kind of novel in epistolary form, describing its author's wanderings through Switzerland and Fontainebleau forest. It contains little plot but is a constant revelation of the author's own sentiments. The hero, like Constant's Adolphe, is a victim of irresolution, and is now interesting chiefly historically as a type popular with the Romantics. *Obermann* is a self-portrait. Its author could say of himself, characteristically, "Perhaps some peaceful days may yet be granted me. But there will be no more charm, no more intoxication, never another moment of pure joy, never! And I am only twenty-one!"

Obermann, neglected for a while, was rediscovered during the height of the Romantic movement, but soon forgotten again.

FRANCE AFTER NAPOLEON

For five and a half decades after Waterloo there was nothing in French national life that could succeed in stirring the interest of the French public comparable to the events occurring between 1789 and 1814. The imagination of the French people was still busy with the issues of the French Revolution and the Napoleonic Empire.

The history of those five and a half decades is one of chaos, for no government during that period proved able to win the support of more than one minority or another. There was a great deal of oratory, a great deal said about "Liberty, Fraternity, Equality," and there was more than one coup d'état. But few issues excited the fervor of the nation as a whole. Even in our own time the chaos of French politics has continued; France has never learned how to govern itself even though it taught the world the principles of liberty.

After Napoleon the government grew consistently reactionary towards the ideas propagated by the French Revolution until at last another revolution was fomented. Louis XVIII, though a Bourbon, of course could not easily hark back to the standards of his illustrious ancestor, Louis XIV. He saw that the old order could not be restored, but he did try to revive the theory that the king is the final authority in all matters of state. The Charter, as the new constitution came to be called, was bestowed upon the people as his gift, though it technically made France's government a limited monarchy, somewhat on the English model. It was his intention to rule as a liberal king, and he resisted the extreme demands of church and émigrés alike. France began to recover from the losses of the Napoleonic conquest. Though there were some instances of the suppression of free speech, the tendency of Louis XVIII was to be moderate.

His brother, Charles X, who reigned from 1824 to 1830, however, seemed to take seriously the theory of the divine right of kings. He began to pad the pockets of the nobles whom the French Revolution had dispossessed, and disbanded the National Guard. As a result the Liberals grew in strength in the lower house of the legislature. Charles attempted to overrule the constitution in the appointment of his ministers, but could not get the backing of the Legislature. He dissolved the national body, but the people voted them in again. He next attempted a coup d'état, hoping to start a revolution in favor of absolute monarchy (1830). Paris revolted, and in three days he was forced to abdicate and go into exile.

Louis Philippe, the next Bourbon, ruled from 1830 to 1848. He pretended from the first to be a staunch democrat in his principles, a "citizen king." The new constitution modified the 1814 Charter according to the wishes of the Legislature, and thus rendered the king subject to the laws; in many matters it liberalized the old Charter. But Louis Philippe was a man of inferior talents. His supporters were the increasingly wealthy middle class, whose point of view he represented. Under him France took a secondary role in European affairs, and his subjects did not conceal a certain contempt for him. The forbidding of a banquet in Paris to celebrate Washington's birthday in 1848 became the signal for a local insurrection. Though the revolt was limited to a Paris mob, Louis Philippe was terrified, and he fled to the border.

The Revolution of 1848 was much more of a success than anyone could have expected, and the Paris mob, at first uncertain as to what to do next, decided on a coup d'état of its own. It invaded the Legislature and declared for a republic. The Second Republic (1848–1852), as it has been known, was thus established by an accident and supported by a small minority. During it the Assembly contained a majority of Monarchists, who, however, could not agree among themselves. The Socialist Party at this time began to be a fairly important factor in French politics, and for a little while was able to put through certain socialist measures (such as guaranteeing employment to all the unemployed). After a few days of bloody fighting in Paris, the moderate Republicans were in power next, and a republican constitution was adopted, with a president something on the American model, and providing universal male suffrage. The President and the Legislature, though both opposed to the Republic, were ever at odds with each other. Louis Napoleon had been elected President (1848) by a large majority. But the growing fear by the middle classes of the radicals enabled Louis Napoleon to effect a coup d'état (1851) with the assurance of considerable backing, and for several weeks he ruled like an absolute monarch. He then submitted a constitution of his own fabrication, modeled upon that of Napoleon I, though calling the country still a republic, and making him President for ten years. The next year (1852) it was easy enough for him to be proclaimed Emperor. He took the title of Napoleon III (1848–1870), with the approval of something approaching a majority of the people. (Napoleon I's son by his Austrian wife, Napoleon II, never came to the throne. He is the subject of a drama, *L'Aiglon* [*The Eaglet*] by Edmond Rostand.)

Under Napoleon III a great many public improvements were effected to keep the people satisfied: railroads, splendid additions to Paris, canals, new harbors, steamship lines. France grew rich. Its pride was renewed for a brief while too by the defeat of Austria in the War for Italian Liberation, and the defeat of Russia in the Crimean War, as well as by the annexation of Savoy and Nice.

But the opposition to Napoleon III increased, and he was forced to yield to limitations to his power. Most fatal of all, he seemed blind to the enormous strides in military prowess that Prussia had made under Bismarck. When France in an apparently reckless mood went to war with Prussia (1870), the German armies poured across the Rhine, and in seven weeks after the opening of hostilities had captured Napoleon III himself at the crucial battle of Sedan (September 1, 1870). Paris was surrounded, and after a harrowing siege capitulated (January 28, 1871). The success of the campaign saw the fall of the Empire in France, and the formation of the German Empire, which had been Bismarck's dream.

The Third Republic in France started, as had become the custom, with the terrorizing of the Legislature by the Paris mob, who set up a provisional government of their own immediately after the battle of Sedan. In the elections following the fall of Paris, most of the candidates elected were monarchists.

Thiers was intrusted with the executive power temporarily. After accepting the crushing terms of the Germans (1871), the republicans in the Assembly demanded a new election. When the monarchists refused to agree, the Parisians again revolted. These revolutionists, the celebrated Paris Commune, consisted of republicans, socialists, anarchists, and communists. They demanded that every municipality (commune) have the right to manage its own affairs, and that France become a federation of such communes. The rest of the country did not like the idea, however, and Thiers (whose headquarters were at Versailles) ordered Paris bombarded. After weeks of bitter street fighting, Marshal MacMahon established order; hundreds of the revolutionists were executed by the monarchists, and thousands were sent across the world to the criminal colony.

Thiers was elected President of the new republic in 1871, but was soon succeeded by MacMahon. The monarchists failed to succeed in their attempts to compromise on the rightful claimant to the throne. Finally, by a majority of one vote, the form of a republic was legally established in 1875. As the next years went by, the monarchists became weaker and weaker because of the deaths of the various claimants. Correspondingly, republican sentiment grew stronger and stronger until by the close of the century the monarchical point of view was held by only a very small intransigent minority. It has been true, however, that at every national emergency this small minority has been very vociferous in insisting that "only a king can save France."

2
THE HEIGHT OF THE FRENCH AND ITALIAN ROMANTIC MOVEMENT

Romanticism in France reached an amazingly luxuriant flourishing during the last years of Louis XVIII's reign, the reign of Charles X, and most of the reign of Louis Philippe, that is between 1820 and 1843. This period saw a marvelous expansion in the resources of the French language and its literature. After remaining for a century and a half, since the days of Corneille, the center of Neoclassical practice in Europe, France abandoned almost completely its classical traditions and drew closer in its literary tastes to the rest of Western Europe. For subject matter and style it looked now to England, Germany, Italy, and Spain, and even far distant lands. French prose, no less than French poetry, enlarged its former bounds to include tones of greater variety than had seemed possible before. In mediocre hands, it is true, the level degenerated as it could never have done in the Age of Reason. But in the hands of genius French literature took on a new richness.

The number of great figures who appeared within the compass of these years is truly astounding: Lamartine, Hugo, Musset, Vigny, Gautier, Sainte-Beuve, Stendhal, Balzac, and George Sand—nowhere else in Europe could such an aggregation of great literary ability have been found at that time.

ALPHONSE PRAT DE LAMARTINE (1798–1869)

IMPORTANCE

In England it is customary to think of Wordsworth as ushering in the English Romantic movement (1798) although he was preceded by two such full-fledged Romantics as Burns and Blake and a number of lesser poets with strong Romantic tendencies. There is justice in the allegation because Wordsworth's poetry inaugurated a period in which the Romantic attitude towards literature was general among writers. In much the same fashion, although Lamartine was preceded by such

> Romantic writers as Saint-Pierre, Chateaubriand, and Mme. de Staël, he
> is credited, for the like reason, with ushering in the Romantic move-
> ment in France. It has been said of him that he made into poetry what
> Rousseau, Saint-Pierre, and Chateaubriand had already made into
> prose.

Alphonse Prat de Lamartine was born of an ancient noble family, and was
the son of a mother celebrated for her intellect. After the Revolution the family settled at Macon on their estate, where Lamartine had been born. He read
and wrote a great deal in his youth, and in 1811–1812 journeyed to Italy. At
the age of twenty-four he was appointed bodyguard to Louis XVIII (1814),
but did not remain at his post after Waterloo. Instead, he lived the life of a
country gentleman—reading, writing, traveling.

His earlier verses are undistinguished. But a blighted love affair inspired
him to write the first volume of his *Méditations* (1820), which contains some
of his best known poems: "Le Soir" (Evening), "L'Isolement" (Isolation), "Le
Vallon" (The Vale), "L'Automne" (Autumn), and "Le Lac" (The Lake). The very
titles show the pure Romantic. These poems were greeted with the greatest
enthusiasm, an enthusiasm well deserved, for these partly religious, partly
melancholy refections were as chastened in form as original in language.

Louis XVIII now appointed Lamartine as secretary to the Embassy in Florence (1821). In 1823 appeared his *Nouvelles Méditations* (*New Meditations*),
containing one of the best of French lyric poems, the ode on *Bonaparte*, as
well as the beautiful "Le Passé" (The Past), "Les Étoiles" (The Stars), and "Les
Préludes"—the last-named of which inspired Liszt to write his celebrated
symphonic poem. "La Mort de Socrate" (The Death of Socrates) of the same
year is a not very inspired poetical rendering of Plato's *Phaedo*.

The influence that Byron was already exerting on French literature is to be
seen in "Le Dernier Chant du Pélerinage d'Harold" (The Last Song of Childe
Harold's Pilgrimage) of 1825. The subject matter is Byron's last days in Italy,
his fight for Greek independence, and his death at Missolonghi. In Byron's
mouth he puts an indictment of Italy. The line, "Forgive me, shadows of
Rome, if I go to seek elsewhere men and not mere human dust," offended
the Italian exile Colonel Pepe, who challenged Lamartine to a duel which
ended happily.

For five years the poet remained at Florence, and then returned to France.
In 1830 he was elected member of the Academy, and the same year his *Harmonies Poétiques et Religieuses* (*Poetical and Religious Harmonies*) appeared,
containing a few very superior poems: "Hymne du Matin" (Morning Hymn),
"Penseé des Morts" (A Thought of the Dead), "Au Rossignol" (To the Nightingale), "Le Tombeau d'une Mère" (A Mother's Grave), and "Jéhovah."

Lamartine had intended writing a huge epic "devoted to humanity." Of
this the fragment "Jocelyn" appeared in 1836, with the subtitle, "An episode,
found in the journal of a country curate." The theme is that of a youth who

becomes a priest after losing track of the woman he has fallen in love with; they meet again, but too late. The descriptions and the elevated sentiments are beautifully expressed. Another fragment of the same intended epic was published two years later, "La Chute d'un Ange" (The Fall of an Angel). Here an angel who wished to be made into man because of his love for a woman is granted his wish by God, but not her love.

After the fall of Charles X, Lamartine traveled into the Orient (1832). On his return he began his political life with his election to the Chamber of Deputies. He participated in the Revolution of 1848, and as a result was made Minister of Foreign Affairs during the provisional government. But upon the election of Louis Napoleon to President he decided to retire to private life again. In his last years, as a result of his generosity and prodigality, he was in considerable financial embarrassment.

His prose works include *Voyage en Orient* (1835), an account of his travels to Syria, Palestine, Damascus, and Constantinople; *L'Histoire des Girondins* (*History of the Girondins*), which appeared in 1847 and, because of its masterful portraits of some of the leaders of the French Revolution, did much to aid the Revolution of 1848; and *Les Confidences, Graziella, Raphael* (all 1849), a series of romantic autobiographical recollections.

The influences on Lamartine's poetry are varied; touches from Petrarch, Tasso, Macpherson, Rousseau, Chateaubriand, Saint-Pierre, and Byron are discernible. But all of these are fused into the poet's personality, which was one of an almost feminine sensibility. He lacks power and sometimes fatigues with his melancholy; but he is a poet whose lines abound in delicate harmony and a charming picturesqueness.

VICTOR-MARIE HUGO (1802–1885)

IMPORTANCE

There are many solid scholars who have declared that Victor Hugo is the greatest poet and one of the greatest prose writers France has ever had. His creative energies were vast, and he wrote copiously as a poet, novelist, dramatist, critic, and polemicist. No man of his era was so thorough a champion of the Romantic movement. It is not strange that when he died, after a long career that had continued unaffected by newer literary trends, a tendency to disparage his achievement should have begun. Those of classic bent had never liked him; the vagaries of his political views made enemies of others. Yet even those who have taken an attitude of condescension towards his novels and plays have not been able to deny his excellence as a poet. And it is probably true that although the general public for a long time considered him as one of the world's preeminent novelists, it is as a poet that he will figure highest.

As the major literary figure of his century in France it is natural that an elaborate legend should have grown up about Victor Hugo. But the facts of his career are available.

Victor-Marie Hugo was born at Besançon, the son of an officer in Napoleon's army. Later, the elder Hugo was a general under Jerome Bonaparte when King of Spain. The boy lived for a while in that country, and stored his mind with impressions that were later to figure in his works. In 1812 the family moved to Paris; there Victor and his brother Eugène had for their tutors, "an old priest, the garden, and their mother." In 1815 the boy began to attend school, and won a prize in physics. By the time he was fourteen he decided, "I wish to be a Chateaubriand or else nothing." He was already composing verse.

When he was seventeen he began a journal with his brother Abel, *Le Conservateur Littéraire* (1819–1821). The name of the periodical was honest enough, for in his youth Hugo was a royalist and a Catholic in the Chateaubriand tradition. For this publication his pen already showed its fertility: he wrote 272 articles!

At the age of twenty-one he married the beautiful Adèle Foucher shortly after issuing his first volume of verse, *Odes et poésies diverses* (1822). In consequence of this publication he was invited to join the *cénacle* ("literary circle") of a group of young poets editing *La Muse Française*. The young men included Alexander Soumet, Alexander Guiraud, Émile Deschamps, and Alfred de Vigny (the last-named of whom is an important poet). After two years the magazine was discontinued (1824), but these belligerent Romantics continued to meet at the home of the literary jack-of-all-trades, Charles Nodier (1780–1844). Their number was augmented by Sainte-Beuve and Alfred de Musset. Hugo by degrees had assumed the leadership of this *cénacle*, which continued its gatherings until 1834. At the meetings criticism flowed freely and productively; they would, indeed, have been justified by the fact that they formed the basis for the important friendship, personal and literary, between Hugo and Sainte-Beuve.

In 1826 Hugo published his *Odes et Ballades* (*Odes and Ballads*). Many of these ballads are on current political events, but there are few poems that show a growth in lyricism. But neither this nor the earlier volume give much hint of the power Hugo was to demonstrate soon; they are both still under the spell of royalistic sentiment and Neoclassical technique, despite his Romantic convictions. It was by the publication of the drama *Cromwell* (1827), with a famous Preface that became a kind of manifesto for the new dramatists, that Hugo the writer at last emerged as a true Romantic. The play itself has not been acted, for it is more of a novel in dramatic form than a true drama; the blood-and-thunder plot has to do with the ambitions of Cromwell to be crowned king.

Preface to *Cromwell*

Hugo begins with a survey of the history of the development of poetry. With primitive man poetry was first lyrical and rhapsodic. Later with increase of human activity, poetry became epic. Then the playwrights used the epics for dramatic presentation, and poetry became tragedy. Then Christianity discovered for man the duality of his nature: the aspirations of his soul and the evil instincts of his animal qualities; from this self-examination in man poetry became at last drama.

The importance of the discussion is that it affords a key to Hugo's practice throughout his career: his obsession with the antithetical aspect of man's nature, which to him was ever the source of dramatic conflict. Had he said that the Christian era afforded profounder examples of psychological insight than the ancient world, he would have been true enough to the facts, as the examples of Shakespeare and Racine alone would have sufficed to prove.

Hugo then proceeds to argue against the classical practice of separating comedy and tragedy each as a different species of composition. It is the purpose of drama to represent life as an entity; in life tears and laughter, beauty and ugliness, the sublime and the grotesque exist side by side. Let us unite them as Shakespeare has done, Hugo suggests. This remained Hugo's formula in the drama and the novel.

The Preface attracted wide notice, and was discussed by literary critics everywhere in France.

Hernani

Hugo's next volume of poems, *Les Orientales* (1829) was the product of a new wave of interest in the Orient, as a result of the struggle between Turkey and Greece. This volume shows Hugo's poetry improving in power. The influence of Byron is to be seen in a poem modeled on the English poet's *Mazeppa* by the same title. The collection is admirable for its new freedom of rhythm and language.

But it was with the play *Hernani* of 1830 and the novel *Notre-Dame de Paris* of the next year that he achieved the height of his fame, and was universally recognized in France as the leader of the Romantic movement. For the ensuing decade, when he wrote a number of plays for production—*Le Roi S'Amuse* (*The King Amuses Himself*), *Lucrèce Borgia*, *Marie Tudor*, *Angelo*, *Ruy Blas*—and four important volumes of poetry—*Les Feuilles d'Automne* (*Autumn Leaves*) of 1831, *Chants du Crépuscule* (*Songs of Twilight*) of 1835, *Les Voix Intérieures* (*Inner Voices*) of 1837, and *Les Rayons et les Ombres* (*Rays and Shadows*) of 1840—he was king of the literary world. By degrees he was converted to a moderate republicanism and became an admirer of Napoleon Bonaparte, and this change too won new admirers for him. He began to be, indeed, surrounded by too many adorers for his own good.

It has been said that a knowledge of the productions of 1830–1831, *Hernani* and *Notre-Dame de Paris*, would be enough to give one a good idea of Hugo. In both these works Hugo's characteristic greatness and defects are plentifully in evidence. His incomparable power to depict tragic passions, his dynamic control of magnificent language, the irresistible flow of his style, the unforgettable pictures—are all here. Here, too, are a sense of over-abundance, lack of balance, deficiency in a saving sense of humor.

Hernani breaks completely with the past of French drama in its subject material, its plot, its variety of style. The occasion of its first presentation at the Théâtre Français on February 25, 1830 proved historic and resulted in what came to be known as "The Battle of *Hernani.*" Its subject, verse, style, period, setting were the topics of heated debate between adherents of the old classicism and the Romantics. Even the scenery for *Hernani* was romantic in the extreme: now an old Spanish palace, now dim dungeons, now a city street lit by the reflections of flames in the distance, now a ballroom scene.

The plot of the play concerns a Spanish nobleman who has become a bandit under the assumed name of Hernani. He is an inveterate enemy of King Carlos, the future Emperor Charles V. Hernani loves Donna Sol, who is betrothed to her guardian, an old Spanish nobleman, Don Ruy Gomès de Silva. The king also falls in love with Donna Sol. The three men are each thus required by chivalric tradition to aid one rival against the other. Pretending to be a pilgrim, Hernani comes back to court, so he can see his beloved. The king saves Hernani from her guardian-lover. Hernani is soon saving the king against *his* enemies, and Carlos becomes Emperor. Carlos now goes in chase of Hernani, but is prevented from success by Don Gomès. To pay for this kindness, Hernani offers to surrender his life whenever it is demanded, and presents Don Gomès with his horn, the sound of which is to be the signal that Hernani's life is forfeit. Having taken on all his old dignities and title, Hernani is in the midst of the joyful celebration of his marriage to Donna Sol, when the horn sounds. Hernani and Donna Sol die together by drinking poison, and Don Gomès stabs himself by their side.

The plot of this play will strike anyone today as ridiculous but it is even less so than the plot of *Le Roi S'Amuse* and the still popular *Ruy Blas.* The success of Hugo as a dramatist has been owing to the energy of his style, the color he evokes, and the power with which he represents passion.

Notre-Dame de Paris

Hugo's novel *Notre-Dame de Paris* (1831), known to Americans as *The Hunchback of Notre Dame*, is characteristic of its author in its power, its poetic passages, and its violent imagination. It is a brilliant and withal somber evocation of medieval life. The focus of interest in the novel is the great cathedral that gives the book its name. The reader is made to feel how the life of the people centered around Notre Dame in the fifteenth century. Hugo recreates in prose the very aisles and towers of the church, the squares and crooked streets nearby, and every important structure then standing in Paris.

This, the first of Hugo's important historical novels, shows the great vogue that the historical novels of Sir Walter Scott were already having on the Continent. Scott may be said to have fathered the school of historical novelists in

Europe. It is interesting, in passing, to note that Scott's *Quentin Durward* (1823) is laid in the same era, and also contains a portrait of the clever, but treacherous, King Louis XI of France.

The leading idea in the novel is a noble one: God has created man in but an imperfect likeness of Himself; yet, though man is limited by his animal self and social institutions, Love can enable him to be spiritually free. To exhibit the thesis, Hugo employs, as usual, a series of violent contrasts in character and situation.

In expectation of the marriage of his heir to Margaret of Flanders, Louis XI is awaiting, in the opening month of 1482, the arrival of her ambassadors. The day, Epiphany, also marks the celebration by the people of the Festival of Fools, when the noisy Parisian crowd will choose the Prince of Fools and witness a play. Gringoire, a famished poet, orders the play to begin when the ambassadors have not yet arrived, but the performance is halted by the royal procession. No longer desirous of seeing the play concluded, the mob shouts that it is time to select the Prince of Fools, who by tradition must be remarkable for his ugliness. Various shady characters appear for the honor, until the bellringer of Notre-Dame, the hunchback Quasimodo, appears. He is deaf, built like an ape, with an enormous nose, and tusk-like teeth; he is chosen for the honor, and robed in ridiculous garments for his role. Pleased, yet suspicious, he is lifted over their heads, while the crowd marches through the streets. The celebration pauses to watch the dancing of the enchanting gypsy girl, Esmerelda, and her little goat. Later that same night, the impoverished poet Gringoire, despairing of shelter from the cold, witnesses the abduction of Esmerelda by a black-hooded man who is accompanied by Quasimodo. Just then a horseman riding down the street takes in the situation, and demands Esmerelda's release. Her abductors flee. Her rescuer turns out to be Phoebus de Chateaupers, a captain. Esmerelda falls wildly in love with him.

We now discover that the hooded man has been none other than the archdeacon of Notre-Dame, Claude Frollo. Formerly an upright man, who had befriended Quasimodo when abandoned as a baby, Frollo now is tempted by experiments in magic and alchemy. Quasimodo, in gratitude, would have given his life for Frollo, whose intention had been to enjoy Esmerelda without molestation from others in his cell.

Gringoire, continuing his aimless way, is set upon by some thieves, and faces death unless some one of the thieves' women is willing to marry him. None of these dames wants any part of him, and he is about to be strung up, when Esmerelda appears, declaring she will have him. Having rescued him, Esmerelda refuses to give herself to him later, determined that none but Phoebus shall be her mate.

The scene shifts. Quasimodo, whose admiration for the "witch" Esmerelda has been noted, and who is known to be almost a slave of the man suspected of witchcraft, is arrested, and tried on the charge of associating with dangerous people. He is sentenced to a flogging and the pillory. In the pillory

Quasimodo is seized with a terrible thirst, but the crowd only jeers and throws stones at him because of his ugliness. But brave Esmerelda climbs the scaffolding, and gives him to drink. Touched to the quick, Quasimodo's eyes pour tears down his grotesque face. Frollo has been a witness to the entire proceedings, and Quasimodo realizes that his benefactor has left him a prey to the cruelty of the mob without interfering.

Sometime later, Phoebus sees Esmerelda again dancing in the square, follows her, and arranges a meeting the next night. Frollo, having learned that she is only technically the wife of Gringoire, follows Phoebus, and offers the captain money if the latter will permit him to hide in the chamber where the lovers are to meet. Phoebus agrees. Seeing that the girl is indeed the Esmerelda whom he so much desires, Frollo dashes from his place of hiding and stabs the captain, though not identified by Esmerelda. As she faints Frollo makes his escape. A mob collects, exclaiming that the witch has slain the captain. Esmerelda is taken off to prison. In court she is found guilty of witchcraft. Her punishment is to do public penance before Notre-Dame and thence to be taken to be hanged.

En route to Notre-Dame, the gypsy sees the recovered Phoebus on horseback, but he ignores her. To avoid being involved in a scandal, he has kept out of the way during the proceedings. She appears before Frollo to do penance, and he offers to save her if she will give herself to him. She refuses.

Suddenly, Quasimodo appears, lifts the girl up, and carries her into the cathedral. The law of sanctuary now protects her as long as she can remain within. She is hidden by her rescuer in his own poor cell, and brought food by him. He locks the door to keep her safe, and shields her from the horror he knows she must feel for him by appearing only at mealtimes with his own food, which he brings to her. Frollo procures a key to Quasimodo's cell, and tries to overpower the girl. Quasimodo, hearing the struggle, comes in and drags out the priest, but allows him to free himself from his infuriated grasp.

A few days later, a mob collects outside Notre-Dame to demand Esmerelda's release from the church. Quasimodo bars the doors. The mob now tries to force the doors with a ram; Quasimodo climbs to the tower, and pours melted lead on their heads. Ladders are now fetched, and the men start climbing, but Quasimodo pushes the ladders from the wall, killing hundreds in the act. Now the royal guards come upon the scene to end the fray. Quasimodo imagines they have come to save the girl from the mob. He runs to the cell, and finds it empty. Gringoire, given the key by Frollo, has persuaded Esmerelda to fly; he takes her to a boat where Frollo is waiting. In fear Gringoire runs off. Again the priest offers to save her if she will yield to him. She flees from him, but the soldiers catch her, and drag her off to be hanged the following day.

Quasimodo, searching in miserable worry for the girl, comes upon Frollo on the tower watching with glee the erection of a gibbet in a square below. Quasimodo sees the rope placed over the girl's head and the trap sprung. In fury he picks up Frollo and hurls him over the wall. At last Quasimodo understands Frollo's machinations against the gypsy, and he weeps. Thereafter Quasimodo is no more seen.

Many years later when a vault is opened to find the remains of a famous dead man, there are found the skeletons of a woman who had been dressed in white and of a man whose arms were tightly clasped about her—the long-dead Esmerelda and Quasimodo. When an attempt is made to separate the bodies, they crumble into dust.

Hugo as a Lyric Poet

As has been said, during the decade of his preeminence Hugo published four volumes containing his greatest poems, *Autumn Leaves* (1831), *Songs of Twilight* (1835), *Inner Voices* (1837), and *Rays and Shadows* (1840). These "immortal volumes," as they have been called, establish him as a great lyrical poet.

He is to be seen here as a man who could write with the utmost tenderness and pathos without ever being less than virile. He is the master of the exquisite as much as he is the master of the awesome or the mystical moods which Nature can evoke in us. No other French poet has such a range.

Several distinguished English poets have made renderings of Hugo's verse. The reader is recommended to enjoy: Andrew Lang's versions of "More Strong Than Time," "The Grave and the Rose," and "The Genesis of Butterflies"; Francis Thompson's translation of "A Sunset"; and Swinburne's "The Poor Children."

In 1841 Hugo was elected to the French Academy, after being rejected several times. Two years later he suffered a heavy loss, the death of his daughter by drowning.

Now he entered upon a period of his life when he turned aside from poetry to participate in politics. Becoming a supporter of Louis-Philippe, "the citizen-king," Hugo was elevated by the monarch to the peerage (1845). Unfortunately, Hugo was wholly unsuited to politics, but he was surrounded by too many worshippers to take a just view of himself. After the Revolution of 1848 he was elected to the Constituent Assembly, and began to work on his vast novel, *Les Misérables*. He was at first a partisan of Louis Napoleon's, but after the latter's coup d'état in 1851, which ended in the Second Empire (1852) he became an inexorable enemy of "the little Napoleon." Banished by the monarch, he fled to Brussels, and then to Jersey and Guernsey—islands in the English Channel.

In 1853 at Jersey he issued *Les Châtiments* (*Chastisements*), which contains some spirited abuse of Napoleon III and his allies in the government. Despite the personal invective of the satires in this collection, there are some fine poems, such as "L'Expiation" with its stirring description of Waterloo. He remained in bitter exile until 1870.

In 1856 appeared *Les Contemplations*, an uneven collection of poems and fragments, some of them labored and obscure, some—especially those inspired by his grief at the death of his daughter—equal to his best. Free of politics, Hugo began to write again as assiduously as formerly, pouring forth from his pen a vast collection of verse, novels, and criticism.

In 1859 he issued the first part of an amazingly ambitious work in which his marvelous imagination is seen at its most breath-taking, *La Légende des Siècles* (*The Legend of Centuries*), of which the second and third parts were published in 1877 and 1883. The work is subtitled, *Petites Épopées* (*Little Epics*), Hugo's epic intention being to make a series of poems that would illustrate the destinies of the human race as seen in characteristic heroes. But not many of the poems are truly narrative, and the lyrical mood, of which he is a world master, predominates. He shows a preference for heroic periods: We find poems on *Genesis*, the war between the Titans and the Gods, Pan, Roland, the Cid, Dante. Characteristically, the golden ages of Athens or Rome do not tempt him. Everywhere he simplifies history to bring more sharply into focus the conflict between good and evil. His republicanism now seems to have become complete, for kings are always on the side of wickedness. Yet, despite historical indifference to the dividing line between fact and fancy, Hugo's reconstructions of the past are vivid and compelling beyond criticism, and his command of verse is more astounding than ever. Swinburne's rhapsody on this work, though not to be taken literally, is an index of how a great English poet was affected by it:

> Opening with a vision of Eve in Paradise which eclipses Milton's in beauty no less than in sublimity—a dream of the mother of mankind at the hour when she knew the first sense of dawning motherhood, it closes [the first part of *La Légende*] with a vision of the trumpet to be sounded on the day of judgment which transcends the imagination of Dante by right of a realized idea...the idea of real and final equity; the concept of absolute and abstract righteousness. Between this opening and this close the pageant of history and of legend, marshalled and vivified by the will and the hand of the poet, ranges through an infinite variety of action and passion, of light and darkness, of terror and pity, of lyric rapture and of tragic triumph.

La Légende is the summit of Hugo's achievement as a poet. It shows all his genius and all his defects.

Hugo's Last Years

After the fall of Napoleon III, Hugo returned to Paris (1870), and was with his compatriots during the terrible siege of that city, the harrowing experiences of which he recorded in verse in *L'Année Terrible* (*The Terrible Year*), published in 1872. He now was regarded as "the grand old man" of the country; few men have been accorded the hero-worship he knew for his remaining days. Now a confirmed republican, he was elected Senator by the city of Paris, and his eightieth birthday (1882) was the occasion of a national celebration. The very fact of his having entertained so many different kinds of political opinions made him appear the personification of his country's rapidly changing fortunes. His death in 1885 was mourned by the entire nation, and his remains were buried, with state, in the Pantheon.

His pen was active to the last. After his return to France, he published in 1877 *L'Art D'Être Grandpère* (*The Art of Being a Grandfather*), a charming, simple book; in 1878 appeared *Le Pape* (*The Pope*), in which the teachings of Christ are contrasted with the institutions of the Church; in 1879 came *La Pitié Suprème* (*The Supreme Pity*), a plea for charity towards tyrants, who are inevitably perverted by their own despotism; in 1881 he issued *Religions et Religion* (*Religions and Religion*), a poem in protest against the violence done religion by religious dogma; in the same year appeared *L'Âne* (*The Ass*), a satire against pedantry; in 1882 a very ambitious poem was published, *Les Quatres Vents de l'Esprit* (*The Four Winds of the Spirit*), a brilliant poetic exposition of the poet as satirist, dramatist, lyricist, and maker of epics—one book being devoted to each species.

Hugo as Dramatist

We have already discussed Hugo's earlier plays, *Cromwell* (1827) and *Hernani* (1830), and mentioned among others *Marion Delorme* (1829) and *Le Roi S'Amuse* (1832). *Marion Delorme* was delayed on the stage by the censorship; the hero is a Byronic character, and the setting the age of Louis XIII. *Le Roi S'Amuse* (*The King Amuses Himself*) finds Hugo employing his favorite formula: the opposition of the sublime and the grotesque. Here a buffoon is a desperate, devoted father who speaks with rapturous eloquence, and King Francis I, a vicious scoundrel. The public best knows this play as the libretto to Verdi's *Rigoletto*. From 1833 to 1835 Hugo wrote in prose the three dramas already noted, *Lucrèce Borgia*, in which too much poison is administered and too many antidotes supplied; *Marie Tudor*, more oratorical than dramatic; and *Angelo*, a melodrama on the tyrant of Padua.

When Hugo returned to writing poetic drama, he produced the most popular of his plays in the modern repertory of French drama, *Ruy Blas* (1838). It contains his usual antitheses. As in *Hernani* the setting is Spain. Its hero, Ruy Blas, is a lackey of the noblest kind of character; Don Salluste, a nobleman of Spain has "the soul of a lackey." Ruy Blas is made Premier of the land, wins the love of the Queen, and introduces many important reforms. Though now a grandee himself, Ruy Blas is faithful to his master Don Salluste, who is consumed with a desire for vengeance against the Queen. Don Salluste reveals to the Queen Ruy Blas' former status, and tries to force her to elope with him. Ruy Blas thereupon is compelled to kill Don Salluste, and he poisons himself. As foolish as the plot is, the play holds its place in the French theater by reason of the power of individual scenes, and the brilliance of the verse. It is probable that it is the poetry of *Ruy Blas* that has maintained the popularity of the drama.

Les Burgraves (*The Burgraves*) of 1843 was so completely a failure that Hugo for a long time thereafter clung to his determination to write no more plays. For once the grandiosity of the poet was too much even for the romantic public. The "epic drama" was even parodied by many rivals.

A handful of short plays was published many years later, in 1866, under the title of *Théâtre en Liberté* (*The Free Theater*), some of the pieces having real charm. Finally, in 1882 Hugo published the play, *Torquemada*, a powerful study of the Spanish Inquisition, though confused in plot.

Hugo's plots, taking his dramatic output as a whole, are all too much contrived to make convincing drama. He was also deficient in the delineation of character: He was too much preoccupied with the business of presenting violently opposed extremes of human conduct to create any living men and women. He is particularly weak in what we now most demand: psychological insight. It is rather in the power and energy with which individual scenes are written that Hugo's plays are admirable; and even more, his genius as a poet is everywhere evident.

Hugo as a Novelist

Before *Notre-Dame de Paris* (1831), which we have already considered at length, Hugo published two unimportant romances and *Le Dernier Jour d'un Condamné* (*The Last Day of a Condemned Man*)—the last, issued in 1829, a fervent attack on capital punishment. *Claude Gueux* (1834) returns to the same subject.

Les Misérables (*The Wretched Ones*), written in exile and appearing in 1862, though one of his most unequal performances, has captured the imagination of the non-French world more than any other of his books. (Perhaps because of its bulk?) Swinburne has called it "the greatest epic and dramatic work of fiction ever created or conceived; the epic of a soul transfigured and redeemed, purified by heroism and glorified through suffering; the tragedy and the comedy of life at its darkest and its brightest, of humanity at its best and at its worst." If one cannot agree with Swinburne that *Les Misérables* is the "greatest" of such conceptions, one certainly will admit that it is one of the greatest. For *Les Misérables* is one of the most moving appeals ever made in the history of literature to our common humanity; only a great soul could have written it. It is, indeed, a collection of novels rather than a novel—a wonderful, somewhat monstrously overwhelming gallimaufry of plot and character. But it contains superb pages, pages which will ever be remembered; among the most famous of these are the passages recreating the Battle of Waterloo, the flight of Jean Valjean, the portrait of the Bishop, the drama of the candlesticks, the description of the Benedictine monastery.

It would take a book to outline the plot of *Les Misérables*. Here it is possible only to give an idea of the central story. Jean Valjean is the hero. He is a convict sentenced to the galleys for stealing bread for his starving sister's family. Because of his numerous attempts to escape, his term of slavery is always increased. At last he is free, begs his way, and meets with unexpected kindness at the hands of the Bishop of D——. His soul brutalized by his servitude, Jean Valjean steals the bishop's silver. The police catch up with him, and the Bishop now proves that he is a true Christian by telling the police that he had given the loot as a present to Jean Valjean.

Overwhelmed by this kindness, Jean Valjean changes the whole course of his life. He prospers so well that years later we find him, under the assumed name of Monsieur Madeleine, mayor of his town. The police inspector, Javert, however, a man of strict but narrow mind, has not abandoned the trail of Jean Valjean, as an escaped convict. When another man is falsely arrested in his place, Jean Valjean surrenders himself to the police, and goes back to the galleys.

Once more he escapes. His goodness unaffected, he rescues little Cosette, the daughter of a prostitute whom he had before befriended, from the family that is torturing her, and raises her as his own child.

When she grows into young womanhood, she falls in love with handsome Marius. Jean Valjean, fearful of losing the girl, removes to another dwelling. He is betrayed into the hands of robbers by Cosette's former tormentors, but manages to escape. Marius begs Valjean, when he finds Cosette again, for the girl's hand; Valjean refuses.

The populace in Paris are having an uprising; Marius joins them at the barricades. Javert is taken and bound as a prisoner. Valjean, his pity for the young lovers awakened, comes to the barricades too. He discovers Javert bound, and frees him. The barricades fall, and Jean Valjean comes upon the wounded Marius. Through the sewers of Paris he carries him for hours. When he emerges he meets Javert, who arrests him. Jean Valjean asks only to be allowed to bring Marius home safely.

Javert agrees, waits at the door, but his conscience torn between duty and gratitude to the man who has saved his life, he turns to the river and drowns himself in the Seine. Marius and Cosette are soon married with Jean Valjean's blessing, and the old man reveals that he is not her true father. Confessing he is an escaped convict, he finds himself banished from Marius' house.

When Marius at last learns that it was Jean Valjean who had saved him when he lay unconscious, the couple go to Jean Valjean, only to find him dead. His last words had been an acknowledgment of his indebtedness to the Bishop. He was buried in a grave without a stone to mark its place.

In 1866 Hugo published *Les Travailleurs de la Mer* (*Toilers of the Sea*), a novel that reveals the great poet who wrote it. It is an exquisite work dedicated to the island of Guernsey, "my present asylum." The story deals with the fortunes of the steamboat La Durande, which operates between St. Malo and Guernsey. The descriptions of the sea, the storms, the bottom of the ocean are brilliant in the extreme—like an "apocalypse," said George Henry Lewes.

L'Homme Qui Rit (*The Man Who Laughs*) appeared in 1869, another historical novel. Its hero Gwynplaine was disfigured in childhood by cuts around his mouth which left him looking as though he were perpetually grinning in a horrible way. The Duchess Josiana, a headstrong woman, falls in love with him just because he is such a monster. But he is loved also by a blind girl, Dea, whom he rescued from the snow in her infancy, and who worships him. Her love empowers him to withstand the wicked Duchess. When Dea dies, he commits suicide.

Quatre-vingt-treize (*Ninety-three*) appeared in 1874, his last important novel, and deals with the tumultuous year 1793 in France. Among the characters are Danton, Robespierre, and Marat. The chief characters are Lantenac, a monarchist émigré, who represents the past; Cimourdain, citizen-priest, who represents the present; and Gauvain, man of mercy, who points the future. The chief interest of the novel is the masterful way in which Hugo shows three children caught in the torrential events of the Revolution.

Hugo as Critic and Journalist

Besides this enormous outpouring of books, Hugo was the author of four volumes of *Actes et Paroles* (*Deeds and Words*), appearing 1875–1885, the record of his exile, his speeches in the Assembly and in the Senate, and much autobiographical material. His attacks on Napoleon III will be found in *Napoléon le Petit* (*Little Napoleon*) and *Histoire d'un Crime* (*History of a Crime*) of 1852 and 1877 respectively.

In 1864 he published his eloquent tribute to Shakespeare, *William Shakespeare*.

ALFRED DE MUSSET (1810–1857)

After Hugo, the most gifted poet of his generation and the most passionate was Alfred de Musset. Born in Paris of a family already known to literature, he became a member of Hugo's *cénacle* when very young, where he was considered to be the wonderful prodigy of the group.

When only nineteen he published in 1830 a volume, *Contes d'Espagne et d'Italie* (*Tales of Spain and Italy*), which at once proved him a poet of great abilities. It is characteristic of the capriciousness of Musset's talents that the volume should have contained a hilarious parody on the Romantics, of whose inner circle he was a member; the "Ballad to the Moon" ridicules the school by comparing the moon above a steeple to a dot over an *i*. The volume occasioned a great deal of discussion.

He had already made a translation of DeQuincey's *Confessions of an English Opium-Eater*—no easy task. In December, 1830 his one-act comedy *La Nuit Vénitienne* (*The Venetian Night*) was hissed off the stage, probably by prearrangement. Unfortunately for French drama, Musset's predominant failing was weakness of will. He became discouraged and at once gave up his ambitions to write for the stage.

Musset wrote plays thereafter, but never for performance, though some of them found their way to the stage. He now seems to us the best playwright

France produced in his era; but it is obvious that a public that could become excited over Hugo's plots could never have cared much for Musset's. He had the wisdom to see that something between the classical and the Romantic extremes was possible to drama. There is an artful mixture of the grotesque and the comic in his plays, and he is a master of brilliant dialogue.

From time to time he published his plays in the magazine, *Revue des Deux Mondes* (*Review of Two Worlds*). The first of these to appear was *André del Sarto* (1833), and, in a matter of weeks, the best comedy of its time, *Les Caprices de Marianne* (*The Whims of Marianne*). In 1834 appeared Musset's Shakespearean drama, *Lorenzaccio;* to the same year belongs *On Ne Badine Pas avec l'Amour* (*You Don't Trifle with Love*). Among his other plays one of the best is *Il Ne Faut Pas Jurer de Rien* (*Don't Swear about Anything*), a brilliant comedy, written in 1836.

But it is as a poet that Musset figures largest in French literature.

Musset as Poet

Musset stands out in the mind of the lover of literature as the most moving lyric poet of his age. A creature of mood and imagination, petulant, unpredictable, wonderfully gifted, his greatest concern in life and letters was with love. His work reveals the man, if any work ever did. In his tempestuous life the chief episode was his tumultuous love affair with the romantic woman who was known to the world as "George Sand."

Many attempts have been made by partisans of one or the other to allocate the blame for the disruption of their violent attachment. But there can be little doubt that the relationship of two such egotists, both living their private lives very much in public, was doomed to failure. Their opposing temperaments destined Musset to fare the worse in the aftermath. George Sand was expansive, generous, and far more solid basically, and hence came out not too much scathed. Musset, with a weak physical constitution, pettish, spoiled, and willful, emerged a wreck. Both, of course, being dyed-in-the-wool Romantics, made literary copy out of the experience.

They met in 1833 and, although she was six years his elder, fell wildly in love. They ran off to Italy and both became ill in Venice. The physician who tended them was soon assuming the role of George Sand's solace for Musset's neglect. Months of altercation and reconciliations followed, until the affair ended.

Musset's friends soon convinced him that he had been the injured party. Love, which was his religion, had been fulfilled in the brief space of their living together, and Musset was determined to destroy himself by extreme dissipation. He succeeded only too well, as his early death indicates. But the poetic fruits of his blighted love affair constitute his highest achievement: the four *Nuits* (*Nights*) and the *Lettre à Lamartine* (*Letter to Lamartine*), as well as his autobiography, *Confession d'un Enfant du Siècle* (*Confession of a Child of the Age*) and the drama *You Don't Trifle with Love*.

IMPORTANCE

Musset's greatness as a poet was achieved almost effortlessly. He reminds one of Byron in his fatal facility, his indifference to real care with his poems, the air of too much freedom in his form, and his unexpected alternations between malicious wit and honest passion. Indeed, Byron was the most considerable influence on his work, and it may be on his life too. Like him he was much too fond of creating the impression of being very wicked and unconventional. But he is more authentically a poet than his English prototype, and more sensitive; his achievement is certainly higher. Byron's lyric poems and poetic drama rarely succeed in making us feel that he is doing more than posing attractively. No lyric poet can wring the heart with the poignancy of his lines more effectively than does Musset; we feel that he is profoundly sincere.

The four *Nuits* (*Nights*) are all wonderful poems (1835–1837). Three of them take the shape of a dialogue between the poet and his Muse. The "nights" of the poem are in May, August, October, and December; each is a masterpiece of lyrical feeling, beautifully sung, and exquisitely moving. *The Night of May*, which has been described as written with "swooning beauty," finds the poet protesting to his Muse that he cannot sing again, as she bids, because of the terrible wound in his heart; the Muse reminds him of all the subjects he could still convert into poetry, but he is not tempted; the Muse recalls to him the truth that "nothing can so ennoble us as a great sorrow"; she reminds him, too, of the legend of the pelican, who was said by tradition to rip open her own breast to feed her young on her blood; but the poet's grief is still too fresh, and he concludes with the insistence that he cannot sing. In the dialogue with her in *October*, he greets her with happiness because his grief is over; but as he recites his recovery, the memory of the blighted love wounds him anew, and he is in passionate grief once more; the Muse succeeds in calming him: "Man is an apprentice to the mastership of grief"; the poet leaves with the Muse to sing now of nature.

Rolla (1835), one of his masterpieces, shows how strong the Byronic influence was upon him. It is "half Faust, half Manfred," the portrait of a depraved man whose heart is ever touched with a love for humanity. He tries living for pleasure; his last debauching experience is with a girl of fifteen, sold by her mother to him for his gold; feeling it his destiny, he dies willingly by the girl's side. Despite its almost lurid romanticism of plot, the poem is brilliant and realistic in its details, convincingly the work of a major poet.

The Letter to Lamartine, in very moving lines contrasts the calm idealism of the older poet's Romanticism with the feverishness of Musset's own muse.

Musset had little interest in politics or religion, although his *L'Espoir en Dieu* (*The Hope in God*) expresses his undefined spiritual cravings. *Sur la Paresse* (*On Sloth*) is a frank confession of his own incorrigible laziness, his dislike for the middle-class values of his time, his preference for the past days of gallantry, and his general credo of living by whim and caprice.

Souvenir returns to the George Sand affair in exquisite verse. He can sing with some tranquillity of it now: "I only say: Here at this hour, one day, I loved, and I was loved....This treasure my soul shall bear to God."

The Confession of a Child of the Age is in the tradition of Rousseau's *Confessions*, but brilliantly written with sometimes excessive candor. In addition to giving us a clear account of his love affair with George Sand, it also is a mirror of public morale at the time as a result of Napoleon's ideas and exploits. Musset realized that he was living in a sick age, and attributed it to the fact that Bonaparte had ruined the world with his ambition. Musset's character, too, is everywhere exhibited in this autobiography in its most characteristic attitudes. Like a spoiled child he reacted with violent disgust to everything in life that was either difficult or unpleasant. It is precisely in that character that he figures as a poet.

Musset is also the author of a series of tales in prose, collected under the title of *Nouvelles* (*Tales*), which are brilliantly written.

During the last years (1851–1857) of his short life he wrote almost nothing, for he passed from youth into senescence before he was forty. His work is entirely the production of a young man. He is, as Saintsbury says of him, "one of the most remarkable [instances] in the literature of Europe of merely natural genius...not assisted in the least by critical power and a strong will."

ALFRED DE VIGNY (1797–1863)

Count Alfred de Vigny, who shares with Hugo and Musset the position of leader in the Romantic movement, was a poet of considerably more objectivity than the latter. His expression is not directly personal, like Musset's; the inspiration for his work, however, did emanate from his experiences.

Born at Loches of a noble family, he married in 1826 a wealthy Englishwoman and thus remained financially independent for the rest of his life. Realizing that the privileges of men of rank were a thing of the past, he had felt called upon to enter the army, which he at last left in 1828 to devote himself to literature. The fruit of these experiences is to be found in *Servitude et Grandeur Militaires* (*Tales of Military Servitude and Grandeur*), which appeared in 1835.

His collaboration with Hugo on the *Conservateur Littéraire* had brought him into close contact with the Romantic movement (1820). His first volume of poems was issued in 1822, and enlarged in 1826 under the title of *Poèmes*

Antiques et Modernes (*Poems Ancient and Modern*). The collection is subdivided into three heads: "Mystical Poems," "Ancient Poems," and "Modern Poems."

Among the "Mystical Poems" are included poems on "The Deluge," "Moses," and one called "Eloa." "Moses" expounds the same idea that Vigny later used as a basis for his play *Chatterton:* Society always neglects the true poet and heaps misfortune on his head. (This notion is also to be found in the works of the English romanticists, Shelley ["Adonais"] and Keats ["Ode to a Nightingale"].) "Eloa" is the narrative of an angel, Eloa, born of one of Christ's tears, who out of divine pity comes to pity Satan, and is thus drawn by the Prince of Darkness into Hell.

Among the "Modern Poems" are two famous poems, "The Horn" and "The Frigate *Serious,*" the former evoking thoughts of the days of Charlemagne and his Paladins.

Thereafter, though busy with his pen, Vigny issued very few verses. His volume had achieved the great success it deserved, but he turned his attention to prose and drama.

Vigny as Poet

IMPORTANCE

In comparison with Hugo and Musset, Vigny strikes us as being far more reflective. His output is small, for there was to be only one more volume of verse by him, *Les Destinées* (*The Fates*), issued in 1864 after his death. His qualities are almost exactly opposite to those of Musset. He was a careful artist in verse; his lines have an exquisite polish and an admirable sense of perfect performance. His last poems are as well done as his earlier, though they open up no new range.

Vigny figures as an outstanding philosophical poet in France, and his work has never suffered the decline in appreciation that has been the fate of his fellow Romantics. On the other hand, his audience has always been smaller and more select.

Vigny, the poet of the inner life, was as limited in the number of ideas he presented as in the number of poems he wrote—both plainly the effect of long consideration. The note he sounds most consistently is one of noble stoicism and pitying pessimism; he is the poet neither of hope (like Hugo) nor despair (like Musset). One constantly meets in his verses the realization of the loneness which a man of superior parts must expect; the leader of humanity must steel himself to find neither love nor understanding. "Samson's Anger," from *Les Destinées*, shows how easily the love of the great man is subject to betrayal. Even Nature is no kind nurse, as "The House of the Shepherd" from the same volume exquisitely sets forth; she is rather our tomb. God is unconcerned with us, we read in "The Mount of Olives," and man can only answer "the eternal silence of Divinity" with his own "cold silence." Let man learn a lesson from the wolf ("The Death of the Wolf"), and enfold himself with an unyielding stoicism. He can find an outlet in pity for his fellows ("The House of the Shepherd").

Vigny as Dramatist

The dramatic productions, like the poems, of Vigny are few in number, but intellectually of some interest. The influence of England is again manifest in the translations he made of *Othello* and *The Merchant of Venice*. An historical play of his, produced in 1831, *Le Maréchal d'Ancre* (*The Marshal of Ancre*) is laid in the seventeenth century. It was not a success. But his *Chatterton* (1835) is a play that still maintains the interest of the public.

It contains one of his favorite ideas: The tragic lot of a poet in the world. To quote the author: "It is the story of a man who writes a letter in the morning, and awaits its answer until night; the answer arrives and kills him." It is the tale of a poet who commits suicide rather than accept degradation. The plot is interesting. Chatterton is pitied in his failure and illness by the wife of John Bell, a cruel manufacturer in whose house he lives. Kitty Bell succors him, but dares not speak to him because his presence disturbs her heart too much. Their love is manifested by the awkward silence between them. In the end Chatterton poisons himself, and Kitty dies silently of a broken heart. It is significant of the Romantic movement that for Vigny the early death of the boy-wonder Chatterton had the same meaning as for the English Romantics: the type of unappreciated genius.

Vigny's dramatic work shows his interest in the historical play shorn of exterior pomp.

Vigny as Novelist

Under the influence of Sir Walter Scott, Vigny in 1826 produced the historical novel *Cinq-Mars* laid in the reign of Louis XIII. In the Preface he precedes Hugo's *Marion Delorme* by several years when he claims the rights of the creator to tamper with historical fact. Though under the influence of Scott, the novel presented a new type of fiction to French readers: a story colored by the trappings and pomp of history, in which Louis XIII, Richelieu, and Gaston d'Orléans are introduced. The hero, young Cinq-Mars, in his attempts to supplant Richelieu and maintain the love of Marie de Gonzague, moves through a series of incidents which are intended to recreate the life of the times described. Vigny is more temperate than Hugo as an historical novelist, but also colder and less racy.

Stello (1832) employs the cases of Chénier and Chatterton to prove that poets are doomed by the insensitiveness of society. It is from this look that Vigny soon drew material for his drama *Chatterton*.

Tales of Military Servitude and Grandeur (1835), Vigny's finest prose works, is, as has been said, the product of his own observations in the army. It is a collection of tales with historical backgrounds.

ALEXANDRE DUMAS *PÈRE* (1803–1870)

The elder Dumas is known as Dumas *père* to distinguish him from his also celebrated son, Dumas *fils*. (*Père* means father, and *fils* is son in French.)

IMPORTANCE

Perhaps of all French writers none has had a greater audience in the English-speaking world than Dumas père, author of *The Count of Monte Cristo* and *The Three Musketeers*. Unfortunately his renown is all out of proportion to his deserts; for, except as typically illustrating the characteristics of the Romantic movement, Dumas *père* has small title to be mentioned in a history of belles-lettres. As a novelist, he was never at any time more than the writer of popular successes, and the novels issued under his name have no distinction of style or characterization. His importance is in bringing the vogue of the Romantic novel to the people.

Everything about Dumas' literary career is fabulous. His father was the son of a black African woman and the French Marquis de la Pailleterie. (Our author adopted the name of Dumas during his literary eminence.) Alexandre Dumas' father had been a brilliant officer under Napoleon I, well known to the army for his strength and daring. Alexandre Dumas himself received hardly any education, and came to Paris at the age of twenty. Procuring a clerkship in the household of the Duke of Orleans, he began writing at once. With such historical information as he could dig out of dictionaries, he composed a play in verse which was accepted, but not acted, at the Théâtre Français. He soon had another play ready, *Henry III and His Court*, and it was produced with great success in 1829. This melodrama, indeed, was so popular that seven rival dramatists petitioned Charles X not to allow such works to invade the dignity of the Théâtre Français. The King replied, "Like all Frenchmen I occupy only one seat in the theater."

Dumas followed these successes with a series of melodramas, too numerous to list. They include: *Christine* (1830), *Charles VII* (1831), *Richard of Arlington* (1831), *The Tower of Nesle* (1832). The dates will indicate Dumas' fantastic productivity as a writer. Sir Walter Scott's influence, which is particularly to be seen in Dumas' novels, is also visible in the "historical" backgrounds for Dumas' melodramas, and is also present in his later comedies, *Mlle. de Belle-Isle* (1839), *A Marriage under Louis XV* (1841), and *The Ladies at Saint-Cyr* (1843).

Dumas' first play precedes *Hernani*; and although it cannot rival Hugo's play in merit on any level, yet it is in that same flamboyant Romantic vein associated with the greater man's name. Dumas' plays, both melodrama and comedy, are too numerous to list. However, profitable though he found dramatic composition, he was soon devoting the major part of his energies to the novel-factory he ran, turning out historical novels in the Sir Walter Scott style by the dozen.

It would take pages to list only the names of these novels. A staff of "collaborators" who often did most of the writing helped him turn out some three hundred volumes. No writer on record has made more money out of books, and none spent more. He lived in such luxury that despite his income he was always in debt. In addition to all this activity, he traveled considerably—and made profit out of that too.

The Three Musketeers (1844), *The Count of Monte Cristo* (1844), and *The Black Tulip* (1845) are his most widely read novels. The importance of the Dumas novels is that they popularized the historical novel at its most swashbuckling. The prose, the psychology, the characterization are often slipshod and empty. But Dumas must be mentioned if only because of the public he reached.

OTHER ROMANTIC POETS AND CRITICS

Théophile Gautier (1811–1872)

Théophile Gautier, a Gascon by birth, at first embarked upon the career of a painter. The effects of that study are to be seen on all his literary works, for the pictorial values in his writing are particularly strong. He was introduced to the Hugo *cénacle* by his poet-novelist friend. Gérard de Nerval (1805–1857), translator of Goethe's *Faust* and author of exquisite prose tales, and he became one of the great man's most ardent worshippers. At the historic opening of *Hernani*, he was prominent among the enthusiasts in his long flowing hair and notorious red waistcoat.

In 1830 appeared his first volume of verse, *Poésies*, revealing a firm hand but little else noteworthy. *Albertus* (1833), a narrative poem in the most exaggerated Romantic manner, followed; this tale of the orgies of a witch is rather Byronic, except for the vivid pictures and firm versification. With his next volume, *La Comédie de la Mort* (*The Comedy of Death*) of 1833, Gautier took leave of this exuberant brand of Romanticism: it deals with its hero's search for ideal love despite his experience with love that is not ideal.

Undertaking the post of dramatic and art critic for *La Presse* (1837), and later the *Moniteur* (1845), Gautier continued to complain bitterly about the quantity of hackwork that he was thereby forced to turn out. Nevertheless, these pieces written by occasion and necessity constitute an important part of the history of the Romantic movement. He was a man of great taste and artistic judgment, a masterful pen, and great enthusiasms. He thus helped formulate the critical criteria for his and succeeding generations.

It is to him that we owe the earliest formulation of the theory of "art for art's sake" (*l'art pour l'art*), which was to figure prominently in later nineteenth century esthetic discussion. For him artistic expression has nothing to do with morality or politics; the purpose of the arts is to present beauty for beauty's sake alone. He himself was indifferent to politics, and therefore had no adjustments to make to France's changing political horizons. On the other hand, his artistic conscience was so inviolable that he threatened instant resignation if his praise of Victor Hugo (when that praise was dangerous to make publicly in France) were not printed.

His more mature creative work, once he had rid himself of Romantic excesses, is almost uniformly admirable. Having begun to elaborate his esthetic theories, he put them into practice. His emphasis on perfection of form and picturesqueness of expression turned the Romantic movement in the direction of the "Parnassians" who were to follow, by leading authors away from egocentric writing to writing as a fine art. Baudelaire was one of his most devoted admirers.

Gautier's volume of poems, issued in 1852, *Émaux et Camées* (*Enamels and Cameos*), exhibits this transition in his poetic art. The poems in this collection are a wonderful combination of perfect chiseling and lightness. Austin Dobson has very well captured the form of the original French in these lines from his translation of the poem, "Art":

> *All passes. Art alone*
> *Enduring stays to us;*
> *The bust outlasts the throne,*
> *The coin, Tiberius.*

As a writer of fiction, Gautier exhibits the richness of a prose heavily laden with imagery at its best. *Mademoiselle de Maupin* (1835) continues unfortunately to be included, like the *Decameron*, among books that are sought after by the salacious-minded adolescent. It is true, of course, that, being an early work, it was intended by its author to be somewhat shocking to the respectable. But for all its eroticism, it is truly a work of art in the jewelled quality of its phrasing and boldness of imagination. Like Gautier's other stories it has weathered time better than the high-minded extravagances of Hugo.

His novel *Captain Fracasse* (1861–1863) is an example of the Dumas-Sir Walter Scott tradition, but far exceeds in merit anything of the former; and it may be said of the latter that he rarely wrote anything as good. Gautier, as a writer of fiction, however, is at his very best in the shorter tale, of which "Le Roman de la Momie" (The Romance of a Mummy), published in 1856, is a fine example; he succeeds in recreating for us a whole vista of ancient Egyptian life.

Gautier's records of his travels are among the finest of their kind: his books on *Spain* (1839), *Italy* (1852), *Constantinople* (1854), and *Russia* (1866) are written with his characteristic richness of style and pictorial vividness.

IMPORTANCE

During the reaction of the later century against the Romantic movement, Gautier's works were somewhat disparaged. But they were disparaged by younger men who obviously owed much of their vocabulary and artistic vision to him. If his limitation is his lack of interest in matters other than esthetic, it is not a serious one for an important writer. He cannot fail to impress one with the integrity with which he practiced his chosen art, and the number of excellent works for which we are indebted to him.

Charles-Augustin de Sainte-Beuve (1804–1869)

Sainte-Beuve was the most important critic of the French Romantic movement; some would say that he was the leading literary critic of his century. The son of an English mother and French father, he received a good education first at his native town of Boulogne, and then at Paris. He acquired a solid grounding in the classics of Greece and Rome, and an easy prose style. For a while he considered entering the field of medicine; those studies (1824–1837) disciplined him in the formation of detached judgments and objective research. Indeed, he later described his own purposes as a critic to be recording the "natural history of minds."

While he was attending lectures in medicine he began, at the invitation of the founder of *The Globe*, his former teacher, to contribute to that paper (1824). By 1827 he was one of its most important writers; his recurring subject was French literature of the sixteenth century, the quasi-romantic writings that preceded the Classic movement of the seventeenth century. These pieces were collected in 1828 as *Tableau de la Poésie Française au Seizième Siècle (Historical and Critical Sketch of French Poetry in the Sixteenth Century)*, a volume that at once established Sainte-Beuve as the acknowledged critic of the Romantic movement. In dealing with the Pléiade, the group of sixteenth century French poets, Sainte-Beuve considers the attempt of Ronsard and du Bellay to raise the French language to the level of ancient Greek and Latin by expanding the native tongue in the realm of exalted poetry. Noting that the Pléiade was not entirely successful, Sainte-Beuve urges his contemporaries to continue the Pléiade's uncompleted task by exploiting the national idiom. He recognized that the new Romantic literature was to a degree already freeing itself of Neoclassical shackles by reviving earlier poetic forms and techniques, but he also knew that the resources of sixteenth century French poetry were limited. In England, he saw, it was necessary only to go back to Shakespeare to revivify the language; in Italy, to Dante. But the French, he says, "have lacked those vast sacred reserves against the day of regeneration, and we have to draw from the present and from ourselves." The value of the old French poets will be to encourage contemporary effort by certain similarities in a "bold and reckless kind of style, without rules or examples, which proceeds by chance as thought directs."

Sainte-Beuve's success and his membership in Hugo's *cénacle* misled him for a time to believe he had the makings of a poet. His *Vie, Poésies, et Pensées de Joseph Delorme* (*The Life, Poetry, and Thoughts of Joseph Delorme*), issued under that pseudonym in 1829, and his *Consolations* (1830), have the elegance of his prose but are not noteworthy. Neither is his 1837 volume, *Les Pensées d'Août* (*August Thoughts*).

Luckily, he did not persist in his attempts at poetry. His critical articles for the *Revue de Paris*, the *Constitutionnel*, and the *Moniteur* form the basis for his reputation. When he was writing his *Causeries du Lundi* (*Monday Chats*) for the *Constitutionnel*, they were eagerly awaited all over Europe. He lectured on the Jansenists at Lausanne (1837–1838), was elected to the French Academy (1844), and after the 1848 revolution went to Liège to lecture on Chateaubriand and his contemporaries. In 1855 he was appointed Professor of Latin Poetry at the Collège de France, but his friendliness to the Second Empire forced his resignation there. In 1865 he was elected to the Senate.

With the exception of the verse already mentioned; a novel, *Volupté* (*Pleasure*), published in 1834; and a massive history of the Jansenists which he worked on for twenty years, *Histoire de Port-Royal* (*History of Port-Royal*) issued between 1840 and 1860—the rest of his work is critical. As collected these later volumes were called: *Chateaubriand et Son Groupe Littéraire* (*Chateaubriand and His Literary Circle*) of 1860; *Portraits Littéraires* (*Literary Portraits*) of 1844; *Portraits de Femmes* (*Portraits of Women*) of 1844; *Portraits Contemporains* (*Contemporary Portraits*) of 1846; *Causeries du Lundi* (*Monday Chats*), issued 1857–1862 in 15 volumes; *Nouveaux Lundis* (*New Mondays*), issued 1863–1870 in 13 volumes; and *Premiers Lundis* (*First Mondays*), issued in 1875 posthumously in 3 volumes.

Before Sainte-Beuve the only tradition existing in France for forming critical judgments was the method of measuring a work by some abstract principles of literary creation. Hugo, in the Preface to the *Orientales* (1829), had already objected to this procedure by declaring that the only business of a critic is to discover the intrinsic merit of a work without regard to any other considerations. But to write such criticism, a wider knowledge of world literature and trends than most Frenchmen had ever had was necessary. Sainte-Beuve was untiring in his desire to be both well prepared and scrupulous in applying Hugo's criterion. He had a vast enthusiasm for research; no labor was too much in seeking out documentary evidence for establishing a true understanding of the biography of writers and men of influence, historical facts, philosophic and religious backgrounds, manners of the time, and private influences. His was the first attempt at what might be called "scientific" criticism.

IMPORTANCE

Sainte-Beuve's critical essays study the author as a man as well as a writer; he takes into consideration the creator's career as a whole when he is judging a particular work. He gives us an idea of the *mores*, the social institutions, the artistic atmosphere of the times, the purposes and ambitions of the author. As a result Sainte-Beuve has been often unjustly accused of excessive detachment, of being more interested in his critical apparatus than in catching the spirit of literary works— charges which, taking his work in all its wide achievement, are entirely untrue. He was bold, honest, modest, and kind—above all, comprehensive. He was not in the least timid about going against the current of opinion, and quite ready to recast an earlier opinion in the light of more mature judgment. Thus, he first accorded, then retracted, and finally reaffirmed Musset's position as a lyric poet of first rank. He delivered some telling thrusts, as when he said of Mme. Constant that she was "still a shepherdess, even at the age of seventy-two," and some notable appreciations, as of Hugo and Vigny. The only serious objection that can be made to his body of criticism is that his interest in detail seems to have prevented his giving any writer a final summing up. Doubtless, he would have felt that such an attempt would have been by its very nature more or less than the truth. And for truth he had a passion.

Pierre Jean de Béranger (1780–1857)

Béranger was a poet of the people, his father being in business, and his grandfather having been a tailor. He earned his own living as a clerk for the government. By political conviction he was part staunch republican, part Bonapartist, and hence was out of favor with the new court for his political songs. Often imprisoned, he became thereby all the more popular. Equally hostile to the "citizen-king," Louis-Philippe, he refused to come to terms with his government, and retired to private life. After 1833 he published no more. The Revolution of 1848 found him in the Assembly, but he soon resigned. He proved equally uncompromising towards the Second Empire, and would take none of its proffered honors.

Béranger's work is entirely in the field of the *chanson* (song). His lyrics, political, satirical, pseudo-philosophical, and amatory were printed in the newspapers, and were widely popular in cafés and parlors alike. Somewhat in the fashion of the Irish Tom Moore, his songs have very Romantic content, and quite stilted classic diction.

Literary critics have almost universally scorned Béranger as being only a vulgar poet (that is, a popular versifier). He was disliked by the Romantics for his vocabulary, by the Catholics for his freethinking, by royalists and republicans alike for his devotion to Napoleon. But the mass of people, who ordinarily never read poetry at all, read him and quoted him. If he is not a great literary figure, he cannot be dismissed as valueless. He can sing with a remarkable range of feeling from wit to pathos; his real patriotism has endeared him to Frenchmen; and a moral wholesomeness pervades his work and lends it an air of naturalness belied by his language.

Among his best pieces are: "Le Grenier" (The Garret), which Thackeray has translated, "Le Roi d'Yvetot" (The King of Yvetot), "Roger Bontemps," "Les Souvenirs du Peuple" (Memories of the People), "La Bonne Vieille" (The Good Old Woman), and "Les Gueux" (The Beggars) —all written with deep humanity.

Béranger's songs were collected in 1815, 1821, and 1833.

Charles Nodier (1780–1844)

Nodier was one of the founders of the Romantic movement. It was at his home that Hugo's *cénacle* met. A man of extraordinary talent but no genius, he was a critic, poet, novelist, and lexicographer of merit. The best of his work is his series of novels and novelettes: *Les Proscrits* (*The Outlaws*) of 1802, *Le Peintre de Salzbourg* (*The Painter of Salzburg*) of 1803, *Jean Sbogar* (1818), *Trilby* (1822), *La Neuvaine de la Chandeleur* (*The Novena of Candlemas*) of 1839, and *Le Chien de Brisquet* (*Brisquet's Dog*) of 1844. These show the Romantic movement's addiction to the fantastic and weird, and were quite influential in shaping that taste. He was much influenced himself by the writers of the English Gothic school.

In his youth he wrote a poem, *Napoleon*, with some bitter invective against Bonaparte which made it quite popular among enemies of the First Empire.

Alexander Soumet (1788–1845)

Soumet was also a member of Hugo's *cénacle*. He had some success as a dramatist with historical plays: *Clytemnestra* (1822), *Saul* (1822), *Cleopatra* (1824), *The Maccabees* (1827), *Joan of Arc* (1827), and many others. His *Norma* furnished the libretto for Bellini's great opera.

Auguste Barbier (1805–1830)

Barbier was a poet of one book. The Revolution of 1830 inspired him to write a number of satirical pieces for periodicals. These were collected in a volume called *Iambes*. The most notable poems are "Le Lion" (The Lion), "Napoleon," "La Popularité" (Popularity), "Quatre-vingt-treize" (Ninety-three), and "La Curee" (The Quarry).

As a satirist Barbier was both brilliant and powerful. His colorful verse aims shafts at the political opportunists of his day. Unfortunately no other volumes of Barbier have importance.

Gérard de Nerval (1805–1857)

Gérard de Nerval, as has been said, was a close friend of Gautier's. A man of delicate sensibility, he was a victim of periods of mental derangement, as well as an omnipresent inability to take himself in hand. He was very young when he translated Goethe's *Faust*. A frequent contributor to the press, he wrote an account of his *Travels to the East* (1851), which was quite successful. Most of his work is in prose, and he is at his best in a series of short tales, fantastic in matter and delicate in style. Of these the best known are "Les Filles de Feu" (Daughters of Fire) (1854) and "La Bohême Galante" (The Gallant Gypsy) (1855). His poetry consists of sonnets and folksongs, written with a characteristic delicacy.

In the mysterious circumstances of his life he has been compared to our own Edgar Allan Poe; he was frequently in bad straits, and he died either by suicide or murder, which it is not certain. He is most the poet, however, in his colorful prose.

Casimir Delavigne (1793–1843)

Delavigne was a poet-dramatist of whom his contemporaries thought very highly. He first made a reputation with *Messéniennes* (*The Messenians*) in 1815 and 1827; by the title he meant, as he says, "a kind of national poetry which no one has yet tried to introduce into our literature." These are a series of odes inspired by political events and history, as in "Waterloo" and "Joan of Arc." His purpose was to show how France had become degraded under the restoration of the monarchy. As a poet he was more of a survivor of classicism than a romantic.

He was notably successful in the drama, where he became well-known for his melodramas. *Les Vêpres Siciliennes* (*The Sicilian Vespers*) of 1819 and *Le Paria* (*The Pariah*) of 1821 are indebted to Voltaire's plays. *Marino Faliero* (1829) is an adaptation of Byron's work on the same subject. *Louis XI* (1832) and *Les Enfants d'Édouard* (*The Children of Edward*) of 1833 are indebted to Shakespeare's *Henry VI* and *Richard III*.

Of all these writers Delavigne has suffered most at the hands of time. We now feel that he was hardly more than a capable practitioner of a mediocre style of composition.

THE ROMANTIC MOVEMENT IN ITALY

With the exception of England, the influence of the French Neoclassical movement had a paralyzing effect upon the literature of Western Europe during the greater part of the eighteenth century. Slavish imitation of French models had, in general, annihilating results in Germany and Italy where, each in its own way, native temperament is essentially foreign to the critical spirit that seems the very life of French culture.

Count Vittorio Alfieri (1749–1803)

In mid-eighteenth century Italy the name of Count Vittorio Alfieri is so outstanding that one critic can say of it that "it is almost as sacred to the Italians as the name of Dante." Yet by nature Alfieri was not particularly a poet.

He is cherished in Italy quite justly, however, for it was he who revived the spirit of national independence in that enslaved peninsula. A patrician with a boundless thirst for political liberty and love of mankind, he was himself domineering and ever at sword's point with the men he knew—as Richard Garnett says, a kind of Piedmontese version of the English Walter Savage Landor. In literature his taste was for classical Latin, and his tragedies are closer to those of Seneca than to those of Racine or Corneille. Matthew Arnold said of him that he is noble-minded but monotonous. His tragedies include *Cleopatra*, *Philip II*, and *Polynices*—which he originally wrote in French prose—; *Antigone*, *Orestes*, *Mary Stuart*, and *Saul*. But the most interesting of his works is his *Autobiography*, which, unlike his rigidly classic plays, places him among the Romantics.

The *Autobiography* is written in something like a foretaste of the Byronic mood, and is fascinating for its candor and honesty. The paradox between Alfieri's noble principles and his personal pettishness and discontent makes engaging reading. Alfieri traveled a great deal in Italy, France, and England; the experiences he records in those countries as well as his cloak-and-dagger love affairs are related with dash and verve.

Alessandro Manzoni (1785–1873)

The Romantic movement, when it last appeared, produced at least two figures of world stature, Manzoni and Leopardi.

IMPORTANCE

Alessandro Manzoni reminds one somewhat of Victor Hugo in the degree to which the Italian Romantic movement centers around his single figure, although the two could hardly have been more unlike in temperament. His work represents a complete break with the pseudo-classicism that had been strangling Italy for more than a century. Inspiration came to him not from his Italian predecessors, but from Shakespeare, and his contemporaries, Byron, Sir Walter Scott, and Goethe. He also broke with the religious skepticism of Italian classicism, and shows a characteristic Romantic return to the Middle Ages for spiritual values; his religion is that of a devout Catholic.

But Manzoni is in some ways one of the most unusual of Romantics: he lacked, happily, the flamboyance of the typical romantic, and possessed a wonderful inner harmony and balance.

Though very religious, Manzoni thoroughly welcomed the Church's loss of temporal power. He was a quiet, gentle man, fortunate in his married life, and living in comfortable, but not affluent, circumstances the life of a gentleman. Though winning an international fame with *I Promessi Sposi*, which his master Sir Walter Scott declared the best of its kind ever written, he wrote no more after the age of forty. He was determined not to jeopardize a reputation by writing what might turn out inferior work. He took no public part in the exciting political occurrences of his day, and in his old age when Italy became at last united, he refused to take on any political duties. His last years were crowned with the same kind of universal reverence accorded Hugo in France.

In 1815 Manzoni issued his first volume, *Sacred Hymns* (*Inni Sacri*), containing poems on the festivals of the Church; some of the best are "The Resurrection," "The Passion," "The Name of Mary," and "The Nativity." Though these fervent pieces attracted little notice at first, Manzoni's stature as a poet was recognized with the publication of "Il Cinque Maggio" (The Fifth of May) in 1821, an ode on Napoleon's death, which Longfellow later translated. The poem is written with eloquence, heat, and compassion, and caught the public imagination.

In the meantime Manzoni had written his first tragedy, *Il Conte di Carmagnola* (*The Count of Carmagnola*) in 1820; in 1822 he followed it with a second tragedy, *Adelchi*. These plays are of great importance to Italian literary history, for they mark the first successful attempt to adapt the Shakespearean drama to the Italian stage. *The Count of Carmagnola* deals with an exciting moment in Venetian history of the fifteenth century; *Adelchi* is laid in Lombardy in the eighth century. Both plays exhibit great poetic power—indeed, they are rather dramatic poems than plays—and are interspersed with stirring lyrics that show how close to Manzoni's heart was the freedom of his country from foreign domination, even if he did choose to live a retired life.

The Betrothed Lovers: Manzoni's real claim to being the foremost writer in nineteenth century Italy comes not by virtue of his being poet and dramatist. It is as author of *I Promessi Sposi* (*The Betrothed Lovers*, as it was called in English translation), published in 1825, the first great Italian novel, that Manzoni is known the world over. As has been said, Scott pronounced it as the best in the school of historical novels which he himself had fostered. Goethe said of *The Betrothed Lovers* that it is as satisfying as fruit that is perfectly ripe.

The novel, inspired by a deep patriotism and a profound sympathy with the lowly and the poor, is something like a complete picture of Italian manners. Though Romantic in being laid in Milan during the Spanish domination of the seventeenth century, it is so close a study of life as it is lived that it must also be described as a great piece of realism. As Adolfo Bartoli says of it:

> The romance disappears; no one cares for the plot....The attention is entirely fixed on the powerful objective creation of the characters. From the greatest to the least they have a wonderful verisimilitude; they are living persons standing before us, not with the qualities of one time more than another, but with the human

qualities of all time. Manzoni is able to unfold a character in all particulars, to display it in all its aspects, to follow it through its different phases....Manzoni dives down to the innermost recesses of the human heart, and draws thence the most subtle psychological reality.

The "betrothed" of the title are the simple peasant Renzo Tramaglino and the village maiden Lucia Mondella. The cowardly priest Don Abbondio refuses to marry them because he is threatened with death if he does so by the licentious nobleman Don Rodrigo. Don Rodrigo wishes Lucia for himself and sends out his bullies to abduct her. But a humble friar, Fra Cristoforo, foils the attempt by putting her under the protection of the haughty nun Gertrude at the Convent of Monza.

In the meantime Renzo is sent by Fra Cristoforo to the Monastery of Porta Orientale in Milan to work and also to escape the vengeance of Don Rodrigo. When the crops fail in 1628, Renzo becomes involved in the uprising against the Spanish oppressors and almost loses his life. He escapes to Bergamo, where his cousin Bortolo, a weaver, welcomes him despite his own financial distresses.

Don Rodrigo attempts anew the seduction of Lucia by the aid of a nobleman living outside the law, "The Unnamed." Gertrude surrenders her charge, and Lucia is carried off to the castle of The Unnamed. But the purity of Lucia converts the outlaw to decency. The latter now abases himself before the Cardinal Archbishop of Milan, a churchman of noble soul, and Lucia is placed in the home of a tailor's family, people of simple goodness of heart; Lucia's mother Agnese joins her there. The Cardinal also severely reprimands the cowardly priest.

Soon Lucia is a member of the household of Donna Prassede, a gentlewoman of exemplary life. And now the girl is at her wit's end for grief; during her imprisonment in The Unnamed's castle she has taken an oath to the Virgin that she will remain a virgin throughout life if she could ever by miracle be restored to her mother. When Agnese hears of the vow, she is greatly distressed, but continues inquiring for Renzo. The wise Donna Prassede pretends to abuse Renzo's character all the time, so that Lucia, rushing to his defense, finds her old love for him more powerful than ever.

In 1630 a terrible plague decimates Milan, though the city was already dying from famine and suffering under the foreigner's heel. The author describes in great and harrowing detail the depredations of the pestilence. Renzo, now in communication with Agnese, has heard of Lucia's vow, but becomes a victim of the plague. He recovers, and determines to find her. He sees Don Abbondio, still unchanged, and Fra Cristoforo, now working busily at tending the sick, and even extending his charity to the dying Don Rodrigo. At last Renzo finds Lucia just as she is convalescing. When Lucia confesses to Fra Cristoforo that she still loves Renzo, the good friar releases her from her vow. The novel ends with a picture of Renzo and Lucia living in married felicity.

Giacomo Leopardi (1798–1837)

The one outstanding poet of the Italian Romantic movement, Giacomo Leopardi, was born the year of Wordsworth and Coleridge's *Lyrical Ballads* in the little town of Recanati, near Rimini, the son of a patrician and parsimonious family. His father was an impoverished nobleman of antiquarian interests, his mother a practical but greedy woman. The family library was young Leopardi's only comfort during childhood; his studies in it were so profound that he afterwards said that he was more at home in Greek than in Roman or Italian thought. Indeed, when he was nineteen he was already the author not only of a number of translations from the classics, but also, a superior Chatterton, the author of some pretended translations from lost Greek works that deceived capable Greek scholars. But he was by then already a prey to the ill-health that ruined his life. His parents, entirely unfit to understand the genius who was their son, and terrified of his advanced opinions, kept him a prisoner at home.

A victim of parental tyranny, of sickness and loneliness, Leopardi led a bitter, uneventful life. Too ill to enter any profession, he made several abortive attempts to escape from home. For a time he was at Rome, at Bologna, Milan, and Florence, but his impoverished condition always forced him to return to the parental prison. His brilliant mind always won him friends; but his deformed body, feeble limbs, and bad lungs and heart made him an object of derision to women. Such works as he did issue were ignored by the public. Leopardi's story is one of unceasing struggle against overwhelming odds.

A skeptic in religion and an ardent patriot in politics, Leopardi could find no vehicle for publication during the days of Spanish and Austrian oppression. He did publish an ode *To Italy* (1818), lamenting the intellectual and political degeneracy of the fatherland, and a collection of poems in 1824. But it was not until after his death that his work as a whole was given to the world when his friend Antonio Ranieri edited his writings (1846–1880).

Leopardi's works are in three categories: philosophy, philology, and poetry. As a philosopher he was, as may be imagined, an extreme pessimist. His bodily ailments made him into a bitter complainer against the evil forces of nature: hunger, thirst, cold, and heat. All the sublimity of man's creative mind Leopardi regarded as a shining falsity invented to cover the hideousness of reality. If his indictment of life cannot win our respect, it does win our pity for a man who suffered outrageously for reasons beyond his control. Moreover, his misery seemed to be the symbol of Italy's miseries as she suffered under domestic and foreign tyrannies.

IMPORTANCE

It is as a poet that Leopardi stands preeminent. His poetry, though small in volume, restored Italian letters to a place of dignity in the world, just as Manzoni managed to do with his great novel. No poet in any language has managed more miraculously to give the ultimate expression to his ideas to the degree that Leopardi succeeded; in him form and idea are truly inseparable. His range of ideas is not great, but his long addiction to the Greeks taught him perfection in expression. There are not striking lines in his poetry; they are far too perfect for that. He was a modern Greek in the best sense. Thus, this almost unrelieved pessimism is compensated for by the impeccable taste he everywhere discloses.

Leopardi's favorite medium was blank verse, and he was particularly fond of the ode. But he was also at home in rhymed forms, including the *terza rima*. His music has sometimes been compared to that of Shelley's. Among his finest poems are "To Italy," "To Angelo Mai on the Recovery of Cicero's De Republica," and "On the Florentine Monument to Dante"—all patriotic, eloquent with scorn of Italy's current condition; "Hymn to the Patriarchs," "The Solitary Swallow," "The Village Sabbath," and "The Broom-Flower."

Leopardi's pessimism has nothing in common with the attitudinizing of Byron, the cynicism of Montaigne, the flippancy of Schopenhauer's *Essays*. He was, above everything else, a moralist. He was moved to bitterness by the circumstances of his own life and by his sensitiveness to human baseness.

Leopardi's prose partakes of the same flawless quality as his poetry, and is unmatched in the prose of his country for that reason.

REVIEW QUESTIONS

THE ROMANTIC MOVEMENT IN FRANCE AND ITALY

Multiple Choice

1. _____ The Romantic movement was
   a. a reaction against Neoclassicism
   b. a repudiation of Nature
   c. primarily a religious movement
   d. primarily a political movement

2. _____ Romantic writers found inspiration most often in
   a. cities
   b. people
   c. cultural centers
   d. natural settings

3. _____ Romantic authors in France
   a. created the concept of "Rights of Man"
   b. opposed the old French political system
   c. foreshadowed the French Revolution
   d. all of the above

4. _____ We owe the earliest formulation of the theory of "art for art's sake" to
   a. Gautier
   b. Sainte-Beuve
   c. Béranger
   d. Nodier

5. _____ Stylistically, Romantic literature focuses primarily on
   a. clarity
   b. freedom and imagination
   c. satire
   d. balance

6. _____ The trademark emotional state of Romantic writers was one of
   a. suffering
   b. disdain
   c. contentment
   d. curiosity

7. _____ Rousseau believed that the primary pathway to truth was found through
   a. reason
   b. the senses
   c. emotions
   d. faith

8. _____ Physiocrats believed that
   a. the physical body is the source of knowledge
   b. Nature is the source of all knowledge
   c. all individuals in a society have the same rights
   d. governments are unnecessary

9. _____ Count Vittorio Alfieri's most important contribution to Italy was
   a. his use of common Italian in literature
   b. reviving a sense of national identity
   c. his role as patron to Italian writers
   d. all of the above

10. _____ Giacomo Leopardi's works are in
    a. philosophy
    b. philology
    c. poetry
    d. all of the above

True-False

11. _____ When it first appeared, Romantic literature seemed startlingly fresh.

12. _____ Romantic literature relied primarily on Neoclassical themes.

13. _____ Romantic authors emphasized the individual over the group.

14. _____ Romantic literature reflected the elegance of Western culture.

15. _____ Jean-Jacques Rousseau distrusted reason as the solution to man's ills.

16. _____ Through his reforms as the Minister of Finance, Turgot was able to allow freedom of work for French laborers.

17. _____ Physiocrats believe in the natural right of buying and selling for all men.

18. _____ French Romantic philosophers were of little importance in the eighteenth century.

19. _____ The philosophes fostered the intellectual atmosphere of the Enlightenment.

20. _____ Alexander Manzoni was primarily a writer of pseudo-classical literature.

Fill-in

21. In France, Romantic literature was not only a literary movement but was also a _____ movement.

22. The Romantic movement in England began with the publication of _____ in 1798 with poems by Wordsworth and Coleridge.

23. Romantic authors were in revolt against the authority of _____, which was a dominant theme in Neoclassical literature, and instead preferred the freedom of imagination.

24. Romantic authors thought that the best education for people was found in _____ .

25. Romantic authors felt that a sensitive poet would be especially aware of the _____ aspects of any situation.

26. Rousseau believed that _____ corrupted man's inherently benevolent nature.

27. Condillac believed that all our ideas are merely transformations of our _____ .

28. The _____ set forth the ideas that the French Revolution put into practice.

29. _____ is an author of the Italian Romantic movement whose life was a constant struggle against ill health, parental tyranny, and poverty.

30. _____ is considered the author who ushered in the British Romantic movement.

Matching

31. _____ Alexander Dumas *père*   a. *Paul and Virginia*

32. _____ Alessandro Manzoni   b. *Corinne*

33. _____ Victor Hugo   c. *The Betrothed Lovers*

34. _____ Rousseau   d. *Count of Monte Cristo*

35. _____ Count Volney   e. *Traite des Sensations*

36. _____ Condorcet   f. *Les Misérables*

37. _____ Condillac   g. *The Confessions*

38. _____ Bernardin de Saint-Pierre   h. *Reflections on the Corn Trade*

39. _____ Mme. de Staël   i. *Atala*

40. _____ Viscount of Chateaubriand   j. *Les Ruins*

Answers

1. a	15. t	29. Giacomo Leopardi	
2. d	16. t	30. Wordsworth	
3. d	17. t	31. d	
4. a	18. f	32. c	
5. b	19. t	33. f	
6. a	20. f	34. g	
7. c	21. political	35. j	
8. c	22. *Lyrical Ballads*	36. h	
9. b	23. Reason	37. e	
10. d	24. nature	38. a	
11. t	25. tragic	39. b	
12. f	26. society	40. i	
13. t	27. sensations		
14. f	28. philosophes		

Part 2

THE GOLDEN AGE OF
GERMAN LITERATURE

WORKS AT A GLANCE

Ewald Christian von Kleist

1749	*Spring*

Friedrich Gottlieb Klopstock

1746, 1771	*The Messiah*

Christoph Martin Wieland

1750?	*The Nature of Things*	1767	*Agathon*
1764	*Don Sylvio von Rosalva*	1780	*Oberon*
1766	*Humorous Tales*		

Gotthold Ephraim Lessing

1755	*Miss Sara Sampson*	1772	*Emilia Galotti*
1766	*Laokoon*	1779	*Nathan the Wise*
1767	*Minna von Barnhelm*		

Johann Gottfried Herder

1767	*Fragments on the New German Literature*	1790	*Spirit of Hebraic Poetry*
1784	*Voices of the Nations in Songs*	1797	*Ideas Towards the Philosophy of the History of Humanity*

Johann Christian Friedrich Hölderlin

1799	*Hyperion*	1801	*The Death of Empedocles*

Johann Wolfgang von Goethe

1773	*Götz von Berlichingen*	1808	*Faust, Part I*
1774	*Clavigo; The Sorrows of Young Werther*	1809	*The Elective Affinities*
		1810	*Theory of Colors*
1788	*Egmont*	1811–1833	*Poetry and Truth*
1787	*Iphigenia in Taurus*	1821	*Wilhelm Meister's Travels*
1790	*Torquato Tasso*		
1795–1796	*Wilhelm Meister's Apprenticeship*	1833	*Faust, Part II*
1798	*Hermann and Dorothea* (with Schiller)		

Johann Christoph Friedrich von Schiller

1781	*The Robbers*	1801	*Maria Stuart*
1783	*Intrigue and Love*	1802	*The Maid of Orleans*
1793	*Naïve and Sentimental Poetry*	1803	*The Bride of Messina*
		1804	*William Tell*
1798	*Wallenstein's Camp*		
1799	*The Piccolomini; Wallenstein's Death*		

Immanuel Kant

| 1781 | *The Critique of Pure Reason* | 1790 | *The Critique of the Power of Judgment* |
| 1788 | *The Critique of Practical Reason* | | |

Friedrich Maximilian von Klinger

| 1776 | *Confusion, or Storm and Stress; The Twins* | 1791 | *Faust's Life, Deeds and Journey to Hell* |

Jakob Michael Reinhold Lenz

| 1774 | *The Housemaster* | 1776 | *The Soldiers* |

Friedrich Müller

| 1778 | *Faust's Life* |

Gottfried August Bürger

| 1773 | *Lenore* |

Jean Paul Richter

| 1803 | *Titan* | 1805 | *The Years of Wild Oats* |

Novalis

| 1800 | *Hymns to Night* | 1802 | *Heinrich von Ofterdingen* |

Karl Wilhelm Friedrich von Schlegel

| 1799 | *Lucinde* |

Johann Gottlieb Fichte

| 1794 | *Theory of Knowledge* | 1796 | *Theory of Natural Right* |

Friedrich Wilhelm Joseph von Schelling

1797   *Philosophy of Nature*

Johann Ludwig Tieck

1798	*Sternbald's Travels*	1812	*Phantasus*
1804	*The Emperor Octavian*	1821–1840	*Tales*

Wilhelm Heinrich Wackenroder

1797	*Overflowings from the Heart of an Art-loving Friar*	1799	*Fancies Concerning Art*

Ernst Theodor Amadeus Hoffmann

1815   *Devil's Brew*

Clemens Maria Brentano

1805   *The Boys' Magic Horn*

Jakob Ludwig Karl and Wilhelm Karl Grimm

1812–1815   *Children's and Household Fairy Tales*

Hans Christian Anderson

1835–1872[*]   *Fairy Tales and Stories*

L. C. A. de Chamisso

1814   *The Wonderful History of Peter Schlemihl*

Friedrich de la Motte Fouqué

1811   *Undine*

Josef von Eichendorff

1826   *The Life of a Good-for-Nothing*

Eduard Mörike

1832   *Maler Nolten*

---

*Dates written

Karl Leberecht Immermann

1836	*The Late Born*	1839	*Münchhausen*

Heinrich von Kleist

1808	*Penthesilea; The Slaying of Arminius; Michael Kohlhaas*	1810	*Katie of Heilbronn; The Prince of Homburg*

Zacharias Werner

1809	*The Twenty-fourth of February*

Adolf Müllner

1812	*The Twenty-ninth of February*	1813	*Guilt*

Franz Grillparzer

1818	*Sappho*	1830	*A Faithful Servant of His Lord*
1822	*The Golden Fleece*	1831	*Waves of the Sea and of Love*
1825	*King Ottocar's Fortune and End*	1834	*The Dream, a Life*
		1838	*Woe to Him Who Lies*

Arthur Schopenhauer

1818	*The World as Will and Idea*

Heinrich Heine

1826	*Book of Songs*	1854	*Memoirs*

Friedrich Hebbel

1840	*Judith; Mary Magdalene*	1856	*Gyges and His Ring*
1850	*Herod and Mariamne*	1862	*The Nibelungs*
1852	*Agnes Bernauer*		

Richard Wagner

1842	*Rienzi*	1865	*Tristan and Isolde*
1845	*Tannhäuser*	1868	*Die Meistersinger von Nürnberg*
1850	*Lohengrin*		
1853	*The Ring of the Nibelungs*	1882	*Parsifal*

3
THE FOUNDERS OF
GERMAN ROMANTICISM

The golden age of German literature was the product of a political rejuvenation under the inspiring leadership of Frederick the Great (1712–1786) and the vitality occasioned by the European wave of Romanticism that had begun to appear in France in the writings of Rousseau and in England in the novels of Richardson. As a result, writers of the new Germany combined the attitudes of their own age with something of the feeling of the earlier Renaissance authors of other European nations.

Since German literature had been moribund for so long, these writers eagerly sought models and inspiration in other national literatures. But instead of being influenced by the limited models available to writers of the Renaissance itself, they devoured Shakespeare, Milton, and Rousseau and were affected by the classics, by Neoclassicism, by eighteenth century English sentimentalism, and by their own medieval minstrels and minnesingers. Consequently, it may be said that the great age of German literature is both classic and Romantic, and that it succeeded as no other literature did in making a fusion of the two.

In its classicism German literature strikes closer to the Greek spirit than did the English and French formalisms of Neoclassicism. But its essential character is nevertheless Romantic in the sense of its greater concern for the individual than for society, its emphasis on emotion and intuition rather than reason, its veneration for nature and the natural, and its interest in the dark hidden forces which motivate human life. Yet in the hands of Germany's ablest writers and thinkers this concern for the individual and preoccupation with the life-spirit was broadened into a quest for national unity and the brotherhood of all mankind.

The strength of the German Protestant movement and its succeeding milder variant, Pietism, indicates something of the essence of the national character. There had been German humanists, German imitators of Renaissance Italy, of the French Pléiade and of French Neoclassicism, but none of them had succeeded in inspiring a national movement. One of the greatest Germans, Immanuel Kant, may well be called a product of the Age of Reason; yet his *Critique of Pure Reason* uses the tools of logic to discredit reason by pointing out its limitations. Furthermore, the tradition of German autocracy was such that German writers were all but forced to remain personal and subjective, and to forego commentary on social or political problems. That the inevitable spirit of revolt, which characterizes romanticism, was seldom turned against the state can be explained by the odd coincidences that Frederick the Great was Germany's savior and that he combined despotism with a very real concern for the welfare of his subjects, including a belief in their right to intellectual freedom.

THE LITERARY REVIVAL

The revival of German literature also owed something to the interest stimulated by a noisy conflict between rival schools of eighteenth century writers. In Leipzig, Johann Christoph Gottsched (1700–1760) had founded the Saxon School of writers in imitation of the French Academy. His German Society, which was devoted to the strict imposition of Neoclassic rules on diction, grammar, and particularly drama, became the arbiter of German literature for some twenty years. In opposition to a school which held clarity and correctness in higher esteem than emotion and imagination, the rival Swiss School, founded in Zurich by Bodmer and Breitinger, began an active disputation with Gottsched in 1740. Johann Jakob Bodmer (1698–1783) and Johann Jakob Breitinger (1701–1776) were essentially scholars and critics rather than creative writers, but their defense of free poetic imagination won a decisive victory over the conscious, highly formalized principles of Neoclassicism, and simultaneously introduced a respect for English poets like Spenser, Shakespeare, and Milton as models for composition.

Meanwhile, many of Gottsched's admirers were gradually shaking off his domination. Continuing to be known as members of the Saxon School, they founded their own periodical, the *Bremer Beiträge* (*Blemen Contributions*), which pursued a kind of middle course between respect for rules and free exercise of imagination. An outstanding example of this middle-of-the-road concept, Christian Fürchtegott Gellert (1715–1769) wrote plays and fables for and often about the middle class and cultivated a style of almost extreme simplicity. Called "the most reasonable of German scholars" by Frederick the Great, he combined natural subjects and sentiments with a high regard for purity of style and, in a broad sense, set the tone for the writers of the great age to come. Included in his circle were the hymn writer J. A. Cramer (1723–1788), the satirist Gottlieb Wilhelm Rabener (1714–1771), and the dramatist Johann Elias Schlegel (1718–1749).

Ewald Christian von Kleist (1715–1759)

The impetus given to literary freedom by Bodmer and Breitinger had more direct results in the formation of a small group of unpretentious poets known as the Halle School, with which Kleist was closely connected. Ewald Christian von Kleist was an officer in Frederick the Great's army who died as a result of being wounded in battle. He began his poetic career by writing in the Neoclassic tradition but soon turned from wit and reason to the inspiration of nature. His best known work is *Der Frühling* (*Spring*), which was intended as part of a longer poem inspired by Thomson's *Seasons*. Taking as a subject nothing more pretentious than a walk in the country, Kleist describes the beauties of nature and the inner delight which they give him. Spring in particular is regarded as the healer and inspiration of mankind.

Friedrich Gottlieb Klopstock (1724–1803)

Of far greater importance in the encouragement of the lyric as opposed to the rational genius of German literature was the inspiration provided by another disciple of Bodmer, Friedrich Gottlieb Klopstock. Born at Quedlinburg in 1724 of a deeply religious family, he had developed an ambition to write a great religious poem by the time he left school in 1745. At Jena where he studied theology for a short time, he followed the plan of Bodmer's translation of Milton's *Paradise Lost* by writing in prose the first three cantos of his proposed epic, *The Messiah (Der Messias)*. In 1746 he went to the University of Leipzig, where he turned his prose version into hexameters and published the first three cantos anonymously in the *Bremer Beiträge*. The name of the author was soon revealed, and Klopstock found himself suddenly the most popular poet in Germany.

In 1750 he was invited to Zurich by Bodmer and, while there, was offered a pension by Frederick V of Denmark to take up residence in Copenhagen. En route, he met Margarethe Moller whom he later married and whose pious writings he edited after her death in 1758. He returned to Hamburg in 1771, published there the last five cantos of the *Messiah*, and was honored by another pension from the Margrave of Boden. After a second marriage in 1792, he died at Hamburg in 1803. In addition to the *Messiah*, he wrote many ardent odes and series of clumsy plays on Arminius and on Biblical themes.

The *Messiah*, inspired by Milton, is an attempt to write an epic with Christ as its hero. In twenty cantos covering only the conclusion of the Scriptural narrative which begins with the ascent of the Mount of Olives and concludes with the ascent to Heaven, the poem ranges loftily and grandiosely from heaven to hell and gives as much space to angelic as to human personages. Lacking the strength and power of a genuine epic poet, Klopstock strains for sublime and highly emotional effects to cover his weakness in narration and characterization. As a result, the poem is seldom read today, but in its own time it appealed to an audience (which was applauding the English Richardson) because of the heavy sentimentalism of the lines and their unrestrained flights of imagination. As is clear from his odes, Klopstock's genius was essentially lyric, and many individual passages of the *Messiah* contain images of great beauty and deep emotion. The revolutionary effect of this epic on its immediate readers is indicated by the experiences of Goethe who, reading it secretly as a child, was carried away by its sublimities and torrential emotions and, in his novel *Werther*, expressed the ecstasy of a pair of lovers by having one of them murmur, "Klopstock!"

CHRISTOPH MARTIN WIELAND (1733–1813)

IMPORTANCE

While Klopstock was responsible for the broadening of German taste in the direction of English emotionalism and moral sentiment, Wieland widened the current of German literature by introducing an almost French charm and an interest in the sensual varieties of human experience.

Christoph Martin Wieland began his career with the same kind of religious fervor that marked the epic of Klopstock. Born in 1733 at Oberholzheim in a clergyman's family, he received his early education from his father. After some years of formal schooling, during which he showed a strong propensity for literature, he moved with his family to Biberach where he fell in love with a young relative, Sophie Guterman, whom he regarded as an angel and who further stimulated his piety. In 1750 he entered the University of Tübingen to study law. Here he wrote his first serious work, *Die Natur der Dinge* (*The Nature of Things*), which was inspired by one of his father's sermons and which was the first of a series of pieces by him devoted to the exaltation of moral and Christian sentiments. Bodmer was sufficiently impressed by his talents to invite him to Zurich where he continued for a time to write in an exalted religious vein but where he began to lose his enthusiasm for asceticism and to find earthly pleasures very much to his liking.

Toward the end of his six years in Switzerland he deserted religious for secular themes, writing a play about *Lady Jane Grey*, part of an epic *Cyrus* (presenting the Persian monarch as a counterpart of Frederick the Great), and a poem *Araspes und Panthea* on material derived from Xenephon's *Cyropaedia*. In 1760 he was appointed Director of the Chancery at Biberach where he continued a platonic devotion to Sophie, who had meanwhile married another, and found much pleasure in the society of men of the world such as Count Stadion. Under these influences his defection from religion was completed, and he turned to a philosophy of Epicureanism in its popular sense, mocking the very moral earnestness which he had formerly held sacred. In 1764 he published a romance *Don Sylvio von Rosalva*, which in imitation of *Don Quixote*, laughed at high principles. In 1766 he followed this with the cynical and vulgar *Komische Erzählungen* (*Humorous Tales*).

From these two extremes of the spiritual and the physical, Wieland's philosophy of life quickly reached a moderate position between the two. Between 1762 and 1766 he translated most of the plays of Shakespeare, which may have stimulated his desire to seek the equipoise of human nature just as his previous investigations of the classics may have recommended the middle road of life. He concluded, at any rate, that enduring contentment lies between the extremes of piety and sensualism, and that gratification of all impulses is a legitimate part of human experience, provided that excess is avoided. These ideas found utterance in his philosophical and autobiographical novel *Agathon*, completed in 1767, and the didactic poem *Musarion* published in 1768. Between 1769 and 1772 he held a professorship of philosophy at Erfurt where he continued a copious production of works modeled on Greek, Spanish, Italian, and Oriental prototypes, ranging from humor to didacticism. The remaining part of his life until his death in 1813 was mostly spent at Weimar where he edited a periodical and continued a prolific output of literary works, the best known of which is his poem *Oberon*, which was published in 1780.

Agathon

From the point of view of influence on later German literature, Wieland's most interesting work is his novel *Agathon*. A handsome young Athenian who has been exiled for political reasons is presented as a symbol of humanity about to see and experience the infinite vicissitudes of life. As he sets out on his journey, he first encounters sensuality when he chances upon a frenzied, wanton dance of maenads who mistake him for Bacchus himself. Rescued by pirates, he is carried to Smyrna to be sold as a slave, but on the voyage he meets Psyche, who had been his boyhood love in a youth consecrated to piety, but from whom he had become separated by the designs of a sensual priestess. Psyche remains a slave to the pirates, but Agathon is taken to Smyrna where he is sold to Hippias, one of the Sophists whom Socrates despised. Hippias attempts to wean Agathon from purity first by preaching materialistic doctrines and, when words prove futile, by introducing him to Danae, type of the beautiful emancipated woman who had exerted so much influence at European courts since the height of the Renaissance. Agathon is overwhelmed by her charms and, believing her to be possessed of a beautiful soul, succeeds in teaching her what true love is.

Alarmed and jealous about this perversion of his plans, Hippias reveals Danae's sordid past to Agathon, who thereupon repudiates her and sets forth on a career in politics. Having become disillusioned in Athens by democracy, he becomes the prime minister of the benevolent tyrant Dionysius of Sicily, at whose court he devotes himself earnestly to the labors of government. He has learned that the ideal does not exist and that men are variable and unstable; yet his newfound toleration and practicality are not sufficiently developed to prevent his overthrow by an unscrupulous palace intrigue. He finds asylum at Tarentum in the home of the Pythagorean Archytas, who preaches the theory of a universe instituted by God, in which the proper function of mankind is to strive for a perfection which will result from the harmonizing of the demands of spirit and flesh. By accepting this doctrine Agathon finds inner peace and simultaneously rediscovers Psyche, who is married to one of the sons of Archytas, and who turns out to be his own sister. Danae, redeemed by Agathon, has also left Smyrna to live in solitude at Tarentum.

She and Agathon are ecstatically reunited, but instead of the expected marriage, she resolves to deny further satisfactions of the flesh for the sake of more intensive cultivation of the "beautiful soul."

Forced and sentimental as much of this is, it provides a foretaste of many of the trends of later German literature. It is particularly illuminating in connection with Goethe's combination of philosophy and autobiography, especially in *Werther*, *Wilhelm Meister*, and *Faust*, and in relationship to the German interest in the growth of the individual through experience. It also dimly anticipates *Faust* in its presentation of the idea that all experiences are valuable and that the ultimate goal of life is not reducible to a one-sided formula.

Oberon

Among Wieland's later works, the best remembered is his epic poem *Oberon*. Combining materials from Shakespeare, Chaucer, and medieval French romance, the long poem is filled with colorful backgrounds, rapid narrative, and varied characters. Its theme is not markedly different from that of *Agathon*, noting as it does the weaknesses of mankind and the expiation required for them, and describing the gradual purification of two beautiful souls through experience.

GOTTHOLD EPHRAIM LESSING (1729–1781)

IMPORTANCE

An essentially greater writer and thinker than either Klopstock or Wieland, Lessing completes the trio of the most prominent writers who opened the great age of German literature. He is most distinguished internationally as the German representative of the eighteenth-century enlightenment, but he also anticipates the breadth and humanity, and the interest in the spirit rather than the letter, which distinguish the finest utterances of Goethe. Like Goethe, too, he was at once national and international, much concerned with specific German problems but ultimately engrossed by the broader concerns of all mankind.

Gotthold Ephraim Lessing was born to a clergyman's family at Kamenz in Saxony in 1729. In his early schooling he showed a remarkable eagerness and capacity for learning. His combined critical and spiritual temperament was revealed in his schoolboy reputation of being at once sharply sarcastic and exceptionally generous. In 1746 he entered the University of Leipzig with the avowed intention of studying theology, but his interests were attracted to philosophy, to the classics, and to the cultivation of the friendship of his fellow students. He also became devoted to the theater at Leipzig and saw a play of his own, *Der Junge Gelehrte* (*The Young Student*) performed there.

His father, meanwhile, became alarmed over reports of his son's worldliness, called him home for a time, and permitted him to return to Leipzig only on the condition that he devote himself to the study of medicine. Lessing studied medicine in much the same way as he had studied theology, and he was able to continue his absorbed interest in the theater.

In 1748 when the theatrical company was dissolved, he went to Wittenberg and then to Berlin where he became a full-fledged literary man. During his three years there, he wrote plays and translations and helped start a periodical. In 1751 he became the literary critic of the *Voss Gazette*. In deference to his father's request, he returned to Wittenberg during the same year to complete his M. A. Taking with him an unpublished volume of Voltaire with whom he had had some contact, he was accused by the French *savant* of intending to pirate the work. A bitter correspondence was exchanged, and Lessing became the unfortunate object of what was undoubtedly unfounded gossip.

During his year at Wittenberg he devoured, he says, all the books in the library and returned to Berlin for three years of strenuous activity. He resumed his translations, his editing of his periodical, the *Theatralische Bibliothek (Theatrical Library)*, and his articles for the *Voss Gazette*, which were directed principally against Gottsched and his followers. He also made friends with other writers such as Moses Mendelssohn, Ramler, Gleim, and Kleist, and published independent critical works and writings of his own, including plays, epigrams, and lyrics. In 1755 his tragedy *Miss Sara Sampson* was so enthusiastically received that he determined to devote himself exclusively to the career of dramatist. He therefore returned to Leipzig where a new theater had been established, but he was distracted from his immediate objective, first by the proposal of a merchant Winkler to go on a foreign tour, and then by the outbreak of the Seven Years' War.

In 1758 Lessing resumed his career as a critic in Berlin, leading the revolt against arbitrary neoclassic standards and exalting the inspiration and naturalness of such writers as Shakespeare over the French classicists like Corneille and Racine. In 1760 he became secretary to General Tauentzien, happy to find a position that was necessary for his support during the lean war years and which gave him the opportunity for deeper scholarly research. He resigned his position in 1765, but the fruits of his retirement appeared in the publication of two of his most important works, the *Laokoon* in 1766 and *Minna von Barnhelm* in 1767. When the institution of a national theater at Hamburg was projected in 1767, Lessing went there to take an active part. The theater failed, but Lessing made a great contribution to dramatic criticism in his *Hamburgische Dramaturgie*, a series of reviews of plays presented at the theater, using individual plays, however, as springboards for discussions of dramatic theory in general. He based his critical opinions on Aristotle, but in directing attention to principles rather than rules, he continued the teachings of the *Laokoon*, finding the true tragic spirit in the Greek dramatists and in Shakespeare rather than in the French playwrights.

In 1770 Lessing accepted the lifelong post of librarian at Wolfenbüttel in Brunswick. In 1776 he married Eva König, but his happiness was cut short by her death in childbirth in 1778. He had meanwhile continued his critical writings and had completed another of his best plays, *Emilia Galotti*. His remaining years were highlighted by a study of religion into which he was drawn by a literary debate with Pastor Goeze of Hamburg on the subject of the Divine nature of the Scriptures. It was Lessing's contention that the Bible is an expression of the religious feeling of the time of its composition, that it is not to be regarded as sacred, and that belief in it is not at all essential for the true Christian. In 1779 he completed his play *Nathan der Weise* (Nathan the Wise), which proclaims in dramatic form the same doctrine, that religion is a matter of feeling rather than dogma and that a love of God and goodness is more important than subscription to any given creed. After completing several other prose pieces which completed his work of broadening and deepening the meaning of religion, Lessing died at Brunswick, after a short illness, in 1781.

Minna von Barnhelm

As has been seen, the most enduring works of Lessing's career are his plays and his critical pieces. Of his plays, *Miss Sara Sampson*, modeled on the English *London Merchant* by George Lillo, set the essential scheme of his later productions by being built on a classical framework but making use of ordinary characters from middle-class life rather than exalted personages, and by drawing both theme and dialogue from the human interests and problems of the time.

Still considered as the first completely German play, *Minna von Barnhelm* simultaneously employs both the contemporary enthusiasm for the army and Lessing's own dislike of false codes of honor and the artificialities of society.

In a plot simple to the point of crudeness, Major von Tellheim is an idealized soldier, honest, firm, high-principled, and compassionate. When he is discharged from the army under apparently disgraceful conditions, he nobly frees the heiress Minna von Barnhelm from her engagement to him. Minna, who is led by her heart rather than by any false notions of honor, money, or position, immediately journeys to Berlin with her maid and uncle to take lodging in the same inn from which the disgraced Tellheim is evicted. Tellheim moves to another hotel, leaving a ring with the landlord in settlement of his account. After Minna has recognized and purchased the ring, she attempts to persuade Tellheim that he should not let an exaggerated sense of honor stand in the way of true love. When honest words fail, she pretends that she has been disinherited, whereupon it becomes her turn to be adamant to his pleas to be permitted to take care of her, haughtily refusing to be a burden to him. As a final gesture, she returns the ring, an act which brings the lovers to each other's arms as a message arrives from the king (shades of Frederick the Great) redeeming Tellheim's honor and restoring him to his former rank. In spite of this banal plot and the overdose of noble sentiment embodied in the character of Tellheim, the air of naturalness and the contemporaneity of the subject make this play an obviously important curtain-raiser to an independent national drama.

Emilia Galotti

A more obvious attempt to adapt the principles of classical drama to native middle-class material is Lessing's adaptation of the Roman story of Virginia in his *Emilia Galotti.* Emilia, on the verge of marriage to Graf Appiani, is desired by the Prince of Guastalla whose chamberlain, Marinelli, holds up the carriage containing Appiani, Emilia, and her mother. After the Count is killed, Emilia is rescued from the supposed robbers and taken to the Prince. When her father learns what has happened to her, he stabs her in order to protect her honor. The character of Emilia is poorly conceived, but the other figures are sharply and boldly characterized, characterization being the strongest point of this essentially artificial play whose action does indeed spring, as Lessing advised in his *Hamburgische Dramaturgie,* from the personalities of the *dramatis personae.* Its timeliness lies in its theme of revolt against autocratic tyranny.

Nathan der Weise

More of a philosophical drama than a good acting play, *Nathan the Wise* is the product of the broad tolerant views on religion that characterized Lessing's closing years. Based on Boccaccio's story of the three rings (*Decameron* I, 3), it tells of a certain ring that is believed to contain magic powers for any wearer who believes in its potency, making such a one "pleasing to God and man." When a certain possessor of the ring did not wish to discriminate among his three sons, he had two identical rings made and gave one ring to each of the three. The ensuing dispute about which son had the genuine ring was settled by a wise judge who advised each of them to believe that he possessed the true ring and to act accordingly.

In Lessing's version, the saintly Jew Nathan is required by the Saladin to state whether Christianity, Judaism, or Mohammedanism is the true religion. His answer is the story of the three rings, which underlines Lessing's belief that dogma has little to do with true religion. Woven around this tale is an artificial plot in which tolerance is seen in practice. Nathan the Jew, who has the wisdom of age and a broad humanity that imparts an almost mystic glow to his character, is rebuffed by a Templar when he attempts to thank him for rescuing his adopted daughter Recha from a fire. His refusal to be insulted by the Templar's disdain, together with an appeal to the Templar's reason, forces the Templar to see the man rather than his religion and to become his fast friend.

Christianity is introduced in the character of a good Friar who had brought the Christian orphan child Recha to Nathan for adoption after Nathan's wife and children had been murdered by Christians. When a rumor that a Christian child is being fathered by Nathan forces Nathan to reveal the entire story, it is discovered that Recha is the lost sister of the Templar and the niece of the Sultan himself. This chain of remarkable coincidences is actually little more than a skeleton for Lessing's disquisitions in a blank verse that, though seldom inspired as poetry, is thoughtful and pungent in its argumentative passages and often deeply moving in Nathan's simple yet dignified and sometimes exalted utterances.

Laokoon

This only completed volume of a projected three-volume critical work stands ultimately as Lessing's greatest single achievement. The writing of *Laokoon*, which holds a very important position in world critical theory, was stimulated by Winckelmann's researches into and analyses of Greek art. Contrasting the statue with Virgil's description of Laocoön in the *Aeneid*, Winckelmann pointed out that the sculptured Laocoön was not represented as uttering the cries ascribed to him by Virgil and that this restraint and portrayal of inner peace was typical of Greek art which aimed at transcendent perfection rather than natural reality. Lessing counters this suggestion by explaining that the differing representations of Laocoön by a Greek sculptor and a Roman poet proceeded not from different conceptions of their subject but from fundamental laws of their respective arts. In sculpture the highest law is beauty, and a mouth permanently distorted in an outcry would be grotesque. The sculptor therefore indicated Laocoon's agony by the muscular contortions of the body. The sculptor who cannot make use of sequence of time is limited to the medium of space and must therefore select a single moment as the basis of all he desires to express.

The poet, on the other hand, conveys emotion not by description but by the narration of action and speech. Space is not at all his medium, and the great poet, like Homer, suggests through selective action rather than attempting lengthy detailed descriptions of a scene. With the presentation of this clear-cut and obviously sensible distinction, Lessing abolished with a single stroke the time-honored maxim of Horace, "*Ut pictora poesis*" ("As painting, so poetry") and checked the growing tendency toward descriptive writing among German authors. He delimited for all time the proper sphere of creative writing and enlarged its scope to include all truth, releasing it from the obligation (then binding on sculpture) to reverence beauty as the highest law in art.

STURM UND DRANG

For ten or twelve years after 1770, a curious wave of excitement known as the *Sturm und Drang* or Storm and Stress period was the leading tendency in German literature. It was as if the stimulation of the Seven Years' War demanded a continued outlet for the aroused energies of the youth of Germany. A fighting spirit, a spirit of rebellion that could be directed against neither a foreign enemy nor a domestic ruler found expression in a pulsing youthful literature whose most outstanding characteristic was its impetuosity. Influenced by the older writers like Klopstock and Wieland, the fledgling authors of the time found excitable inspiration in the English Shakespeare, Ossian, and Young, and in the French Rousseau and Diderot. The result was a literature of revolt against tyranny, against superstition, against any restricting controls. "Nature" and "strong emotion" became almost synonymous with them, and they longed to plumb the depths of "natural impulse," uncontaminated by the dictates of society or the rules of formal composition. The movement took its name from a play by Klinger, *Der Wirrwarr* (1776) which was subtitled *Sturm und Drang.*

Johann Gottfried Herder (1744–1803)

Nearly all young German auhors of the time were affected by the *Sturm und Drang* movement, but the writer who was regarded as its guiding genius was Johann Gottfried Herder. The young Goethe sat at his feet, and together they completed the transition from the classical rigors of the Enlightenment to the new age of "feeling" which was inspired by Rousseau and the English cult of sentimentalism.

Herder was born of poor and pious parents in Mohrungen near Königsberg in 1744. After a childhood of discipline and severities, he entered the University of Königsberg at the age of eighteen to prepare for the ministry. Here an interest in philosophy was awakened by Immanuel Kant and an interest in primitive literature by Johann Georg Hamann whose disconnected mystical writings were expressions of the new theory that Nature expresses herself through the senses and emotions rather than through processes of reason. He became absorbed in speculations concerning the philosophy of history and of human development and was soon launched upon a career that included the ministry an education, and writing of a critical, philosophical, and creative character. After leaving Königsberg he served at Riga as both assistant master of the cathedral school and curate. Here too, in 1767, he published his first major work, *Fragmente über die neuere deutsche Literatur* (*Fragments on the New German Literature*).

Becoming interested in reforming German education, he made an extensive tour through other European nations in 1769 to collect information on teaching methods used elsewhere. Upon his return, he accepted the appointment of tutor and chaplain to the young prince of Eutin-Holstein, a position which took him to Strassburg where he met Goethe, and to Darmstadt where he met his future wife Caroline Flachsland. In 1771 he was appointed court preacher at Bückeburg, where his liberal views met with considerable opposition from both orthodox clergy and laymen. Meanwhile, his continued study of literature as the natural free expression of the people led him to a fascinated interest in James Macpherson's supposed discovery of the ancient Gaelic bard Ossian, in Bishop Percy's collection of medieval ballads, and in the writings of the "natural" genius Shakespeare.

Under influences such as these, he became the leader of the *Sturm und Drang* movement, collaborating with Goethe and others in the publication of a journal devoted to the dissemination of the new anticlassical doctrines. In 1776 he became a court preacher at Weimar where he completed his life in company with Goethe, Wieland, Jean Paul, and lesser members of the brilliant circle of writers which made Weimar the literary capital of Germany. As he grew older, his failing health and essentially puritanical nature led to many quarrels and embitterments which clouded his last years but did not interfere with his literary and scholarly productiveness, which continued until his death in 1803.

The many writings of Herder document the gradual growth and development of a theory which may be said to begin with his *Fragments* of 1767. The theory is later illustrated by his collection of folk poetry, *Stimmen der Völker in Liedern* (*Voices of the Nations in Songs*), and by his best original poem, *Der Cid*, based on Spanish folk tradition. It is strengthened by his work on the *Spirit of Hebraic Poetry* (*Vom Geist der hebräischen Poesie*) and concluded with his total summation, the *Ideen zur Philosophie der Geschichte der Menschheit* (*Ideas Towards the Philosophy of the History of Humanity*).

Although Herder's ideas were necessarily altered during the various phases of their development, the essential core of his theory sees the world as subject to a gradual evolutionary process in which humanity as a whole grows up much as does an individual human being. The whole achievement of humanity is made up of the contributions of individual national units which, in turn, are the products of the individuals who comprise them and whose collective effort builds the national culture, modified by the conditions and experiences through which the nation passes. In literature, infancy is represented by the development of language itself. Youth, the most interesting period to Herder, is the age of poetry when awareness of the wonder of the world stimulates free and natural image-making power and when the rhythms of song are used to express the history, religion, ethics, emotions, and wisdom of the people. Manhood brings regularity and organization in place of spontaneous vivacity, and so prose becomes the concluding vehicle for national expression in the historical cycle. Prose begins with keen analytical power but, lacking the strength and vitality of youth, it soon becomes senile and falls into decay.

IMPORTANCE

Through this theory and through Herder's concomitant studies and revivals of folk literature, enthusiasm was kindled for spontaneity of expression as opposed to the classical cult of regulation and restraint. At the same time, Germans were led to reexamine their own literature and to find inspiration in the early expressions of their own national character rather than in French models. All of this spelled freedom for the development of a national literature, which would spring spontaneously from the artist's nature and which would be valuable, not as the expression of individual idiosyncrasy, but as a contribution to the total national culture, since the artist is both a product of and a spokesman for his people.

JOHANN CHRISTIAN FRIEDRICH HÖLDERLIN (1770–1843)

Hölderlin was born in a small German village on the River Neckar. After the death of his father in 1772, Hölderlin's mother remarried the mayor of a nearby Nürtingen, where young Hölderlin attended school. When his mother again found herself a widow in 1779, he had little choice if he desired higher education but to pursue ministerial education, which was provided free by the State church. He eventually earned his master's degree in theology at the University of Tübingen. During these years he was also reading Greek mythology with increasing fascination and pleasure.

He faced a choice between these spiritual and secular worlds when, upon graduation, he qualified for ordination as a minister. Hölderlin decided not to enter the ministry. Pursuing his new path as a man of literature, Hölderlin was introduced in 1793 to Friedrich Schiller, who helped the young man obtain a position as a tutor and published several of his early poems in *Neue Thalia*, Schiller's literary periodical. Hölderlin's early poetry and fragments of prose centered on heroic themes: the liberation of Greece, the French Revolution, and more general hymns to freedom.

Hölderlin's life took a dramatic turn in 1795 when, as a tutor in the home of a wealthy banker, he fell in love with Susette, his employer's wife. She stimulated a rush of new poetry, including a novel, *Hyperion*, in which she appears as Diotima, the reincarnated spirit of ancient Greece. The affair was discovered by Susette's husband after several months, and Hölderlin was summarily dismissed. Shaken, he turned to the writing of tragedy, *The Death of Empedocles*, and several odes and elegies. Symptoms of manic-depressive disorder and schizophrenia began to appear as early as 1798. When his beloved Susette died in 1802, Hölderlin returned half mad to his family and friends at Nürtingen. There, in various stages of mental imbalance, he wrote verse translations of Sophocles and visionary heroic poetry. His friend Isaak von Sinclair cared for Hölderlin until Sinclair was thrown in jail, under false charges, in 1805. Hölderlin quickly succumbed to complete schizophrenia and divided the remaining three decades of his life between clinics and a halfway house arrangement in Tübingen.

IMPORTANCE

For nearly 100 years after his death in 1843 Hölderlin's dramatic, poetic, and fictional works were virtually forgotten. At the beginning of the twentieth century, however, his work was rediscovered in Germany and recognized for its unique melding of Greek and Christian themes, intense lyricism, and prophetic call for spiritual renewal. Hölderlin ranks now among Germany's greatest poets.

JOHANN WOLFGANG VON GOETHE (1749–1832)

IMPORTANCE

Goethe is one of those rare, powerful, original, creative geniuses who, like Shakespeare and Dante, stands like a colossus among the lesser great figures in European literature. Spanning the entire era of the great period of German literature, he represents so nearly all the phases of German literary development that a history of the age inevitably revolves around him as a central figure. Like his most famous creation, Faust, he was an eternal searcher for knowledge and experience. Nor was his Faustian greed for experience readily satisfied with conventional or easy solutions to the problems of existence; to him each additional piece of knowledge only opened new vistas for exploration. Blessed and, to a degree, cursed by a boundless vitality, he was driven by a restless inquisitive nature during his entire life until, near his death, he more closely approximated the "universal man" than has any writer or thinker since the end of the Renaissance.

Johann Wolfgang von Goethe was born in Frankfurt on August 28, 1749, the only son and eldest child of an imperial councillor. His father was a highly educated but very strict parent whose severity toward his son was somewhat mollified by his more tolerant and vivacious wife. Both parents doubtless expected that their son would follow a family tradition of bourgeois solidity and distinction in government service. Exposed to no formal education as a child, the young Goethe was directed by his father to the classic works in his extensive private library. More by virtue of an innately inquisitive disposition than through parental guidance, Goethe acquired a broad cultural background and made private excursions into the realm of the forbidden and radical new literary movements. He describes in his autobiography the secret reading of Klopstock's *Messiah* with his sister and the tremulous excitement with which he declaimed many of its soaring lines.

Here in his early environment the combined classicism and Romanticism of his later life were stimulated; the classic influence by his father and his father's library, the Romantic by the warm emotionalism of his mother and sister and his private explorations of the new literary rebellion against French Neoclassicism. His early acquaintance with the theater came from a French company of actors who performed in Frankfurt during the Seven Years' War. At the age of fifteen Goethe also experienced his first encounter with love when he became a worshipper at the feet of an innkeeper's daughter named Marguerite or Gretchen, who was somewhat older than he and who apparently treated him pretty much as a child. Although Goethe makes much of this episode in his autobiography and in *Faust*, it is likely that he singled out Gretchen as a symbol of youthful idealistic boy-love that his sensitive spirit doubtless felt more intensely than is usual at that age.

When he was sixteen years old, he left Frankfurt to study law at the University of Leipzig in accord with his father's desires. He gave some attention to legal study but more to the cultivation of writing, which he had already begun to consider seriously as a lifelong vocation. Under the influence of Adam Frederick Oeser, a friend of Winckelmann the archaeologist, Goethe also began to take an active interest in art, studying drawing and etching under him and learning much about the classic ideal of beauty in repose. At Leipzig, too, Goethe's ardent nature found an object of devotion in Käthchen Schönkopf, whom he named Aennchen. Her capricious nature, together with his own youthful experimentations with the emotions aroused by pursuit, quarrel, and reconquest, made of this an affair more stimulating than earnest. Goethe records the experience in his first play, a frail one-act pastoral concerning happy and unhappy lovers entitled *Lovers' Quarrels* (*Die Laune der Verliebten*). Another very grim play, *The Fellow Sinners* (*Die Mitschuldigen*), and a number of sensuous love songs were also products of his three years at Leipzig.

In 1768 Goethe returned to Frankfurt for an unhappy year and a half, during which he was troubled by poor health and distressed by the stiffness and formality of both the family and social life which he had outgrown during his years of freedom. A sympathetic friend of his mother's, Fraülein von Klettenberg, brightened this dismal period by introducing him to the study of alchemy. This new interest, which became an integral part of *Faust*, and an intensified dislike of social conventionality are the only noteworthy results of his nineteenth and twentieth years.

In 1770 he left Frankfurt for Strassburg to continue his studies. Coming in contact with a group of medical students at his boarding house, he soon became engrossed in an enthusiasm for science which led him to take courses in anatomy, midwifery, and chemistry. Plunging simultaneously into a whirl of social affairs, he took dancing lessons, learned to play the cello, and found as much pleasure in a career of gay pleasure-seeking as he had formerly experienced disgust with the cold rigidities of Frankfurt. Here too he became acquainted with Herder, through whom he came to know Ossian, Shakespeare, the *Vicar of Wakefield*, and Herder's doctrine of natural genius.

Probably under the spell of Goldsmith's portrayal of natural simplicity in the *Vicar of Wakefield*, Goethe conceived a passion for Frederike Brion, a pastor's daughter who lived in a village some twenty miles from Strassburg. For an entire winter Goethe was a constant visitor at the rural parsonage, idolizing the sixteen-year-old girl whose unaffectedness and natural sweetness coincided so well with the poet's new literary discoveries. The termination of his stay at Strassburg, coincident with his taking the degree of Doctor of Law, brought about a realization on both sides that their paths in life were too far separated for a consideration of marriage. They parted amiably,

Goethe to cherish for a lifetime this idyllic otherworldly interlude and Frederike to remain single until her death in 1813, saying "the heart that Goethe has loved should never love another."

Upon his second return home in 1770, Goethe found Frankfurt more unbearable than ever. He enjoyed some literary companionship there, but he was mainly engrossed in literary criticism and in the projection of a German historical play that should ignore the Neoclassical unities and follow the freer inspiration and unity of feeling of Shakespeare. The result was his first noteworthy play, *Götz von Berlichingen*, based on the biography of a sixteenth century knight, which had been published in 1731.

In 1772, while *Götz* was still in manuscript form, Goethe took up residence at Wetzlar, a law court center of the Holy Roman Empire, with the not very enthusiastic intention of continuing the pursuit of law as his vocation. While enjoying the congenial society which the city afforded, he formed one of the strongest attachments of his life. The twenty-year-old Lotte (Charlotte) Buff, who was informally engaged to Kestner, the secretary of the Hanoverian legation, fascinated him by her beauty and by her tender womanliness. The second daughter of a large family, she mothered a large brood of younger brothers and sisters. Goethe was welcomed into the family circle and became an intimate friend of the engaged couple. The purity and fineness of this relationship of three noble spirits in defiance of ordinary conventions added stimulus to this unusual arrangement, but stresses inevitably developed, which caused Goethe to make an abrupt break with the couple, though not before they had made an agreement that whoever died first should attempt to return to the others. In spite of his sudden departure, Goethe maintained a distant relationship with both Lotte and Kestner, providing the wedding ring for their marriage, continuing to correspond with Kestner for many years, and seeing Lotte in 1816 when she was sixty-three years old. From Goethe's lonely agonizings over the lost Lotte was born the internationally famous novel *Werther*, which, together with *Götz*, which had been published in 1773, established his reputation as an author. He had also written a number of lesser pieces including a translation of Goldsmith's *Deserted Village*, a series of amorous poems, and some satirical pieces in both verse and prose.

Although he was actively engaged in legal practice, Goethe was now possessed of a mind seething with projected literary works, including the idea of *Faust*. In 1774 he wrote the highly successful play *Clavigo*, based on the trial of Beaumarchais, studied the Koran for use in a play on *Mahomet*, and worked on themes as diverse as those of the *Wandering Jew* and *Prometheus*. Acknowledged as a genius, Goethe now began to be sought out by other notables including Klopstock himself. In December of 1774 he was visited by Karl Ludwig von Knebel who invited him to meet the two young princes of Saxe-Weimar, the seventeen-year-old Duke Karl August and his younger brother. The meeting resulted in a warm mutual admiration which was to be a decisive factor in Goethe's future. At about the same time,

Goethe's intense craving for love resulted in his passion for Lili Schönemann, who led him into a world of wealth and privilege. But after a gay and impetuous courtship, her family's objections to their daughter's engagement with an undisputed but unsettled genius proved so strong that Goethe reluctantly gave her up as he had all the others. He had written several more scenes of *Faust* during this courtship and had also begun his play *Egmont*, which was inspired by the American Revolution.

An invitation in 1775 from Karl August took him to Weimar where the Renaissance ideal of a court as a magnet for scholars and artists was very much in the ascendant. Goethe quickly became an inseparable companion of the young Duke. Together they engaged in a wild round of pleasure-seeking while Goethe was awarded titles and stipends, and also civic responsibilities. He concerned himself with developing natural resources such as mines, reconstructing the army, and augmenting educational programs. Much of his writing was now turned toward the production of occasional pieces for performance at court by an amateur theatrical group made up of members of this society including himself. His amorous disposition found satisfaction in Charlotte von Stein, the thirty-three-year-old wife of a courtier and mother of seven children. To her and for her were written ecstatic expressions of his devout humility before her womanly perfections.

A series of journeys with the Duke culminated in a winter expedition to Switzerland in 1779, undertaken for the sake of the Duke's health. It was an arduous and difficult tour, which had a sobering effect on both Goethe and his master. Upon their return, past frivolities were abandoned for serious work. Goethe undertook the study of history, geology, osteology, and astronomy. He began these studies seemingly from a sense of their importance in the civic life of the Duchy, but his own active curiosity led him to continue them for their own sake. In anatomy he made a discovery of importance to the establishment of the theory of evolution, that the intermaxillary bone found in lower animals also exists in a rudimentary form in the human skull. His interest was always more in speculation, in proposals of broad principles, than in exact research, and, as a result, his theories concerning botany and geology were interesting and original rather than sound. He also continued his interest in art, trying his hand at sketching, painting, engraving, and etching. As would be expected, his writings began to reach toward greater depth and profundity. He worked simultaneously on the completion of *Egmont* and the writing of *Iphigenie* and *Wilhelm Meister*.

By 1786 his life had become too complex in every way for even Goethe's apparently inexhaustible energy. Feeling an absolute necessity for solitude, he satisfied a long nurtured desire to visit Italy by making a two-year trip incognito, and was able at the same time to break the increasingly difficult ties with Charlotte von Stein and with his multifarious friends, interests, and activities. Under the influence of the monuments and atmosphere of classical culture and the Italian Renaissance, he began his metrical version of *Iphigenie* and a revision of his *Torquato Tasso*. From Rome he traveled to Sicily, often described as more Greek than Greece itself, where his interest in Greek culture was so much stimulated that he attemped to render Homer's *Odyssey* in dramatic form in the unfinished *Nausicaa*. His completion of *Egmont* at the same time is a clear indication that Goethe's classicism was, at best, superficial, since *Egmont* is far from the classic ideal of symmetry and coherence.

Upon his return to Weimar in 1788, he attempted to begin a new life, to be devoted solidly to his own artistic integrity without the distractions of public office or social lionization. His already half-broken relationship with Charlotte von Stein was completely severed by a chance meeting with Christiane Vulpius, a young girl who had come to him with a petition on behalf of her brother. Goethe's reaction to her blooming beauty, her natural goodness, and her vivacious temperament seems to have been as instantaneous as it was lasting. He took her into his own house as his mistress, lived with her for eighteen years without benefit of clergy while she bore his children, and finally married her in 1806, apparently for the sake of his oldest son. He also met Schiller in that same momentous year, although his close association with him did not begin until several years later. Meanwhile, he became engaged in studies of colors and of optics about which, as usual, he had his own theories, became interested in the University of Jena, and was appointed director in 1791 of the new Weimar theater where Shakespeare's and other meritorious plays were performed under his rigorous supervision.

During his early years at Weimar he had been connected with military affairs; in 1792 he was given the opportunity to engage in actual warfare when he accompanied the Duke on a campaign in the Ardennes. After experiencing the sensations of being under fire and the monotony of warfare, which he relieved by writing up his theory of colors in his tent, he returned to Weimar to find that a fine new house had been built for him by the Duke during his absence. His writing during this period was confined to short lyric poems and a few satiric pieces such as his reworking of the old folk tale of *Reynard the Fox*.

In 1789 Schiller, who was already known as a playwright, was appointed to a professorship of history at the University of Jena, and the close friendship between the two poets began. In 1794 Schiller fathered a new literary journal, the *Horen*, to which Goethe and many other distinguished authors contributed but which met with adverse criticism and abuse. The two friends collaborated in answering their critics by composing a series of epigrams, the *Xenien*. Further co-authorship resulted in the idyllic poem *Hermann und Dorothea* and a series of ballads published in 1798 in the *Musen Almanach*. As individual enterprises, Goethe also completed his novel *Wilhelm Meisters Lehrjahre*, was engaged in researches in the morphology of plants and insects, continued his studies in color and biology, and was ceaselessly active in the conduct of the theater. He also did a number of translations, including Cellini's autobiography and the *Mahomet* and *Tancred* of Voltaire.

In 1805 Schiller's death ended a period of mutual stimulation which, although it had produced nothing of outstanding merit from Goethe's pen, had marked the height of Schiller's productivity and influence on German literature. Goethe arranged a memorial performance of Schiller's *The Bell*, to which he added his own epilogue. Since then the names of Goethe and Schiller have always been linked. A pair of statues of the poets in the square in front of Goethe's home commemorates their association.

The death of Schiller coincidentally marked the conclusion of Weimar's glory. In 1806 Napoleon conquered at the Battle of Jena and occupied Weimar, whose court had fled from the city. Goethe's home and property were respected by the conqueror, whose admiration for the poet was expressed at a later meeting in 1808 when Napoleon exclaimed to Goethe, "*Vous êtes un homme!*" ("You are a man!") In the same year a thirteen-volume edition of Goethe's works was published, including Part I of *Faust* in its complete form. This most unusual work was a lifetime preoccupation. Goethe had been writing bits of it at intervals during his entire career. It inevitably lacks the coherence of a work begun and completed with a single idea and written in a particular frame of mind. It is unique in the history of world literature in that it became the repository of the varied and changing attitudes and ideas of a man who lived so full a life.

In 1809 he finished *Die Wahlverwandtschaften* (*The Elective Affinities*), a story that probes into the eternal attacks made upon morality and conventional arrangements by the uncontrollable insistence of human passions. In 1810 he published his *Farbenlehre* (*Theory of Colors*), which rejected the theory that white is the combination of all colors and attempted to demonstrate that light (white) is a pure uncompounded essence of which the other colors are modifications, rendered impure by the medium through which the light passes. Although this theory then ran and still runs counter to all accepted views, it is an excellent illustration of Goethe's unwillingness to accept standard solutions and of the restless inquisitiveness of his mind.

With the end of the Weimar regime and the publication of his collected works, it was natural for Goethe to think of summing up the manifold experiences through which he had passed. Publishing his autobiography in three installments between 1811 and 1814, he gave it the highly suggestive title *Dichtung und Wahrheit* (*Poetry and Truth*), which simultaneously implies "facts and fancies" and "life and writings." Goethe's impatience with literal truth makes the autobiography a very uncertain source of the chronology of his activities, but it remains rich in its delineation of the atmosphere of his time and in its vivid descriptions of the processes of human growth.

Goethe's essential dislike for the mundane details of human life kept him remote from the rising of the German people against the imperialism of Napoleon, and his all-but-complete indifference to this movement is typical of the growing interest in theory and abstraction which marked his later years. Yet at the age of sixty-five, Goethe's mind was still capable of being attracted to new interests. Becoming acquainted with the oriental poetry of Hafiz, he wrote a series of amatory poems, which, together with a side reference to Napoleon's campaign in Russia, were published as a book entitled

Timur. The love poems were addressed to Suleika, an oriental pseudonym for Goethe's latest inamorata, Marianne von Willemer, the newly married wife of an old friend. His *West-östliche Divan* (*West-Eastern Divan*) consists of a similar series of poems with oriental settings and colorings.

The concluding years of Goethe's life, after his seventieth birthday, were occupied by critical analyses of other literatures and by the writing of *Wilhelm Meisters Wanderjahre* and the second part of *Faust.* He had become by now a kind of oracle, visited, honored, and deferred to as the acknowledged titan of European literature. The early death of Byron deepened Goethe's admiration for the English rebel, who is included in *Faust* as Euphorion. In his last years, Goethe had the misfortune to outlive nearly all of those who were dear to him, including his wife who died in 1816, Charlotte von Stein who died in 1827, and Duke Karl who died in 1828. He continued to work on an autobiographical memoir *Tages und Jahrsheften* (*Daily and Yearly Journals*), which was to be supplemented by the work known to English readers as *Conversations with Eckermann* (*Gespräche mit Goethe*) by John Peter Eckermann (1792–1854), who had become his secretary in 1823 and who remained with him until his sudden death from a cold on March 22, 1832.

Goethe's Distinctive Qualities

Goethe's writings differ from the works of the world's other acknowledged literary masters chiefly in their autobiographical nature. They are the record of the manifold experiences and the intellectual and emotional reactions of an extraordinary seeker after truth and knowledge. He was always in love with theories and rather resented the tedious minutiae of exact scientific research. This is to say that Goethe was a poet in the fullest sense of the word. His grasp of truth was intuitive and immediate; his conception of truth was that which is universally felt by mankind; his writing was the recreation of human truths in language no more literal than truth itself. He changed his mind often in the sense that new experiences altered or enlarged his conclusions concerning the nature of man and the universe, the microcosm and the macrocosm. But he gave to the world with freshness and spontaneity his beliefs and perceptions as they came to him.

Unlike the carefully weighed and planned compositions of Dante, Goethe's writings have always the sense of immediacy and enthusiasm. He was a constant experimenter with life, with ideas, and with forms of writing. For the same reason, his works seldom have the qualities of finish or formal beauty which distinguish the masterpieces of Dante and Virgil. He came to love the beauties of classicism, but these were never an essential part of his make-up. Instead, the urgency of the moment, the spirit of the thing, guided his pen. As a result, nearly all his works have serious flaws of structure, of inconsistencies, of excesses and redundancies and extraneities.

In the large sense, Goethe represents the fullest development of the Romanticist. It has been argued that he should not be so designated because he so clearly matured and outgrew the kind of romanticism exhibited by Wordsworth, Shelley, and Keats. Shelley and Keats died young; Wordsworth lived narrowly and abandoned his early attitudes. In contrast, Goethe lived abundantly and developed his faith in the spirit, his understanding of nature and human nature, and his reliance on feelings as man's essential motivating force. The result was an all-encompassing vision of reality and a philosophy of life broader and deeper than the partial visions and attitudes of other romanticists. Yet the spirit of youthfulness, the impatience with close reasoning or "logic-chopping," and the continued faith in nature remained his to the end, together with an occasional waywardness and impulsiveness and a disregard of artistic or logical propriety which savor strongly of romantic individualism. Since so many twentieth century thoughts and attitudes are similarly based on the stimulus of the Romantic movement, Goethe stands as particularly the poet of the modern man as Dante stood for medieval man and as Shakespeare for the man of the Renaissance. A survey of his principal works will indicate more specifically the development of his growing perceptions.

Götz von Berlichingen

Near the beginning of Goethe's career when his enthusiasm for Shakespeare was at once the excitement of new discovery and a reflection of the championship of the human spirit in opposition to the formalities of Neoclassicism, he happened upon the autobiography of Götz von Berlichingen, a sixteenth century robber knight who represented himself as a defender of justice and righteousness in the midst of treacherous and Machiavellian princes and nobles. Inspired by these idealistic sentiments, by the new patriotic spirit, and by a strong Rousseauistic conviction in regard to the goodness of the natural instincts of man, Goethe attempted to imitate Shakespeare's use of historical characters by writing a play about a rather obscure figure in German history. Creating an authentic sixteenth century background, Goethe also projects something of the *Sturm und Drang* sentiments of revolt as the rebellious hero fights against the treachery and meanness of his age.

The plot revolves about the feud between Götz and the Bishop of Bamberg. A former schoolmate of Götz, Adalbert von Weisslingen, who now belongs to the Bishop's faction, is being held a prisoner in Götz's castle. There he falls in love with Götz's sister Maria, and determines to transfer his allegiance to Götz for her sake. Returning to Bamberg to settle his affairs, he succumbs so completely to the intrigues of his former associates as to forget Maria and marry the beautiful Adelheid von Walldorf, who is attached to the Bishop's court. The peasants' revolt, headed by Götz, is defeated, and the original situation is reversed when Götz is condemned to die by Weisslingen's command. When Maria attempts to save her brother by appealing to Weisslingen in memory of his former love, he grants her request only to be poisoned by his jealous wife. She is condemned as a result, and Götz dies of wounds incurred in battle.

The play is loosely organized and often uncertain in its direction. Its fifty-eight scenes, tragic and comic, are a deliberate flaunting of time-honored principles of good dramatic structure. But it has all the feeling of restless violence associated with the *Sturm und Drang* period. Götz rebels and takes the peasants' side against the artificialities and venality of a clerical court. Weisslingen is perverted and then destroyed by associates who are incapable of perceiving the fineness of his character. Where the spirit is pitted against the corruption of society, society wins; but the applause goes to the victims, and their martyrdom is an inspiration for all mankind. Goethe knew that nobility of spirit is as rare as intelligence or force of character; hence he was no democrat. The peasants should have a master, but good leadership should exist for the benefit, not the exploitation, of the people.

The Sorrows of Werther

Die Leiden des jungen Werther (*The Sorrows of the Young Werther*), published in the following year, intensifies the basic conflict of *Götz von Berichingen* by bringing it into the contemporary world and applying it to a more commonplace experience. If *Götz* reflects the struggle of the noble spirit against mundane falsities and worldly guile, *Werther* exemplifies the same *Sturm und Drang* sentiments in a much more intimate way. Omitting the historical and nationalistic qualities of *Götz*, *The Sorrows of Werther* is a direct outpouring of Goethe's heart and is therefore the most perfect example of the *Sturm und Drang* emotional ferment. Following the mode already established by Rousseau and Richardson for such intimate revelation, the novel is composed almost entirely of letters purporting to have been written by Werther to his bosom friend Wilhelm, who then edited them for publication. The effect of verisimilitude so established led many readers to believe that they were reading a real rather than a fictional correspondence. Actually, Werther is Goethe himself, and the story is based upon his own love affair with Lotte Buff.

The first letters describe Werther's retreat to a beautiful countryside to find balm for his heavy-heartedness engendered by a growing awareness of the suffering in the world and particularly of the suffering of one Leonora, who had conceived a hopeless passion for him, which, he blames himself, he had unwittingly encouraged. The beauty and peace of nature are described as supplying that much-needed comfort and tranquility which the society of his former friends and acquaintances had failed to afford. He finds ample delight in reading his beloved Homer amidst the natural surroundings and in drawing close to the common people, particularly the children. A nearby village called Walheim also attracts him because of a small inn kept by a good old woman, where he can drink coffee and read Homer.

After a series of almost daily letters describing these new-found joys, a two-weeks' break in the correspondence is followed by the glowing announcement that he has met an angel. He explains that he had been invited to a country dance and had arranged to hire a carriage to take a girl of his acquaintance and her aunt as chaperon. On their way they stopped at a hunting lodge near Walheim to pick up Charlotte, the daughter of a district judge who had retired there with his children. The first sight of the lovely simple girl surrounded by the six other children to whom she had become a second mother filled Werther's heart with tenderness. His enchantment with her warmth, her gracefulness, her simplicity, her rich dark eyes, warm lips, and glowing cheeks was intensified by the almost immediate discovery that she too was an admirer of Goldsmith's *Vicar of Wakefield*. Although he knew that she was engaged to be married to an absent young man, he could not resist devoting himself to her at the dance where the harmony of her heart, soul, and body expressed itself in her graceful movements. When a storm suddenly broke, the terror of the guests was dispelled by Charlotte's proposal of a game. Then, following her to a window, he was transported into an almost unbearable state of rapture when the magical effect of soft rain and distant thunder caused her to place her hand on his and murmur, "Klopstock!" From that moment it has been clear to Werther that their souls are as one and that the truth and power of nature is greater than the artificialities of society.

Werther now has time or interest for nothing but Charlotte. He sees her every day and continues to be enchanted by her great-heartedness, as evidenced by her visits to the old and the sick. He can scarcely endure having her out of his sight; the touch of her hand excites him wildly. The return of Albert, her fiancé, accentuates the hopelessness of his case. In spite of sound advice from Wilhelm, he can neither give her up nor hope to win her for himself. His admiration for Albert and for his infinite tact and understanding serves only to intensify his anguish. He is finally driven to the realization that he must leave Walheim, and asks Wilhelm to secure a government position for him. He puts off his departure as long as possible, tells no one of his plans for fear that a leave-taking would be unendurable, engages in a last most tender conversation with Charlotte and Albert, and sees them depart together in the moonlight. He throws himself on the ground weeping, jumps up to run after them for a last glimpse of her white dress, stretches out his arms to her, and sees them vanish.

Book II of this short novel describes his new position with an ambassador. For a time his work keeps his mind occupied, but soon he begins to hate the contemptible inanities of rank and property. He writes a distracted letter to Charlotte asking her about her true feelings for Albert and receives an answer from Albert that they are married. Having resigned his distasteful court position, he attempts to escape from himself by accepting the invitation of a young prince to spend the summer on his country estate. But his passion will allow him no peace anywhere, so he returns again to Walheim to be at least near the object of his adoration.

His first meeting with Albert and Charlotte leaves him with the awareness that Albert does not truly appreciate the ineffable qualities of his wife and that Charlotte's marriage is superficial compared with the true union of his and Charlotte's souls. Charlotte pities Werther, and Albert is not without sympathy, but the wild darkness that has taken possession of Werther's heart finds comfort only in reading Ossian, who has superseded the majestic calm of Homer in Werther's heart. Then Charlotte suggests that he see her less frequently. He begins to drink more wine than is good for him, and his visits to her become an unendurable anguish.

The story is concluded from the accounts of others. On one occasion, Werther had gone to Charlotte's home, where he heard of a peasant who had killed another peasant because of jealousy. When Werther found himself unable to save the unfortunate victim of his passion whose case so closely resembled his own, he was plunged into even deeper despair. After writing a farewell letter to Charlotte, he nevertheless visited her again in a wildly excited condition. She attempted to soothe him by having him read Ossian to her. When Charlotte was moved to tears by the mournful beauty of the lines, Werther seized her in his arms and covered her lips with passionate kisses. The next day he borrowed a brace of pistols from Albert and shot himself that night. When Charlotte heard of his death, she collapsed at Albert's feet. Werther was buried by laborers without priestly attendance in a place which he himself had selected.

From a cold-blooded viewpoint, *The Sorrows of Werther* is the worst kind of sentimentalism, without dignity or restraint. Written, as Goethe says, from the heart, it represents Werther as wallowing in uncontrolled emotions ranging from extravagant ecstasy to suicidal gloom. His moods of melting tenderness, excessive adoration, and maudlin self-pity make the sentimentality of Rousseau, Richardson, and even Chateaubriand almost dignified by comparison. Yet there is a sense of honesty and sincerity through the book which redeems it. Admitting that uncontrolled emotions constitute a kind of sickness, one must admit that youthful sentimentalism is a very human and very common ailment. Being a phase through which many sensitive young idealists like Goethe inevitably pass, its quality and its intensity are fully realized when described by an artist who experienced within himself a superabundance of emotional fervor. For here is the complete revelation of the dangerous delights of enjoying one's own emotions, including the most somber ones, to such an extent that the normal realities of life are submerged by torrents of feelings and theatrical extremes. From still another point of view *The Sorrows of Werther* is a fine example historically of the emphasis on natural feeling that constituted a basic element of the Romantic movement in Europe.

Iphigenia in Tauris

The change from the tempestuous emotionalism of *Werther* to the calm certainty of *Iphigenia* is evidence of a considerable step in Goethe's development. In a play based on Euripides and loosely following the pattern of Greek drama, he asserts the universal appeal of moral law which operates within man and which has power to soothe both inward and outward violence. *Iphigenie auf Tauris* was written in prose in 1779 and performed at the Weimar theater. Then, after several experimental revisions, it was shaped into its final form under the influence of Shakespearean iambic pentameter.

Euripides' *Iphigenia* describes the combination of cunning and divine assistance by which Agamemnon's daughter and her brother Orestes escaped from the barbaric Taurians. At the beginning of the Trojan war, when Iphigenia had been offered up for sacrifice by her father Agamemnon to obtain a favoring wind, she had been snatched away by Artemis (Diana) and placed in Aulis as priestess to Artemis' stolen image which was in a temple there. Years later, Agamemnon's son Orestes, who had avenged his father's death at his wife's hands, was doomed by the furies to torment until he should retrieve Artemis' statue. The Greek play concerns the arrival of Orestes at Tauris with his lifelong friend Pylades, the recognition of brother and sister, and the ruse by which their escape is made.

Following the general pattern of the Greek play, Goethe places the emphasis on character rather than on external forces. Orestes is tortured by his own sense of guilt and finds release in the pure, clear spirit of his sister whose beautiful soul (a concept deriving ultimately from Plato) has been so persuasive that it has even turned the barbarian king Thoas away from his previous custom of slaughtering all strangers. When her purity so moves the king that he asks her to be his wife and meets the meek refusal of a devoted priestess, his wrath causes him to restore the old custom and insist that two newly captured strangers, Orestes and Pylades, be sacrificed by the priestess of Artemis.

In recognition of his own past kindnesses to her, Iphigenia frankly reveals her own origin but is unable to move the monarch's heart. When Orestes reveals himself to her and verges on madness in confession of his matricidal guilt, she finds new hope in her ability to restore his peace of mind and in the ingenious scheme for escape proposed by the Ulysses-like Pylades. But at the last crucial moment, her moral sense will not allow her to deceive the king who has protected and trusted her. She reveals to him the entire plot, and her appeal to moral principles and the essential brotherhood of all humanity is so powerful that he allows them all to depart in peace.

Just as the ancient Greek furies who pursued Orestes are here turned into psychological terrors, so too the statue that is rescued is actually the image of truth in Iphigenia's heart. Autobiographically, the play represents something of the peace that the tormented Goethe found in the love of Charlotte von Stein and the new-found sense of universal law that he believed to be intuitive rather than logical. From the standpoint of literary history, *Iphigenia* is at once one of the most notable examples of the German adaptation of Hellenic models and one of the clearest indications of the growing German interest in individual personality as reflecting not national but universal principles of humanity.

Torquato Tasso

Begun like *Iphigenia* in prose, *Torquato Tasso* was later completed as poetic drama in 1789. The romantic legend of the Italian poet Tasso, whose career is described in the first volume of this study, attracted Goethe as a striking example of the fluidity of the artistic temperament in conflict with the rigidity of the conventional world of society. In a play that has almost no action, Goethe presents much of his own temperament and sense of frustration. As a somewhat grown-up Werther possessed of extraordinary talent, Tasso is supersensitive and almost morbidly emotional. As an artist, he prefers solitude and the inner satisfaction which comes from his own achievement. But as a human being, he craves applause and recognition, human companionship, and the love of an understanding woman.

The play is modeled on the Greek conception of dramatizing the moment of crisis rather than, as in Shakespearean plays, the entire event. Tasso has completed his masterwork. At an apex of emotional and artistic excitement he is crowned by the princess Leonora, whom he adores but who is beyond his orbit. Sublimated by the moment he receives a merited rebuff from Antonio, the man of the world. A challenge to a duel is interrupted by the Duke, Goethe's idealized ruler, who is a man of mature judgment, patience, and understanding. But the Duke's mild penalty of imposing upon Tasso a temporary confinement to his own quarters so rankles upon the psyche of a man who knows himself to be a genius that he breaks the bounds of conventionality by attempting to clasp Leonora in his arms. Repulsed by her, however gently, he is a completely lost soul who at last finds solace in the proffered friendship of Antonio, who has been incited by the Duke to this act of generosity.

The concluding reconciliation of Tasso and Antonio is unsatisfactory from any point of view. Nothing has been solved, and the likelihood of such a reconciliation seems extremely remote. But in using his characters as symbols, as he does, Goethe seems to imply that both artist and man of affairs have their places in the world and that each must learn to recognize the value of the other. Biographically, the play reveals a great deal of Goethe's own feeling about his relationship with Duke Karl and his attitude toward the ladies of the court. In action and motivation the play leaves much to be desired, but psychologically it presents a very real understanding of the essentially irresponsible and temperamental nature of the creative urge. It is also a kind of prelude to *Faust* in its refusal to place blame on any variety of honest human endeavor and in its implied message that the meaning of life is in the interrelationship of many different kind of abilities. Tasso's inability to meet the stresses of human relationships was the cause of his frustration, as was also true of Werther. The complete man would be a combination of Tasso and Antonio.

Goethe's Lyric Poetry

Goethe's shorter poems, written throughout his life, are in themselves reason enough for his reputation as Germany's greatest poet. He was essentially a lyrist in whatever he wrote, and these highly personal poems, bound by no strictures such as the conventionalities of plot, projection of character, staging, and the like, flow directly and spontaneously from the poet's heart. Nearly all of them came into being as the result of the inspiration of a moment's powerful feeling. Like all good lyrics they defy translation, but they are of interest even when rendered into English because of their revelation of the powerful fluid emotionalism of Goethe, his earnest quest for the meaning of life, his extraordinary flashes of insight, and his almost total preoccupation with humanity.

Many of the poems have to do with nature, yet even these have as their focal point the relationship of nature and man. Some of the pieces are tempestuous outbursts; others are quiet, gentle, and restrained. In most of them is expressed or implied Goethe's mystic sense of the unity of all life in which the individual is part of an endlessly varying moving pattern, the significance of life being not in its goal but in the actual experience of living. Even the love poems, which are the nearest to being expressions of pure emotion, are apt to contain allusions to the aspiring nature of man, to his instinct for idealization, or to the loneliness of the individual desiring to feel himself part of the fabric of life. To Goethe the love of a woman meant vastly more than sexual satisfaction. It provided a definite object as an implicit symbol for his Platonic yearning for goodness and beauty, and it also allowed him to break the barriers of individuality to find union with another part of the world spirit.

Wilhelm Meister's Apprenticeship

Wilhelm Meisters Lehrjahre (1796) is a long loosely knit novel on Goethe's favorite subect, the development of personality through experience. As a deep-feeling, sincere, and striving young man, Wilhelm Meister begins his experiences with a devotion to the ideal of creating a German theater, an idea which was more than esthetic because it was believed by many that Germany could thus achieve cultural unity even if political unity was not immediately to be realized. Even in the overworked sense that "all the world's a stage," the theater appealed to the imagination and instinct for idealization of a young man who had reached that period of human growth when, as was true of Werther, nearly everything is conceived in theatrical terms. It also represents a kind of opposite extreme from the world of business into which his father attempts to guide him.

From his childhood delight in puppet shows and an early love for an actress Marianne, he becomes connected with a theatrical troupe and writes a play that is well received. He reaches the zenith of this part of his career through his intoxicating discovery of Shakespeare. It becomes the mission of his life to translate *Hamlet* and to act the leading part. While he is in the course of achieving this goal, the author takes the opportunity to engage in an almost complete and rather formidable discussion of Shakespeare's play, a commentary which, however interesting or intrinsically valuable, is entirely out of proportion when inserted into the history of Wilhelm Meister's development.

At the height of his success, Wilhelm Meister's instinct tells him that he must not relax in the luxury of achievement but must reach forward to greater challenges. He therefore quits the theater and becomes connected with the Society of the Tower, a group of earnest seekers after truth who have pooled their distinctive individualities in a common cause. From them he learns that self-cultivation is only the first step in attaining maturity. He must learn to be active in his relationships with his fellow men and to lose himself in devotion to others. He then makes the astounding discovery that the child Felix to whom he had been attentive is his natural son by his first love. Accepting his responsibilities as father and guide, he feels in his devotion to the boy a revelation of the continuity of life. The fact that his past is thus linked with the present and that his efforts in educating the boy will have effect on the incalculable future makes him aware of the process by which the world continues to form itself through a meaningful, continuous, self-made pattern of development. With a little too much coincidence for complete comfort, he also marries Natalie, whose beautiful soul offers a reward for and a final experience in his attainment of maturity.

The novel also provides a highly romantic element in the figure of the ethereal Mignon, with her passionate insatiable yearning for Italy, and concludes with her death after the discovery that she is the daughter of an almost equally strange character, the Harper. These lonely and appealing figures may have been meant to provide by their tenuous hold on reality a contrast to the growing purposefulness of Wilhelm's career. This part of the novel formed the basis for the libretto of the perennial favorite in opera, *Mignon.*

Wilhelm Meister's Travels

In no real sense a continuation of the earlier novel, *Wilhelm Meisters Wanderjahre*, written late in Goethe's life (1821–1829), has only a formal connection with *Wilhelm Meister's Apprenticeship*. This relationship is created by the device of having Wilhelm Meister accompany his son and the Harper's brother on a journey to Mignon's home in Italy. The novel also continues the original theme by having Wilhelm choose a profession as a means of being useful to society. He thereby limits himself, but at the same time becomes more effective in terms of practical and positive achievement. Having chosen the medical profession, he is confirmed in his choice (the long arm of coincidence again) by his ability to save the life of his own son, with which event the novel concludes.

But this thread of story and theme is the barest skeleton of the book. The flesh and blood are supplied by a wealth of discussions, comments, and descriptions in which Goethe airs his views on anything that occurs to his mind. The strictures imposed by any exended form or plan or design were always something of a bugaboo to Goethe; in this work he succeeded in ignoring them almost entirely.

Faust

Goethe's greatest achievement and his greatest poem, which is cast in dramatic form, is *Faust*. Begun at the age of twenty-three and not completed until the age of eighty-three, it became the poetic record of his life, his experiences, his musings, and his philosophical inquiries. Although a large portion of Part I has received theatrical and operatic presentation, *Faust* is essentially a play for the imagination which entirely disregards the limitations of the stage. Much more subjective and incomparably looser in organization than the *Divine Comedy*, it nevertheless parallels the work of Dante in many ways. It is not an allegory; yet it has many meanings. Like the *Comedy* it is at once a personal record and a mirror of its age, becoming thereby the epic of modern man in his search for an understanding of the world about him.

Instead of being composed of a tightly knit progression of scenes, this universal drama is a composite of very nearly as many ideas, attitudes, and viewpoints as it is varied in its versification. Always a foe of little-mindedness and conventional thinking, Goethe is here more the explorer than the dogmatist, and, even though he uses well-known symbols such as God and devil, he is striving to reach an all-embracing definition of the forces in the universe that play upon the life of man.

As a convenient and suggestive framework, he builds on the medieval legend of the man who sold his soul to the devil in exchange for magical powers. There is evidence that early in the sixteenth century there actually existed an adventurer who called himself Faustus the Younger and who was supposedly carried away by the devil in 1525. Later books of magic refer to Faustus, and one such book was supposedly written by him. An anonymous biography of Dr. Johann Fausten, published at Frankfurt in 1587, became the standard version of the story, including Mephistopheles, the anticlerical tradition, and the connection with classical mythology. Faust thus became a symbol for free thought and for the investigations of the Renaissance man in opposition to the dogmas of the medieval Church. Christopher Marlowe's *Dr. Faustus* is the first effective artistic and dramatic use of the legend, consigning the protagonist to hell after his enjoyment of earthly delights. The attractiveness of the story led to the production of many other versions, such as Lessing's lost play. A popular puppet play also helped keep the subject alive, and there was a picture in Auerbach's Cellar in Leipzig that depicted the feats of Faustus the Younger.

Using also the medieval conception of macrocosm (the great world) and microcosm (the little world), Goethe divides the play into two parts. Part I (separately published in 1808) concerns the individual man who, although essentially good, is tempted by his desire for knowledge of earthly experience to experiment selfishly with life and to end in a hell of his own making. Part II (sealed by Goethe for posthumous publication) broadens the scope of the inquiry to encompass Modern Society (society after the Renaissance) and to offer final redemption to man as a reward for the good and social intentions of his earthly strivings. Because *Faust* is both personal and lyric, a neatly demonstrable series of interpretations cannot be arrived at; even more than is to be expected of all good poetry, the meaning and the effect of *Faust* become a matter of the relationship between the poet and each individual reader. The following commentary is offered, therefore, as being suggestive rather than didactic.

Part I: *Prelude on the Stage:* Goethe, mindful of his experiences as a theatrical director, opens the play with a disquisition on the practical demands of pleasing an audience. The manager knows that he must offer something important which shall at the same time appear novel and entertaining. The poet scorns the crowd and seeks to write sublimely for posterity. The clown rebukes the poet for his idealistic attitude and bids him learn to appreciate the variety and gusto of everyday experience.

At first sight the Prelude seems to stand outside the play and to be a half rueful and very realistic account of Goethe's knowledge of human nature and of the nature of the theater. Yet even here are suggested some of the essential ideas of the entire play. For the play is about mankind, and an audience comprises a fair sample of human qualities and desires. Here, in short, is the stage of the world operated by the manager who presents what his audiences require of him; namely, both poet and clown. The poet, be it noted, is the dreamer, the idealist, who strives after eternity. He is rebuked, as the Lord is later to be rebuked by Mephistopheles, for being somewhat stuffy. The clown, in contrast, is the realist who lives for the enjoyment of the moment. Both are part of life, and both are necessary to the manager, the God of the theater, who plans to present the universe on his stage, beginning with Heaven and progressing through the world to Hell, a summary of the scheme of Part 1.

Prologue in Heaven: Suggested by the Biblical narrative of *Job*, the Prologue opens the play by presenting the opposing forces of the Lord and Mephistopheles together with the contract that sets the play in motion. The pulsing song of the three archangels underscores Goethe's conception of a dynamic universe where motion is the law of nature as it is of man. Mephistopheles, who is not concerned with celestial glories, bitterly upbraids the Lord for the state of man whose divine gift which he calls reason only serves to debase him more. The rebuttal is to point out the Lord's servant Faust. When Mephistopheles describes Faust as a restless, insatiable seeker after perfection in both heaven and earth, the Lord replies that he is only temporarily confused and will find his own way to ultimate understanding. The conclusion of this very important scene explains man's mission in life as an endless striving filled with mistakes but leading inevitably toward the good. The Lord, like the poet in the Prelude on the Stage, represents the somewhat humorless eternal ideal. Mephistopheles, on the other hand, is the denying spirit, critical, derisive, Voltaire-like, and accordingly interested in earthly pleasures of the moment like the clown in the Prelude. The Lord knows that the goad of denial and cynicism is necessary to keep man active and striving. He therefore permits Mephistopheles to have a free hand with Faust, calmly assured that Mephistopheles is incapable of turning man wholly aside from his immortal vision.

Night—Faust's Study (I): Faust's bewildered state of mind suggests that the Prologue in Heaven might very well have taken place within Faust's own mind. With a God-like yearning for absolute knowledge, he is already possessed by the spirit of Mephistopheles in his cynical appraisement of the limitations of human knowledge and the misery on earth. Yet his impelling urgency drives him to have recourse to magic for possible enlightenment. The mysterious sign of the Macrocosm (the universe) fills him with rapture in the contemplation of the magnificent harmony of the world. His disgust returns when he ruefully admits that it is magnificent but meaningless. Turning impatiently to the Earth-Spirit, he is filled again with that earthy energy and vitality which makes man explore and examine. When summoned, the Earth-Spirit defines himself as the fluctuating vibration of physical life. Faust's awareness that he as an individual is part of the flow of universal life causes him to seek kinship with the Earth-Spirit. He is flatly rebuked. The Earth-Spirit's enigmatic reply seems to mean that man is the sum total of all his awareness, or perhaps that his spiritual nature removes him from the sphere of pure earthiness.

Faust's spirituality is emphasized by the sudden entrance of Wagner whose dull but honest pedantry, shallowness, and bourgeois respect for the greatness of Faust create an effective contrast to Faust's (and Goethe's) poetic grasp of meaning and significance, to which is coupled a scornful impatience with petty details. Wagner seeks knowledge or the show of knowledge, but Faust seeks understanding. Wagner's entrance also serves to rescue Faust from despair at his being unable to give up his God-given individuality in order to lose himself in the nonrational power of the life-force. But Wagner's lack of perception and the sight of a skull remind Faust again of human impotence, and he is about to commit suicide when the sound of Easter bells brings back childhood memories of his own lost faith and renews dimly flickering hope with its implied promise of the rebirth of spring from death and earthly corruption.

Before the City Gate: A rapid survey of the world of the common man presents the impulses of pleasure, joy, and desire for conquest which flow from the vitality of earthly spring. Faust is cheered by the people's unthinking joy and by their adulation of him. But he becomes envious of their simple acceptance of life in contrast to his own sense of ignorance and inadequacy. He confesses his own dual nature and the strength of both the earthly and spiritual urgencies that battle within him. When a black poodle's strange behavior excites Faust's interest, his sharp intuition perceives more than just a dog. The literal-minded Wagner, however, convinces him that the dog's actions have nothing of the occult in them.

Faust's Study (II): Followed by the poodle, Faust enters his study in a somewhat more placid frame of mind, momentarily seduced from his gloom by the simple pleasurable earthly sensations. He begins to translate the New Testament *Gospel of John* into German. He renders the first line as "In the beginning was the Word," the most obvious and least meaningful translation of the original Greek. Dissatisfied, he substitutes "Thought" or "Idea" for "Word," but realizes that thought does not create. He tentatively substitutes "Force," and concludes with "In the beginning was the Act." This brief passage specifies the conception which is everywhere in the play that action is the law of the universe; only in rest are death and damnation.

Disturbed by the whining of the poodle, Faust uses an old book of magic to effect the transformation of the dog into the shape of Mephistopheles in the guise of a traveling scholar. It is true that Mephistopheles has sought him out, but it is important that Faust must first dimly recognize him and then deliberately invoke his presence. The spirit of denial that Mephistopheles represents is actually in the universe and within man. Faust, having become discouraged by his efforts in a positive direction, here begins to nurse and encourage a negative and cynical state of mind.

Goethe's interest in medieval magic is responsible for a trifling bit of by-play connected with the power of the pentagram, the five-pointed star made of one continuous line such as every child has drawn, in preventing the passage of evil spirits. A break in the outward point of Faust's pentagram had allowed Mephistopheles to enter, but the continuity of the line on the inside keeps him a prisoner in Faust's study. Mephistopheles defines himself as the spirit of negativism, part of the darkness and the physical from which light and spirit emerged. This statement matches the angelic song of the earlier scene describing Christ's rise from corruption. It is the hope of Mephistopheles that the creative power that rose from chaos will ultimately exhaust itself in its struggles and resign itself again to the inaction that is the nature of chaos and darkness.

Mephistopheles charms Faust's senses with a beautiful lullaby made up of a fugue-like series of sensuous images sung by spirits who are unidentified but who would presumably be earth-spirits. While Faust sleeps, Mephistopheles makes good his escape by summoning mice to nibble away an inner point of the pentagram. Upon awakening, Faust is convinced that he has been deluded by a dream. By this brief concluding soliloquy Goethe again hints that Mephistopheles is an outward visible symbol of something that is a part of Faust's own nature.

Faust's Study (III): Mephistopheles again appears and is again invited into Faust's study. His recommendation to Faust of a life of pleasure-seeking calls forth a response that again evokes Faust's awareness of the dualism of his own nature, describing himself this time as too old to enjoy unintellectual pleasure and too young to be entirely free from fleshly desires. Faust's despair makes him willing to accept Mephistopheles' offer of a life of pleasure in exchange for an eternity after death as Mephistopheles' servant, but his knowledge of reality causes him to be entirely skeptical of Mephistopheles' ability to provide him with satisfaction. He therefore insists on making a specific contract to the effect that Mephistopheles may possess his soul only when he is completely satisfied, only when the moment is so perfect that he has no desire for a more complete satisfaction in the future, only when he is content to rest.

Mephistopheles of course accepts the wager because it is no more than a statement of his own admission that man becomes entirely negative and part of his domain of darkness only when he ceases to act. Mephistopheles admits a doubt of his own effectiveness by remarking that a poet (as in the Prelude on the Stage) would have a better chance of satisfying Faust's boundless aspirations.

When a student comes to consult Faust, Mephistopheles necessarily assumes the role of Faust since the spirit of denial is in the ascendant in Faust's personality. His advice to the student reveals all of Faust's cynicism regarding the futility of learning and the pettiness, superficiality, and grossness of humanity. He concludes by pointing out the serpent's advice to Eve in the Garden of Eden, "You shall be like God, knowing good and evil." Since the devil is regarded by Goethe as an essential part of the Divine Purpose, the devil is here speaking the truth. Man comes to know the Whole that is God only by experience; he comes to know good partly by experience with evil. Dante had to pass through Hell in order to reach Heaven. But to Dante knowledge of evil was apparently sufficient; Goethe insists on actual experience as the only way to knowledge, as is already evident from his ridicule of book learning.

Auerbach's Cellar: Mephistopheles' first attempt to satisfy Faust is to try to make him lose himself in the blissful irresponsibility of drunkenness. As is true of all the remaining events of Part I except the restoration of Faust's youth, Mephistopheles does nothing for Faust that he could not or would be unlikely to do for himself. Goethe's choice of Auerbach's Cellar was determined by the fact that the painting of the deeds of the historical Faustus the Younger decorated one of its walls. The students whose senses are befogged with alcohol are easily deluded by Mephistopheles' pranks. When Mephistopheles calls to Faust's attention the freedom attained by drink, Faust's awareness that this is a freedom only to act like swine impels him to nothing except a desire to get away.

The Witches' Kitchen: A sharp transition to the Witches' kitchen, where Faust is to have thirty years removed from his age (he was about fifty at the beginning of the play), intimates that Faust's previously confessed trouble of being too old to enjoy physical pleasure is about to be remedied in order that he may lose himself in sensuous delights. It also serves Goethe's purpose of reviewing his own and mankind's normal experiences by beginning with youth when fleshly appetites are strongest. Faust is disgusted by the foulness of the scene and inquires if man's science hasn't evolved a less repulsive method for restoring youth. Mephistopheles replies drily that there is the natural method of simple rustic living.

The paraphernalia of this chaotic scene is a composite of the witches of *Macbeth* and medieval magic. In spite of Goethe's own mockery at attempts to find symbolic significance in the scene, it is impossible to ignore the appearance of such common symbols as the ball of the universe and the crown of reason. Throughout the scene, also, are suggestions of the theory of evolution and an all-but-inescapable implication that Faust in regaining his youth is moving backward in time toward the ape and toward the primeval slime from which the world of organization and reason arose. He is also abandoning more mature reason for animal appetites. Under such influences he sees a vision of desirable womanhood in a mirror, implying that what he sees is his own projection and that, as Mephistopheles says at the end of the scene, nearly any woman looks like Helen of Troy in the eyes of youth.

A Street: The first woman Faust passes in the street inevitably corresponds to the image in the mirror. When Margaret (Marguerite or Gretchen) rejects Faust's brazen overture, Faust insists that Mephistopheles procure her for the satisfaction of his desire. Mephistopheles confesses that he has no power over her innocent purity. Faust in his youthful self-confidence insists that he requires only seven hours with her to break down her resistance and needs only practical help, such as the providing of jewelry, from Mephistopheles.

Evening: A Small Tidy Room: Conveyed by Mephistopheles to Margaret's room, Faust reacts in exactly the wrong way from Mephistopheles' point of view. The order and neatness of the household stimulates Faust's moral sense of all that is good and wholesome and orderly and enduring about family life. Faust's first instinct is to abandon his selfish plan of seduction, but his sensual nature causes him to waver when encouraged by Mephistopheles. The casket of jewelry is therefore placed in Margaret's clothes chest. When she enters, she is oppressed by the unhealthy atmosphere of the room but is delighted as only a poor girl could be by the glitter of the jewels that she finds.

A Walk: In a very brief scene, Mephistopheles tells Faust that Margaret's mother was so suspicious of the origin of the jewels that she turned them over to a priest. He also indulges in some cynical observations on the material rapacity of the Church.

The Neighbor's House: Martha, a worldly woman whose husband has deserted her, is effective contrast to the innocent Margaret, who runs to tell her about the finding of another set of jewels in her chest. Even Margaret is learning something by experience; this time she confides in Martha rather than in her mother. Martha is advising her to keep them and wear them secretly when Mephistopheles enters to hasten the seduction of Margaret to worldliness by flattery and by establishing a friendship with Martha. His excuse for calling is that he brings news of Martha's husband's death. He offers to return with a young friend who will corroborate his testimony.

A Street: Mephistopheles prevails on Faust to abet his scheme by lying about his supposed knowledge of the death of Martha's husband. When Faust indignantly refuses to lend himself to such a gross deception,

Mephistopheles effectively presses him with Faust's own past scholarly pronouncements concerning vast universal principles for which he had as little real evidence as for the death of Herr Schwertlein. The argument is another reminder that Faust's loss of faith in the meaning of life leads him to the logical sequel that human responsibility or moral sense is pointless. If life has no greater meaning than is implicit in physical existence, one might as well eat, drink, and be merry regardless of who pays the bills. Plato probably had something of this sort in mind when he warned in the *Phaedo* against rejecting all arguments because some arguments are found to be invalid. The poet in Faust is still active and seeks in Margaret a proof of his ideal of a spiritual and everlasting love; his cynicism, proceeding from the lips of Mephistopheles, makes him simultaneously skeptical about finding any such constancy either in a woman or in his own emotions.

Martha's Garden: The double courtship of Faust and Mephistopheles highlights again the essentially spiritual and idealistic nature of Faust and the worldly cynicism of Mephistopheles. Faust's original desire to possess Margaret has grown to what he believes is an enduring love. Margaret's appeals to him are rapidly sketched in this scene: her purity, her guilelessness, her domestic virtues, and her motherly solicitude for her baby sister. In contrast is the arch sparring of Martha and Mephistopheles. The conflict between the poet's yearning for eternity and the cynic's interest in the moment is cleverly suggested near the end of the scene when Faust's ecstatic remarks about the eternity of love are followed immediately by the flat practical statements of Martha and Mephistopheles to the effect that night is approaching and the *tête-à-tête* must be broken off.

A Summer House: In a brief postlude to the preceding scene that is probably intended to take place a few days later, Goethe reinforces the conventionality of Margaret's mother, who apparently would not tolerate Faust as a suitor. He also makes it clear that Margaret is completely and submissively in love with Faust.

Forest and Cavern: Faust, being human, is torn between his idealistic love for Margaret and an urgent physical desire to possess her body. Stimulated by nature, he thanks the Earth-Spirit for the ecstasy of his desire. Mephistopheles adds the reminder that man is saved from despair, as Faust was saved from suicide, by being able to take vacations from intellectualism, morality, and spiritual aspiration. It is necessary for Mephistopheles' purpose that Faust regard the proposed seduction of Margaret as a purely fleshly affair. He scarcely succeeds in convincing Faust that his love is no more than common sexual desire, but he so stimulates him by his loose talk that Faust is ready to plunge both himself and Margaret into ruin to satisfy his physical urgency.

Margaret's Room: The well-known "Spinning Wheel Song" implies that the seduction will soon take place and that it will scarcely be a seduction in view of Margaret's eagerness. She is now entirely overmastered by her desire for Faust, love having become for her "woman's sole existence."

Martha's Garden: Margaret's skepticism about Faust's companion (or about the Mephisthophelean element in Faust) leads her to question him about his religion. Although Faust is unwilling to tamper with the creeds of anyone else, he admits his dislike of conventional religion or a conventional God. His own definition describes God as an active moving force embracing all things and infused in all things, which can be known only by feeling rather than by indoctrination or ritual. Much of this is Goethe's own belief, but it must be remembered that Faust in this scene is very much under the influence of Mephistopheles as Margaret perceives. God is indeed "all-enfolding," but Faust's conception of the "all" is at this moment limited by his preoccupation with sense experience.

Enslaved by her own feeling Margaret agrees to administer to her mother what Faust implies is a sleeping potion in order that Faust may safely spend the night in her bedroom. The scene concludes with a brief but pungent dialogue between Faust and Mephistopheles in which Faust's insistence on the spirituality of Margaret's love evokes the very keen diagnosis by Mephistopheles that the spiritual quality of Margaret is acting as an added inducement to the satisfaction of Faust's momently self-centered and mainly sensual desires. Faust feels the lure of Margaret's goodness but is sufficiently under the spell of Mephistopheles to brush off with an insultingly casual word her expressed loathing of his companion.

At the Well: Considerable time has elapsed since the preceding scene. Aware of her own pregnancy Margaret hears the kind of scornful gossip usually accorded the fallen woman. She is made more deeply aware of her own plight by the reference to the unlikelihood that the fallen woman's gallant will marry her. She has also learned the lesson of compassion by experience, thus exemplifying part of Goethe's philosophy.

By the City Wall: Before an image of the Virgin Mary, Margaret pours out her anguish.

Night: Before Margaret's Door: The destruction in this scene results from inexperience, conventionality, and from Faust's now-degraded moral status. Valentine, shallow and conventional, is more upset by the slur on his own reputation than concern for his sister, and sets out to kill Faust without giving a thought to whether Faust's death will please Margaret or even remedy the situation in any way. Faust is so completely degraded that he asks for more jewels, listens to Mephistopheles' song, and is plainly interested in further satisfaction of his sexual appetite. He finally avails himself of Mephistopheles' assistance in his cowardly murder of Valentine.

Cathedral: The death of Valentine is followed by the revelation that Margaret's mother has also died from the effects of the sleeping potion that Margaret herself had administered on her fatal night of love. This death was also caused by Faust's degeneracy, but a contributing factor was the mother's own conventionality, which forbade anything but a secret relationship between the lovers. The Evil-Spirit that has gained possession of Margaret makes her unable to take advantage of the healing powers of religion.

Instead, she is stifled by the negative suggestions of fear concerning her approaching disgrace and probable damnation. Her swooning at the end probably results from a combination of her morbid thoughts and her advanced condition of pregnancy.

Walpurgis Night: By an old German tradition Walpurgis Night, April 30, was marked by an annual festival of witches held on Mount Brocken. Faust is led to view this obscene assembly presumably in an attempt by Mephistopheles to have him shake off all last traces of moral human nature. The scene itself is hectic, introducing traditional evil spirits like the classical Baubo and the Hebrew Lilith together with pure fantasy and a hidden reference to a disliked contemporary, Friedrich Nicolai, by including him as the Proctaphantasmist or "Rump-Visionary." Nicolai was the sponsor of a method for vanquishing ghosts by affixing leeches to the rump of the victim. His attempt to disperse the devils of course meets with failure.

When Faust is encouraged to join the sensual dance, the sight of a red mouse in the mouth of his partner reminds him that he is still somewhat removed from and can be disgusted by pure animalism. His moral nature is thereby sufficiently restored to bring to his mind the emprisoned Margaret, whom he seems to see chained in the midst of the carnival. Mephistopheles quickly attempts to distract Faust by telling him that the horrible woman is Medusa who was beheaded by Perseus, and leads him away to a theater.

Walpurgis Night's Dream: The play that Faust and Mephistopheles attend is omitted in some editions of *Faust* and might well be entirely expunged from the play. It has no connection of any kind with the action or the ideas of the drama, being composed of a series of satiric verses directed at Goethe's contemporaries. Planned originally as a separate publication and then arbitrarily inserted here, this piece represents the height of Goethe's occasional arbitrary flaunting of artistic standards.

Dreary Day: Open Country: The sudden shift to violent prose marks Faust's sharp recovery of his moral nature. Concerned now for Margaret rather than for himself, he forces Mephistopheles to make an attempt to set her free from the prison where she has been placed because of her misdeeds.

Night: Open Field: With extreme brevity, the effect of Faust's moral regeneration is symbolically represented by the appearance of angelic spirits. Faust and Mephistopheles are now completely antagonistic. It is only a momentary glimpse as they gallop along on their way to rescue Margaret, but Faust's brief remarks bespeak his enchantment at the sight and are punctuated by Mephistopheles' suggestions that another witches' meeting is taking place.

A Prison: When Faust and his diabolical servant arrive at the prison to rescue Margaret, they find her insane and learn that in her insanity she has drowned her baby. Her love for Faust is still so complete that his appearance momentarily restores her sanity. Entirely willing to accept the punishment due her and even the probability of eternal damnation, she is concerned only for Faust and her child. While Faust is attempting to persuade her to seek freedom with him, she becomes aware of the presence of Faust's companion, completely repudiates any freedom connected with Mephistopheles, and gives herself up unreservedly to judgment.

In contradiction to Mephistopheles' apparent certainty that her deeds will insure her damnation, a voice from above calls her "saved." Her salvation is assured presumably because her acts had never proceeded from sinful intention but rather from the most generous of motives. In her love for Faust she had followed her natural instinct which was creative and good. Her crimes were essentially the result of her innocence. It is also clear from this last scene that her sense of moral responsibility, which had momentarily lapsed, has been completely restored. As Faust departs with Mephistopheles, he hears her voice calling his name. This can certainly not be taken as the expression of a selfish desire to have him return to her. Rather, her last concern is to call him away from his evil companion and to beckon him to a more affirmative view of life.

Although this drama is but the first part of a larger play, it is entirely complete in itself. Mephistopheles has clearly lost both his wager with Faust and his compact with the Lord. Faust, far from accepting any moment as completely satisfactory, has in the end been forcing Mephistopheles to aid him in an attempted good deed. The Lord's faith in man is also vindicated in that Faust has never become completely animalistic. His momentary lapse into sensuality had only served to repeat the Easter message of the rise of the spirit from corruption. Margaret's original physical appeal had been quickly overshadowed in Faust's mind by the appeal of her character. With her last repetition of his name ringing in his ears, there can be no doubt that Faust will be made thoroughly aware of the disasters caused by his selfish desires and that his experiences will convince him that man must follow the call of his spiritual destiny. As is specifically stated at the end of Part II, his redemption will be the culmination of this first all-important lesson taught him by the "eternal woman-spirit," which is the purest earthly embodiment of heavenly love, and which provides a constant earthly reminder of the right pattern for human behavior by its instinctive generosity and concern for others.

Part II: Whereas the first part of *Faust* is devoted to highly personal experiences, the second part is concerned with society as a whole. Faust can no longer be enslaved by sensual passion, but he is still susceptible to the lures of worldly power and preeminence. But there is a decided difference in his relationship with Mephistopheles. Having experienced and overcome the strongest possible diabolical lure of the flesh, Faust is never again completely victimized. Mephistopheles is now much more the servant of Faust's ambitions than the director of his destiny. Faust himself becomes less an individual and more a symbol of the striving Germanic spirit, which first made itself felt in Europe in the Middle Ages.

ACT I. *A Pleasing Landscape:* The tortured soul of Faust is revived by contact with the spirit of Nature which fills man with vitality to rise again after each defeat. He is no longer insistent on knowing ultimate truth, but he is as restless as ever to explore the knowable world.

The Emperor's Palace: In the midst of troubled times Mephistopheles appears to the Emperor as the new court jester, the role suggested in the Prelude on the Stage. Being representative of the momentary and the physical, he suggests as a cure for the woes of the realm the mining of gold, which he says is hidden beneath the land.

A Spacious Hall: In this masquerade of all varieties of worldliness and of all the elements that make up human experience, a chariot enters driven by a Boy who symbolizes Poetry, accompanied by Faust disguised as Plutus, the god of wealth, and Mephistopheles as avarice. When the Emperor is attracted to Faust's magic chest of molten gold only to have his beard set on fire by it, Faust extinguishes the flame and establishes himself as a master magician.

Pleasure Garden: Faust's great impression on the Emperor bears fruit in the issue of paper money based on the unmined gold. The results of this easy money are briefly suggested at the close of the scene by the thoughtless eagerness and frivolity with which it is received by the people.

A Dark Gallery: In the first private conversation of Faust and Mephistopheles in Part II, Faust reveals the Emperor's desire to have the ideal man and woman, Paris and Helen of Troy, invoked by magic art. The superficiality of the Christian devil is here revealed by his inability to penetrate into the classical world. Mephistopheles can only suggest the method of going back to the Mothers, the basic essential mystery of life that existed before man created gods or God in his own image. The woman-spirit is again invoked as the ultimate key to the mystery of life, and the procreative function of the Mother is an ideal symbol of a universe which must eternally create. Mephistopheles is perfectly fulfilling his role of spurring on creative action by denial. By his denial of the Christian Deity, he forces Faust into the search for a more profound conception of the Author of the Universe.

Brightly Lighted Halls: A humorous interlude precedes the return of Faust from the Mothers. Mephistopheles is exhibited in his most playful mood while the court eagerly anticipates Faust's return.

Hall of the Knights: In an impressive theatrical pageant Faust returns with Paris and Helen, the basic archetypes of the eternal will striving for human perfection. Although they are unimpressive to the superficial taste of the audience, Faust sees in Helen the essential nature of all Beauty. Spurred on by the Astrologer's remarks to save her from so trivial a destiny as to become the mistress of her contemporary Paris, Faust attempts to force a blending of the ancient and modern world by seizing her. His failure is symbolic of the difficulty of grasping easily the mystery of life which is a blending of many forces. The sense of the "all" cannot be so easily achieved.

ACT II. *A Gothic Chamber Formerly Faust's:* The lesson of the concluding scene of Act I is reinforced by a return to the scene of Faust's own youth where the sophomoric young are secure in their superficial knowledge. The concluding words of Mephistopheles to the audience are freighted with meaning. True insight comes only by penetration to the essence of life, by examination of its earliest archetypal manifestations. Such research would scarcely be undertaken if it were not for the Mephistophelean spirit of denial in the world which makes earnest men unwilling to accept conventional or facile explanations.

Laboratory: The creation of the Homunculus or test-tube man is a tribute to the plodding meticulous scientist who had been so scorned by Faust in Part I. Wagner's creation, like Helen and Paris, is also archetypal and gets to the roots of things. Not being limited to the Gothic imagination of Mephistopheles and Faust who still sleeps in his Gothic chamber, the Homunculus can lead Faust back to the classic past.

Classical Walpurgis Night: In place of Germanic witches, the figures of Hellenic mythology are here assembled on the eve of August 9, commemorating the battle of Pharsalus won by Caesar against Pompey. This victory solidified the position of Caesar and paved the way for Imperial Rome under Augustus.

By the Upper Peneus: Beside the most beautiful river in Thessaly, Faust searches for Helen while Mephistopheles continues his flippant role of wanton. The double wooing of Margaret and Martha of Part I is repeated with the great difference that a now very mature Faust is searching for an ideal, and Mephistopheles is reduced to a trivial self-seeking buffoon who can exert no real power in the realm of Faust's mind. The profusion of mythological and historical creatures which populate these scenes gives Faust respect for the free and bold imaginings of the Greek mind. The Sphinxes direct Faust to Chiron for aid in his quest for Helen.

By the Lower Peneus: The god of the river is stirred by the first tremors of an impending earthquake. Faust mounts behind the ancient centaur Chiron to cross the stream. Chiron, the great mythical educator of the Greek age of fable, is another symbol of unresting creative activity. After further references to Greek legends, Chiron illuminates Faust's mind by explaining that the Helen he seeks is a poet's conception (perhaps the inspired projection by an ancient poet of an ideal to be realized in later aeons of evolution), an ideal, not a fleshly woman. Approving of Faust's quest for the absolute, Chiron carries him to Manto, the wise daughter of the renowned Greek physician Aesculapius. She also approves of Faust's yearning for the impossible and enables him to descend to Hades. Faust is learning that one must approach the ideal by degrees (Plato's theory), repeating nature's own process.

By the Upper Peneus (II): Leaving Faust for the moment but contributing to his and the reader's education, Goethe presents a cosmic drama of creation. Seismos, essence of restless upward striving, produces an earthquake which rears up a beautiful and majestic mountain, asserting that he is responsible for the creation of earth from Night and Chaos. Then appear the earth-born peoples, hoarders, graspers, fighters, who attempt to grasp earth's treasures for themselves. Mephistopheles perceives that evil is as ancient as the world and ultimately assumes the form of a Phorkyad, symbolic of absolute ugliness in contrast to Helen, in order that he may continue his effectiveness in this alien world. Meanwhile, in this scene concerning the origins of things, the Homunculus, a spirit or an idea or an archetype seeking realization, is searching for a way to break from his test-tube phase and to come into being. He listens to a debate between the early Greek philosophers Thales and Anaxagoras. Anaxagoras, who held that fire was the basic essence, upholds the view of Seismos that volcanic eruptions forced the earth's surface above the water. Thales, who believed that water was fundamental, expresses Goethe's own view that creation was fluid and gradual, the earth's surface having been formed by alluvial deposit. The violence of the earthquake has produced violent and little people, a creation scarcely worth the effort.

Homunculus refuses the offer of Anaxagoras to be made king of the ants; his own deeper and higher aspirations cause him to ally himself with Thales, accepting Goethe's idea of gradual evolution. A meteor from the moon extinguishes the creations of Seismos who have been quickly created by violence and are as suddenly destroyed by force; such is the fate of the upstart apparent lords of the earth. Thales then leads Homunculus toward the sea.

Rocky Caves of the Aegean Sea: Amidst the most enchanting evocations of the spirit of nature, Homunculus is led to Nereus, a god of the sea, who advises him to seek out Proteus, symbol of change and also an ocean deity. The ever-changing Proteus tells Homunculus that he must begin as nature began with the smallest forms of marine life. Changing to a Dolphin, he carries Homunculus out to sea on his back. Nereus meanwhile summons Galatea, Pygmalion's ideal which had achieved realization through the power of love. Life came from the sea but, in Greek theogony which Goethe is only too happy to subscribe to, Light and Form were brought out of Night and Chaos through the moving power of love. In more scientific terms, the earliest forms of marine life continued to reproduce themselves and evolve through the mystery of sex. Homunculus throws himself into the sea at Galatea's feet where he is perceived as an active vibrant flame of love giving birth to life in the sea.

ACT III. *Before the Palace of Menelaus in Sparta:* The preceding act has pretty well fulfilled Goethe's promise that in Part II the macrocosm would be surveyed. Faust has been sufficiently educated to be able to meet Helen with understanding, so the action of the play is ready to proceed. The tone of this act with its chorus is very close to that of a Greek tragedy as Helen is depicted returned to her home by Menelaus after the fall of Troy. Through the offices of Manto, Faust has apparently released Helen from Hades to reenact the closing scene of her earthly life.

Desire for possession of beauty has brought about destruction, a lesson Faust might have learned from the Greeks before he experienced the same results in his own desire to possess Margaret. Mephistopheles reappears in his new role of Phorkyas to resume his cynical commentary on the destructive powers of beauty. Knowing that Menelaus, who had desired possession of beauty, could never brook the sharing of it with others, Phorkyas tells Helen that she is to be the victim of the sacrifice she has been ordered to prepare. She accepts his offer of refuge in the castle of a barbarian lord who is, of course, Faust.

The Inner Court of the Castle: In a Gothic castle Faust as a medieval Germanic knight receives Helen as his guest. His conquest of the ancient world and wooing of Helen are symbolic of the destruction of Graeco-Roman civilization by the Germanic hordes who then sought to possess the classic serenity an beauty personified in Helen. (There is another possible overtone implied in the rescue by the Germanic poet of the memory of Helen from obliteration.) Lynceus seems to be the symbol of the migratory urge of the early Germans in their disorganized search for loot. Their lawless violence is quelled by new-found adoration of Helen's spirit of the beauty of restraint and order. Faust, still aware that life demands continued action rather than blissful repose, proposes that they leave the shelter of the castle and venture forth to Arcadia, symbolic of the youth of the human race, where, unfettered by later codes and conventions, they may work out human destiny from the beginning. The marriage of Faust and Helen implies the union of Germanic vitality with Greek serenity and balance. It is specifically connected with the rediscovery of Greek culture at the time of the Renaissance.

The Scene Changes: Arcadia: The marriage of Faust and Helen has produced Euphorion (Byron, who mingled Romanticism and Classicism in his verses). But again it is emphasized that change cannot come suddenly. Euphorion's wild poetic temperament produces extremes of longing and violent rebelliousness. Like the earlier Faust he too attempts to seize beauty and to fly to the aid of others before he has really learned to walk. His sudden death, which is like the early death of Byron, is possibly intended to symbolize the demise of Romanticism because of its excesses.

In view of later scenes Euphorion's entirely poetic temperament may be considered as unfit for continued life because of inability to adjust to the sober demands of prosaic labor. As the spirit of poetry Euphorion is also a beautiful image of an ideal to be held, like Helen, in memory rather than to become exclusively the object of life. With Euphorion's death, therefore, Helen also vanishes. The chorus, instead of returning to Hades, prefers to become identified with nature, thus reiterating Goethe's conception of the universe as an all-embracing whole, which is not compartmented but fluid and growing in a perpetual mingling and merging of spirit and body. At the end of the scene which concludes the classic episode, Mephistopheles resumes his original form.

ACT IV. *A High Mountain Range:* With the image of Helen in Faust's mind, Mephistopheles' offers of unlimited enjoyment and glory fall on deaf ears, but Faust now desires to exercise his new-found understanding and is lured by his new sense of power to the vision of a vague scheme for controlling the sea. Mephistopheles reveals to him that his prior easy-money plan has created nothing but discord and riot, so that the very throne of the Emperor is in danger. Faust disclaims any knowledge of military strategy but accepts the help of Mephistophelean destructive knowledge of war and the Three Mighty Men who fought with David against the Philistines, it being occasionally necessary to employ force against barbarism. Goethe renames them to signify Youth, Maturity, and Old Age, implying again that even the destructive powers of man have eventual use as in David's righteous war.

On the Headland: Faust dissuades the Emperor from his noble but foolish project of leading his troops. His distribution of the Three Mighty Men is a further indication that all human talents have their use if they are well placed. All of this is the wisdom that Faust has derived from Greece. Through the magic of Mephistopheles, nature is also enlisted on their side, flooding the plain and producing a curtain of sheet lightning, a tribute perhaps to the natural vigor and ingenuity of the Germanic peoples.

The Rival Emperor's Tent: The deserted tent of the opposing Emperor is being looted by his own defeated troops as Faust's Emperor takes possession. The Emperor confers honors, assuming that the victory has been won by his generals, receives a warning from the Archbishop for having used diabolical assistance, and atones by promising to serve the Church's rapacity, but rewards Faust by giving him a strip of worthless seashore, which is mostly under water.

ACT V. *Open Country:* Faust's great project of draining marshes and reclaiming from the sea land for useful healthy human habitation is being carried out. Philemon and Baucis, greeting a wanderer whom they had previously saved from drowning, describe the mammoth labor, and also express fear of eviction from their cottage because of Faust's violent determination to have his own way.

Palace: Faust, now a hundred years old, has all but consummated his dream of mastering nature by the creation of a thriving port from which, however, the Three Mighty Men sail forth in deeds of piracy. The everlasting peccadillos of human nature have not been cured either in Faust or in the general population. As for him, any hindrance to his determined will rankles excessively. Opposed not by nature but by humanity and his own conscience, he momentarily forces justice to submit to his lawless desire by ordering the eviction of Philemon and Baucis in order to possess their linden trees. Mephistopheles explains the significance of the scene by alluding to the Biblical story of Ahab and Naboth's vineyard. Great accomplishments can scarcely remain free of unlawful use of power. It is an eternal law of life.

Deep Night: Faust suffers from his own impulsive rashness when his command for the removal of the old couple to a pleasant farm is carried out by the impulsiveness of others to the point of death for the couple and the wanderer and the burning of house and trees. This violent event mars the beauty of the world which is so feelingly celebrated in the watchman's opening song.

Midnight: In an allegorical scene, the soul of Faust is examined. Want, Guilt, Distress, and Care hover about him. Want, Guilt, and Distress turn away, unable to enter a wealthy house, but only to herald the approach of their brother Death. Faust, who strangely believes himself free of Want, Guilt, and Distress, communes with Care because he knows now that his ultimate freedom as a man depends on his dismissal of the magical assistance of Mephistopheles. Man must carve out his destiny without the aid of illusory shortcuts. He fights against Care with his knowledge that man must live and achieve from day to day, without attempting to fly beyond his own abilities or comprehension. But blinded by Care, the aged Faust orders the continued work of digging to be pressed forward immediately to finish the great enterprise before his death. Moral concerns are removed from his mind by the urgency of accomplishment itself, which Goethe apparently thinks is of much more value than brooding over past guilt, however justified such brooding may be.

Great Outer Court of the Palace: While the Lemurs obey Mephistopheles' command to dig Faust's grave in anticipation of his imminent death, the care-blinded Faust, believing that the work of his own great project causes the sound of shovels that he hears, comes the closest he ever has to losing his personal wager with Mephistopheles. Envisioning the future welfare of a free and active population, he actually utters the fatal words, "Stay, thou art so fair," but speaks them not in relationship to the present but to the unrealized future. Overconfident, Mephistopheles takes the sound of the words, without regard to meaning or context, as assurance of his own complete victory.

Burial: Mephistopheles as the spirit of negation pays unwilling tribute to the persistence of the life-urge. While directing his diabolical legions, he sees his own defeat in the descent of flights of angels. True to character he lusts after them in as primitive a fashion as he had lusted after Martha. Remembering the clown and poet of the Prelude on the Stage, we see again the contrast between earthly momentary selfish enjoyment of sexual desire and the enduring creative urgency which is stimulated by the imaginative spiritualization of love. The angels possess the soul of Faust because Mephistopheles has lost both his wager with Faust and his agreement with the Lord; Faust has never rested in his pursuit of experience, knowledge, and achievement. He has made grave errors and caused great misery, but in Goethe's evolutionary vision Mephistophelean errors are as necessary to growth as realization of ideals. Through cynical doubt the individual arrives at a more secure faith. Through destructive criticism and serious opposition he learns to struggle more effectively and to build more enduringly. The whole includes many apparently conflicting elements, but the Divine conclusion toward which creation moves is greater than the sum of its parts because it is the triumphant world spirit, not the individual, which ultimately counts.

Mountain Gorges: The concluding reception of Faust in heaven is a many-voiced paean to the power of love. As in the *Divine Comedy* love is the moving creative force which vibrates through the universe; it vibrates too through the succession of glowing lyrics of this closing scene. After a brief suggestive contrast between earthly conflicts and spiritual peace sung by Chorus and Echo, Pater Ecstaticus, Pater Profundus, and Pater Seraphicus represent three phases of exalted human desire for holiness, described respectively as ecstatic yearning for the ineffable, anguished desire to understand the Divine glories manifested in nature, and the perfected spirit of contemplative love found in such men as St. Francis of Assisi.

Spirits of children who died at birth are present, possibly to contrast their inexperience with Faust's fully awakened earthly knowledge. Because of their ignorance they must receive instruction before ascending. Doctor Marianus, whose earthly function was to give instruction concerning the Virgin Mary, prepares for the vision of the Queen of Heaven. Three penitent women from Scripture introduce the spirit of Margaret, who draws Faust to her in imitation of the magnetic power of the perfect love of Mary. The concluding mystic chorus sums up the meaning of the scene and part of the meaning of the entire play in its glorification of the eternal woman-spirit, the spirit of pure and unselfish love which is not only the moving force of all man's moral and useful accomplishments, but also the nurse and guardian of his spiritual nature, teaching him to reject the earthy and the transitory for the spiritual and the eternal. The Lord of the Prologue does not appear in this scene; in place of an anthropomorphic deity, Goethe substitutes here an all-inclusive moving spirit of love.

JOHANN CHRISTOPH FRIEDRICH VON SCHILLER (1759–1805)

IMPORTANCE

Although the names of Goethe and Schiller are always connected as leaders of Germany's greatest literary age, the achievements of Schiller are clearly secondary to those of his friend and rival. For although Schiller is like Goethe in many ways and although each man undoubtedly stimulated and inspired the other, Schiller's imaginative powers have less range and depth. Unendowed with Goethe's massive faculty for including all the universe within his vision, Schiller was a poet of ardent but limited enthusiasms. He too was interested in ideas, but he lacked Goethe's ability to express these ideas through the words and actions of vital, lifelike characters. Most of his works have consequently faded considerably with the passing of time because they become remote and artificial when the theme itself has lost its power to move the reader.

The relatively brief career of Johann Christoph Friedrich von Schiller began at Württemberg in 1759 when he was born the second of six children of a rather stern army surgeon and a remarkably sweet-tempered mother. A very affectionate child, he responded eagerly to the private tutoring of a village clergyman before being sent to the Latin School at Ludwigsburg, where his family had taken up residence. An early fondness for poetry and the desire of his parents that he should become a clergyman were both discouraged by the wish of the Duke of Württemberg that he should be sent to a military academy, where he remained until he was twenty-one. Although he was made miserable by the rigid military discipline, he found interest in the study of law and medicine and was fascinated by his independent reading of such authors as Rousseau, Klopstock, Goethe, Shakespeare, and Macpherson. He found himself closely akin to these "revolutionary" spirits and was ready to join in the contemporary battle against Neoclassicism and conventionalism; he wrote most of his play *Die Räuber* (*The Robbers*) before leaving the academy.

In 1780 Schiller became a medical officer, finding himself in a post for which he had little enthusiasm or talent. He was more concerned with finishing his play, which, when completed, was published at his own expense in 1781 and performed the next year at the Mannheim theater. Since neither the Duke of Württemberg nor Schiller's immediate superiors looked favorably upon this escapade, inevitable frictions developed, which soon forced Schiller to abandon a military career for the uncertain livelihood of a creative writer. After the rejection of a second play, *Fiesco*, he besought and was granted temporary sanctuary at the home of an old friend Frau von Wolzogen, where he wrote a great deal of rather crude lyric poetry and two more plays, *Kabale und Liebe* and *Don Carlos*. In 1783 his efforts were rewarded by an appointment as dramatic poet of the Mannheim theater, where *Fiesco* and *Kabale und Liebe* (*Intrigue and Love*) were both performed. *Fiesco*, the dramatization of a revolution, proved to be a failure; *Kabale und Liebe*, describing a great love destroyed by class prejudice, exhibited the same revolutionary tendencies as *Die Räuber*, and, being much more dramatically effective, met with great success.

After a period of financial stress and great anxiety about his future, during which time he published the periodical *Thalia* and moved within a small circle of warm admirers, he went to Weimar in 1787. There he wrote a notable history of the revolt of the Netherlands, became a professor at the University of Jena, and in 1790 married Charlotte von Lengefeld, by whom four children were later born. A severe illness the following year resulted in a chronic state of poor health for the remainder of his life. A year of rest, made possible by monetary grants from members of the nobility, was followed by studies and writings in philosophy to which he had been attracted by the powerful influence of Kant. Schiller's contributions were mainly in the field of esthetics; his most notable work, *Die Naive und Sentimentalische Dichtung* (*Naïve and Sentimental Poetry*), specifies the basic principles of classic and romantic art. In 1793 he composed an essay on the characteristics of the *schöne Seele*, the beautiful soul, in which he explains that the beautiful soul comprises a state where the instinctive moral sentiments entirely possess the emotions, thus creating a mode of life which is intuitively and inescapably good.

Although he had met Goethe as early as 1788, he did not become a close friend until 1794 when he returned to lyric and dramatic poetry, stimulated to a "second youth," as he called it, by association with the older writer. In an idealistic frame of mind he set to work on a great dramatic trilogy on the life of Wallenstein. When completed, these three plays, *Wallensteins Lager* (*Wallenstein's Camp*), *Die Piccolomini* (*The Piccolomini*), and *Wallensteins Tod* (*Wallenstein's Death*) were so enthusiastically applauded that Schiller determined to devote his talents thereafter mainly to dramatic poetry. In 1801 he presented his *Maria Stuart*, a portrait of Mary Stuart that was compounded more of honest craftsmanship than poetic inspiration. Much more successful was his treatment of Joan of Arc in *Die Jungfrau von Orleans* (*The Maid of Orleans*), which appeared about a year later. In 1803 the Weimar theater presented *Die Braut von Messina* (*The Bride of Messina*), which attempted to combine classical and romantic elements with little success. His final work, *Wilhelm Tell* (*William Tell*), which was presented in 1804, was a fitting climax to a life of poetic endeavor devoted to man's struggle for freedom.

Schiller's rhetoric, poetry, inspiration, and ability in dramatic construction had meanwhile made him famous. In 1802 he was made a member of the nobility; in 1804 his salary in connection with the court theater was doubled. But his health continued to fail, and a high fever, which he contracted upon returning from the theater on the night of April 29, resulted in his death on May 9, 1805.

Although he lacked both the sense of humor and the breadth of knowledge and experience that distinguished his friend and rival Goethe, Schiller was the possessor of a feverishly idealistic temperament which exacts a ready response from his readers. He is the master of a glowing eloquence which infuses his characters with vitality. Essentially a poet, Schiller had little interest in humdrum reality and little ability to delineate the human trivialities on which other playwrights rely to give their characters a sense of human solidity. More of a rhapsodist than a thinker, Schiller was fortunate to strike the perennially sympathetic chords of human aspiration, yearning for the ideal and for freedom. These motifs form the basis of three of his best-known plays:

Die Räuber

Faintly reminiscent of the Robin Hood tradition, *The Robbers* expresses the violent personal rebellion of a young son against the machinations of a cold-blooded and artificial society. The youthful protagonist, Karl Moor, has been vilified by a tangle of lies instigated by his villainous brother Franz. When he believes himself to be rejected by his own father, he seeks refuge in the forest, where he becomes the leader of a band of robbers and proceeds to make war against society, whose vileness he has so deeply experienced.

While thus attempting to reestablish justice in the world, a yearning to see his fiancée, Amalia, leads him to return home, where he discovers that Franz has imprisoned his father and is starving him to death. The rescue of his father comes too late to save his life, but Franz commits suicide, and Karl gives himself up to justice, realizing that law must depend upon more than the desires or even the valor of the individual.

The play is violent, bombastic, and filled with improbabilities. Both plot and speeches sometimes read like a series of misquotations from Shakespeare. Yet it has a kind of authority in the sheer earnestness and power of its dialogue and in the rapid motion of its scenes. Its contemporary success relied heavily on the *Sturm und Drang* sentiments it echoed in its portrayal of an individual like Goethe's Götz or Werther whose recognition of his own spiritual rightness was so at odds with the artificial codes of society.

Wallenstein

Based on the tragic career of Wallenstein, the leading imperialist figure of the Thirty Years' War, the three parts of this historical drama are an essentially objective account, in the manner of Greek tragedy, of the workings of fate. Acting as a prologue, the first play, *Wallensteins Lager*, describes by the deft use of character types the varied elements that composed Wallenstein's army as it lay before Pilsen in the winter of 1633–1634. It also throws some light on the character of this young man whose deeply serious nature and a miraculous escape from death have intrenched in him a deep religiosity and an exalted sense of his own importance in the eyes of Providence. Thereafter, the play becomes the tragedy of a man who refuses to obey his inner voices of faithfulness and honesty in order to ride the tide of fortune's favor by whatever means that offer themselves.

Die Piccolomini presents Wallenstein well on his way to achieving his ambition of being made King of Bohemia. With the powerful army that has been his own creation, he believes that he needs only a secret alliance with the Protestant Swedes into which he is about to enter. To make assurance doubly sure, two of Wallenstein's friends, Field Marshal Illo and Graf Terzky, take advantage of a drunken banquet to obtain the signatures of the regiment leaders to a document that swears their allegiance to Wallenstein in any eventuality. The Italian leader, Octavio Piccolomini, sees through Wallenstein's character because of this vainglorious action and tries to warn his son Max. But Max is blinded by his personal devotion to Wallenstein and is further ensnared by his love of Thekla, Wallenstein's daughter.

All of this serves as preparation for the inevitable catastrophe of *Wallensteins Tod*. When Wallenstein's plan to join the Swedes is discovered, this man who is devoted not to principle but only to his own, rising star, dares to join the enemy, depending on the allegiance of the Piccolomini. The love of his daughter and the respect of his friends are to him only tools to further his own rise to power. Relying blindly on the Piccolomini in the most crucial moments, he is amazed to find himself deserted by both Octavio and Max.

When he seeks final refuge with Butler, whom he has treacherously served in the past, he finds that Butler too has been informed by Octavio of his past double dealing and he meets death at Butler's hands. A final touch is supplied by the arrival of a messenger from the Emperor to confer on Octavio the title of "Prince."

Wilhelm Tell

William Tell, based on a well-known Swiss legend, is the final full-length statement of Schiller's revolt against tyranny. In a panorama of scenes that depict not so much a person as the character of an essentially free people in revolt, Schiller tells the story of this common man's defiance of the established order. The oppression of authority had been demonstrated in many ways. When Wolfshot, a nobleman, had taken liberties with Baumgarten's wife, Baumgarten had split open his skull and attempted to find safety across Lake Lucerne. A rising storm filled the ferryman with fright, but William Tell, the fearless hunter, undertakes to ferry him across. When the pursuing soldiers find that the fugitive has escaped, they take vengeance on the sympathetic peasants.

As the Viceroy of the Emperor of Austria, Gessler meanwhile attempts to break the spirit of the proud Swiss by placing a cap on a pole in a public place and ruling that every man bow before the cap. When Gessler's subordinates attempt to take a team of oxen from Henry of Halden, his son Arnold beats them off and then is forced to go into hiding. When his father's eyes are put out, Arnold becomes one of a number of active revolutionaries led by Fürst, Tell's father-in-law, for the overthrow of the Viceroy. Further signs of the rising conflict become obvious at the mansion of Werner, where his nephew Ulrich refuses to drink the morning cup of friendship with the people, partly because he is lured by the luxury of the Austrian court and partly because of his love for the wealthy Bertha.

The ancient Diet is revived under the leadership of Fürst, but immediate action is postponed until after the traditional Christmas meeting of the peasants in the castle. Ulrich, meanwhile, is rejected by Bertha because of her patriotic Swiss feeling. When William Tell, accompanied by his sons, neglects to pay homage to the symbolic cap, he is about to be carried off to jail when Gessler happens to ride by. Gessler displays his vicious spirit by ordering Tell to shoot an apple from the head of his son Walter. In the midst of Ulrich's protests, Tell prepares two arrows and with the first shot hits the apple. When Gessler asks him why he had two arrows in readiness, promising him immunuity no matter what the answer may be, Tell admits that if his first arrow had missed, the second was intended for Gessler's heart.

The enraged Gessler sentences Tell to life imprisonment and personally accompanies him on the boat trip to his castle. Meeting the fury of a storm, Gessler has Tell unbound and makes him the helmsman. Tell makes good his escape by leaping to shore and then lies in wait with his bow beside a pass through which Gessler must travel. He meets there a plaintiff woman who, with her children, is also awaiting Gessler to plead for her imprisoned husband. After waiting for her to confront Gessler and receive the expected denial, Tell shoots the Viceroy and vanishes in the forest.

With the death of Gessler, Werner is looked up to as a popular leader. Age and illness, however, prevent him from remaining alive even long enough for his nephew Ulrich to arrive. But upon Ulrich's appearance, the people find in him a new leader, aroused because Bertha has been abducted by the Austrians. He assumes command of the revolt of the Swiss Forest Cantons. Then the news comes that the Emperor has been killed by Duke John of Austria, whose estates had been confiscated. When John seeks refuge with Tell, he is rebuffed because Tell is concerned with principles rather than personal revenge. Duke John is nevertheless allowed to go his way to find refuge in Italy, and Tell's bow is put away when news comes that the Count of Luxembourg has been elected emperor. With the restoration of human dignity to the Swiss, Bertha signalizes the new and peaceful and friendly relations by accepting Ulrich as her husband.

In this decidedly episodic pageant, Schiller speaks his last great word as the defender of liberty, not as the expression of individual whim but as an essential principle for the fulfillment of humanity's highest mission. The characters, including Tell himself, are scarcely intended to be regarded as individual personalities; rather they are embodiments of human idealisms and passions which are given fervent expression by Schiller in this adaptation of the simple sixteenth century folk-tale of Aegidius Tschudi.

IMMANUEL KANT (1724–1804)

Although celebrated as a philosopher rather than as a man of letters, Immanuel Kant had a profound influence on literary men throughout Europe for more than half a century. In Germany the effect of his writings in stimulating thought has been compared to the electrifying effect of Darwin's *Origin of the Species* in England. It is certain that the trend of nearly all nineteenth century German writing is foreshadowed in his three most important works, *The Critique of Pure Reason* (*Kritik der reinen Vernunft*) (1781), *The Critique of Practical Reason* (*Kritik der praktischen Vernunft*) (1788), and *The Critique of the Power of Judgment* (*Kritik der Urteilskraft*) (1790).

Kant's philosophical system begins with an apparent identification with both the *Sturm und Drang* and the Romantic movement in its emphasis on the individual. Like the Platonists he held that all human knowledge is subjective in character. Objects can be known only by their qualities: hardness, squareness, color, etc. These qualities are not inherent in the things themselves but are expressions of human reactions to them. Hence, the function of the intellect is to sift, coordinate, and arrange these sense impressions into a meaningful pattern. It is the human intellect, therefore, that imposes and, in a sense, creates the order of the cosmos.

This much of Kant's theory seems to make each individual a sole arbiter of reality and a God-within-himself of the universe. But Kant drew attention to that other human power known as the Will which manifests itself in a constant striving toward the verities of the spiritual or moral world which are unrelated to sense impressions and are consequently unknowable to the intellect. Whereas the intellect draws impressions of the outward world to itself, the will reaches outward to an external reality with a certainty that it exists. This is the reality of a universal moral law, of a sense of absolute goodness which can exist only in the will, being incapable of demonstration by reason. It operates within the individual as a "categorical imperative," which determines rightness and directs action without reference to reason and sometimes even in opposition to the rational process.

Here is at once a philosophical demonstration of the nature of the "*schöne Seele*" and a condensed history of the progress of German thinking from the extremes of Romantic individualism to a collectivism in which all human souls are united in a sense of goodness and in a yearning to reach out toward the Divine. God is no longer an Old Testament or Calvinistic Jehovah imposing law upon man. Instead God is a Universal Spirit whose reality is felt within the consciousness of all mankind by which all men are united in a striving toward a common goal of goodness and ruled by an innate moral law of duty. This is the law that Goethe's Faust comes to recognize after his quest for personal satisfaction leaves part of his nature in active revolt against purely sensuous delights.

MINOR CONTEMPORARIES OF GOETHE

The excitement of the period during which Goethe began his career stimulated a host of writers who became well known in their own time but whose glories have become dimmed by the passing of years and by their essential inferiority to Goethe and Schiller.

Friedrich Maximilian von Klinger (1752–1831)

One of the most noteworthy of these was Friedrich Maximilian von Klinger, who, like Goethe, was an enthusiastic devotee of ideas. During the *Sturm und Drang* period, it was his play *Der Wirrwarr, oder Sturm und Drang* (*Confusion, or Storm and Stress*) (1776) that gave the movement its name. A second play, *Die Zwillinge* (*The Twins*) (1776), which revolves about the conflict between two brothers, is equally notable for its earnestness and for the violent seething of emotionalism which courses through it. Klinger also wrote a version of Faust in his *Fausts Leben, Thaten und Höllenfahrt* (*Faust's Life, Deeds and Journey to Hell*) (1791), which emphasizes the plight of the common people and the spirit of rebelliousness against arbitrary authority.

Jakob Michael Reinhold Lenz (1751–1792)

Jakob Michael Reinhold Lenz, whose name is usually associated with that of Klinger, was an imitator of Shakespeare and Goethe. The best of his plays, *Der Hofmeister* (*The Housemaster*) (1774), which describes the thwarted love of an impoverished intellectual for a nobleman's daughter, and *Die Soldaten* (*The Soldiers*) (1776), which attacks the licentiousness of the swaggering military caste contain sharp and realistic delineations of contemporary life and its problems but are marred by shapelessness and complete lack of artistic restraint and intellectual objectivity.

Heinrich Leopold Wagner (1747–1779) and Friedrich Müller (1749–1825)

Heinrich Leopold Wagner also concentrated on representations of everyday life in crude but realistic and often effective dramas. The poet and painter Müller, sometimes known as Maler (Painter) Müller, wrote idylls that are marked by truthful observations on common life. He was typical of his age in dividing his attention between classical figures like Niobe and modern ones like Faust. His *Fausts Leben* (*Faust's Life*) (1778) is a play that finds in Faust a spirit of rebellion akin to his own refusal to accept the conventional restrictions of his time.

Gottfried August Bürger (1747–1794) and the Grove Brotherhood

Gottfried August Bürger was a member of a Göttingen organization of idealistic young disciples of Klopstock who called themselves the *Hainbund* ("Grove Brotherhood"). He became the outstanding member of this coterie by the creation of a national ballad. *Lenore* (1773), a translation of which was Sir Walter Scott's first published work, entitled *William and Helen*, is a kind of German *Ossian* in its attempt to recapture the wild fantastic imagination of an earlier age. Written in a portentious tone and shrouded with ghostly images, this highly atmospheric masterpiece of ballad style begins with the rebellion of Lenore against God when her lover fails to return from battle. When at the nadir of her despair, she is startled by the midnight appearance of her lover at her bedside, an appearance heralded by the clang of the drawbridge, hoofbeats, and heavy steps up the castle stairs. Carrying her to his horse, he takes her on a wild moonlight ride to his bridal bed. Giving cryptic and baleful answers to her hysterical queries, he urges the frantic steed to a churchyard and gallops over tombstones to the edge of an open grave where his flesh dissolves, leaving Lenore's arms entwining a ghastly skeleton. The judgment of Heaven is fulfilled when she too dies in the midst of a spectral dance of howling spirits.

Of the other members of the Göttingen Brotherhood, a few achieved momentary prominence by virtue of individual talents rather than by their commonly held theories. Johann Martin Miller (1750–1814) wrote the sentimental novel *Siegwart* (1776) which is a rather pallid imitation of Goethe's *Werther.* Johann Heinrich Voss (1751–1826) produced a good translation of Homer and a number of natural and quietly moving idylls of German life, the best known of which is his *Luise* (*Louise*) (1784), which revolves about the homely and deeply human minute details connected with the marriage of a young village clergyman. The consumptive and short-lived Ludwig Hölty (1748–1776) was possessed of a dreamy, melancholy nature which, together with a genuine devotion to nature, suffused his over-sentimental verses with a gentle and often highly effective spiritual glow.

Followers of Wieland

Early opposition to these imitators of Klopstock came from a number of other writers who made Wieland their model. Of these Wilhelm Heinse (1749–1803) composed the tumultuous romance *Ardinghello* (1787) which, in its title character Ardinghello, extols the completely free and natural man. A close friend of both Wieland and Goethe, Frederich Jacobi (1743–1819) was something of a philosopher and a very minor novelist. His best-known romance, *Woldemar* (1779) is mildly sentimental but essentially moral and philosophical in nature.

Jean Paul Richter (1763–1825)

Jean Paul Richter, better known by his first two names, was a highly prolific author whose keen sense of humor, active imagination, powerful emotionalism, and obvious sincerity have kept alive novels which are otherwise marred by constant extravagances and complete lack of self-criticism. After a long series of novels, idylls, and romances, he reached the summit of his genius in two memorable novels. His *Titan* (1803) is a kind of biography of an enlightened German prince whose sanity is in striking opposition to the emotionally unbalanced characters who surround him. His uncompleted *Flegeljahre* (*The Years of Wild Oats*) (1805) is much closer to reality and to Richter's examination of his own two-sided nature in its portrayal of the twin brothers Walt and Vult, the one dreamy and impractical, the other energetic and aggressive. In all of his novels a contempt for form leads to constant intrusion of digressions and to the use of a vocabulary which ignores the fitness of words to their subject in order to gratify the author's own momentary impulse. Among English novelists, Laurence Sterne is his nearest analogue.

4
THE DEVELOPMENT OF GERMAN ROMANTICISM

As in other nations all German literature was affected by the current of Romanticism that swept through Europe at the end of the eighteenth century. But a number of Goethe's contemporaries may be singled out as composing the main stream of this movement in Germany. Although the Romantic emphasis on the individual and the impatience with imposed form and conventions are evident in nearly all the writers of the time, more specialized evidences of the directions taken by the Romantic school are somewhat in opposition to the main trend of German thought, which, as has been seen, came to subordinate individualism to the more mature concept of nationalism and collective responsibility.

Such German Romantics were therefore those who sought refuge from the responsibilities of their own age by turning back to the Middle Ages, which they visualized in a roseate poetic glow of simple piety and devoted loyalties. A similar passion for the remote and the exotic led to studies of Sanskrit and Persian poetry and to imitation of oriental literature. Believing that the spirit of writing was more important than form and was often stifled by the strictures of rules of composition, they took as their guides Shakespeare, Calderon, and the anonymous authors of the medieval ballads. Many of them actually joined the Catholic Church in an attempt to experience actively the medieval spirit of submissive piety. In contrast to the vigorous adventurousness of Goethe, they often seem to be reactionaries and escapists; yet they were responsible for a renewed appreciation and understanding of medieval culture, and they expressed an all but universal human nostalgia for the haunting beauty of a world of dreams.

NOVALIS (1772–1801)

The prophet of the Romantic school was Friedrich von Hardenberg, better known as Novalis. Born of deeply religious Moravian parents, he early displayed the shy, thoughtful, and imaginative nature that made up the peculiar fascination of his poetry. After studying at the University of Jena, where he attracted the favorable attention of Schiller, he embarked on the study of law. But the death of his fiancée in 1797 plunged him into extreme dejection and left him temporarily without desire or ambition for the future. He had meanwhile been employed in his father's salt works and consequently attended the academy of mines at Freiberg, where he became engaged for a second time. Returning to the salt works in 1799, he was on the verge of marriage when the appearance of blood from his lungs was the harbinger of his early death in 1801.

His writings, which were published posthumously, are fragmentary expressions of deep feeling and gracious tenderness. He is best known for his unfinished romance *Heinrich von Ofterdingen* (1802) on the legendary medieval poet, and the delicate poetic prose of his *Hymnen an die Nacht* (*Hymns to Night*) (1800). His best lyrics are of a religious character, breathing forth a pure and simple faith untouched by creeds or dogmas.

CRITICS AND PHILOSOPHERS

August Wilhelm von Schlegel (1767–1845) and Karl Wilhelm Friedrich von Schlegel (1772–1829)

The leading critics of the Romantic school were the brothers Schlegel. The older brother Wilhelm possessed scarcely any real creative ability but exerted a wide influence by his translations of Shakespeare and Calderon and by his oriental studies. As a critic he became internationally known for sympathetic appreciation and interpretation of widely diversified works of art. The principal novelty of his conception of criticism was his insistence that neither praise nor blame but understanding was the chief business of a critic.

His younger brother Friedrich was an effective critic in much the same vein. But his creative writing was somewhat superior, and he made a considerable impression with his romance *Lucinde* (1799) which preached to his contemporaries the sermon of injecting more individualism and freedom into their everyday lives. The brothers edited a literary journal, the *Athenäum*, which was for a time a kind of official organ for the expression of the Romantic position and represented a remarkable intellectual group at Jena that included, besides themselves, Fichte, Schelling, and Tieck.

Johann Gottlieb Fichte (1762–1814)

Another philosophical figure active at the height of German Romanticism, Fichte is considered the first of the transcendental idealists. Having attended university in Leipzig and Jena, Fichte became the first rector of the University of Berlin in 1810. His work is often divided into two distinct periods, the first of which gave direction to the progress made on Kant's philosophy by post-Kantian idealists. Kant, Fichte's major influence, also published Fichte's first text and helped to establish Fichte as an important thinker and essayist.

Alongside Kant, Fichte is viewed as one of the pioneers of idealist epistemology. Fichte refused to start a discourse with an abstract notion. Splitting with Aristotelian empiricism, he based certainty on reason and intuition, the source of which is the free activity of the Ego. Will and Ego are closely related in Fichte's system, and his *Theory of Knowledge* (*Wissenschaftslehre*) (1794) and *Theory of Natural Right* (*Grundlage des Naturrechts*) (1796) established his views on the origin of reason and explicate the states that constitute the realization of the practical ego.

Friedrich Wilhelm Joseph von Schelling (1775–1854)

Although the philosophy of Fichte was both an echo and a basis for the spiritualization of nature that was a prominent Romantic tendency, the movement owed its philosophical basis mainly to the works of Friedrich Wilhelm Joseph von Schelling. His *Naturphilosophie* (*Philosophy of Nature*) looks upon all of nature as a completed whole possessed of an outer reality and a soul. The striving of the inner spirit in both man and nature is a single phenomenon that brings about incessant change and development. The duality of nature and spirit is in itself an imperfection and implies that these are expressions of God rather than being ultimate realities themselves. God is an Action, an Impulse, or Will, of which the external world of nature and the inner world of spirit are manifestations. Human beings may reach this Ultimate Spirit through art, where nature and spirit are united in the World Soul (*Weltseele*).

MINOR GERMAN ROMANTICS

Johann Ludwig Tieck (1773–1853)

Johann Ludwig Tieck was the most prolific and probably the most careless of the writers of the Romantic school. Born in Berlin in 1773 of a sarcastic, realistic father and a gentle, mystically inclined mother, he seems to have inherited the characteristics of both his parents. He was early fascinated by Shakespeare, and, after a distinguished schooling at the University of Halle, he determined to make literature his career. After the composition of a few melodramatic tales (*Märchen*), he formed a friendship with Wackenroder which solidified his interest in the Romantic movement and led to the creation of an unfinished novel *Franz Sternbalds Wanderungen* (*Sternbald's Travels*) (1798). This book owed much to Goethe's *Wilhelm Meister* but also became a prototype for the Romantic novel, describing the journey of Dürer's pupil through Holland and Italy; it delights in nature and rhapsodizes about art. This was followed by a series of fairy tales, the best of which is *Der blonde Eckbert* (*Fair Eckbert*). Like the others, this is a mystical and dreamy tale in which nature and human nature are inseparably united.

In 1798 Tieck was attracted from Berlin to Jena to join the circle of the Schlegels. Inspired by their interest in Spanish literature, he made some translations and wrote some very undramatic plays like *Kaiser Oktavianus*

(*The Emperor Octavian*) (1804), which are mainly lyric in nature. Physical distress, caused by rheumatic gout and the trials of a rather unsuitable marriage, beset him after 1804 and considerably hampered his productive powers. After a trip to Italy he continued to write stories and plays that do not entirely abjure mysticism but are more direct, realistic, and often caustic and satiric. He meanwhile collected some of his earlier narratives, pieced them into a connected narrative in the manner of *The Decameron*, and published them under the title *Phantasus* in 1812.

A period spent in study was followed by a long series of *Novellen* (*Tales*) written between 1821 and 1840, using materials from everyday life, realistic, ironic, and satiric by turns, but marred by improbabilities and ineptitudes. In 1851 his rapidly failing health forced his retirement from active life until his death in 1853. He remains best known for his earlier *Märchen*, which are fine examples of the Romantic fairy tale, a genre in which German writers have been particularly gifted.

Wilhelm Heinrich Wackenroder (1773–1798)

Wackenroder, who lived a scant twenty-five years, was an essayist who wrote stimulating essays on the fine arts and music, regarding the arts from the Romantic viewpoint of searching for their spirit rather than analyzing their forms or techniques. In love with medieval art and with Raphael's Madonnas, he extols art as the expression of the divine. To Wackenroder all life should be itself a beautiful art with religion as its guide, as he believes it to have been in the Middle Ages. His views were published together with essays by Tieck in two volumes, *Herzensergiessungen eines kunstliebenden Klosterbruders* (*Overflowings from the Heart of an Art-loving Friar*) (1797) and *Phantasien über die Kunst* (*Fancies Concerning Art*) (1799).

Ernst Theodor Amadeus Hoffmann (1776–1822)

The favorite Romantic blending of the real and the imaginary was carried to an extreme in the ghostly tales of Ernst Theodor Amadeus Hoffmann. Painter, lawyer, composer, and author, his versatility prevented his reaching very great eminence in any field, but his romances have been remembered for their frenzied demonic horrors. Although an adherent to the deeper theories of Romanticism, he was essentially a superficial writer who used cleverness and carefully planned effects to instill morbid terror in his readers. Apart from his many tales, his most celebrated longer work is the novel *Die Elixiere des Teufels* (*Devil's Brew*) (1815). This is the story of a violent series of monstrous crimes committed by a Capuchin monk as the result of his having sampled a mysterious drink that had been preserved for years in the monastery.

Clemens Maria Brentano (1778–1842)

Brentano also composed bizarre and strange tales in which fantastic imaginings vie with exotic modes of expression. One of the small Heidelberg group who constituted a younger generation of Romantics, he made his greatest contribution to German literature in collaboration with his brother-in-law, Von Arnim, in the collection of tales and poems, *Des Knaben Wunderhorn* (*The Boys' Magic Horn*) (1805), the great German book of *Volkslieder* (folksongs).

Ludwig Achim von Arnim (1781–1831)

In his introductory essay to *Des Knaben Wunderhorn*, Arnim touches on the patriotic fervor of the later Romantics as well as their constant emphasis on the spirit. In song, he says, all classes and kinds of people are united, and the German folk song is thereby an important expression of the national consciousness. His own tales, which are not particularly inspired, though clear-cut and healthy, follow the prevailing mode of constant employment of the supernatural and the marvelous.

Jakob Ludwig Karl Grimm (1785–1863) and Wilhelm Karl Grimm (1786–1859)

The antiquarian interest of the Romantic movement, which was responsible for reviving old German folk songs, created the prose complement to *Des Knaben Wunderhorn* in the universally known "Grimms' Fairy Tales." The brothers Grimm were essentially scholars whose joint researches resulted in lasting contributions to German philology and early literary history. The tales which make up the *Kinder- und Haus-Märchen* (*Children's and Household Fairy Tales*) (1812–1815) were collected from old books and manuscripts and often from the lips of people who had heard them from their parents. With exquisite taste they set them down in the simple language of childhood sincerity. Although the work was a collaboration, much of its charm is owed to Wilhelm's understanding of children and to his flair for selecting those stories which particularly appeal to a young audience.

Wilhelm can be considered the more literary of the brothers Grimm, whereas Jakob made several important contributions to philology and to the beginnings of modern linguistics. Using the oral folk tales as his starting point, Jakob began compiling data for the colossal *Deutsches Worterbuch* (*German Dictionary*), the definitive dictionary of the German language, which was only completed in the 1960s. The Grimm's grammar of German again uses the tales as a partial textual basis, and their new approach to literature as a source of knowledge, not only cultural but linguistic, established their place as the founders of the science of folklore—a tradition continued by Russian formalists such as Vladimir Propp, whose *Morphology of the Folktale* (1928) in turn influenced the structuralist school of critics. Jakob also delved into the study of phonology. As a result of his investigations came Grimm's law, which describes the consonant shifts in German and other Indo-European languages.

Hans Christian Anderson (1805–1875)

The other literary figure primarily identified with children's literature in this period was Hans Christian Anderson. Rising from the slums of Odense,

Denmark, Anderson received a scholarship through the help of Jonas Collins, a prominent Danish director. As a teenager, Anderson wrote many plays, all of which were rejected by the Royal Theater. He then turned his hand to poetry, travel sketches, and novels. His fame, however, came with the periodic publication of his *Fairy Tales and Stories*, written between 1835 and 1872. Numbering 168 in all, these tales include some of the most familiar to Western readers: "The Tinderbox," "The Princess and the Pea," "The Emperor's New Clothing," "The Ugly Duckling," "The Little Mermaid," and "The Snow Queen."

L. C. A. de Chamisso (1781–1838)

When Arnim and Brentano moved from Heidelberg to Berlin in 1808, they found a number of new writers with whom they entered into a third period of the Romantic movement, which was much more productive than the two earlier phases. The finest lyrist of the group was a French nobleman, L. C. A. de Chamisso, who was a refugee from the French Revolution and who became known in Germany as Adelbert von Chamisso. A master of folk song and ballad, he created truly German lyrics on the most common and deeply human themes of family life. He also composed the extraordinary tale *Peter Schlemihls wundersame Geschichte (The Wonderful History of Peter Schlemihl)* (1814). *"Schlemihl"* means an unlucky person, and Peter was unlucky enough to have the devil rob him of his shadow. The simply told narrative is the pathetic account of Peter's good-natured pessimism in his attempt to cope with the world in spite of the remarkable difficulties that encumber a shadowless man. Its allegorical overtones make it also an autobiographical account of Chamisso's own rather unhappy and somewhat ineffectual personality.

Friedrich de la Motte Fouqué (1777–1843)

The most popular prose writer of the Berlin group was Friedrich de la Motte Fouqué, who wrote many rather crude and entirely conventional romances on historical and mythological themes. But he created a genuine masterpiece in his delicate and beautiful fairy tale *Undine* (1811), which tells the story of a gentle water sprite who acquires a soul by being married to a mortal but who reverts to the fairy world.

Josef von Eichendorff (1788–1857)

Although not associated with the Berlin circle, Josef von Eichendorff belongs to this last phase of the Romantic school. Gifted with a rich lyric genius, he was especially a poet of nature. He too felt deeply the appeal of the Middle Ages, but the effectiveness of his lyrics lies chiefly in their evocations of moods in which the effects of nature on human emotions is given rich expression. Eichendorff also wrote a number of novels that all but ignore plot and construction in their emphasis on emotions and states of mind. His brief *Aus dem Leben eines Taugenichts (The Life of a Good-for-Nothing)* (1826) is an entirely improbable story of the romantic wanderings of a young musician, but it has become something of a classic because of its infectious light-heartedness and its expressions of the delights and yearnings of an inveterate dreamer.

Johann Ludwig Uhland (1787–1862)

An offshoot of the Romantic movement was begun in Swabia by Johann Ludwig Uhland. A patriotic professor and a scholar, he was deeply interested in German antiquities. But he was also a realist who was well informed and vitally concerned with the problems of his day. Described as "the classic of the Romantic movement," he composed concise and metrically perfect patriotic songs and ballads in the medieval tradition, with no sentimentalizing of the people and no effect of nostalgic yearning for a romanticized past. Without extravagance or mistiness of any kind, this quiet conscientious artist created masterpieces of honest sentiment rather than sentimentality and expressed the essential goodness, loyalty, faithfulness, and valor that are imbedded in the German character and are the intrinsic characteristics of the great figures of German folklore.

Eduard Mörike (1804–1875)

Among Uhland's many imitators, his friend Eduard Mörike possessed a delicacy and charm that raise him in the minds of many very close to the first rank of German lyrists. He was a quiet village pastor whose poetic output was small and unpretentious. His fragile lyrics are filled with delicate insights voiced with rare simplicity and restraint, giving off the rich overtones that are the clue to the mysterious effectiveness of all great lyric writing. An unfinished novel, *Maler Nolten* (1832), is as structureless as the majority of the novels produced by the Romantic school but is far from being undistinguished because of the same fineness of perception and the effective suggestiveness of his style.

Karl Leberecht Immermann (1796–1840)

Much the same kind of sanity and signs of health that began to appear toward the close of the Romantic movement distinguish the novels of Karl Leberecht Immermann, who was also a poet and dramatist of considerable ability. The best of his novels foreshadow the greater concern for social problems that became a dominant note in German fiction during the last part of the nineteenth century. *Die Epigonen* (*The Late Born*) (1836) is an account of his own life and reactions to the world about him. *Der Oberhof* (*The Village Magistrate*), which forms part of the longer novel *Münchhausen* (1839), is a remarkable story of peasant life and forecasts the many novels about the peasantry which constitute some of the best of later German fiction.

The Patriotic Poets

An eddy in the main current of German Romanticism was created by the fervor with which German youth rallied in 1813 to the Prussian march against Napoleon and by the subsequent German liberation. More spirited and enthusiastic than richly poetic, these poets of the "*Befreiungskrieg*" (The War of Liberation) well expressed for their time the sense of Germany's potential greatness and vigor, a sense that had been encouraged by the antiquarianism of the Romantics but had been almost necessarily limited to the world of dreams. Of these youthful poets, the best were Körner and Arndt. Karl Theodor Körner (1791–1813) was an enterprising young poet and dramatist who fell in battle when he was only twenty-three years old. His war songs, published the year after his death, became immensely popular, partly because of their intense fervor and partly, no doubt, because of the author's sacrifice of his life in the cause that he celebrated. Ernst Moritz Arndt (1769–1860) was a more mature and more critical composer who molded the German folk song into an expression of contemporary patriotism and of his own deeply held religious convictions. His lyrics have strength and solid power and contain occasional flashes of genuine poetic inspiration.

ROMANTIC DRAMA

Heinrich von Kleist (1777–1811)

The outstanding dramatist of German romanticism was Heinrich von Kleist. Born at Frankfurt an der Oder of a military family and subjected to military discipline as a lieutenant in the Prussian army, he escaped to literature and philosophy only to find little comfort in either. His study of Kant plunged him into despair because it pointed out the apparent futility of ever finding any objective reality. His career as a dramatist awarded him little contemporary recognition and seemed often futile even to himself because of his inability to rival the greatness of Schiller. After protracted wanderings through Germany, Switzerland, and France, he settled down to the writing of poetic dramas as a lifework, using a wide variety of subjects to echo his own tragedy of unattainable dreams. He finally committed suicide in 1811.

His first really effective play, *Penthesilea* (1808), evokes the vanished mores of the Amazons, which required the woman to vanquish her lover on the field of battle. When the Amazon queen Penthesilea finds herself mastered by her beloved Achilles, her own sense of frustration causes her to cap a night of ecstatic lovemaking by plunging an arrow into his breast, setting her hounds upon him, and drinking his blood. Only then is she overcome by the monstrosity of her actions and sinks into death, a passionate Germanic type of heroine scarcely heard of since the time of the *Nibelungenlied*.

Less original and less violent is *Das Käthchen von Heilbronn* (*Katie of Heilbronn*) (1810), in which a medieval heroine is so overpowered by the inner compulsion of love that she is as if bewitched by blind devotion to Ritter von Strahl.

Affected by the spirit of revolt against Napoleon, Kleist echoed the popular feeling in his *Hermannsschlacht* (*The Slaying of Arminius*) (1808) in which the ancient Arminius recognizes within himself a propulsion toward action and leads the Germans against Rome. Surrounded by sluggards he is willing to sacrifice honor, wife, and children to find consummation for his maddening passion for freedom. When his wife Thusnelda is also subjected to Roman arrogance in the person of Ventidius, the Roman legate, she equals her husband's violence in a Penthesilea-like revenge upon him.

Der Prinz von Homburg (*The Prince of Homburg*) (1810) is Kleist's last and probably greatest play. Based on the historical Prince Friedrich von Homburg, who won the battle of Fehrbellin in 1675 in defiance of the commands of the Elector of Brandenburg, this description of an inner conflict reflects much of the German spirit and also Kleist's own struggle toward maturity. The ideals of the young Prince include a desire for the favor of the Elector, a yearning for fame, and a passion for the Princess Natalie. At a moment of decision in the war against the invading Swedes, the images of his dreams cause him to flaunt both orders and sane advice to sweep to victory with his squadrons. A rumor that the Elector himself has fallen in battle leaves him intoxicated with his own preeminence, but he quickly changes from a glorified hero to a sniveling suppliant when the Elector, very much alive, orders him to be court-martialed. Willing to renounce Natalie and utterly degraded in his pleas for mercy, he is offered the opportunity to sit in calm judgment upon his own willful disregard of the plans or safety of others. Thus confronted, he regains his manhood and comes to understand the moral responsibility of the individual. He decides his own guilt and sentences himself to death as a willing sacrifice to world order. Only then has he achieved maturity and proved himself worthy of being pardoned.

Although less distinguished as a novelist, Kleist also composed at least one fine work in his *Michael Kohlhaas* (1808), also based on a historical figure, a sixteenth century horse dealer who magnified a personal grudge against a nobleman to the point of almost fomenting a civil war. Kohlhaas is outwardly nothing more than an ordinary commonplace merchant, but there burns in him an idealistic fervor that cannot be suppressed when a series of blatant personal injustices makes him aware that the law is always on the side of the rich and the powerful. After he buries his devoted wife, who died in an effort to secure justice for him, he deliberately and calmly settles his worldly affairs and begins a systematic campaign of vengeance. He plunges the entire countryside into the terrors of conflict but fulfills his purpose when justice is finally accorded him and the nobleman is placed in prison. Kohlhaas then willingly submits to his own execution as a rebel, having achieved his higher purpose of restoring moral law.

The characters and plots of Kleist are extreme to the point of absurdity; yet his inspired language and the inner reality of his feelings and the solidity of his idealism make his writings powerful expressions of an earnest striving spirit which shares none of the dreaminess of the lesser Romantic poets. Although his extravagances aroused the antipathy of Goethe, his basic philosophical background and his impetuous expressions of what he believed to be true indicate that he had much in common with the greater writer. By virtue of his expression of the smoldering national resentment of oppression and his adoption of the conception of the importance of moral law for all mankind, he deserves to be reckoned as an important figure in the communal growth of Gernan culture.

Zacharias Werner (1768–1823)

Werner was a Romantic dramatist who attempted to imitate the manner of Schiller. He produced patriotic and religious plays that substitute sensationalism and exotic effects for any real depth of feeling or genuine power. He is nevertheless remembered for his creation of a type of drama that enjoyed momentary popularity. The whole series of plays known as "fate-tragedies" (*Schicksalsragodiën*) seem to have been inspired by his *Vierundzwanzigster Februar* (*The Twenty-fourth of February*) (1809), which concentrated a series of coincidental horrors into a single fateful day. The favorite murder weapon of these fate-tragedies was a knife or sword that had once been similarly used in the history of the family and that is visible to the audience from the beginning of the play.

Adolf Müllner (1774–1829)

The outstanding "fate-dramatist," Adolf Müllner followed Werner's play with his *Der Neunundzwanzigste Februar* (*The Twenty-ninth of February*) in 1812, and in 1813 produced the most famous work of this type, *Die Shuld* (*Guilt*). In this play a young Spaniard who is fated to kill his brother is nurtured far away in northern Europe. But on a chance return to Spain he falls in love with a married woman. Only after he has murdered her husband does he discover that he has killed his own brother.

Franz Grillparzer (1791–1872)

Beginning his career as a fate-dramatist, Franz Grillparzer did much to establish the reputation of the Viennese theater that made the Austrian capital the center of the German dramatic world throughout the nineteenth century. He became the author of a series of tragedies that approach the level of masterpieces through their powerful expressions of tragic frustrations that echo Grillparzer's own rather barren life.

Born in Vienna in 1791, he was intended to become an advocate like his father. But a kind of inactivity of will and an abnormal shyness doomed him to retire to an unexciting civil position under the bureaucracy of Metternich. A few journeys abroad were his only breathing spells from a stifling atmosphere of petty censorship under which he apparently never dared carve out his own destiny even in the theater, where he wavered between the classic and romantic styles. Becoming interested in the stage partly through the fascination exercised over him by the Spanish playwright Calderon, he produced his first play in 1816. Its great popularity encouraged him to write a series of highly effective serious plays until, in 1840, his attempt to write a comedy was such a dismal failure that he retired from the stage. He was apparently unable to credit his own popularity and was amazed at the honors showered upon him on his eightieth birthday. When he died in 1872, he was accorded one of the most ceremonious funerals ever bestowed upon a private citizen of Vienna.

His first play, *Die Ahnfrau* (*The Ancestress*), gives highly effective dramatic treatment to the hackneyed materials of the fate-tragedy. The ancestress is a lady who was killed by her husband for infidelity and who is doomed to haunt her family until the last descendant is destroyed. Using scenes of terror and horror, including a secondary action in which an outlaw is discovered to be the brother of his fiancée, Grillparzer shows mastery in his creation of stage effects and in the power and beauty of many of the lines.

Distressed at being classed as a fate-tragedian, Grillparzer deliberately turned to a classic subject for his second play. *Sappho* (1818), like Goethe's *Tasso*, concerns the dilemma of the artist and uses the celebrated Greek poet to glorify the struggles attendant upon Grillparzer's own art. Unmarried himself and undistinguished in the world of affairs, Grillparzer portrays in Sappho the artist whose poetic achievements are paid for at the price of renunciation of earthly love and other normal human relationships.

The Golden Fleece: His most ambitious undertaking in the classical manner was a trilogy entitled *Das Goldene Vlies* (*The Golden Fleece*) (1822) in which he attempted to stage the entire legend of Jason and Medea instead of concentrating on the final revenge as was done by Euripides and succeeding dramatists who had worked with the subject. The first play of the trilogy, *Der Gastfreund* (*The Guest-Friend*), is a one-act treatment of the killing of Phryxus by Medea's father. Phryxus was the original possessor of the golden fleece, and his murder caused the fleece to become a bane to anyone who later possessed it. The succeeding play, *Die Argonauten* (*The Argonauts*), is a full-length description of Jason's quest of the fleece and the pledge of eternal love made to Medea in exchange for her invaluable assistance in procuring the golden fleece.

Medea, which is the best of the series, becomes a highly effective conclusion, particularly for an audience who would not be otherwise acquainted with the background of the catastrophe. Having established so completely the relationship between the lovers, Grillparzer finely weaves the strands of the conflict that develops between them: the inevitable undercurrent of antagonism between the barbarian Eastern passionate woman and the civilized Western ambitious man, the scorn of the Corinthians for Medea when Jason returns home with her, and Jason's enchantment with the princess Kreusa, who would make him a much more suitable wife from every point of view. When Jason plans to marry Kreusa, forgetting his vows, the violent emotionalism of the wronged Medea reaches the heights of fury as she kills her children and sets the palace on fire. Taking her last bitter farewell of Jason, she sets out to Delphi in order to return the fleece to its divine source.

King Ottocar's Fortune and End: Turning momentarily from ancient Greece to the past of his own nation, Grillparzer next wrote a national historical drama entitled *König Ottokars Glück und Ende* (*King Ottocar's Fortune and End*) (1825). With the figure of Napoleon dominating the attention of all Europe, the rise and fall of Ottocar of Bohemia in his conflict with Rudolf I, founder of the Hapsburg dynasty, was a singularly timely subject for a play. Although the drama suffers from that looseness of structure that besets most historical or chronicle plays, it is very successful in its evocation of the period and in its delineation of character. Its force derives from the conflict between the brilliant unscrupulousness of Ottocar and the quiet self-possessed righteousness of Rudolf, whose ultimate triumph is at once a glorification of Austrian government and an indictment of Napoleon.

Grillparzer followed his success in this genre with the distinctly inferior play *Ein treuer Diener seines Herrn* (*A Faithful Servant of his Lord*) (1830). Except for the self-revelatory treatment of the conflict between a sense of duty and a weak will, this depiction of a historical devotion of a servant to his king has little to recommend it and brought upon Grillparzer vehement accusations of servility.

Waves of the Sea and of Love: Returning to ancient Greece, Grillparzer found in the story of Hero and Leander a very happy subject for the same kind of modern psychological interpretation of ancient characters that he had used so effectively in *Medea*. The title, *Des Meeres und der Liebe Wellen* (*Waves of the Sea and of Love*) (1831), suggests the working out of a rather ingenious theme in which Leander's drowning, while literally true, is suggestive of the loss of his own personality which has become submerged in waves of love. Leander's character is first presented as being weak-willed and passive like Grillparzer's until he is fired by catching sight of the child-like Hero to swim the Hellespont to be with her in her temple cell. Leaving her after a particularly touching love scene, he makes a second attempt to swim across, guided by the light in her window. He might even have surmounted the storm that arose if the light had not been treacherously put out. The next morning his body is washed up on the shore, and Hero dies from grief.

Last plays: Grillparzer's dramatic career was concluded with an adaptation of Calderon's *Life is a Dream* and an attempt to write a comedy. His version, *Der Traum, ein Leben* (*The Dream, a Life*) (1834), marked a partial return to his earliest manner by withholding from the audience the revelation that the horrors that seem to be real are actually only the phantoms of a dream. The protagonist Rustan rises to power by treachery and violence, endures the horror of seeing his baseness discovered, and as he flees for his life he awakens to a realization of the emptiness of fame purchased at such a price. *Weh dem, der lügt* (*Woe to Him Who Lies*) (1838) was the ill-fated comedy, the poor reception of which so embittered Grillparzer that he renounced his theatrical career.

IMPORTANCE
At his best Grillparzer is master of a dramatic technique whose characters are made to seem extraordinarily genuine, partly because of the restraint of their dramatic utterances at moments of high emotional crisis. For that same reason, he has been accused of being essentially pallid, preaching safe morals and making his plays a mirror of his own unaggressive nature. His language is seldom inspired, but his choice of metrical speech became in his hands a pliable and very natural means of dramatic expression.

GERMAN LITERATURE AFTER GOETHE

After the vital literary activity of the age of Goethe, the cultural development of Germany tended to turn to other directions. While the nation was developing a sense of national unity and an aggressive patriotism through a series of wars that ultimately reached the proportions of world conflicts, the genius of the German people was most marked in philosophy, music, scholarship, and science.

The achievements of German philosophy and literature as well were very much stimulated by the speculations of Immanuel Kant (1724–1804) and Georg Wilhelm Friedrich Hegel (1770–1831). Hegel was technically an idealist, but his main interest was in delving into the nature of the actual world. He held the evolutionary concept that the universe is a process of becoming or of realizing itself. Mind or the seeds of mentality existed from the beginning. The natural world evolves as one manifestation of this process, and the world of spirit grows from the nexus of nature and mind. He applied this basic and all-but-inexpressible idea to all spheres of history, science, and human activity, creating a massive unification of apparently mutually exclusive spheres by finding in all of them cognate expressions of the movement of the "world-soul" (nature and mind growing and finding self-realization).

Arthur Schopenhauer (1788–1860)

Schopenhauer actually did his finest work during the lifetime of Goethe but did not become known until after the middle of the century. His eventual popular reception was owing partly to the appeal of his pessimism and his antifeminism and partly to his firm and lucid prose.

One of two children of the bourgeois aristocracy of Danzig, he was born in 1788 into a family whose mutual incompatibility created a childhood atmosphere of strain and suffering. His parents arranged to see little of each other, and for two years, soon after the birth of his sister in 1796, he was boarded out in France where he came to know French nearly as well as his mother tongue. He showed an early leaning toward books and scholarship, but his father, who scorned "impractical pursuits," tried to divert his interests by sending him on a trip to England in 1803 and by placing him in a Hamburg merchant's office in 1805. Three months after Arthur had been forcibly introduced to the world of business, his father committed suicide.

Cynical, morbid, and feeling much abused, Schopenhauer turned eagerly to the pursuit of scholarship. After a few years of private study, he entered the University of Göttingen in 1809 where he acquired his reverence for Plato and Kant. After two years he moved on to Berlin to continue his studies for an equal period of time under Fichte and Schliermacher. Still very much of a malcontent, he nearly joined the rising against Napoleon, but his cynicism forced him to change his mind in order to ponder over the human lust for power which was so spectacularly exemplified in the Emperor's career. In 1813 he received his doctorate from Jena and published the first of his strangely unnoticed books.

The years that followed included a rupture with his mother, the formation of a friendship with Goethe, and the publication in 1818 of *The World as Will and Idea*. The lack of response even to this, his now most famous work, increased his bitterness and his violence. His hatred of women denied him the comforts of domesticity, his impatience lost him a professorship, and ill-health added to his sense of being persecuted by the entire world. His later publications, consequently, became principally added illustrations and defenses of his earlier work. It was not until 1851 that recognition began to be accorded to the originality of his thinking. Not becoming widely known until he was seventy years old, he died two years later of a heart attack in 1860.

Schopenhauer's philosophy, which is basically stated in *The World as Will and Idea* (*Die Welt als Wille und Vorstellung*), derives from Kant and is an attempt to correct and complete his system. Agreeing that all objects are known only as intellectual relationships, he notes that the apprehension of a world of objects constitutes intelligence which is possessed alike by man and animals. The power of generalizing these apprehensions is reason, an exclusively human faculty. But reason is ultimately only a method of classification and is incapable of arriving at the ultimate or inner truth of things. Scientific proof consists only of convincing the mind that a new idea harmonizes with convictions already held by the mind.

The inner reality that defies explanation by reason is felt in human beings by the consciousness of exerting a force that we call will. But the self-consciousness of exerting will is perceived by the mind as corporeal action. Thus, all apprehensible objects are the result of will. The human body is the objectification of the human will, and similarly all objects of perception proceed from will. Creation is an eternal process by which will produces in its different degrees all the varieties of inorganic and organic matter, the human brain being its highest achievement. What is known to science as force is one manifestation of will; music is the expression of will in human beings in its least objective form.

Since all life is a phenomenon of will, the basic "character" of any individual is unalterable, and human beings are but impotent slaves to the specific manifestation of the eternal will that has chosen to express itself through their personalities. Intelligence can make slight modifications in direction but can never alter fundamental urgencies. Life thus becomes an endless battle between individuals who are victim of the strivings of a blind, purposeless, and unintelligible force. Happiness is a negative quality, attained only in momentary relief from the pain of being victimized by uncontrollable desires. To the few who can lose egoism in an understanding that they are but minute expressions of the whole, peace can be attained by deliberate withdrawal from the lust for individual life. By benevolent reaching out to others in self-sacrificing pity for the human plight, by a total asceticism, such enlightened souls may attain freedom by abandoning the personal objectification of the will and lapsing into the infinite quietude of nothingness; there the incessant striving of the will for objectification does not exist.

Heinrich Heine (1797–1856)

The greatest German lyric poet since Goethe, Heinrich Heine was born at Düsseldorf of Jewish parents. An extremely shy and sensitive member of an oppressed people, he was a lonely and indifferent pupil at the gymnasium, but learned considerable French and English. During these same years he acquired a boundless admiration for Napoleon, who was then at the height of his career. Intended for a business vocation, he was employed by his uncle Solomon Heine at Hamburg when he finished school. Neglecting his work to write poetry, he made it clear that commercial enterprise was not at all to his liking, whereupon he was sent by his uncle to the university at Bonn at the age of twenty-two on the sole condition that he prepare himself for the law.

Attending lectures on literature and history, he was a zealous student who was now privately preparing himself for a career in writing. He composed numbers of poems, some of which he sent to Goethe without receiving any response, and wrote his well-known lyric "The Grenadiers" as the result of a walking-trip on a road which Napoleon had traveled. Leaving Bonn for Göttingen, he seems to have gotten in trouble because of a duel and probably quit the university for that reason to repair to Berlin. While continuing his studies at the university, he also found publication for some of his poems and mingled in a stimulating literary and social circle. But his shyness made him generally ill at ease with women, and the urgings of the flesh prompted him to seek out the professional caresses of street girls. At this same time he began to suffer from constant headaches and a state of nervous tension which made even the ticking of a clock unbearable to him.

After a brief rest cure, he finally fulfilled his part of the agreement with his uncle by returning to Göttingen to take a law degree. In order to be admitted to the bar he was forced to accept Christian baptism, a meaningless formality that undoubtedly intensified his already rather cynical disposition. He seems never to have made any serious attempt to practice law. His high-strung temperament caused his discharge from a briefly held position as a teacher, and Heine's income thereafter depended on literature and journalism. His journalistic writings, brilliant, impudent, irreverent, blasphemous, and gentle by turns, were recklessly radical for their day, and his apparent fear of reprisals caused him to seek refuge for a short time in England. Upon his return, he quarrelled with his uncle, thus cutting himself off from further financial assistance, but earned wide acclaim through the publication in 1826 of the *Book of Songs* (*Buch der Lieder*), one of the most popular collections of lyrics in all world literature.

His sudden fame brought him the post of Associate Editor of the *Allgemeine Politische Annalen* (*General Political Annals*) through which he supplemented his poetry of freedom by propagating radical ideas. A constant propagandist in "humanity's war of liberation," he leveled attacks against church and state, against institutions and individuals. As denunciations of his writing became more frequent and more violent, he sought refuge in debauchery, which probably contributed to his increasing nervous and physical maladies. At the age of thirty he suffered a hemorrhage of the lungs. Shortly thereafter, when he was officially proscribed as "blasphemous, indecent, subversive against the state, and replete with *lèse majesté*," he fled to Paris in May 1831, where he was enthusiastically received and later awarded a small government pension.

His unbounded delight with the country of liberty, equality, and fraternity is ecstatically recorded in his *Memoirs*. Always an enthusiast, he soon became an ardent convert to the cult of Saint-Simonism, which exalted a pagan love of the flesh and preached the holiness of beauty. At the age of thirty-seven, he became infatuated with the nineteen-year-old Crescentia Eugénie Mirat. He attempted to break away from her but returned to live with her until his death, finally marrying her when he was forty-four years old. The worst possible mate for the nerve-tortured poet, she was extravagant, bad-tempered, jealous, and noisy. Although suffering from incessant headaches, Heine continued to write. When his books were suppressed in Germany, his writings were smuggled in under school textbook covers.

"The horrible thing is dying, not death," he wrote during his last agonized years of gradual physical decay. He became blind in one eye and had to hold up the drooping lid of the other. Gradual paralysis withered his left hand and took possession of his entire face, depriving him of the power of taste and almost of speech. As his lower limbs began to shrink and his back became an open running sore, his seven-year "mattress grave" was rendered tolerable only by copious doses of morphine and by the devoted attentions of a young German girl, Camille Seldon, who nursed him, soothed him, and took his dictation. Nevertheless, he somehow found the power to write or dictate some of his finest poems. He died in 1856, having remarked, "God will forgive me; that's his business."

IMPORTANCE

Of Heine's voluminous writings the majority are too journalistic and momentary to be of enduring interest. In prose his *Memoirs* (*Geständnisse*) are of interest partly because of the vicissitudes of his life and partly because of their abrupt variations of mood. Quixotic and temperamental, they include poetic observation, mysticism, heavy sentimentalism, satire, humor, and propaganda. The same variety even within a single short piece is the distinguishing mark of his lyrics. Finely and delicately finished, they give the effect of spontaneity as they move from moods of rare tenderness, touching pathos, or inspired adoration to sharp sarcasm or pungent wit. Many of his best-known poems lead the unsuspecting reader into an elevated mood only to drop him sharply to the ground with a neatly turned cynical, caustic, or earthy conclusion. His principal topic is love, which is treated ardently, sensually, nostalgically, frivolously, and cynically, sometimes all at once. This combination of sentiment and wit makes Heine unique in the history of German literature.

Young Germany

Inspired and influenced by Heine and the effects of the July Revolution of 1830 in France, a group of writers known as "Young Germany" carried on a similar revolutionary crusade. The best of the group, Karl Gutzkow (1811–1878), wrote a series of plays and novels, mainly historical and designed to inculcate revolutionary fervor. Lesser members of the group were Heinrich Laube (1806–1884) and Theodor Mundt (1808–1861). Although effective at the time and important in the history of German political and social development, they have received little attention outside of Germany because of their essentially local and temporary subjects.

Friedrich Hebbel (1813–1863)

In the theater Grillparzer's best known successor was Friedrich Hebbel. Born in Schleswig-Holstein of peasant parents, he discovered within himself poetic talent and found a means to acquire a university education at Heidelberg and Munich. In 1840 he published his first prose tragedy *Judith* under the auspices of "Young Germany," in which the rights of the individual are proclaimed in a violent, crude, but often strikingly powerful play. *Maria Magdalena* (*Mary Magdalene*) (1840) also uses a scriptural character to enforce a contemporary moral. Concerned with lower class life, this more sober and more carefully constructed drama revolves about the then favorite theme of the conflict between convention and natural impulse.

Turning from prose to blank verse, Hebbel in anticipation of Ibsen inaugurated a new and greater phase of his career with a psychological and sociological treatment of marriage. Using the old Jewish story, *Herodes und Mariamne* (*Herod and Mariamne*) (1850) creates an intense conflict between the powerful, masterful, and possessive love of the man and the resistance of the woman in her attempt to preserve her own individuality.

Belief in the sanctity of the individual became Hebbel's dominant theme, which he worked out in further highly imaginative variations. *Agnes Bernauer* (1852), in prose, turns to the Renaissance to depict the sacrifice of a historical personage to the maintenance of the state. *Gyges und sein Ring* (*Gyges and His Ring*) (1856), a highly effective tragedy in blank verse, uses the story told by Herodotus to underscore the inviolability of woman's right to her own dignity.

His last work, a trilogy in blank verse, was an attempt to dramatize and fill in the psychological details of the German epic. *Die Nibelungen* (1862) fails to achieve its purpose partly because of its attempt to adhere precisely to a long and complex story and partly because of the dramatist's efforts to be faithful to the essential simplicity of the leading characters.

Hebbel possesses a keen sense of the theater in his presentation of memorable characters, forceful conflicts, fervent passions, and excellent situations. His uniqueness, which is appealing to some and repellent to others, lies in his predilection for the strange, the bizarre, and the unpleasant.

Richard Wagner (1813–1883)

Although not primarily a writer, Richard Wagner came closest in his music dramas to the realization of the German ambition for a great national drama. Born in Leipzig of parents who were very much interested in the theater, he combined the study of music and drama to produce such early music-dramas as *Rienzi* (1842), *Tannhäuser* (1845), and *Lohengrin* (1850), which deviate little from the usual romantic tradition of grand opera.

His most original and greatest works evolved from the concept that the highest form of national drama was that of Greece in which acting, music, and painting were combined to give voice to a national heritage. From this broad vision he daringly relegated voice to a position not notably superior to that of any given instrument in the orchestral combination and concentrated on language and dramaturgy as much as on the music. The resulting vast tetralogy *Der Ring des Nibelungen* (*The Ring of the Nibelungs*) (1853) is made up of *Das Rheingold* (*The Rhine-gold*), *Die Walküre* (*The Valkyrie*), *Siegfried*, and *Götterdämmerung* (*The Downfall of the Gods*). Blending the highly poetic and mystical elements of the *Volsung Saga* with the fierce and gloomy narrative of the *Nibelungenlied*, he achieved the best and most effective version ever written of the Germanic epic material.

Having also voiced the mood of pessimism of his age, he was particularly receptive to the philosophy of Schopenhauer with which he became acquainted after his completion of the *Ring*. *Tristan und Isolde* (1865) is an intense, finely unified, and highly economical tragedy made from the old discursive medieval romance. *Die Meistersinger von Nürnberg* (1868) was a deliberate and highly successful attempt to realize the ideal of a national comedy. In his final work *Parsifal* (1882) the pessimism of *Tristan* is still present, but it finds relief in a serene and noble otherworldliness.

Wagner's text, particularly in its use of alliteration, is written with the demands of music always in mind and can scarcely be divorced from it. There is nevertheless no doubt of his first-rate dramatic talent or of his brilliant achievement in creating an essentially new and moving art form.

REVIEW QUESTIONS

THE GOLDEN AGE OF GERMAN LITERATURE

Multiple Choice

1. _____ German literature of this period was
   a. a reaction against Romanticism
   b. both classic and Romantic
   c. inspired by Renaissance writers
   d. a rejection of English sentimentalism

2. _____ German literature is Romantic because it
   a. values the individual over society
   b. emphasizes emotion and intuition
   c. shows interest in dark human motivations
   d. all of the above

3. _____ Klopstock was responsible for adding which of the following to German tastes?
   a. Impressionistic poetry
   b. Moral sentiment and English emotionalism
   c. French charm and interest in sensuality
   d. An interest in the varieties of human experience

4. _____ *Sturm und Drang* was
   a. a play by Lessing
   b. a movement that emphasized rules and control
   c. a school of youthful German writers
   d. a series of dramas about the Seven Years' War

5. _____ The Saxon School of writers was
   a. founded by Johann Gottsched
   b. an imitation of the French Academy
   c. strict in its imposition of Neoclassic rules of literature
   d. all of the above

6. _____ Goethe is considered
   a. a "universal man"
   b. a strict moral philosopher
   c. a product of a strict formal education
   d. a predictable and conventional writer

7. _____ Christian Fürchtegott Gellert
   a. wrote dramas for and about the upper class
   b. cultivated a style of extreme simplicity
   c. emphasized exotic subjects and scenes
   d. tutored the young Goethe

8. _____ Christopher Wieland wrote
   a. tales satirizing Christian sentiments
   b. a philosophical treatise mocking patriotism
   c. a romance that imitated Don Quixote
   d. all of the above

9. _____ Schiller's work was distinctive for
   a. its ability to encompass the universal themes
   b. its breadth of knowledge
   c. a feverishly idealistic temperament
   d. delineation of human failings

10. _____ Hegel was interested in
    a. expressing rigid moral and religious constructs
    b. investigating the nature of the actual world
    c. promoting patriotism through pamphlets
    d. using metrical speech

True-False

11. _____ Classic German literature is less like Greek literature than like English or French Neoclassicism.

12. _____ German Romantic literature venerated political leaders and parties.

13. _____ For Germany's ablest thinkers, concern for the individual and preoccupation with the life-spirit was more important than national unity and the brotherhood of man.

14. _____ Conflicts between rival schools of writers in the eighteenth century helped revive German literature.

15. _____ Klopstock's epic *Messiah* was inspired by Milton's *Paradise Lost.*

16. _____ Lessing is considered the German writer most representative of the eighteenth century Enlightenment.

17. _____ Franz Gillparzer defied censorship throughout his career.

18. _____ Goethe's work was never autobiographical.

19. _____ A play by Klinger gave the movement *Sturm und Drang* its name.

20. _____ Heine is considered the greatest German lyric poet after Goethe.

Fill-in

21. The tradition of German autocracy forced German writers to remain personal and _____ .

22. In his *Critique of Pure Reason* Immanuel Kant uses the tools of _____ to discredit reason by pointing out its limitations.

23. Johann Gottsched's _____ was the arbiter of German literature for about twenty years.

24. Founded by members of the Saxon School, _____ was a periodical that balanced a respect for rules with a free exercise of imagination.

25. After a life in which he practiced the extremes of highly moral behavior and the gratification of his physical desires, _____ came to the conclusion that enduring contentment lies between the extremes of piety and sensualism.

26. _____ is a writer who represents nearly all of the phases of German literary development.

27. _____ wrote about the concept of the beautiful soul in which instinctive moral sentiments entirely possess the emotions.

28. Because his work stimulated thought in so many literary men throughout Europe, _____ has been compared to Darwin.

29. _____ was an Austrian playwright whose dramatic expressions of tragic frustrations reflected his own life.

30. In his work *The World as Will and Idea*, _____ explains that both man and animals have intellects, but only man has reason.

Matching

31.	_____ Ewald von Kleist	a.	*Faust*
32.	_____ Herder	b.	founder of the Saxon School
33.	_____ Gottsched	c.	fate-dramatist
34.	_____ Goethe	d.	world-soul
35.	_____ Schiller	e.	Halle School
36.	_____ Grillparzer	f.	pessimist and antifeminist
37.	_____ Müllner	g.	*Sturm und Drang*
38.	_____ Hegel	h.	the beautiful soul
39.	_____ Schopenhauer	i.	opera
40.	_____ Wagner	j.	Viennese theater

Answers

1.	b	15.	t	29.	Grillparzer
2.	d	16.	t	30.	Schopenhauer
3.	c	17.	f	31.	e
4.	c	18.	f	32.	g
5.	d	19.	t	33.	b
6.	a	20.	t	34.	a
7.	b	21.	subjective	35.	h
8.	c	22.	logic	36.	j
9.	c	23.	German Society	37.	c
10.	b	24.	*Bremer Beiträge*	38.	d
11.	f	25.	Wieland	39.	f
12.	t	26.	Goethe	40.	i
13.	f	27.	Schiller		
14.	t	28.	Kant		

Part *3*

THE RISE OF REALISM AND NATURALISM

WORKS AT A GLANCE

Stendhal (Henri Beyle)

1822	*About Love*	1839	*The Abbess of Castro*
1830	*The Red and the Black*	1839	*The Charterhouse of Parma*

Honoré de Balzac

1829	*The Last of the Chouans*	1835	*Séraphita*
1830	*The Wild Ass's Skin; A*	1837	*César Birotteau*
	Passion in the Desert	1839	*Lost Illusions; The Village*
1831	*The Unknown Masterpiece*		*Curé*
1832	*Colonel Chabert*	1841	*A Secret Affair; Ursule*
1833	*Droll Stories; Eugénie*		*Mirouet*
	Grandet	1844	*Modest Mignon; Béatrix*
1834	*The Search for the Absolute;*	1846	*Cousin Bette*
	The Duchess of Langeais;	1847	*Cousin Pons*
	Old Goriot		

Gustave Flaubert

1857	*Madame Bovary*	1874	*The Temptation of Saint*
1862	*Salammbô*		*Anthony*
1869	*Sentimental Education*	1881	*Bouvard and Pécuchet*

George Sand (Lucile-Aurore Dupin)

1831	*Indiana*	1845	*The Miller of Angibault*
1832	*Valentine*	1848	*The Haunted Pool; Little*
1834	*Lélia*		*Fadette*
1840	*Spiridion*	1852	*The Master Bellringers*
1842	*Consuelo*	1860	*The Marquis de Villemer*

Prosper Mérimée

1825	*Plays of Clara Gazul*	1833	*The Double Mistake*
1829	*Chronicle of the Reign of*	1840	*Colomba*
	Charles IX	1847	*Carmen*
1830	*The Etruscan Vase*		

Émile Zola

1864	*Tales for Ninon*	1872	*The Quarry*
1867	*Thérèse Raquin*	1874	*The Conquest of Plassans*
1871	*The Rougon Family*		

Émile Zola (continued)

1875	The Markets of Paris; The Transgression of Abbé Mouret	1883	The Ladies' Paradise
		1884	How Jolly Life Is
		1885	Germinal
1876	His Excellency Eugene Rougon	1886	The Masterpiece
		1888	Earth; The Dream
1877	The Dram Shop	1890	Human Brutes
1878	A Love Episode	1891	Money
1880	Nana	1892	The Downfall; Doctor Pascal
1882	Piping Hot		

Guy de Maupassant

1880	Some Verses	1887	Mont-Oriol; Le Horla
1881	The Tellier House	1888	Mme. Husson's Rosebush; Pierre and Jean
1883	Mademoiselle Fifi; A Life		
		1889	Stranger than Death
1883–1884	Clair de Lune; Miss Harriet; The Rondoli Sisters; Yvette; "The Necklace"	1890	Our Heart; Useless Beauty
1885	Tales and Novelettes; Monsieur Parent; Tales of Day and Night; Bel-Ami		

The de Goncourts

1857	Intimate Portraits of the Eighteenth Century	1862	Women in the Eighteenth Century
		1864	Renée Mauperin
1859–1875	The Art of the Eighteenth Century	1865	Germinie Lacerteux; Henriette Maréchal
1860	Charles Demailly	1869	Madame Gervaisais
1861	Sister Philomène	1878	Mme. du Barry
1867	Manette Salomon	1887–1896	Journals

Alphonse Daudet

1858	The Amorous	1881	Numa Roumestan
1866	Letters from My Mill	1884	Sappho
1868	Little Nobody	1885	Tartarin on the Alps
1872	The Astonishing Adventures of Tartarin of Tarascon	1887	Thirty Years of Paris
		1888	The Immortal; Recollections of a Literary Man
1874	Fromont Jr. and Risler Sr.		
1877	The Nabob	1890	Port-Tarascon
1879	Kings in Exile		

Hippolyte Taine

1858	Essays	1869	The Ideal in Art
1863	History of English Literature	1872	Notes on England
1865	New Essays; Philosophy of	1875	The Old Regime
	Italian Art	1894	Last Essays
1866	Travels in Italy		

Eugene Scribe

1833	Bertrand and Raton	1849	Adrienne Lecouvreur; The
1842	The Glass of Water		Battle of the Women

Émile Augier

1848	The Adventuress; Gabrielle	1864	Maître Guérin
1854	Mr. Poirier's Son-in-Law	1868	Paul Forestier
1855	Olympe's Marriage	1872	Jean de Thommeray
1856	The Golden Girdle	1876	Madame Coverlet
1858	A Fine Marriage		

Alexander Dumas *fils*

1847	Sins of Youth	1857	The Question of Money
1848	The Lady of the Camelias;	1858	The Natural Son
	The Romance of a	1859	The Prodigal Father
	Woman	1867	The Ideas of Mme. Aubray
1851	Diane de Lys	1871	Man-Woman
1855	The Demi-Monde	1873	Claude's Wife

Victorien Sardou

1873	Rabagas	1880	Let Us Divorce

Karl Marx

1847	Communist Manifesto	1867, 1885,	Capital
1867	Critique of Political	1895	
	Economy		

Friedrich Nietzsche

1883–1891	Thus Spake Zarathustra	1886	Beyond Good and Evil

Gerhard Hauptmann

1883	The Lot of a Promethean	1898	Teamster Henschel
1889	Before Sunrise	1903	Rose Bernd
1893	The Weavers	1911	The Rats
1896	The Sunken Bell		

Hermann Sudermann

1887	*Dame Care*	1889	*Honor; Home (Magda)*

Arthur Schnitzler

1893	*The Affairs of Anatol*

Rainer Marie Rilke

1905	*The Book of Hours*	1922	*Sonnets to Orpheus;*
1908	*New Poems*		*Duino Elegies*
1910	*The Notebook of Malte Laurids Brigge*		

5
EARLY REALISTS

Literary historians have long discerned three main tendencies in literature: Classicism, which emphasizes form; Romanticism, which emphasizes values of the imagination; and Realism, which emphasizes the depiction of life as it is lived. If the nineteenth century saw the luxurious flourishing of Romanticism, it also witnessed the emergence of Realism as a literary method.

It is important, however, at the outset to observe that as the nineteenth century advanced we find a mixture of tendencies in some writers. In many cases it is not possible to identify authors with the same conviction with which we may safely call Addison, Racine, and Voltaire Classicists, and Shelley, Hugo, and Manzoni Romantics. Flaubert, the author of one of the greatest of all Realistic novels, was a Romantic to his finger-tips, and wrote some works which are Romantic in the extreme; Stendhal, called by some critics the father of the Realistic novel, is by others described as extravagantly Romantic; the same is true of George Sand. Ibsen, though often cited as the chief force behind the new Realistic drama, wrote a number of important plays that are certainly Romantic. From the mid-nineteenth century on, we can often apply these terms with some intelligence to individual works, rather than to authors. Nonetheless, the classifications sometimes break down even here, when we are forced to recognize opposing tendencies in a given work.

THE NATURE OF REALISM

Realism is essentially born of an impatience with Romanticism. It is true, of course, that Classicist, Romantic, and Realist all take their raw materials from life—there is no other way to make literature. But the Romantic sees his material through the lenses of his imagination, and thus presents us a world that may be better or worse than the world we all know, but is never the world as it is actually lived. The Realistic temper has never been quite so far removed from the classic as from the Romantic; the Classicist's need of clarity and directness has often, as we have seen, led him to sharp satire upon actual social conditions; the Classicist, moreover, has always tended to deal with contemporary life, as has the Realist. Nevertheless, the dyed-in-the-wool Realist is often quite indifferent to form or beauty of any kind, and that is his main difference from the Classicist. Rather, we should say, he finds beauty resides only in the depiction of truth.

Realism has been defined by William Dean Howells as "the truthful treatment of material." Realism looks at life with objectivity. The Realistic author refrains from taking sides with his characters. The author seeks to see life according to the facts, and hence presents his interpretation of it by documenting character, story, or picture with facts. Moreover, as has been remarked, Realism deals with contemporary society; the Realist avoids the past or the future since one can see them only through a veil of fancy. The Realist is interested more in character than in story, more in people than in external nature.

Though Realism first made its appearance as a movement in the nineteenth century, it is an attitude toward art that is discernible in earlier periods. Chaucer's *Prologue to the Canterbury Tales*, Ben Jonson's comedies of London life, Defoe's *Journal of the Plague Year* and other journalistic ventures—to mention only a few—are undeniably pieces of realism. There are low comedy scenes in Shakespeare and stories in the Bible that must be described as fragments of Realism. But these are all isolated instances.

The Realistic Novel

It was during the height of the Romantic movement that Realism emerged as a literary trend. Balzac was, after all, born three years before Victor Hugo. And it was in the field of the novel that Realism first became prominent.

As we have seen, the novel emerged as a very important literary form in the hands of the Romantics. Chateaubriand, Mme. de Staël, Benjamin Constant, Nodier, Xavier de Maistre, Vigny, Dumas *père*, and, most of all, Hugo achieved noteworthy successes as novelists—and these names constitute most of the history of the Romantic movement in France. In England, Sir Walter Scott produced a long series of historical novels that did much by their vogue to bring the Romantic movement to the rest of Europe. Goethe himself authored novels that fostered some of the extremest tendencies of Romanticism.

But in this very era, a new type of novel evolved, the Realistic novel, which in the hands of Stendhal and Balzac, and to a lesser degree in the hands of George Sand, achieved literary excellence, and established the new mode.

STENDHAL (HENRI BEYLE) (1783–1842)

Henri Beyle, who assumed the appellation of de Stendhal as a penname, suffered a long period of neglect almost up to the beginning of our own century. He himself had predicted, "I shall be successful about 1880." Now his place as a major novelist is assured.

Had his reputation depended at any time upon his personal character, he would never have been recognized, for he was a man of peculiarly unattractive qualities; he was vain, pretentious, vulgar, and intellectually an opportunist. His very pride in calling himself M. de Beyle during the Empire shows a snobbery towards his own middle-class origins. The same is true of the "de" in his pseudonym.

He was a son of an attaché of the parlement at Grenoble. He served for a time as a soldier during the campaigns at Jena and Moscow. Under the Empire he saw civil service employment. After Napoleon's fall he went to his favorite country, Italy, but was expelled in 1821 by the Austrian police. Thereafter he lived at Paris, contributing to an English magazine in London, and making visits to that city. He had a fine command of English and was a great admirer of English literature. After 1830 he was appointed French consul at Trieste, and later at Città Vecchia. He was at Rome as often as he could manage it, but died at Paris.

His literary works consist of novels, criticism, biography, and travel impressions. He wrote a history of Italian painting (1817); a book on Rome, Naples, and Florence (1814); a life of Haydn (1814), a comparative study of *Racine and Shakespeare* (1824); and biographies of Mozart, Metastasio, and Napoleon.

He is also the author of a curious book *De l'Amour* (*About Love*) (1822), full of cynicism but sharp observation; to Stendhal love meant forthright and brutal sensuality—it is in that sense he always refers to it. "Love has always been for me," he says, "the most important business in the world, or, rather, the only one." He despised, in a Byronic manner, all convention as so much dishonest prudery. *Bégueulisme* ("haughty prudery"), as he called it, "is the art of being offended for the sake of being credited with virtues one does not possess." This indifference to moral codes came to be known as "Beylism."

However unacceptable Stendhal's posing as an immoralist may be, there has been no question about the value of his best novels. He is the first major Realist and one of the earliest psychologists in the French novel. It has, indeed, been said of him that he is a Romantic too; certainly his eccentricities of character, his stress on love, his dislike of the Neoclassicists (in *Racine and Shakespeare*)—all are Romantic enough. But his method as a novelist is to accumulate innumerable small facts and details concerning his characters rather than to weave an exciting plot—and that constitutes what we know as Realism. Balzac was one of the earliest to recognize his greatness, and said of him that he was "one of the most remarkable writers of our times."

In addition to a collection of tales, *The Abbess of Castro*, Stendhal's most important fiction is to be found in the novels, *Le Rouge et le Noir* (*The Red and the Black*) (1830) and *La Chartreuse de Parme* (*The Charterhouse of Parma*) (1839).

The Red and the Black

The "red" of Stendhal's title refers to the military spirit as typified by the Napoleonic ambition; the "black" is the ecclesiastic, a power that the author detested. The hero, Julien Sorel, the son of a peasant, is an unattractive, thoroughly unsentimental opportunist, who, feeling that the road to power is closed to the military after Napoleon's fall, seeks it in the church.

Julien, a highly intelligent hypocrite, pretends so effectively to piety that he is appointed tutor to the children of the mayor of the little town of Verrières, M. de Rênal. Mme. de Rênal, a good woman, falls in love with Julien, and he, to gain ascendancy over her, pretends he is smitten. He enjoys so much the sense of power over his mistress that he rejects the offer of his friend Fouqué to go into business partnership. A corrupt local politician, once an unsuccesful suitor of Mme. de Renal, writes an anonymous letter to the mayor revealing his wife's infidelity with the tutor.

The mayor ends the affair by sending Julien to the seminary at Besançon. Mme. de Rênal, filled with remorse, becomes very religious after her lover goes away. Julien, disgusted with the hypocrisy of his fellow students, is disliked by them because of his critical intelligence, but he makes a friend of the Abbé Pirard. The latter, a man of ethical conduct, is fired from the seminary because of his support of the Marquis de la Mole against the bishop. When the Marquis procures a living for the Abbé in Paris, he also appoints Julien as his own secretary.

En route to Paris, Julien stops off to see Mme. de Rênal. At first she repulses him, and then yields. Just in time Julien avoids discovery by the mayor when he jumps out of the window.

Julien is now an intimate of the Marquis' home but is bored with the intellectual vacuity of Paris. Surreptitiously he borrows books from the Marquis' library, and devours them in the solitude of his room. One day he finds out that the nobleman's proud daughter, Mathilde, is doing the same thing. The two become friends and the girl, tired of the stupid young men of rank she knows, falls in love with the clever Julien.

She gives herself to him, but soon feels she has degraded herself to sleep with a servant. Infuriated at the insult, Julien plans to win power over the whole household.

An old friend advises him how to proceed. He begins to ignore Mathilde and to pay court to another woman who frequents the Marquis' home. Mathilde realizes how deep her love is for him, and abases herself before him. Now that he has won power over her he means to keep it, and treats her with some disdain.

Mathilde is delighted when she becomes pregnant. Now Julien will have to marry her, and she can make the sacrifice for him of her social position. The Marquis, enraged at first, takes the only way out he knows: he settles a fortune on Julien, and procures a title for him and a commission in the army. Delighted, Julien pays small attention to Mathilde. But Mme. de Rênal, in a fit of penitence, ruins her former lover's career by telling the Marquis of Julien's perfidy, with the result that the nobleman refuses to sanction the marriage. Out of his mind with wrath, Julien rushes to Verrières, seeks out his former mistress in the church, and fires twice at her. He admits his guilt, when arrested, and is ready to go to the gallows. He even repulses the attempts of Mathilde and Fouqué to procure his release or escape. At his trial he is given the death sentence.

Mme. de Rênal, recovered from her wounds, and more violently in love than ever, visits him in prison, and begs him to appeal his case. He now feels that she is his true love, and that Mathilde only irritates him. Julien pays the penalty, and Fouqué fulfills his request to be buried in the mountains. Mathilde buries his head with her own hands, and later has a marble memorial erected on the spot. Mme. de Rênal dies of grief three days after her lover's end.

The Red and the Black is written in a firm prose, shot through with irony.

The Charterhouse of Parma

In *La Chartreuse de Parme* the hero, Fabrice del Dongo, is a kind of Italian Julien Sorel; the motif of *Le Rouge et le Noir* is also repeated here, except that the hero makes the opposite journey: he begins as a soldier at Waterloo, and, after a life of intrigue, becomes a priest. *The Charterhouse of Parma*, laid in Stendhal's beloved Italy, is more picturesque than its predecessor, and is for that reason preferred by many readers. Here, too, the overtones are more Romantic, perhaps because of the Italian locale.

When Fabrice, son of the Marquis del Dongo, whose villa is situated on Lake Como, reaches the age of seventeen, he is determined to become a soldier under Napoleon. This is a decision shocking to the family; the Marquis, a fanatic and a miser, loathes everything French—particularly Napoleon. The Marquis, finding the boy unalterable, forbids his wife to give Fabrice any money for his expenses; but Fabrice's aunt, Gina, is able to secrete some diamonds in his coat.

Pretending to be a dealer in astrological instruments, Fabrice reaches Paris, follows part of the army out of the city, and is arrested as a spy, but is released through the kindness of the jailer's wife. Acquiring a horse, he rides into the thick of the fight at Waterloo. Dismounted, Fabrice joins the ranks of the infantry and manages to kill a Prussian officer.

When Fabrice returns to Lake Como, he is arrested on the charge of possessing a false passport, but his Aunt Gina, now a Countess, puts matters to rights for him when they go to Milan. She takes him to Parma, and thence sends him to Naples to the seminary to study for the priesthood.

At the end of his studies Fabrice has become not the least pious, but is a thoroughly worldly minded young ecclesiast. At the theater he is smitten with the charms of the actress Marietta Valsera, and arouses the hate of her protector, Giletti. To rescue him from further difficulties in the affair, his aunt's lover, the prime minister of Parma, sends him to the country on an archeological expedition. While out hunting, Fabrice comes upon Marietta and Giletti in a carriage; in a jealous fit Giletti rushes at Fabrice and is killed by him. The young priest runs off with Marietta to Bologna, and supplied with funds by his aunt, lives in amorous felicity with his mistress. But because of the prime minister's enemies, Fabrice is tried at Parma *in absentia* and condemned as a murderer.

His lust for Marietta sated, Fabrice follows the singer Fausta to Parma, and is there arrested. But he is content enough in prison because he is able to communicate with Clelia, the jailer's daughter, whom he had met once before. With Clelia's help Aunt Gina plots to smuggle ropes to Fabrice to enable him to escape. He makes a successful flight for freedom, and goes to Piedmont.

Gina has also succeeded in having the ruling prince of Parma poisoned. She returns with her nephew to Parma, and the new prince eventually makes Fabrice his archbishop. His eloquence is soon drawing a large attendance.

Clelia, now married to a nobleman, comes to hear the archbishop preach, and succumbs to her love for him. Fabrice makes love to her every night. A child is born to them, and Fabrice brings the baby to his own establishment. But the child dies, and Clelia soon follows it. Tired of a life of intrigue, and sorrowed by her death, Fabrice resigns his office, and retires to the Charterhouse of Parma, a Carthusian monastery, to end his days in study and reflection.

IMPORTANCE

To study the differences between the methods of Realist and Romantic, one has only to compare the Battle of Waterloo as described by Stendhal in this novel and as painted by Hugo in *Les Misérables*. Stendhal sees the conflict only in terms of the details affecting his hero; Hugo recreates the action of the battle as a totality of vast movements.

Concerning Stendhal's contribution to literature, the great critic Taine said of him, "No one has taught us better how to open our eyes and see."

HONORÉ DE BALZAC (1799–1850)

It is doubtful whether in the whole annals of literary creativeness there is a record of indefatigable labor to equal Honore de Balzac's. "This prince of novelists," as he has been called, planned one hundred and thirty-eight novels and novelettes to form the series of the *Human Comedy* (*La Comédie Humaine*), and actually completed all but some thirty of them. The story of his life is largely the story of unending literary composition, which he would begin at two in the morning and continue uninterrupted through seven in the evening, to the accompaniment of innumerable cups of coffee. When he died at the age of fifty-one it was from complete exhaustion and enervation.

Obviously such a life left little time for complicated experience. Yet, although Balzac saw much less of the world and of people than most of his celebrated contemporaries, he has excelled them all in the fidelity to and knowledge of the intricacies of human experience. He had an almost incredible ability to objectify his own experiences, as limited as they were, so that he could use them with perfect impersonality in his novels.

He came of peasant stock (the *de* in his name was later addition), inheriting from his father a sturdy physique, and from his mother a mystical turn, which, oddly enough, was part of his nature. Indeed, one would have prophesied from the beginning of his career writings of a purely Romantic character.

Though his parents did not encourage his pursuit of literature, his sister Laura was sympathetic. Honoré's youth was spent in sunny Touraine, associated with the great figure of Rabelais, and the boy never forgot the vivid impressions he gathered there. Later in life he was to write of the manners of Touraine; and in one book, his gayest, and one of the wittiest and bawdiest ever written, he was to salute Rabelais by telling a series of tales that the old Titan would have relished, *Contes Drôlatiques* (*Droll Stories*) (1833).

The boy was sent to Paris to study for the law, which he did not like. At last, when he was twenty he was allowed to try his hand at literature, his father imagining that living in a garret on a trifling allowance would bring sense into the lad's head. The elder Balzac proved to be quite in error. However, the law studies and the apprenticeship to a notary were to stand the novelist in good stead. There is probably no novelist in the world whose plots revolve so much about affairs of business as do Balzac's.

His first productions, after a tragedy that he had been counseled to burn, were a series of over-emotional novels that he had the good sense not to prize above their worth, and therefore issued under various fancy pseudonyms (Viellerglé, Lord R'hoone, and Horace Saint-Aubin). Balzac never tired of hoping he would someday be very rich—though that ambition never interfered with his integrity as a writer—and went from one foolish speculation to another, all of them ending disastrously. With the small sums he had procured for his early novels, he joined fortunes with a printing concern; his activities as publisher, printer, and type founder resulted in his accumulating a debt that took decades to discharge. These early novels are, despite their number, usually considered outside Balzac's career proper, and are rarely printed, even in editions of his complete works. The disastrous printing experience, however, proved good material for later novels.

To escape from the annoyance of debt, he went for a visit to Brittany, and there found the inspiration for the first novel to which he was willing to sign his name, the earliest of the *Comédie Humaine* series, *Le Dernier Chouan* (*The Last of the Chouans*) (1829)—later renamed *Les Chouans*; it is romantically colorful, laid in the period of the French Revolution, and in the Sir Walter Scott tradition. The same year (1829), with which his literary career truly begins, saw the publication also of his analytical satire, *La Physiologie du Mariage* (*The Physiology of Marriage*). This treatise is fairly fundamental to Balzac's thinking. In a Rabelaisian spirit, he examines the nature of the marriage relation—the recurring subject in many of his novels—under various heads: "A Treatise on Marital Politics," "Customs," "Essay on the Police," "The Budget," "Civil War," "Of Allies," "Conjugal Peace," "Principles of Strategy." Pretending to consider marriage as a constitutional state, he manages a diverting mixture of the ludicrous and the profoundly earnest.

In the two decades of life left to him Balzac turned out a library of volumes, allowing himself just enough nonlaboring hours to know a little of personal love and a great deal of financial failure. He earned vast sums, spent vast sums, and engaged in the maddest kind of financial speculations, which kept him plunged in inextricable debt. Three women figured in his life. When he was young the aristocratic Mme. de Berny, very much his senior and the mother of nine children, did much to develop his tastes; she sat as the model for Mme. de Mortsauf in *Le Lys dans la Vallée* (*Lily of the Valley*), and was close to him until her death in 1836. The Marquise de Castries, the model for his less moral ladies of society, tired of him soon after bestowing her favors. The most important of these women was a Polish Countess, Evelina Haska, who began writing to him in 1832. For the last eighteen years of his life he corresponded with her, idolized her, and for her sake made several trips to Russia. It was largely for the purpose of putting himself in the position of marrying her that he indulged in many of his wild business ventures (which included digging in abandoned Sardinian mines, and traffic with the Great Mogul). Finally, just a few months before his death they were married.

Before we consider Balzac's novels, we should observe that this phenomenal laborer in the vineyards of literature also wrote enough plays, essays, and stray pieces to make up several volumes during those two decades, and also penned, almost single-handed, the contents of a journal, the *Revue Parisienne*. The dramas, with the possible exception of the still-performed *Mercadet*, are all unworthy of him. The shorter prose pieces are full of interest.

By 1833 Balzac had already determined that his novels were to be social studies, and that they should form a vast design by the means of employing characters that interlock in various stories. In 1842 he issued a *Plan* of the entire series, which was to be given the general title, *La Comédie Humaine* (*The Human Comedy*). He planned his works, in short, to complement Dante's *Divine Comedy*. Prof. Van Laun has magnificently caught Balzac's purposes in these words:

> With the true spirit of a Pantagruelist he sees a tragedy, identical, or at least conterminous with human existence; he is penetrated by it, he becomes the seer and the prophet of a new revelation; and, far from raising the cry of a Jeremiah, or a John in the wilderness, he proclaims to his generation and to posterity a gigantic comedy. He has been at the point of weeping at the thought of all that is implied in the central social bond...[but] he prepares to make them [his fellow men] laugh.

The plan of the Human Comedy is divided by the author into three main heads, the first division being subdivided into six:

1. The largest division, Studies of Manners (*Études de Moeurs*):
   a. Scenes of Private Life (*Scénes de la Vie Privé*)—*Gobseck, Colonel Chabert, Old Goriot (Le Pére Coriot), Béatrix.*
   b. Life in the Provinces (*Vie de Province*)—*Eugénie Grandet, Pierrette, Lost Illusions (Illusions Perdues), Lily of the Valley (Le Lys dans la Vallée).*
   c. Life in Paris (*Vie Parisienne*)—*The Duchess of Langeais (La Duchesse de Langeais), Cousin Bette (La Cousine Bette), Cousin Pons (Le Cousin Pons), Triumphs and Miseries of Courtesans (Les Splendeurs et Misères des Courtisanes).*
   d. Political Life (*Vie Politique*)—*A Secret Affair (Une Ténébreuse Affaire).*
   e. Military Life (*Vie Militaire*)—*The Chouans, A Passion in the Desert (Une Passion dans le Désert).*
   f. Life in the Country (*Vie de Campagne*)—*The Peasants (Les Paysans), The Country Doctor (Le Médecin de Campagne), The Village Curé (Le Curé de Village).*

2. Philosophical Studies (*Études Philosophiques*)—*The Search for the Absolute (La Recherche de l'Absolu), The Wild Ass's Skin (La Peau de Chagrin).*

3. Analyical Studies (*Études Analytiques*)—*The Physiology of Marriage (La Physiologie du Mariage).*

In a study such as this it would be neither necessary nor wise to list all of Balzac's fiction. It would be inconceivable that a man who wrote so copiously in twenty years could write always on an equally high level. What is astounding is the quantity of masterful novels and stories by Balzac worthy of everyone's attention. These we list, in order of publication: *The Chouans* (1829), *The Wild Ass's Skin* (1830), *A Passion in the Desert* (1830), *The Unknown Masterpiece (Le Chef-d'Oeuvre Inconnu)* (1831), *Colonel Chabert* (1832), *Eugénie Grandet* (1833), *Droll Stories* (1833), *The Search for the Absolute* (1834), *The Duchess of Langeais* (1834), *Old Goriot* (1834), *Séraphita* (1835), *César Birotteau* (1837), *Lost Illusions* (1839), *The Village Curé* (1839), *A Secret Affair* (1841), *Ursule Mirouet* (1841), *Modest Mignon (Modeste Mignon)* (1844), *Béatrix* (1844), *Cousin Bette* (1846), and *Cousin Pons* (1847). It is safe to say that no novelist in the world could claim that many excellent novels to his credit. And yet, our list excludes many other novels of some quality! Moreover, there were still more novels in Balzac's head (since the whole design of the *Human Comedy* was projected by him years before his premature death), novels never to be written.

IMPORTANCE

There are many of Balzac's admirers who insist upon certain Romantic traits in the work of this great Realist. And it is true that novels like *Séraphita,* *The Wild Ass's Skin,* and *Lost Illusions* are Romantic in the best sense of the word, for they exalt the imagination and the passions. Very often, too, when Balzac describes a scene he will let loose a flood of rhapsodic rhetoric. But, nevertheless, when taken as a whole the *Human Comedy* is the world's most imposing Realistic creation in literature. Courageously the pioneer in the depiction of middle-class life in town and country, at home and in public, he emphasizes the materialistic pursuits just as they are emphasized in middle-class lives. Money and business transactions figure largely, as they do in life as it is lived; so do eating, and work at a trade or profession. He pauses constantly to describe such objects of furniture and clothing as constitute the most familiar sights in everyday living, and often makes one feel that they are important to the plot. His interest in "documenting" life also causes him to stress the force of environment in shaping conduct and character. A modern reader will sometimes find the author's careful citing of contemporary events and some of his descriptions needlessly long; but it must be remembered that those very passages were important to Balzac's intention of presenting a complete picture of society.

Others find defects in the style, complaining that the prose is sometimes as pedestrian as the types Balzac is writing about. But in this respect he sins far less than most of the Realists who came after him— far less, for instance, than some of the most admired of our American Realists. A great American artist, Henry James, said of Balzac that he was "the master of us all."

Perhaps only in one respect have his followers improved upon the manner Balzac invented: They learned not to intrude upon the story with their private disquisitions. This old habit of novelists Balzac adhered to, nor can it be said that he knew how to make those interruptions invaluable as did the English satirist Fielding.

The reason for these personal intrusions is not far to seek. Balzac, master realist though he was, wrote always with a point of view. He is above all, like all the world's greatest writers, concerned with conduct good and evil. No one has excelled him in the depiction of viciousness; wicked misers like old man Grandet or Gobseck, the corrupt Hulot, the jealous Bette, the parasite Pons, the spiteful Mlle. Gamard, the vain Mme. de Nucingen. He is perhaps less successful with his noble characters. But one is aware, behind his objectivity, of his hatred of evil, despite his dispassionate approach. Nor does he succumb to the desire to give his stories happy endings. He knows too well how often malice triumphs in the world, and the emphasis of the *Human Comedy* is tragic.

He has been compared with Shakespeare as one of the world's greatest creators of character. He is at home in every milieu—on the fashionable boulevard or in the slums, in a salon or in a dive. He had an ear for the kind of speech that brings each of his types to life—and it is the ever-present sense of reality that, after all, bespeaks the great artist, whatever Balzac's defects. It would be fair to say, taking his total accomplishment, that he is the world's greatest representative novelist.

To select for particular notice even a handful of the novels in the *Human Comedy* is to incur inevitably the just wrath of readers who have other favorites in that vast undertaking. But the world has fairly well agreed in singling out as its favorites *The Wild Ass's Skin, Eugénie Grandet, The Duchess of Langeais, Old Goriot,* and *Cousin Bette.*

The Wild Ass's Skin

La Peau de Chagrin (1830) begins in 1829 when a young man, who has made a complete failure of his life thus far, is trying his luck at gambling. He is at the lowest depth of despair when he meets an ancient man who shows him a piece of skin with an Arabic inscription promising the possessor the granting of his every wish. But there is a limit to this gratification, too, for at every wish granted the skin becomes smaller in size.

The youth is enchanted with the idea, even though he learns that there is a penalty attached to owning the magic skin. As the skin lessens in size so will the life of the owner shorten. The happy young man seizes the skin with a cry, "A short life but a merry one!"

The brief years pass, and with them we move through scenes of life among Parisian politicians, journalists, and artists. Our hero Raphael is possessor of the magic skin, and through it has become very wealthy. He has succeeed, too, in winning the love of Pauline, and has every apparent reason for being happy. Yet all that he could enjoy is embittered for him when he thinks of the skin. Works of art, the theater, his interest in science—all end by becoming meaningless to him.

At length he seeks out a very wise man, Lavrille, and brings him the magic skin. After an examination Lavrille remarks that it is the skin of an ass. But what Raphael wishes is some means of stretching the skin so that he may lengthen his own days. No strength of hand can do it, nor can chemical experiments. All the time the skin is diminishing. At last Raphael dies.

This novel shows Balzac at his most Romantic, and in some respects his least finished style. But the power of the central idea sustains the plot and lends the book fascination.

Eugénie Grandet

Eugénie Grandet (1833) shows Balzac's method at its best; there is a lucky absence in it of prolixity of detail. The leading characters are M. Grandet, a psychopathic miser, and his daughter Eugénie, who is forced by her father's behavior to lead a lonely life of self-deprivation.

In this masterful study of provincial life the scene is the town of Saumur. Grandet has succeeded in piling up a fortune for himself, once he had married the daughter of a wealthy merchant. Under the Republic he had seized the opportunity to buy up some valuable property formerly belonging to the Church. When Napoleon was Consul he became mayor and was richer than ever. During the early days of the First Empire he fell heir to three fortunes through his wife by the death of her mother and grandparents. By 1811 he was able to purchase the estate of an impoverished nobleman.

His miserliness is already legendary, but he is respected in the town nonetheless, largely because of the extreme thriftiness and simplicity of his habits. His wife, Eugénie, and himself are served by only one domestic, Nanon, who is his devoted slave. His wife also toils away despite the fact that her husband loves her in his own way. Every birthday little Eugénie is given one gold piece, but she is expected to save it, for each New Year's Day her father asks to see what she has saved. He measures the bread and sugar they use for food, and has the household freezing until November because of his refusal to have fires earlier.

As Eugénie reaches the age when she is eligible to think of marriage, she has two suitors, the banker's son and the notary's son. Both call on her the night of her birthday in 1819, when Grandet's nephew Charles suddenly appears. Charles' father has also been wealthy, and Charles does not hesitate to patronize the provincials with his Parisian airs. Eugénie is so much impressed with him that she risks her father's anger by her use of firewood and candles.

But Charles does not know that the letter he has brought Grandet from Paris announces the fact that Charles' father has become penniless, that he has written it just before taking his own life, and that he has asked Grandet to befriend the young man. When informed of the catastrophe next day, Charles remains in his room weeping bitterly. He asks a friend in Paris to dispose of his property and settle his obligations, and he gives some small gifts to Eugénie and her mother. Sympathy for Charles has already stirred Eugénie, and his little kindness makes her fall in love with him.

Grandet sends the local banker to Paris to act for him in his brother's affairs. Eugénie, knowing her father's intention of getting rid of Charles as soon as possible, gives her cousin her little treasure of gold coins to enable him to start out in life. When Charles leaves, the two swear undying love.

Next New Year's Day Grandet, as usual, asks to see Eugénie's coins. Her mother has kept her secret, but Grandet suspects the truth. He orders her to her room, and declares himself through with her and her mother. However, the little town is now rife with rumors that Mme. Grandet is dying because of her ill-treatment, and Grandet relents, making peace with both his women. Moreover, he understands that on Mme. Grandet's death Eugénie could insist on having her money in her own right, if she chose to do so.

Mme. Grandet dies, and her husband easily persuades Eugénie to sign over her share to him.

Five years pass. During them no word has come to Eugénie from the West Indies, where Charles went to seek his fortune. In his eighty-second year Grandet has a stroke, and dies. Eugénie, now a wealthy heiress, is living with the old servant Nanon, confident that she will some day hear from Charles.

At last Charles writes to her, asking to be released from his promise to marry her. He has some hopes of marrying the daughter of a nobleman, and of securing by royal grant his prospective father-in-law's title. She releases him. But hearing from the banker that Charles' father's debts are not yet paid, and that Charles will not be acceptable to the nobleman until they are, she pays the sum herself.

Eugénie is now resigned to solitude. At last she agrees to marry the former notary's son, now a government official, with the proviso that their marriage be one in name only. Soon after she becomes Mme. Cruchot, her husband dies. She is now wealthier by the addition of his holdings. Living only with Nanon, she is so accustomed to the Spartan régime of her father that she desires no other. Her great wealth holds no meaning for her.

The Duchess of Langeais

La Duchesse de Langeais (1834) is a powerful picture of the Parisian aristocracy of Balzac's own day. It is a study of how the upper classes have lost their power in the country through their own shortcomings; they have taken no advantage of their birth and education.

The young Duchess of Langeais is a typical Parisian noblewoman, very feminine, fickle, a coquette to the core. The center of her life varies from the ballroom to the boudoir. Her husband, whose interests are military, takes little note of her comings and goings, and the Duchess enjoys flirting with large numbers of young men, alternately encouraging and discouraging each of them. But Armand de Montriveau will not endure such treatment. He is a man of fierce pride. Discovering that she has been only playing a game with him, he forces her to see him, and in anger calls her the murderer of his faith in life. When he leaves her, the Duchess suddenly realizes that she is madly in love with him.

She now writes him begging for forgiveness, but she receives no answers to her letters. Desperate, she determines to go to him, and leaves Paris just as he arrives to see her.

For five years he searches everywhere for her. At last he comes upon news of her in Spain, when he learns that she is imprisoned, as he feels, in a convent. He is determined to rescue her at all costs, and finally makes his way to her cell, the cell of "Sister Thérèse." And there she lies dead.

This novel shows Balzac depicting with his usual precision the life of the Parisian aristocracy.

Old Goriot

Père Goriot (1834), like Shakespeare's *King Lear*, is the most devastatingly pathetic work of its author, and has often been compared to it because of its theme. Old Goriot is like another Lear with his two ungrateful daughters. On the other hand, the portrait of the social climber, Raslignac, is one of Balzac's master-strokes of characterization.

The setting is in Paris during the 1830s. Old Goriot, a retired merchant of means, has married off his daughters to men of rank: Anastasie to the Count de Restaud, and Delphine to the Baron de Nucingen. He himself has taken the best rooms on the first floor of Madame Vauquer's modest boarding house. The good lady who runs the pension considers him as a possible catch. But after two years when old Goriot moves to cheaper quarters on the second floor, the inmates of the pension decide he is an old cheat and miser. It is in vain that old Goriot has explained that the two elegant young women who on rare occasions have paid him fleeting visits are his daughters: the general verdict is that they are the old skinflint's mistresses.

At the end of his third year old Goriot moves to still cheaper lodgings on the third floor. His young ladies come almost never, and he is the butt of many jokes in the establishment.

One night when the poor law student, Eugène de Rastignac, comes home late to the pension, he peers through the keyhole of Goriot's door, and finds the old man melting down some silver plate. Next day Rastignac learns that a fellow boarder, Vautrin, has seen Goriot selling silver to a money lender. Neither of these two has any idea that the money is to go to the Countess Anastasie, whom Eugène is delighted to have met at a ball the night before. Indeed, Rastignac this day goes to call on the Countess, just as old Goriot is leaving. Anastasie's husband and lover are there too, and they all welcome Rastignac because he is the cousin of the wealthy Mme. de Beauséant. But his unfortunate mention of old Goriot results in the visit's being cut short, and the Count's telling the servant that he would no more be at home to Rastignac.

It is Mme. de Beauséant who explains to her cousin that old Goriot has settled his entire fortune on his two daughters, that the girls are anxious now to break all ties with their father, and that they obviously would not care to know anyone acquainted with their middle-class past. To make up for the snub her cousin has received at the hands of the de Restauds, Mme. de Beauséant suggests that Rastignac tell Goriot to invite his other daughter to her home, where she knows Delphine will be only too anxious to be received; Delphine will, in consequence, be grateful to Rastignac.

Eugène is presented to Delphine de Nucingen next night at the theater by his cousin, and soon receives an invitation to the Baroness' home. Before dinner he takes Delphine to a gambling house, where he wins a lot of money for her. She explains that her husband keeps her impoverished, and that she needs the sum to pay off the debt owing to an old lover of hers.

In the meantime Eugène is concerned about his own lack of funds. At the pension Vautrin has offered a solution. Their fellow boarder, Victorine Taillefer, disinherited by her wealthy father, is taken with Eugène, and Vautrin offers to arrange the murder of Victorine's brother so she can inherit a fortune; then

Eugène can marry her. Eugène has been hesitant about agreeing to the scheme, but now that he knows Delphine, he feels the need of money, and he agrees. Vautrin is busy explaining the details of the duel that is to finish off Taillefer, when Goriot comes in with the news that he and Delphine have set up better lodgings for Eugène.

Eugène, now sorry about the crime about to be enacted, tries to send word of warning by Goriot, but Vautrin has drugged their wine at dinner, and they both fall asleep. The next morning news comes that Taillefer has been mortally hurt in a duel, and Victorine rushes off to see her brother. It now turns out that one of the boarders is a police agent; she drugs Vautrin's coffee; when he collapses and is carried upstairs, the brand on his body proves he is the notorious criminal, Trompe-la-mort. The police arrive and take him away.

Goriot is planning to take a room over Eugène's new apartment. The two men are preparing to leave the pension when Delphine comes to announce that her husband's money is so involved in investments that he cannot settle an independent allowance on her, as Goriot's lawyer has planned. Anastasie also arrives to tell that her husband has discovered that she has sold the family jewels to pay her lover's debts; in revenge her husband demands complete control of her dower money. Eugène, overhearing the account, rushes into Goriot's room with a check forged in Vautrin's name to the amount she requires. She merely insults him for eavesdropping.

Goriot at last has no more strength to keep up with his daughters' wickedness, and Eugène, after a session with Delphine, finds him too ill to move from the pension. His last possessions are gone to pay for a gown for Anastasie. Goriot's illness does not prevent his daughters from attending Mme. de Beauséant's ball, and Eugène goes too.

The next day Goriot is in a serious condition. Neither daughter is in a hurry to come to him. When Eugène tries to borrow money for a decent burial from the two daughters, they both profess to be too ill to be seen. The following day Goriot is buried in a pauper's grave. The daughters do, however, send their empty carriages as a final tribute to their good father.

Père Goriot shows its author's style at its most direct and pitiless. It is one of his most brilliant achievements.

Cousin Bette

Many critics consider *La Cousine Bette* (1846) the pinnacle of Balzac's achievement as a Realist. Certainly, he never drew a more powerful indictment of vice than in this picture of nineteenth century Paris. The plot is rather more involved than in most of Balzac's Realistic novels. But the energy with which the characters are drawn, particularly the jealous Bette and the corrupt Hulot, gives the book unity, and makes it one of the most memorable of all novels. Balzac himself called it a "serious and terrible study of Parisian manners."

Bette is the poor cousin of the Baroness Adeline Hulot; she has been raised in Paris and treated very kindly by the Baron's family. She earns her living by making lace and embroidery, yet she is made to feel always welcome by Adeline. Ugly in appearance, Bette, now a spinster of thirty-five, only resents the kindness done her, and is envious of her cousin's station in life. But it is to her advantage to conceal her jealousy, and she manages to do so. Her closest attachment in the Hulot home is to Adeline's daughter, Hortense.

Bette is secretly in love with Count Wenceslas Steinbock, a Polish refugee with a great gift as a sculptor, who lodges in the same humble house as she does. In a fit of despondency Count Steinbock is ready to attempt suicide, but is saved by Bette. In gratitude the sculptor allows her to domineer over him in her uncouth, affectionate way.

Adeline's husband, Baron Hulot d'Ervy, sixty years of age, is one of the worst debauchees of Paris. He makes a religion out of the care of his personal appearance, and spends all he has on his pleasures, dyeing his hair and whiskers, corsets, and clothes. He has, indeed, become impoverished through these expenditures, even though his wife valiantly tries to keep up appearances. The Baron's inveterate enemy is Crevel, a retired perfumer: Hulot, by bestowing the major part of his money on Crevel's former mistress, has won her away from him.

Crevel calls on Adeline, one summer's day in 1838, to ask her to be his mistress. She rejects him. Crevel swears revenge on the Hulots. Because of Hulot's extravagance Hortense has no dowry, and hence no matrimonial prospects. Bette, in a moment of recklessness boasts of having a lover in Count Steinbock; Hortense has made her the butt of many jokes because she is a spinster. Hortense's curiosity about the sculptor is stirred.

That night Baron Hulot entertains his brother, Colonel Hulot, and the Colonel's son and daughter-in-law, Victorin and Célestine, at dinner; Célestine, Crevel's daughter, is fond of the Hulots. Later in the evening, the Baron escorts Bette home, goes to see his mistress, and finds that he has been superseded by a wealthy nobleman.

The Baron now undertakes to seduce the wife of a clerk in his employ, Marneffe. Hortense, in the meanwhile, has found the young sculptor, flatters him, and purchases one of his sculptures. He is invited to call at her home. Her parents think, all matters considered, that the young Count might be a good catch for their daughter.

Having arranged to have a rendezvous with Valérie Marneffe in Bette's rooms, the Baron moves the clerk and his wife to a more elaborate dwelling, and Bette goes along with them. Mme. Marneffe reveals to Bette that Hortense is to marry Count Steinbock. Bette, robbed of the thing she prizes most in the world, the sculptor's love, vows eternal vengeance on the Hulots. In this undertaking Valérie Marneffe promises her assistance.

The rest of the novel is largely devoted to the working out of Bette's hate. She first arranges a meeting between Valérie Marneffe, "the Circe of the story," and Crevel—for Marneffe himself is a disgusting creature who is willing to allow his wife complete freedom as long as he can profit from it. Next,

Bette has the Count imprisoned for debt, pretending to Hortense that he has decided to go back to Poland. Nobody guesses that Bette has been responsible for his incarceration. Her plot, however, fails; the Count wins his freedom through the good offices of friends.

Baron Hulot, always in debt, succeeds in raising some money; part of his method is stealing money through his position in the War Office, making Adeline's uncle the victim by sending him to Algiers. The Count and Hortense are now married, and the Hulots take a simpler dwelling, since the Baron needs plenty of money to keep Valérie Marneffe contented. That siren is, however, also having an affair at the same time with Crevel. But suddenly an old lover of hers, Baron Montès, turns up, and Hulot is not admitted to her apartment. Crevel, also indignant, tells Hulot that he has been sharing Mme. Marneffe. The two enemies make a truce, and go together to the lady's home. Valérie informs Crevel that she may consent to marry him if her husband should ever die in time; but to Hulot she says that their relationship is over. Eager for more conquests, Valérie urges Bette, in furtherance of her revenge against Hortense, to arrange Count Steinbock's coming to see her.

The Count, hard-pressed for cash, is counseled by Bette to borrow from Mme. Marneffe. He visits the latter and succumbs to her blandishments.

Valérie Marneffe now finds herself with child. She assures each of her lovers that he is the father. Hortense, convinced that it is her husband who has earned that doubtful honor, returns to her mother, and refuses her father, in a stormy scene, when he asks her to return to the Count. Bette sides with Hortense. Vowing that she can no longer abide the wickedness of Mme. Marneffe, Bette undertakes keeping house for old Colonel Hulot, with the intention of getting him to marry her, for he is the only man of means left in the Hulot family.

Adeline's uncle writes from Algiers that Hulot's peculations have been discovered, and that money will be needed to quash an investigation. Valérie, in the meantime, plots with her husband to advance Marneffe; in a fit of pretended outrage he intrudes upon Hulot and his wife (Hulot being, for the purpose, restored to her favors) with the police, and threatens prosecution unless he is promoted. Hulot is forced to comply. But the scandal in Algiers cannot be averted, and Adeline's uncle kills himself. Colonel Hulot, hearing at last of his brother's infamy, pays the needed sum to save what is left of the family honor, and dies soon after of a broken heart. Bette has triumphed in her revenge.

Hulot now seeks refuge with his earlier mistress, who gives him some money and her seamstress as a substitute mistress. He dwells in a shabby neighborhood under a false name. Victorin, who has inherited his mother's fine character, now begins to recoup slowly the family's fortunes. Mme. Marneffe's child dies at birth; her husband follows soon, and she decides to marry Crevel. Baron Montès in revenge deliberately infects them with a tropical disease, and the newlyweds die soon thereafter.

Adeline, now doing social work, comes upon her husband in the slums, and brings him home. Cousin Bette, suffering from tuberculosis, dies soon after his return. He reforms for a while. But one day Adeline finds her husband pursuing the new cook, a peasant girl. Adeline dies soon thereafter. The Baron leaves Paris and marries the cook.

One of the most remarkable portraits in this remarkable novel is that of Valérie, Mme. Marneffe. The great critic Taine said of her:

> Balzac loves his Valérie.... He does not labor to make her odious, but intelligible.... She is perfect of her kind. Balzac delights to paint her only for the sake of his own picture.... He details her gestures with as much pleasure as if he were her waiting-woman.... After a violent scene he pauses at a spare moment, and shows her idle, stretched on her couch like a cat, yawning and basking in the sun. Like a physiologist, he knows that...the beast of prey...only ceases to bound in order to sleep. But what bounds! She dazzles, fascinates; she defends herself..., refutes evidence, alternately humiliates and glorifies herself, rails, adores, demonstrates, changing a score of times her voice, her ideas, her tricks, and all this in one quarter of an hour.... To proportion her fortune to her vice, he leads her triumphantly through the ruin, death, or despair of twenty people, and shatters her in the supreme moment by a fall as terrible as her success.

Taine also made an interesting comparative study between her and Becky Sharp, the little devil who rules the world in Thackeray's *Vanity Fair*.

GUSTAVE FLAUBERT (1821–1880)

Many lovers of literature of the most discriminating taste would say that the greatest of all Realistic novels is, beyond question, *Madame Bovary*. The history of the composition of this amazing novel is in itself a fascinating story, for its author, Gustave Flaubert, was temperamentally an incorrigible Romantic, and another book, *The Temptation of Saint Anthony*, which he spent almost a lifetime planning, is one of the most completely Romantic works ever written.

In a manner of speaking, Flaubert's great novel was written in despite of his own character, and he confessed hating its composition. Everything about Flaubert's nature prepared him to be the perfect Romantic. He hated the city, avoided it whenever possible, and adored the country. He loved the past and the exotic, and early came to worship Chateaubriand. Gautier was a particular favorite of his, and he shared with the older man a love of color, of the exotic, and of the grotesque. He carried even further Gautier's hatred of the commonplace and the values of the solid middle-class citizen. Indeed, he was so much of an esthete in taste that it was he who evolved the theory of "le mot juste" (the perfect word), a theory that very few of his followers in

Realism have respected. In his judgment there is only one right way of expressing any given idea, and he was tireless as a writer in his search for the ultimate word for his need.

He was born of Norman stock in the old town of Rouen, the son of a doctor. The city is one of the most romantic in all France, but Gustave disliked it because of its middle-class life. At the age of nineteen he came to Paris to study law, but he detested the capital, and soon paid a visit to the Pyrenees and Corsica. In his early twenties he formed the plan of writing an elaborate work on the temptations of Saint Anthony, and in his own mind all he wrote thereafter was a kind of discipline for what he intended should be his masterpiece.

When he was twenty-five, after the deaths of his father and his dearly loved sister, he settled down at the family estate at Croisset, on the Seine, near Rouen to devote himself to writing. Thereafter with only one notable exception he spent most of his life there. At the age of twenty-eight, however, he indulged a great desire to see exotic lands, and traveled with Maxime du Camp to the Near East; Greece and Egypt particularly fascinated him. The next year (1850) he began working on *Madame Bovary*. He had written much, but had published practically nothing.

Madame Bovary

Flaubert spent six agonizing years over his great novel. Though his total output as a writer is small, his devotion to his task is almost comparable to Balzac's, even though the latter issued a flood of volumes. He worked slowly but incessantly. His rate of accomplishment was thirteen pages a month. "What a miracle it would be," he exclaimed, "if in one day I could write two pages!" But he would be satisfied with nothing less than perfection.

Madame Bovary first appeared in the *Revue de Paris* in installments in 1857. The government, which was trying to ingratiate itself with the middle class as being a pillar of respectability, brought action against the publisher and author for immorality. Flaubert had some trouble with the editor, who was anxious to delete passages. But he was acquitted by the court, and when the novel appeared in book form it was a great success. One can only wonder today at the stupidity of the charge against Flaubert, for there is not a word in the book that could offend anyone. It was felt by the government that he had outraged female modesty. What he actually had done was to draw an amazingly truthful portrait of a woman.

IMPORTANCE

There has never been a novel written with such perfect objectivity. "I want," Flaubert said, "my book to contain not a single agitated page." It is a faithful picture of all that the author detested in middle-class vulgarity; yet there is a complete avoidance of satire in the tone in which Flaubert has painted his picture.

It remained for the young poet Baudelaire to be almost the first to understand Flaubert's genius. In a study of the novel when it appeared, Baudelaire imagined himself to be the author, and saying to himself during its composition: "We must employ a style that is terse, vivid, subtle, and exact on a subject that is banal. We shall imprison the most burning and passionate feelings within the most commonplace intrigue. The most solemn utterances will come from the most imbecile mouths."

But the author also admitted that the portrait of Emma Bovary was a self-portrait. If he hated sham emotions in others, he also knew how easily sham emotions had risen in his own bosom. His picture of Emma was a species of self-laceration.

In his portrait of Madame Bovary, Flaubert did not intend to depict Every-woman, as some nineteenth century critics insinuated. It would be absurd, and a distortion of Flaubert's art, to extend Madame Bovary's characteristics to other members of her gender generally. Flaubert above all is interested in capturing here an original portrait, not a type.

Madame Bovary opens by introducing us to Charles Bovary as a boy at school, where he is a mediocre student who finally manages to pass his examinations in chemistry. His mother finds him a widow twice his age with a little money, and marries him off to her. Charles settles at Tostes as a doctor, henpecked by his ugly wife.

Called to a prosperous farmer's bedside over a minor matter, Charles meets the daughter, Emma Rouault. He begins to frequent the Rouault home, much to his wife's unhappiness. But his wife dies suddenly, and the emancipated young man begins to court Emma. He is accepted and they are married to the accompaniment of a lavish wedding feast on the Rouault farm.

Emma has been rendered a sentimentalist by her education, and is prepared for a life of ecstasy and thrills. Soon she finds her husband boring and prosaic. He, in his happiness, is utterly unaware of her dissatisfaction. They are invited to spend a weekend at the Marquis d'Andervilliers' estate; the Marquis is trying to gather goodwill before the coming elections to the Chamber of Deputies. At the estate Emma is enraptured by contact with the nobility, and is stirred by the symptoms of amorous intrigue that she senses going on around her. When a nobleman drops a cigar case, she secretes it, and treasures it as a memento of the great occasion.

Back in Tostes, she lives in a dream world of her own fantasy, grows increasingly listless and slovenly, and becomes ill. Charles, in alarm, decides to move to a larger town that he hopes will make life more interesting for her, and chooses Yonville l'Abbaye.

In Part Two, the Bovarys are flattered on their arrival at Yonville by the attentions of the inhabitants, particularly those of Homais the druggist, and

Léon, a young law clerk. From the beginning Emma and Léon are aware of a sympathy of interests; they are both sentimentalists and vaguely unhappy in provincial surroundings.

Emma's little girl, Berthe, is born, and put out to nurse. Charles's practice is not doing very well. Léon is soon infatuated with Emma, but lacks the courage to speak up. She, on her part, falls desperately in love with him, but suppresses all signs of her feelings. Instead, she overdoes the role of a good wife to Charles. Léon is convinced that she is unobtainable, and Emma, in her frustration, begins to hate Charles and his complacent happiness in their marriage. At length Léon, tiring of his unspoken love for Emma, decides after much postponing to go to Paris, as he had planned, to complete his studies. He leaves her without declaring himself. The memory of Léon, heightened by absence, becomes the center of Emma's unhappy thoughts.

Rodolphe Boulanger, who has recently purchased a large estate nearby, having occasion to visit the doctor, meets Emma. A brutal sensualist, a shrewd observer of women, he guesses that Emma is bored and pining for excitement. He decides to make her his mistress, wondering at the same time how he will eventually manage to get rid of her.

Yonville is chosen as the scene of an agricultural fair. During it, Rodolphe leads Emma to the deserted council room of the town hall; as they sit by the window, to the accompaniment of pompous political speeches and the awarding of prizes for livestock and fertilizers, he breaks down Emma's reserve with sentimental talk, and declares his passion for her. She lets him know that she is not unwilling to reciprocate. Rodolphe makes her wait six weeks, and then on a horseback ride, which Charles urges her to take with Rodolphe for her health's sake, she gives herself to her lover in the woods. Soon she is incautiously stealing out at dawn to go to Rodolphe's home to be with him.

Within half a year, her lover is tiring of her, gives up all his pretty speeches, and resumes his natural brutality of manner. Emma's disillusionment begins, and she even wishes she could love Charles. She is just seeking an excuse for becoming a good wife again, when the occasion seems to present itself. Homais talks Charles into performing an operation on Hippolyte, the club-footed stableboy of the inn, to make him normal. The operation is to bring fame to him and Yonville. Emma makes herself believe that perhaps her husband has great ability after all. Charles's incompetence results in a terrible case of blood poisoning; the dim-witted stableboy's leg must be amputated by another surgeon to prevent Hippolyte's death. Emma is so revolted at Charles's stupidity that she bitterly regrets having tried to love him.

She returns to Rodolphe's arms. She smothers him with love, and grows daily more abandoned and more beautiful. Now she presses her lover to elope with her, and in a fit of passion he agrees. The day they are to leave, however, he sends her a note telling her, hypocritically, that it would be too unjust to her that he accept such a sacrifice from her, and that he is going to exile himself for a while.

Emma becomes violently ill for months, and Charles nurses her tenderly. As a diversion he takes her, on her recovery, to Rouen to hear the opera. There, after three years, they meet Léon again by accident.

In Part Three Léon and Emma continue their relationship from where they had left it. Charles has insisted that Emma stay over a day in Rouen to enjoy the theater since Léon is willing to accompany her. She allows herself to be persuaded. After a sentimental talk with Léon, she arranges to meet him next morning at the Cathedral. Léon, now confident of a conquest, finally bustles Emma into a cab, ordering the driver to go wherever he pleases. In the carriage, during the course of the afternoon, Emma surrenders to Léon. When she returns to Yonville she learns that her father-in-law is dead.

In the meantime Emma has fallen into the habit of using the services of a scoundrel, Lheureux, as a broker for extravagant purchases and as a money-lender, without the knowledge of Charles. Lheureux, since her bills have not been paid, urges Emma to get power of attorney from Charles. She submits a form to her husband, and he suggests that to be sure of its legality they had better consult Léon. Thus Emma has an excuse to go to Rouen, and lives there for three days with her young lover, a kind of honeymoon.

Emma now coerces Charles into allowing her to go to Rouen once a week for piano lessons. This hoax enables the lovers to meet weekly. She begins to lie about everything in order to cover her movements. One day in Rouen Lheureux sees her leaving the hotel on Léon's arm. In a few days the old scoundrel is demanding more of his money, and he insinuates the idea that she use her power of attorney to sell some of Charles's inherited property through him. She is easily tricked into signing all kinds of documents, which are gradually building up a fortune for Lheureux. Emma becomes more and more reckless in her meetings with Léon and even calls for him at his office. By degrees he seems to be becoming her mistress, rather than she his, and is enthralled to her every wish.

One fatal day Homais the chemist pays a surprise visit to his old friend Léon in town; it happens to be Emma's day, and Homais takes up all Léon's time, and will not be shaken off. After that Emma becomes more and more dissatisfied with Léon, and, in consequence, more and more possessive. He begins to resent his subjection to her.

As her debts press more and more on her, Emma uses every device to raise more money, and borrows from everyone. Her lover is not able to keep up with her lavish tastes in town, and Emma defrays most of their expenses. His mother, having heard that he is having an affair with a married woman, begs his employer to warn him. That worthy does so, and Léon commences to find his love affair a possible obstacle to a good future in law. It is time to settle down, he reflects. His middle-class nature asserts itself, and romance suddenly loses its enchantment for him.

They are both tiring of each other, though Emma keeps up all appearances of sentiment. After a night's debauch in Rouen, Emma returns to Yonville to find that Lheureux has taken out a judgment against her with the right to seize on all her belongings. When she pleads with him for more time, he refuses. Charles is unaware of what is happening, as well as of the inventory made of all the Bovary possessions during his absence. Emma begs Léon's help, and even urges him to steal the sum needed from his employer. He shrinks from the crime, but promises to find some money for her by the next day.

Back in Yonville, Emma finds a bill publicly posted authorizing the sale of the Bovary furnishings. She appeals to the Yonville notary, an old lecher, who hints that he can help her if she will be his mistress. She recoils at the idea. For her the worst prospect is having to accept the forgiveness of Charles when he learns the facts of their financial ruin. Rather than face that, she tries tempting the old tax collector, who repulses her as though she were Satan. Léon, of course, does not appear with his promised help. Wild with despair, as a last resort she goes to Rodolphe, and like a prostitute reawakens his old passion in the hope that he will succor her. When she asks for 3,000 francs, he admits grimly that he hasn't got them. She leaves him in contempt for what she erroneously believes his miserliness.

With the courage of despair, she steals into Homais' shop, through the help of the chemist's assistant, who adores her. Plunging her hand into the jar of arsenic, she eats handfuls of it, and goes home. She writes a letter to Charles, and lies down to die. It is too late to save her by the time her husband understands that she is poisoned. Last rites are administered to her by the priest, and she dies.

After her funeral the chemist's boy weeps on her grave. Mme. Bovary Senior quarrels with Charles about Emma, and they break permanently. He, engulfed with bills, tries for a while to live up to Emma's extravagant ideas. Léon marries. Charles, corrupted by Emma from beyond the grave, is gradually forced to sell everything he owns. Eventually he comes upon Léon's letters, then Rodolphe's, and can no longer conceal from himself the truth. But he loves her still. He begins to degenerate in his habits, and spends all his time weeping over his loss of her. In a chance meeting with Rodolphe he says, "I don't blame you now." The next day Charles is found dead of a broken heart. In a few years his daughter Berthe is working in a cotton factory to earn her living, and Homais, the intellectual fraud, is granted the utmost of his dreams, the award of the Legion of Honor.

Flaubert as Romantic and Realist

The writing of *Madame Bovary* cost Flaubert his youth and his health. When he began it, he was young and physically stalwart. He came out of it, though still in his thirties, an ill, middle-aged man. But his arduous care over his writing continued. He had only one love affair of consequence in his life, the tempestuous one with Louise Colet, a woman who in her time was vastly overrated as a poet and who was essentially shallow and opportunistic. The fact that Flaubert saw through her pretenses and understood her mediocrity only made him more bitter. His life was that, as he said himself, of a monk of letters.

In 1859 he went to Carthage to gather material for his next book, and studied diligently at archeology so that he might write it with complete authority. He worked on *Salammbô* constantly until it appeared in 1862. That novel has been called the greatest and most beautiful failure in literature. In it there is a marvelous display of erudition, and the color and pageantry of ancient Carthage have been reproduced with dazzling brilliance. The love story that forms the plot is a very moving and romantic one. But, oddly enough, the characters fail to come to life: they are smothered by the magnificence of the detail and the jeweled opulence of the setting.

Everything about *Salammbô* is Romantic—the story, the setting, the idea— except the method. Here again we find Flaubert's perfect objectivity in revivifying for us a completely lost civilization with unerring historical accuracy.

On his next book Flaubert worked for seven years. *Sentimental Education* (*L'Éducation Sentimentale*) (1869) was intended to be the portrait of the male counterpart of Emma Bovary. But the novel has none of the virtues of Flaubert's masterpiece; its form is not tight and much that is related, though truthful, is dull. Here, it is to be observed, Flaubert comes close to the school of Naturalism that is to be found exemplified in the novels of Zola in France and Dreiser in America, where artistic selectivity is sacrificed to the "scientific accuracy" of the picture of life. In this respect *Sentimental Education* must be pronounced a success, for it recreates faithfully and vividly the epoch of the Revolution of 1848. But the dynamic power due to the superb artistry of *Madame Bovary* is lacking.

The year of the great catastrophe to France, 1870, saw the beginning of Flaubert's collapse as a man. Most of those dearest to him were dead. In 1872 his mother, to whom he had been very close, died. It is true that he enjoyed, however, the literary friendship of some eminent writers: George Sand, Daudet, the de Goncourt brothers, Zola, and Turgenev, his letters to George Sand being of particular interest.

At last in 1874 his life's ambition, *The Temptation of Saint Anthony* (*La Tentation de Saint-Antoine*), was published. It is a book, says Saintsbury, which deserves "to rank at the head of its class—that of the fantastic romance." It has been compared to a wonderful opium dream, and the display of learning is once more astounding. With it the insatiable Romantic in Flaubert was at last placated.

In 1877 appeared a remarkable collection of stories, *Three Tales* (*Trois Contes*), showing both sides of its author's temperament. *A Simple Heart* (*Un Coeur Simple*) is Flaubert's most deeply humane work, a movingly realistic account of the faithfulness of an old servant. *Hérodias,* on the other hand, is akin to *Salammbô* in its Oriental splendor; it was the source for Oscar Wilde's *Salomé*, which tells the same story in a very diluted form. *The Legend of Saint Julien l'Hospitalier* (*La Légende de Saint-Julien l'Hospitalier*) is in Flaubert's erudite vein.

Flaubert's last years were spent on an unfinished satire, *Bouvard and Pécuchet* (1881), a depressing book to read, the purpose of which was to show how universal mediocrity is. But its author's faculties were too much deteriorated by that time to do justice to the subject. It presented just such another opportunity as *Madame Bovary* to expose the middle-class values that were anathema to Flaubert, but nothing can be more unlike than the power of the earlier work and the feebleness of this last.

In the last analysis, Flaubert is likely to be remembered as the author of one book, but it is a book that has no rivals in the nineteenth century.

GEORGE SAND (LUCILE-AURORE DUPIN) (1804–1876)

Lucile-Aurore Dupin, who wrote under the name of George Sand, is a novelist who defies classification. Perhaps the sanest view of her work is that taken by the critic Rocheblave when he said: "Don't seek in the work of George Sand for a school...; here is just a woman who observed her own life, and gave it expression.... She wrote as she breathed."

From that point of view she belongs prominently, of course, among the Romantics. She has often been described with justice as a follower of Rousseau in the extent to which she made literary capital out of her experiences; like him she had a highly emotional nature. She possessed, too, more than a little of the Chateaubriand *mal du siècle* and a Byronic spirit of revolt against convention. On the other hand her interest in the psychological novel and her attacks on social institutions set her apart from the purely Romantic novelist.

Her father's mother was the daughter of the famous Marshal Saxe and her father himself was a brilliant officer in Napoleon's army; but he had married a common woman of loose life. Aurore's childhood was in consequence disturbed by a constant quarrel between her arrogant grandmother and vulgar mother. At sixteen she married a stupid country squire, Baron Dudevant. After a few years, she could no longer bear the restraint of living under the domination of her coarse and faithless husband. She left him and went to Paris to live the life of a bohemian. For years she had a series of intense love affairs with some of the most noted men of her times: first Jules Sandeau, the dramatist, with whom she collaborated on her first book, *Rose et Blanche*, and because of whom she took the name of Sand; later with Alfred de Musset and with Chopin, to mention only a few. In her relationship with men of greater genius than her own, she had the remarkable faculty of ruining their peace of mind, while coming out unscathed herself from the experience. Her reputation grew with the years, not without justice; for, though she wrote without effort, her novels do not lack quality. Among her close friends she numbered Sainte-Beuve, Dumas *fils*, Liszt, the great painter Delacroix, and Flaubert. Her correspondence with the author of *Madame Bovary* is today as interesting as anything she ever wrote.

After 1839 she returned to the country of her childhood at Nohant, where she soon won the reputation of a solid citizen and, later, an indulgent grandmother.

Her novels are of four kinds: from 1832 to 1836 she wrote novels dealing with *la femme incomprise* (the misunderstood woman), like those of Mme. de Staël, but involving stories of great passion—*Indiana* (1831), *Valentine* (1832). *Lélia* (1834); from 1840 to 1848 she wrote novels of a socialistic bent, often tinctured with mysticism—*Spiridion* (1840), *Consuelo* (1842), *Le Meunier d'Angibault* (*The Miller of Angibault*) (1845); from 1848 to 1860, she wrote chiefly pastoral romances—*La Mare au Diable* (*The Haunted Pool*) (1848), *La Petite Fadette* (*Little Fadette*) (1848), *Les Maîtres Sonneurs* (*The Master Bellringers*) (1852); from 1860 to her death, miscellaneous novels without her earlier emphases—*Le Marquis de Villemer* (1860). This is but a small sampling among the hundred and more books she authored.

The novels of the first period particularly assert the doctrine of free love, which she herself practiced, and which caused a great scandal at the height of the Romantic movement (*Indiana, Lélia*). Having absorbed much political radicalism and some religious mysticism, she exploited these points of view during her second period. They show a broad humanitarianism, particularly in *Le Meunier d'Angibault*, in which, as has been observed, a great deal of arson is carried on so that at the end a workingman can be free to marry a wealthy widow. She was an enthusiast for the Revolution of 1848 and edited the *Bulletins de la République*; but the coup d'état that followed disillusioned her with politics, and prompted her change of interest to pastoral themes.

It is precisely in her pastoral works, where she has no thesis to promulgate, no reform to advocate, that she is at her best. She was very familiar with rustic life from her childhood days, and though her characters are somewhat idealized, she writes about the country with a great deal of charm. It is this part of her work that is most enduring because of the authentic spirit of poetry that hovers over her pages. *La Mare au Diable* and *La Petite Fadette* contain unforgettable pictures of the beauty of rural France, and her psychological insight into the lives of its simple folk is admirable.

IMPORTANCE

George Sand's worst faults proceed from a fundamental superficiality in her imbibing from her friends their political and social ideas, and her habit of writing by, as she herself put it, "turning on the faucet." But she is important in the history of the social novel. Also, she made literary contributions of real value to her country in her pastoral novels, written with tenderness and deep sympathy for her subject.

PROSPER MÉRIMÉE (1803–1870)

IMPORTANCE

Mérimée, one of the finest stylists in French prose, was the earliest writer to compose under the influence of Stendhal. Choosing material that is often Romantic in the extreme, he wrote in a manner coldly detached and ironically objective, in the best Realist tradition.

Though a contemporary of the leaders of French Romanticism, Mérimée had little sympathy for their ideas, political or literary. He had English blood in him, and more than a little of Anglo-Saxon reserve in his make-up. In his twenties Mérimée proved with two clever hoaxes how easy it was to turn out the kind of Romanticism the public wanted: *Théâtre de Clara Gazul* (*Plays of Clara Gazul*) (1825), purporting to be plays in the native syle by a nonexistent Spanish actress; and *La Guzla*, an anagram of the same name, which pretended to be a collection of verse and prose from Illyria. Both were eminently successful. It was with his novel, *Chronique du Règne de Charles IX* (*Chronicle of the Reign of Charles IX*) (1829) that he became known in the world of letters. This novel has been called the triumph of the historical school of novelists. But unlike Sir Walter Scott and Hugo, Mérimée has the great virtue of conciseness and brevity in his descriptions; here, too, instead of the rhapsodic tone of the Romantic school, we find the calm aloofness of the Stendhal tradition. It has been admired as the best-considered historical novel of its period in France, both for its excellent characterization of historical persons and its calm firm style.

Mérimée now enjoyed for some years the life of a Parisian gentleman, and in 1830 went for a visit to Spain. There he became on close terms with the family of the future Empress of France, Eugénie. He had enough of a fortune to be able to write as he pleased. Fundamentally disliking democratic ways, he took kindly to the Second Empire, and was an important adjunct to the court of Napoleon III, particularly because of his friendship with the Empress; he also served as Senator during this period.

Brunetière has aptly described Mérimée's Romantic air up to this point in his career as being the product of a man "who pretended to believe in Romanticism...to be able the better to ridicule it." In the *Vase Etrusque* (*The Etruscan Vase*) (1830) and the *Double Méprise* (*The Double Mistake*) (1833) Mérimée discarded Romantic pretenses altogether—both tales being frankly works of sophistication. By now his reputation was made, chiefly through the series of stories which he issued between 1829 and 1840 in the *Revue des Deux Mondes* and the *Revue de Paris*. Among the most celebrated of these are *L'Enlèvement de la Redoute* (*The Siege of the Redoubt*), *La Partie de Trictrac* (*The Backgammon Match*), *Venus d'Ille*, and *Matteo Falcone*. The last-named is a calm presentation of violent passions in Corsica, the kind of tale in which Mérimée was to achieve his two greatest triumphs: *Colomba* (1840) and *Carmen* (1847).

Carmen, having furnished the text for Bizet's immortal opera, is too well known to require comment; the story of the heartless, tempestuous gypsy is the best of its kind ever told. *Colomba* is of the same species, a story of Corsican vendetta, and possesses all the fine restraint characteristic of Mérimée's prose at its very best—a medium which serves to underscore the fury of its contents by its very coldness.

Mérimée is also important to French letters for having been one of the first to introduce Russian literature to his country. He translated, among other notable works, Pushkin's *Queen of Spades*, Gogol's *The Inspector-General*, and pieces of Turgenev. He left, too, a vast amount of interesting correspondence.

6
THE NATURALISTS AND OTHER EXPERIMENTERS

After Flaubert's superb accomplishment in *Madame Bovary*, the Realist movement underwent a new and important variation. Zola, the leader of this development, claimed descent from Balzac (whom he described as having been a student of the physiology) and Stendhal (whom he described as a student of the psychology of "human documents"). This newer tendency of Realism, which flourished in the works of Zola, the de Goncourt brothers, Guy de Maupassant, and (in a quite different manner) Alphonse Daudet, has been recognized as constituting in effect a new school, the school of Naturalism.

Zola, at any rate, claimed for it a new method. The distinguishing trait of this school is the rejection of the "art" of the Romantics and earlier Realists like Flaubert; instead these writers stipulate for a "scientific" method. The de Goncourt brothers described themselves, for instance, as setting up a "medico-literary clinic" of the life of men and women.

Certain attributes of the Naturalist school are clearly decipherable: these writers tend to emphasize the more brutal aspects of existence; their manner of presenting such material is intentionally often revolting; they refuse to accept ideals as a part of human character; they make small pretense to weaving a plot in the older sense of the word; they are interested in presenting only what they believe to be the facts of a life; they do not recognize the existence of romantic love; they believe themselves to be applying to their books the scientific method; they often present many facts connected with the operation of a certain trade or industry as part of their "documentation"; they maintain an attitude of pessimism towards life; and philosophically they are deterministic.

Naturalism has had a powerful effect upon late-nineteenth century and twentieth century literature, particularly in the United States. The differences between Realism and Naturalism can be seen in contrasting among twentieth century American novelists the realism of Willa Cather with the naturalism of Theodore Dreiser and James T. Farrell.

Generally speaking, Naturalism has had the great virtue of honesty and intellectual integrity. But it has had very considerable failings too. By denying the presence of artistry in writing, it has banished one of the greatest sources of pleasure in literature—but, of course, some Naturalists would deny the rights of readers to pleasure too. Also, taking into account the actual productions of this school, we must charge its writers with being blinder to life than they have known, for the picture they give of it is almost uniformly gloomy and depressing. Zola said that wherever he looked he could see only the beast in man, and that has been the whole bent of Naturalism. According to the Naturalist, the pleasure to be derived from reading such works is in the excitement created by the author's revelation of the ultimate truth about mankind.

Yet there are many clear-eyed people, guiltless of any glib optimism towards life, who feel that not everything about men and women is seamy, not everything revolting. If the latter are right, then the Naturalists have not presented anything like the real truth about life after all. Indeed, this realization is becoming so strong and the term "Naturalism" becoming so much less than admired, that many practitioners in that school are objecting vehemently to the term, and are insisting that their work be called "realistic" rather than "naturalistic."

ÉMILE ZOLA (1840–1902)

Émile Zola was born in Paris, the son of a Frenchwoman and an Italian engineer. The boy spent a number of years at Aix, which figures in his novels constantly as Plassans. First at Paris and later at Marseilles Zola tried in vain to procure a bachelor's degree. After several years of extreme poverty, he obtained a position as clerk in the Hachette publishing house in Paris (1862). His first book, *Contes à Ninon* (*Tales for Ninon*) (1864) made some impression, and within a year or so he decided to devote himself to writing as a profession.

Zola began to contribute a series of articles on his literary theories for the periodical *L'Événement* and issued his first novel, *La Confession de Claude*. His first important novel, *Thérèse Raquin*, appeared in 1867, a gruesome but powerful work.

He now began to plan a long series of novels to supplement the *Human Comedy* of Balzac; his intention was to give a picture of French life under the Second Empire just as Balzac had given one for the earlier decades of the nineteenth century. His method was inspired by Claude Bernard's *Introduction to Experimental Medicine* (1865); he would use the laboratory technique on his experiences and observations. The claim, of course, is more fanciful than actual, for no one has yet explained how a novel could be written in that fashion. The very nature of literary composition is creative, no matter how analytical the writer is concerning his characters.

The *Rougon-Macquart* Series

Nor did the greatest of the Naturalists operate with the perfect objectivity which he claimed for his method. He did not, like Maupassant, merely observe and record. He had a "scientific" theory to demonstrate: the theory of heredity. The *Rougon-Macquart* series, which runs to twenty volumes, and which purports to trace the "natural and social history of a family under the Second Empire," is a study of the devastating effects of their heredity upon the descendants of the alcoholic Macquart and the subnormal degenerate Adelaïde Fouqué of the town of Plassans. It should be needless to point out what short work modern psychology would make of the scientific validity of the vast undertaking.

The first novel in the series was *La Fortune des Rougons* (*The Rougon Family*) (1871) and the last *Doctor Pascal* (1892). The twenty novels record the life stories of all kinds of men and women: a city worker, a farmer, a miner, a soldier, a scholar, a prostitute, an artist, a public official.

La Fortune des Rougons: *La Fortune des Rougons* has as its central character Adelaïde Fouqué, daughter of an insane man. In 1786 she marries Rougon, a stupid gardener, and bears him a son, Pierre. Her husband dies, and she bears two illegitimate children, Antoine and Ursule, to the smuggler Macquart, an incorrigible drunkard. Antoine becomes an alcoholic too, and marries a drink-loving marketwoman. Ursule marries a decent workingman, Mouret. Pierre by underhanded means procures control of the family property and sells it; he marries a merchant's daughter and through her is able to enter an old established business house.

La Curée: *La Curée* (*The Quarry*, translated into English as *Rush for the Spoil*) (1872) deals with Pierre's son Aristide, who has changed his name from Rougon to Saccard. The setting is the business world of Paris. Aristide's elder brother Eugène helps him accumulate a fortune through his own political career. The new boulevards are being laid out in Paris by Haussmann, and Aristide buys up property that will be extremely valuable, in this fashion becoming very rich.

La Conquête de Plassans: *La Conquête de Plassans* (*The Conquest of Plassans*) (1874) is laid again at Plassans. Marthe Rougon is married to Ursule's descendant, François Mouret. The Abbé Faujas manages to get Marthe under his thumb, and François, on the pretense that he is insane, is confined to an asylum. He does become insane there. Determined to escape, he manages to get free, sets fire to his home, and destroys the Abbé and himself in the process.

Le Ventre de Paris: *Le Ventre de Paris* (translated as *The Markets of Paris*) (1875) deals with Lisa Macquart, a marketwoman. The novel is a study of the central marketplace in Paris.

La Faute de l'Abbé Mouret: *La Faute de l'Abbé Mouret* (*The Transgression of the Abbé Mouret*) (1875) is a study of the religious life and the mystical temperament. Serge Mouret is the victim of a terrible passion. In its depiction Zola is at his best. After falling in his battle against temptation, the Abbé Mouret repents, and even officiates at the funeral of the woman he adored.

Son Excellence Eugène Rougon: *Son Excellence Eugène Rougon* (*His Excellency Eugène Rougon*) (1876) is centered around the court of Napoleon III. His Prime Minister, Eugène Rougon, is the central character in this study of politics.

L'Assommoir: *L'Assommoir* (*The Dram Shop*) (1877) is one of the most powerful in the cycle. It is laid in Paris, and undertakes to show the ruinous effects of the neighborhood dispensary of drink upon the working class. Antoine's daughter Gervaise is the central character. Gervaise is already pregnant when fourteen and is driven from her father's home. She and her lover go to Paris. After she bears him another child he deserts her.

Later she marries Coupeau, a tinsmith, and seems on the road to happiness. But the inheritance of viciousness and the poverty they cannot overcome corrupt their life, and they degenerate into the worst kind of wretchedness.

We here have Naturalism at its most pessimistic. But this was the novel that brought its author fame and fortune.

Une Page d'Amour: *Une Page d'Amour* (*A Love Episode*) (1878) is a study of woman's passion. The heroine is Ursule's daughter, Hélène. She is torn between mother love and a love for the doctor who has saved her child's life. She gives herself to him. But the child is waiting for her at an open window, and catches its mortal illness.

Nana: *Nana* (1880) is a study of the prostitute, a daughter of Gervaise and Coupeau. Educated in the streets of Parisian slums, Nana leads a vile life until her beauty attracts the notice of a theatrical producer who specializes in lewd spectacles on the boards. Without a shred of theatrical talent, she becomes a great success because her physical provocativeness enchants the men in the audience. She makes money but spends more than she can earn.

Utterly without scruples, she cheats all her lovers, and runs through the fortunes they squander on her. They all end in financial, physical, or spiritual ruin through her. Still young, she dies a miserable death when she contracts smallpox.

This novel, because of its subject matter, has been the most frequently reprinted of all of Zola's works, although it is not the equal of *L'Assommoir* or *Germinal*. It would seem, therefore, that, after all, the charge that Zola's popularity proceeds less from his own great moral earnestness than from the viciousness that he has chosen for his subject matter, is a fairly just one.

Pot-Bouille: *Pot-Bouille* (*Piping Hot*) (1882) turns to study the middle class. The hero is Octave, the son of François Mouret, the incendiary who had destroyed himself with his home. The setting is in a typical middle-class flat, and the relations between the servants and their employers are fully dealt with.

Au Bonheur des Dames: *Au Bonheur des Dames* (*The Ladies' Paradise*) (1883) is a study of life in a huge department store. Octave, hero of the preceding novel, has married the widow Hedouin. On her death he becomes owner of the store. Zola treats us to a detailed account of the way a department store is run, how smaller shops fight for their lives against the tentacles of the large owner, and how Octave makes a success out of his business.

La Joie de Vivre: *La Joie de Vivre* (translated as *How Jolly Life Is*) (1884) finds Zola, in despite of his theory, writing a novel that approaches something like real tragic grandeur. The daughter of Lisa, the marketwoman (of *Le Ventre de Paris*) is Pauline Quenu, one of the few truly admirable women Zola has drawn. A human being of great personal dignity, she is capable of sacrifice. First she surrenders her lover to her friend, then accepts their child after they separate, and rears it tenderly as though it were her own. She is alone, however, in her quality, for everyone else is self-seeking and complaining, while she makes a life for herself without help or egotism.

Germinal: *Germinal* (originally translated as *Master and Man*) (1885) is one of Zola's best achievements, a study of miners. The son of Gervaise, Étienne Lanier, Nana's brother, works in the mines. He is a socialist, and leads a strike against the operators because of the shamefully low wages and excessive fines imposed on the miners. He is moderate in his demands and advises the miners to use discretion. But starvation causes the workers to run riot. There is a desperate clash, and a number of miners are killed. He is blamed for the catastrophe, and sentenced to deportation. The miners, after their bitter struggle, are as badly off as ever.

L'Oeuvre: *L'Oeuvre* (*The Masterpiece*) (1886) is a study of the artist's life. The hero is a brother of Étienne's and Nana's, Gervaise's illegitimate son, Claude Lanier, a painter. He is an artist of great vision and ambition, but he lacks the technique to express his great conceptions. In a fit of despair, unable to finish a picture, he hangs himself.

La Terre: *La Terre* (*Earth*) (1888) caused the greatest scandal of any of Zola's novels. It has been called "the climax of unnecessary obscenity." The picture is of the peasantry at their most degraded and avaricious. In the struggle for acquiring land, hatred makes the peasants behave on a subhuman level. In the end Jean Macquart's wife is murdered by her own sister.

La Rêve: *La Rêve* (*The Dream*) (1888), by way of reaction, was the author's attempt to prove that it was not necessary for him to deal with vulgar subjects only. The heroine is appropriately named Angélique; she is the illegitimate daughter of Sidonie Rougon, and is raised in a foundling home.

Later she is adopted by a family that is occupied with the making of vestments for the church. A child that lives in a world of fantasy, she falls in love with the painter of the church's windows. Her lover is the son of the bishop. The latter, who had entered the church after the death of his wife, objects to the young man's marrying a girl of humble station.

But he relents when Angélique is dying and he is called to administer the last rites of the church to her. The girl dies united to her sweetheart. This idyllic story has nothing in common with the rest of the series; but one is forced to admit, by comparison, that it was wiser for Zola to adhere to his revolting subjects.

La Bête Humaine: La Bête Humaine (*Human Brutes*) (1890) is a study of life on the railroads. The hero is Jacques Lanier, an engineer, who has inherited the streak of insanity running in his family. In his case it takes the terrible form of a lust to murder women. There are many exciting scenes in this book.

L'Argent: L'Argent (*Money*) (1891) is a study of the stock exchange and the complexities of financial dealings. Aristide Saccard (né Rougon), the hero of *La Curée*, has lost his fortune. He organizes a company for floating various financial dealings in the East. After all kinds of nefarious manipulations, his "Banque Universelle" becomes the most powerful on the exchange. Millionaires vie with poor widows to pour their money into its shares. For a while Saccard is fabulously wealthy. Then comes the unification of forces among his enemies. He is ruined along with all his investors.

La Débâcle: La Débâcle (*The Downfall*) (1892) is one of the very finest in the *Rougon-Macquart* cycle. It is a truly brilliant study of the Franco-Prussian War and the terrible Siege of Paris. Here the setting is military, but the great national issues of the time are intermingled with a powerful love story. Jean Macquart is a corporal in the French forces; his close friend is Maurice Levasseur, a lawyer who has enlisted under him. Macquart is in love with Levasseur's sister, Henriette, whose husband is killed at Sedan. During the siege Macquart kills Levasseur without knowing who he is. This catastrophe makes marriage between Henriette and Macquart impossible. The latter is determined to devote the rest of his life to help build a new France.

Docteur Pascal: Docteur Pascal (1892) concludes the cycle, and is one of the best. Pierre Rougon's son, Pascal, has made a study of the history of his family, and brings the offspring up to date on his records. Jean Macquart is married again, and heads a healthy family. Octave is doing very well as a merchant. Saccard is an editor. Eugène is in the national Legislature. Adelaïde Fouqué is insane. The Doctor understands the symptoms of his own disease, and records an hourly diagnosis of it. When he feels that the end is coming, he puts the finishing touches to his genealogical account. His niece, however, he knows is to bear him an illegitimate child, whose destiny is still unpredictable.

Other Novels of Zola

After *L'Assommoir* Zola became one of the most successful as well as the most-argued-about, writers in France. When the *Rougon-Macquart* cycle was completed, he launched a new series on the influence of the clergy, entitled *Trois Villes* (*Three Cities*): *Lourdes, Rome, Paris* (1894–1898). His last novels were intended as another cycle, *Les Quatres Évangiles* (*The Four Gospels*); *Fécondité* (*Fruitfulness*), against race suicide, and *Travail* (*Work*) were issued before his death; *Vérité* (*Truth*), on the Dreyfus case, was published after his death; and *Justice*, though planned, was never written.

The Dreyfus Case

In connection with the Dreyfus Affair, it would be unjust to Zola's memory to omit reference to the noble role he played in it, and because of which Anatole France called him "a moment of the conscience of man." For, whatever one may think of Zola's novels, there can only be admiration for the integrity of the man.

Captain Alfred Dreyfus, the son of a Jewish manufacturer, had served in the French artillery with great honor, when he was charged in 1894 with the grave accusation of selling documents of military value. The evidence was an intercepted letter. Dreyfus was convicted on falsified evidence, stripped of his military honors and rank, and sentenced to life imprisonment on Devil's Island. At the public ceremony, the mob yelled for his death. Dreyfus answered in a clear voice: "I am innocent. Some day you shall know the truth. Long live France!"

Three years later the incriminating letter was definitely established as having been penned by a notorious blackguard, Esterhazy. But Dreyfus continued to suffer terrible hardships in his prison. The high officials of the French military were interested only in saving their face and refused to reconsider their verdict. The whole nation was stirred up, and the rest of the world agitated. In France families were torn asunder as members took sides. Zola, at the height of his fame, was convinced early of Dreyfus's innocence, and with the deliberate intention of inviting a libel suit so that the whole matter would have to be aired publicly in the courts, he wrote a now-celebrated letter to the newspaper *Aurore* on January 13, 1898. Because a number of its paragraphs begin with the phrase *J'accuse* (*I accuse*), the document has come to be known by that name.

In his letter Zola named the army officers whom he held responsible for the injustice—one for "having been the diabolical agent of the judicial error,"—another for being an accomplice "probably through weak-mindedness,"—another of having concealed the proof of Dreyfus's innocence "to save the face of the General Staff,"—one of being an accomplice "through religious prejudice," and another through "esprit de corps,"—and still another of composing a report that is "an imperishable monument of naïve effrontery." Zola concluded with the admission that he was fully aware that he was exposing himself to the Libel Laws, and expressed a fond wish to be subpoenaed to the court of appeals.

For *J'accuse* Zola was immediately brought to trial, on the charge of criminal libel. Riots broke out all over the country. During the trial Zola and his friends were in danger of mob violence. Zola was not allowed to bring in any evidence about the Dreyfus case during this mockery of a trial, and he was sentenced to a year's imprisonment and a large fine. On the advice of friends, he escaped to England.

During Zola's exile, one of the culprits admitted forging crucial documents that had incriminated Dreyfus and committed suicide. Esterhazy also admitted his guilt. In 1899, having been a victim on Devil's Island for six years, Dreyfus was brought back and "pardoned" for "treason under extenuating circumstances." But it was not until July 21, 1906 that he was fully exonerated, reinstated in the army, and decorated on the same spot on which he had been degraded. By then Zola had been dead for four years. He had never met the man for whom he had fought so well.

The *Soirées*

Zola, in addition to his novels, left some volumes of other works, of which the most significant is the *Soirées de Médan* (1880). He had acquired a piece of property in the suburb of Médan, and from there was launched a series of pieces by some of the leaders of the new Naturalistic Movement, of whom the most important, excluding himself, were Maupassant and Huysmans.

IMPORTANCE

A final estimate of Zola's value as a writer is still not possible, for he is as much adored by our own Naturalists as he is underprized by the Romantics and esthetes. He had considerable power and little taste; his prose has energy but no grace or quality. He can be more boring, page by page, than almost any other writer of equal fame. Yet, one is puzzled in making a final judgment. If Zola does bore one page by page, he usually succeeds in having impressed one at the conclusion of a novel. The cardinal question here is whether it is justifiable that a reader submit to being bored during the reading of a long novel so that he may be impressed by the sum total when he has finished. The answer to that question would probably afford the answer to the question of the worth of much twentieth century writing.

GUY DE MAUPASSANT (1850–1893)

Guy de Maupassant was a follower and admirer of both Flaubert and Zola; the former took him under his wing and the latter admitted him to the Médan circle. His private life, indeed, might very well have made him a candidate as a subject for one of Zola's "documented" novels. A Norman by birth, like his great predecessor, the author of *Madame Bovary*, he inherited both a powerful physique and the germs of a mental disease. His earlier years are pleasant to record: his passion for the water and for fishing as a lad; his acknowledging himself willingly as Flaubert's disciple at the age of twenty-three, after having already seen service in the war; his living a carefree outdoor life, and his love of secluded country places. In the meantime he was serving in various smaller governmental posts. Then, when he decided to devote himself to writing, and worked at it at a prodigious rate, he began to lose his health and his cheerfulness. He began to grow melancholy, engaged on a course of violent dissipation, took opium and hashish, traveled for his health, and was suddenly stricken insane in the Riviera. A year and one-half later he was dead of general paralysis, at the premature age of forty-three.

In the field of the short story he became France's most preeminent writer. His first tale, "Boule de Suif" (*Ball of Tallow*) already shows him a Naturalist; it was published in the *Soirées de Médan* (1880), a collection of pieces, already mentioned, by Zola, Huysmans, and other naturalistic authors. The story was noted, and much admired. It was at this point in his life that Maupassant determined to live by his pen. Practically all of his works were composed during the next ten years.

Maupassant accepted the doctrine of *le mot juste*, which Flaubert had formulated, and his style owes much to the latter. He also wrote with such perfect objectivity that he seems to belong more to the Naturalists than to the Realists. Like Zola's, his subjects are largely somber and coarse, and his greatest preoccupation is with the more brutal aspects of sex.

The year of the *Médan Soirées* (1880) Maupassant issued a volume of poetry *Des Vers* (*Some Verses*), naturalistic in tone, with the result that the public prosecutor took measures to have the book suppressed. Flaubert, who had had a similar experience with *Madame Bovary*, sent him a letter of congratulation. No one, however, thinks of Maupassant as a poet.

It is astonishing to observe that his first story, "Boule de Suif," finds its author in full command of his medium, and showing to perfection his best qualities as a writer. A volume of stories, *La Maison Tellier* (*The Tellier House*) (1881) followed; next came *Mademoiselle Fifi* (1883). The same year appeared his first novel, *Une Vie* (*A Life*) (1883); the plot is the life story of an unhappy woman, unlucky in her husband and her son, meeting misery at every turn of events, ruined of all hope of joy in life, vainly clinging at the end to a hope in her grandson. This book was threatened with prosecution, too, with the natural result that it and its author became more celebrated than ever. Between 1883 and 1884 Maupassant published *Clair de Lune, Miss*

Harriet, Les Soeurs Rondoli (*The Rondoli Sisters*), and *Yvette*. In 1885 he published three more collections of tales, *Contes et Nouvelles* (*Tales and Novelettes*), *Monsieur Parent*, and *Contes du Jour et Nuit* (*Tales of Day and Night*). In the same year appeared one of his most elaborate works, *Bel-Ami* (1885), a novel telling the success of a loathsome scoundrel who goes far because of his good looks.

Volumes of tales continued to flow from his pen, but it was at this time that symptoms of his fatal malady began first to appear. The novel, *Mont-Oriol* (1887) is equal to his best, but *Le Horla* (1887) contains such gruesomeness that it is likely that Maupassant realized the dreadful fate awaiting him. Nevertheless *Le Rosier de Madame Husson* (*Mme. Husson's Rosebush*) (1888) finds the author at his best in a collection of tales running over with Rabelaisian humor. The series of novels which now followed are examples of Maupassant's technique at its best: *Pierre et Jean* (1888), *Fort comme la Mort* (*Stronger than Death*) (1889), and *Notre Coeur* (*Our Heart*) (1890)—all touched with a compassion unknown to his earlier work. This same tragic sentiment is to be found in what is practically his last important volume of tales, *Inutile Beauté* (*Useless Beauty*) (1890).

Some of Maupassant's predominant themes and narrative techniques can be seen clearly in his best-known short story, "The Necklace" (1884). This is the story of Mathilde Loisel, a pretty young woman who is deeply dissatisfied with her lower-middle-class existence and marriage to a junior clerk. In a constant state of resentment over the things and social position she doesn't have, Mathilde begins to avoid more fortunate friends, especially Mme. Forestier, a former classmate.

When her husband brings home an invitation to a party at the Ministry of Public Instruction, Mathilde plunges to new depths of despair over what to wear. Her husband gives her 400 francs, which he had been saving for a new gun, so that she can buy a new gown. With that problem resolved, Mathilde frets about her lack of jewelry. Her husband suggests that she borrow some from Madame Forestier. Mathilde gets up the nerve to ask Madame Forestier for the loan of a lovely necklace, apparently studded with diamonds, and Forestier gladly complies.

At the party, Mathilde's dreams of beauty, status, and showy wealth all seem to come true. She is noticed, complimented, and lionized. Upon returning home, however, she finds that she has lost the necklace. She and her husband search for it frantically, but to no avail. After several delaying tactics while they figure out what to do, they end up buying a replacement at the enormous cost of 36,000 francs. To raise this money, they must liquidate an inheritance and take on several crushing loans. But the necklace is returned to Madame Forestier.

The heavy burden of debt wears upon Mathilde and her husband both physically and spiritually. Under the grind of domestic labor, Mathilde loses her youthful beauty. Years pass, and at last the debt is paid in full—but at the expense of a life spent in endless, arduous work and worry.

Mathilde, now a harried hag, happens upon the still-beautiful Mme. Forestier one day on the boulevarde and resolves to tell her about the necklace episode. In a mixture of pity, horror, and disbelief, Mme. Forestier takes Mathilde's hands and tells her the awful truth: the necklace was fake jewelry, hardly worth 500 francs.

Maupassant revels in such ironies: Those who have little yearn to have much, but fail to recognize that those who have much often have less than it would appear. Entire lives are spent in fruitless efforts to create appearances and keep others from the truth. We learn, often too late, that we have spent ourselves, body and soul, pursuing false goals. Facing the painful but undeniable truths of our existence, Maupassant suggests, is vastly preferable to a life of lies, most of them told over and over to ourselves.

Soon after that he became subject to spells in which his reason gave way. His behavior grew increasingly more unusual, and in January 1862 he tried to commit suicide. His death the next year at Paris in its miserable circumstances would have provided all the necessary material for a Naturalist novelist.

In addition to volumes of tales not listed, Maupassant was the author of two volumes of travel books, *Au Soleil* (*In the Sun*) (1884) and *La Vie Errante* (*The Wandering Life*). But it is not for these, nor even for his excellent novels that Maupassant will be most remembered. He is the only writer of short stories of the Realistic kind who has ever threatened the supremacy of the Russian master of that form, Anton Chekov. But his Naturalism goes much further than the Russian's, or for that matter, than Zola's. It has been said of him that he destroyed Naturalism by pushing it to its logical extreme. As Prof. J. Fitzmaurice-Kelly has said of him: "He had no psychology, no theories of art, no moral or strong social prejudices, no disturbing imagination, no wealth of perplexing ideas.... His marked limitations made him the incomparable artist that he was." It is probable that Maupassant never described anything he had not himself seen. He had known intimately the peasantry, the artists, the workingmen of Paris, and Parisian society; he had seen the inside of governmental offices, newspapers, farmers' homes—and he has set it all down precisely as he saw it.

IMPORTANCE

In all ranks and places Maupassant found men equally brutal and cunning. He seems even not to dislike the bad or to prefer the good. He merely records, with perfect objectivity in a style that is remarkable for its directness and clarity. That is his great virtue as well as his one weakness. The limitation of Maupassant's work is that it implies no interpretation of life. One feels, after reading him, that life does not merit an interpretation. That trait sets him apart from nearly all the world's greatest writers.

EDMOND LOUIS ANTOINE HUOT DE GONCOURT (1822–1896) AND BROTHER JULES ALFRED HUOT DE GONCOURT (1830–1870)

The de Goncourts wrote always as collaborators until the death of Jules. Up till that time it is not possible to isolate the work of each. Indeed, their method of composition indicates the completeness of the collaboration; each would write his version of an incident in a novel in progress, and then both versions would be incorporated into one. It is probable that the closeness of these brothers is unparalleled in literary history. From the time of the death of their mother, when Jules was eighteen, they were inseparable. They first intended to be painters, and traveled together through France and Algiers, but later turned to writing.

There was something spinsterish in their temperaments, and they were proud of their fastidious tastes as demonstrated in their private collection of French and Japanese art of the eighteenth century, paintings and bibelots. Their interest in that epoch is to be seen in their three volumes on *L'Art du XVIIIᵉ Siècle* (*The Art of the Eighteenth Century*) (1859–1875), dealing with Watteau and his school; and in their histories, *Portraits Intimes du XVIIIᵉ Siècle* (*Intimate Portraits of the Eighteenth Century*) (1857), *La Femme au XVIIIᵉ Siècle* (*Women in the Eighteenth Century*) (1862), and *La du Barry* (*Mme. du Barry*) (1878). The same intellectual temper that created the novels went into the composition of these historical and critical studies. The de Goncourts collected their evidence from a painstaking research into documents, letters, costumes, pictures, music—everything (no matter how trifling) that could relate to the subject. The same, almost psychopathic, preoccupation with the minutiae of their daily lives and sensations is to be found in their highly self-revealing *Journals* (1887–1896).

After the death of his brother Jules, Edmond claimed that they had invented the Naturalistic novel; thereafter it has often been declared that they were Zola's master. The matter is not important enough to be worth a discussion, for, in any case, their method is not similar to Zola's, and infinitely distant from Flaubert's.

Their theory of the novel was that it should be made up of a countless number of details. As Arthur Symons has eloquently described it, the de Goncourts desired to "give the sense of the passing of life, the heat and form of its moments as they pass." In their novels no details seem more important than others, and the chapters are often very short, each a record of some happening or emotion calling for attention. The powerful unity that Flaubert achieved in *Madame Bovary* and the effect of unity provided in Zola by his "scientific" documentation of the workings of heredity, therefore, have nothing in common with the de Goncourts' purposes, which were to break up deliberately the appearances of life into fragments of momentary sensation.

They wished, they said, their novels to be "a medico-literary clinic of those illnesses of the liver, the heart, the lungs, so connected with and so neighboring to the emotions and ideas of the sickness;" their novels would "present all the revolutions of the soul in the sufferings of the body."

Their earliest novel, *Charles Demailly* (1860) and a later one, *Manette Salomon* (1867) are studies of the ruinous effects of women upon the creative life. *Soeur Philomène* (*Sister Philomène*) (1861) investigates life in a hospital and the mystical proclivities of a nun. *Renée Mauperin* (1864) is considered their best novel, and their sensitiveness in this case succeeds in delineating very well the plight of the modern young Frenchwoman of their times. *Germinie Lacerteux* (1865) is closer to the field in which Zola chose to operate; it deals with the life of a servant girl, and the vicissitudes to which she is exposed; it actually antedates by a few years Zola's earliest attempts. The clinical method is seen in *Madame Gervaisais* (1869), a study in religious monomania. After his brother's death Edmond de Goncourt alone wrote *La Fille Elisa* (*The Girl Elisa*) (1878), *Les Frères Zamganno* (*The Brothers Zamganno*) (1879), *Faustin* (1882), and *Chérie* (*Dearie*) (1884).

The de Goncourts were not very popular until 1865, when their play *Henriette Maréchal* caused so much discussion that their name became known to the entire literary world of Paris. On his death Edmond left money to found an academy of ten prominent writers, the Académie des Goncourts, which awards prizes to novels it deems of merit.

ALPHONSE DAUDET (1840–1897)

Daudet proved that one can be a Naturalist and yet delightful—if one is willing to note that not all of life is vicious and to sacrifice something of the typical Naturalist's complete impersonality. Zola himself called him "a charmer." Daudet wrote somewhat in the manner that Charles Dickens might have employed had he been tempted by Naturalism. Indeed, Daudet was accused of imitating Dickens (there are worse models!), and though he denied the charge, there can be little doubt that he was influenced by the English master. What Sir Frank Marzials observes about Daudet's work might be said of Dickens' as well: "It struck a note...comparatively new. Here was a writer who possessed the gift of laughter and tears, a writer not only sensible to pathos and sorrow, but also to moral beauty."

Alphonse Daudet was born at Nimes, the son of a silk manufacturer who never managed to make a success of his undertakings. At sixteen the boy went south to try his hand at teaching school, but he came to hate the task of disciplining his pupils to such an extent that he was haunted for a long time afterward by dreams in which he found himself still facing a classroom.

After a year he came to live with his older brother Ernest, three years his senior, who was trying to earn a living in Paris as a journalist. Alphonse began to write too, and when he was only eighteen produced a volume of poems, *Les Amoureuses* (*The Amorous*) (1858). The volume won him employment on the *Figaro*. After writing several plays he attracted the notice of Napoleon III's minister, the Duke de Morny, who appointed him his secretary until Morny's death in 1865. The position allowed Daudet to make trips to the south of France and to Algiers, vacations demanded by his delicate health.

In 1866 Daudet published an enchanting collection of tales and sketches, *Lettres de Mon Moulin* (*Letters from My Mill*), which brought him many admirers. From this he turned to the form of the novel with *Le Petit Chose* (*Little Nobody*) (1868), full of pathos and largely autobiographical, dealing with his own experiences as a youth trying to teach at a boys' school. In 1872 appeared one of his most celebrated works, *Les Aventures Prodigieuses de Tartarin de Tarascon* (*The Astonishing Adventures of Tartarin of Tarascon*); this, with its sequels *Tartarin sur les Alpes* (*Tartarin on the Alps*) (1885) and *Port-Tarascon* (1890), which shows the hero as a colonizer, is a mighty, mirthful prose epic, genially satirizing the temperament of his native southern France, with the predilection of the Méridional to being the victim of his own imaginative boasting. The year of the first *Tartarin* also brought his three-act drama, *L'Arlésienne* (*The Woman of Arles*), for which Bizet wrote some of his most moving music.

The work, however, that brought Daudet great fame was *Fromont Jeune et Risler Aîné* (*Fromont Jr. and Risler Sr.*) (1874); it is a novel that finds Daudet turning to the milieu in which he did some of his best work—the life of the humble. Against the setting of the operations of a business partnership it tells the story of how stupid but vain Sidonie Chèbe, a girl of Paris, deceives her husband; one of the most beautiful creations of fiction is to be found in this novel, too—old Delobelle, a poverty-stricken actor living in a world of his own fantasy.

Thereafter Daudet issued a great many volumes, with considerable success. His novels and tales have been classified into three kinds: those dealing with his native soil in the south of France and with the characters peculiar to that locale; those dealing with Parisian life; and, cutting across both categories, those which particularly deal with simple folk.

The volumes dealing with the south of France include *Lettres de Mon Moulin* and the three *Tartarin* novels.

Those dealing with Parisian life—and no one has described it with more brilliance—include *Le Nabob* (*The Nabob*) (1877), in which a southerner, Jansoulet, comes to Paris under the Second Empire with his millions newly made in Africa, there to become the prey of every kind of adventurer—a picture enriched by Daudet's observations when secretary to Mornay; *Les Rois en Exil* (*Kings in Exile*) (1879), fashioned on the experiences of the dethroned King of Naples; *Numa Roumestan* (1881), in which a braggart politician from Provence, a good fellow notwithstanding (Gambetta stood for the portrait), is sent to Paris as deputy by his adoring countrymen; *Sapho* (1884), one of his best novels, dealing with the life of a Parisian courtesan, and which may be compared to advantage with *Nana* to show that one can be realistic on such a subject without being distasteful; and *L'Immortel* (*The Immortal*) (1888), the sole example of bitter satire in Daudet's work, in this case at the expense of the French Academy, to which he was never elected; it is said that the persons of this last story were nearly all modeled on actual members of that august body.

Those volumes dealing with humble people are set sometimes in the south, sometimes in Paris. Daudet is always moving when he writes about them. These books include *Le Petit Chose; Fromont Jeune et Risler Aîné, Jack* (1876), which owes something to Thackeray as well as to Dickens in its story of an illegitimate child's suffering at the hands of its selfish mother—here again Daudet drew upon his own painful recollections of a boys' school; and *L'Évangéliste* (*The Evangelist*) (1883) a satire on religious fanaticism.

In addition Daudet wrote volumes of reminiscences, thoroughly engaging to read: *Trente Ans de Paris* (*Thirty Years of Paris*) (1887) and *Souvenirs d'un Homme de Lettres* (*Recollections of a Literary Man*) (1888).

Daudet was an intimate friend of Flaubert and the great Naturalists Zola and the de Goncourts. Unlike any of them, however, his faithful representation of life as it is lived did not exclude tenderness or charm. For that reason he has been more admired than the other Naturalists among the English-reading public. It is true, of course, that his life was on the whole, despite poor health, happier than theirs. His marriage in 1867 to Julia Allard, herself an able writer, was a felicitous one.

His delightful stories for children should be mentioned, particularly the tale of an old boat and its crew, *La Belle Nivernaise*.

HIPPOLYTE TAINE (1828–1893)

IMPORTANCE

Taine bears the same relationship to his generation of writers that Sainte-Beuve did to the Romantic movement. He was a man of original mind, but dogmatic and intractable; he evolved the principles of his beliefs while still a youth and at no time changed them. That was his weakness and his strength; it lends conviction to his utterances, but renders them all one-sided. It would, nevertheless, be impossible to overestimate the effects of his teaching upon his contemporaries.

He was a materialist and a determinist. According to him "everything and everybody" could be accounted for as a product of three factors: *moment* (time), *milieu* (environment), and *race* (race). He was a man of vast erudition. From Hegel he accepted a philosophy of history and the concept of the unity of all science. From Comte and from the English Utilitarians he drew his general philosophy.

> As a critic his first endeavor was to "purge" criticism of all esthetic and moral purposes, and to see it as a branch of natural history. Taine insisted that there was nothing new about his view that time, environment, and race are the determining factors in culture; but it is true that he was the first to make that synthesis and to perceive whither it led. The creator thus becomes not particularly his own spokesman, but rather the voice of his period. To a degree, twentieth century criticism has not recovered from that dogma.

As regards the creator, Taine accounted for him in the same rigidly deterministic way. In addition to the all-controlling factors of time, environment, and race, a man himself, Taine believed, is dominated by one faculty so powerful, what he called the *faculté maîtresse* (the predominating faculty), that it regulates the man's activities, forces it into a particular direction, and subordinates all other faculties to it.

To illustrate his theories Taine wrote his long and influential *Histoire de la Littérature Anglaise* (*History of English Literature*) (1863). It is only just to note that very much that is vital and true can be found in these four volumes despite the very serious limitations of what Taine has to say. Scholarship of the more recent kind, with its emphasis on dates, has invalidated by its findings many of Taine's pronouncements. More serious still, English literature is far less adapted to the creed of "race, time, and environment" than French, for our literature has never had much respect for tradition, and it is precisely the expression of personal convictions that has made English letters as great as they are. Taine far too often summons up the "Anglo-Saxon" and the "Norman" nature, the English climate and soil, to account for great English works. Nevertheless, except to the pedantic, Taine's massive work remains *in toto* one of the most brilliant and sensitive collections of appreciations ever penned about English literature. He had a deep knowledge and a great affection for it, and luckily his enthusiasms and esthetic sensibilities sometimes sweep aside his "scientific" pretensions. It is unfortunate that Taine worked so relentlessly Sainte-Beuve's practice of accumulating all the facts available in order to understand a work of literature; Sainte-Beuve did that without the obstruction of a theory or the need of forcing a conclusion. It is Taine's weakness that he operated under the disadvantages of both impediments.

In 1864 Taine was appointed Professor of the History of Art and Esthetics at the École des Beaux Arts. In 1866 he received the medal of the Legion of Honor. At the conclusion of his lectures at Oxford on Corneille and Racine, the English university conferred on him the degree of D.C.L.

His critical essays on French literature are to be found in the three volumes of collected pieces: *Essais* (1858), *Nouveaux Essais* (*New Essays*) (1865), and *Derniers Essais* (*Last Essays*) (1894). In them he applies the same method to La Fontaine, Racine, Balzac, and Stendhal.

Taine's other works include *Philosophie de l'Art en Italie* (*Philosophy of Italian Art*) (1865), *Voyage en Italie* (*Travels in Italy*) (1866) and *Idéal dans l'Art* (*The Ideal in Art*) (1869)—all devoted to the subject of art, in discussing which he employs his favorite theories and evokes some very vivid pictures through his great gifts at description; and *Notes sur l'Angleterre* (*Notes on England*) (1872), the fruit of a long stay in England during 1858 and another visit in 1871.

The events of 1870 and 1871 stirred Taine so deeply that he decided it was his duty to devote his talents thereafter to French interests exclusively. Having seen the effects of mob violence during the days of the Paris Commune, he became very critical of the Jacobin temper. In 1871 he wrote a pamphlet on *Universal Suffrage*, and this it was that determined him to begin a study of France's history of political ineptitude. From 1871 to the end of his life he was engaged on a vast work, *Les Origines de la France Contemporaine* (*The Origins of Contemporary France*), in which he undertook to prove that the roots of France's political vicissitudes could be traced to the Revolution of 1789. In 1884 he gave up his professorship to devote all of his hours to the composition of this work, but he did not live long enough to complete it. The first volume, on the *Ancien Régime* (1875), has been called his masterpiece. In his desire to show that the French Revolution did not destroy absolutism, but merely caused absolutism to pass into other hands, and that, on the other hand, the French Revolution did not destroy French liberty, the patriot in Taine assumed ascendancy over the theories, and his pet ideas are constantly pushed aside; he allows himself to become excited and his lines often glow with deep feeling.

Taine, indeed, tried valiantly to abide throughout by his fundamental trust in the validity of the scientific method as applied to philosophy and criticism. He is rarely enthusiastic and never bitter; his preferred attitude is one of disenchanted resignation. He had studied mankind untiringly and could only condemn what he found. He was to a degree the victim of his own love of abstraction. He said that every man and every book could be summed up in three lines; he once admired a sonata of Beethoven for being "as beautiful as a syllogism." Luckily, however, his own imagination was better than he knew. It is characteristic of him that his own preferences were for the giants in art—Shakespeare, Rubens, Titian.

His kinship with the Realistic attitude towards literature makes it easy to understand his approval of Stendhal, Balzac, Flaubert. The Naturalists declared themselves disciples to his method and his pessimism, Zola and Maupassant particularly.

FRENCH POST-ROMANTIC DRAMA

After the flourishing of Romanticism in its most absurd aspects in the plays of Victor Hugo, a reaction set in during the 1840s. Hugo's *Les Burgraves* of

1843, as we have seen, was a failure. As a consequence the rather dull *Lucrèce* of François Ponsard (1824–1867), a young dramatist of limited imagination, was wildly applauded at the Odéon only a month or so later, as though it were the center of a new movement. What the audience was approving was Ponsard's lack of ornamentation and extravagance, and what seemed to be the inauguration of a new classicism. Ponsard, although he had some continued success with other plays, is important only for the one moment when he typified the public's weariness of Romantic excesses.

Eugene Scribe (1791–1861)

Meanwhile, indifferent to movements and trends in literature—indeed, indifferent to literature—Eugene Scribe was making a fortune for himself by providing the middle-class public with the kind of plays they liked to see. He was merely an entertainer, who managed, with the aid of collaborators, to turn out more than four hundred plays, not one of them with any quality. Nevertheless, he must be mentioned in any history of literature, for it was he who made famous the concept of "the well-made play." With no gift for language and little for characterization, Scribe learned to perfection the management of plot. As Wright says of him, "He was unequaled in finding solutions to apparently insoluble problems." He made no pretense to having important ideas, but Ibsen, who had plenty of them, and simply took over the form Scribe had perfected, found Scribe's labors useful in providing for him the medium he required.

His collaborators included Legouvé, Dupin, Delavigne, and many others. He was well known to be extremely generous to them, often sharing the entire proceeds from a success with a man who had merely given him an idea. Caramouche said, "I've written a dozen or fifteen vaudevilles in collaboration with Scribe, and I can truthfully say not a word in those pieces is mine."

It was in the *vaudeville* piece that Scribe first acquired his technique—one-act "sketches" written for the lowest common denominator of the theater-going public. Later he was more than welcome within the lofty precincts of the Théâtre Français. His average was often ten plays a month. The values of Scribe's plays are those of his audience: virtue is rewarded by a wealthy marriage.

Nevertheless, in so far as he approaches any school, he must be classed as a Realist for he generally sees man as actuated by petty motives, motives that were common to the daily lives of Scribe's middle-class audiences.

It has also been said that Scribe inaugurated the modern "debunking" attitude towards erstwhile glittering historical personages. *Le Verre d'Eau* (*The Glass of Water*) (1842) shows how the mere overturning of a glass of water alters the course of history.

His best known plays are *Bertrand et Raton* (1833), *Adrienne Lecouvreur* (1849) and *La Bataille des Dames* (*The Battle of the Women*). He was fortunate in having the great actress Rachel appearing in various roles he created for her. Scribe also wrote the libretti for a good many operas, of which still popular are *Robert le Diable* (*Robert the Devil*), *La Juive* (*The Jewess*), and *Les Huguenots* (*The Huguenots*).

Émile Augier (1820–1889)

Augier carried the trend towards Realism to a higher plane than Scribe. A man solidly middle class in his point of view, his virtues, and his prejudices, he made a false start in his career by writing a series of classical plays in verse. He had no gift as a poet, and he did not find himself until he turned to prose.

In *L'Aventurière* (*The Adventuress*) (1848) his essentially anti-Romantic temperament vented itself for the first time. In *Gabrielle* of the next year, he courageously stepped forth as the defender of the family—after the orgy of the Romantics before the altar of Passion, it took courage to resist it as Augier's heroine does and prefer the soberer virtues of family life.

Once he had discovered his own convictions, Augier continued to sing— in able prose—the hymn of respectability. *Le Mariage d'Olympe* (*Olympe's Marriage*) (1855), shows the dangers of moral mismating; the heroine is not elevated by her marriage with a decent man, but still longs for the slime. *Ceinture Dorée* (*The Golden Girdle*) (1856) shows how much more difficult it is for a wealthy girl to make a good marriage, particularly when she has a conscience about the unscrupulous manner in which her father has made his money. *Un Beau Mariage* (*A Fine Marriage*) (1858) introduces us to the folly of an intellectual's marrying into a family that loves only frivolity. *Paul Forestier* (1868) and *Jean de Thommeray* (1872) expose the cynicism and idleness of the younger generation. *Madame Coverlet* (1876) is on divorce. But Augier will always be remembered for two plays above all others: *Le Gendre de M. Poirier* (*Mr. Poirier's Son-in-Law*) (1854) and *Maître Guérin* (1864).

Le Gendre de M. Poirier has been described by Brander Matthews as "the chief modern exemplar of high comedy, of which Molière made the pattern in *Tartuffe*." He also remarks that "it is the masterpiece of French comedy in the nineteenth century; and it is unmatched in the dramatic literature of any other language." This is high praise, but not entirely undeserved. For Augier, despite the undercurrent seriousness of his middle-class temperament, had a great flair for dialogue and characterization; he was, moreover, a man of extraordinary sanity of perspective—and no quality is more indispensable to the writing of good comedy.

The play is a collaboration between Augier and Jules Sandeau, the material coming from a novel of the latter. But the actual writing of the drama bears throughout the stamp of Augier's manly style. In the transition between Scribe and Ibsen, Augier is here seen as the most important link; he took Scribe's "well-made play" and gave it social content. In *Le Gendre de M. Poirier*, Augier had a subject full of timely interest: the contrast in the moral values between the old and now generally impoverished aristocracy, and the new wealthy middle class. Like a good Realist he caricatures neither, but shows both in their attractive and unattractive attributes. The heroine's father, a wealthy man of middle-class origins who dotes on his daughter, is anxious to cross the line into the nobility, as many of his fellows were doing; he is Molière's M. Jourdain as he would have been in the nineteenth century—not covetous of the nobleman's elegance but of his title and influence. Yet M. Poirier is fundamentally a man of straight morals and honest habits, and kindness itself when his fatuous ambition is asleep. His son-in-law, on the other hand, is a fast-living rake, ungrateful for the love of his wife and the generosity of her father, and only too conscious of his condescension in marrying a girl of the merchant class. Nevertheless, when honor is involved he is quite capable of sacrificing his happiness and his best interests on a scruple, to a degree that M. Poirier could not begin to understand. In the end, Augier shows that there is common meeting ground between these two—an optimistic conclusion for which his compatriots must have been grateful.

Maître Guérin is the stronger of the two plays, but not authentically in the comic spirit. It gives a fine portrait of a man of inexorable will, who gains riches and power at the expense of his family's affection and esteem. Unable to endure living with him any longer, they leave him. He dies alone, surrounded by leeches of low character.

Alexandre Dumas *fils* (1824–1895)

The younger Alexandre Dumas, illegitimate son of the novelist, had an unhappy childhood until his celebrated father took him in hand to give him a whirl of Parisian life. But Dumas *fils* found little pleasure in these gaieties, and encumbered by his debts, took to literature. He started with a volume of verse, *Péchés de Jeunesse* (*Sins of Youth*) (1847). The next year he published a novel reflecting the frivolous kind of life his father had introduced him to, *La Dame aux Camélias* (*The Lady of the Camelias*) (1848), which had considerable success, and was followed by *Le Roman d'une Femme* (*The Romance of a Woman*) (1848) and *Diane de Lys* (1851).

With the pressure of debts heavy upon him, he dramatized his first novel, *La Dame aux Camélias*, the play now known to the world as *Camille* (1852) and the basis for Verdi's *La Traviata*. Its success was enormous, and it has held the boards ever since, probably because it affords leading actresses a wonderful opportunity to exhibit the range of their abilities in the starring role. What once seemed like an extreme piece of Realism now seems less so because of the sentimentality with which the plot is weighted.

After this success, Dumas' popularity continued through a series of plays: *Diane de Lys* (1853), which has adultery as its subject; *Le Demi-Monde* (*The Demi-Monde*) (1855), which, like *La Dame aux Camélias*, is a picture of the world inhabited by kept women and their lovers; *La Question d'Argent* (*The Question of Money*) (1857), which shows the power of money to corrupt; *Le Fils Naturel* (*The Natural Son*) (1858), in which he draws from his own bitter youth the knowledge of what it means to be illegitimate, and which is the first of his "thesis-plays;" and *Le Père Prodigue* (*The Prodigal Father*) (1859).

Up to this point Dumas, having learned from Scribe how to construct a play brilliantly and having mastered the manipulation of clever dialogue, had by degrees come to be the leading writer of the drama of manners of his century. But he was, in addition to being of the Realist persuasion, a born moralist. His father, in fact, accused him of loving to preach too much. Dumas *fils* himself wrote that all literature that does not tend to the "moral uplifting of society" is unhealthy. Thus, after *Le Fils Naturel* he began to write plays with a definite thesis in view—a practice that Ibsen adopted. *The Natural Son* urges the need of new laws to protect the illegitimate.

His later plays all have a thesis, but the point argued is not always consistent with others of his plays. *Les Idées de Madame Aubray* (*The Ideas of Mme. Aubray*) (1867), preaches clemency for the woman who has sinned, and the obligation of the seducer to marry his victim. *La Femme de Claude* (*Claude's Wife*) (1873), on the other hand, pleads the justice of the deceived husband's killing with his own hands his faithless wife. This point of view Dumas also argued in a pamphlet, *Homme-Femme* (*Man-Woman*) (1871).

The technical skill and brilliant dialogue of Dumas' plays have made them very popular. He is historically important as the first leading dramatist of the "problem play." But his eternal preoccupation with the fallen woman and with adultery becomes rather tedious on closer acquaintance, and what in his own time seemed like very advanced thinking has become today a little old-fashioned.

Victorien Sardou (1831–1908)

Sardou was an enormously prolific writer of plays, a true son of Scribe in his technical mastery of plots and his skill in untying dramatic knots. It has been said of him humorously that all his plays might have been entitled *All's Well That Ends Well*. He was at his best in the observation of current foibles in politics and life. One of his best plays is *Rabagas* (1873), a satire on demagogues. But on the whole Sardou was too much interested in supplying the current market to figure as an important literary man. *Divorçons* (*Let Us Divorce*) (1880) shocked the public just enough to delight it. Like Dumas *fils*, he was fortunate in having great stars like Sara Bernhardt to enact his plays, and he was kept busy supplying them with "vehicles." His *La Tosca* furnished Puccini with a libretto for one of the most popular of operas.

POST-ROMANTIC TRENDS IN GERMANY

Sociological Fiction

German writers of fiction after 1830 tended to continue the early pattern of novels of ideas or to build on the interest in the common man that had been awakened by the Romantic movement. Whether singly or in combination, these themes reflected the total European pattern of the time which considered fiction the handmaid of sociology. A mixture of the two modes is to be found in the sincere and realistic stories of the Swiss Pastor Albert Bitzius (1797–1854), better known by his pseudonym Jeremias Gotthelf. Berthold Auerbach (1812–1882) became famous for stories and novels that combine ideas of sociological progress with the naive atmosphere of peasant simplicity. Gustav Freytag (1816–1895) turned to the bourgeoisie with his fine novel *Soll und Haben* (*Debit and Credit*) (1855), which shows the influence of Dickens in its doctrine of commercial success through honest industry, and simultaneously glorifies the sober diligence of the German people. Gottfried Keller (1819–1890), who was also a lyric poet, was at his best in depicting with sympathy, humor, and insight the trials and tribulations of the lower classes and in minute perceptions of natural phenomena which he believed to be the expression of God.

Theodor Storm (1817–1888) developed from the idyllic and widely read *Immensee* (1852) to a more realistic treatment of contemporary psychological problems. Paul Heyse (1830–1914) achieved a mastery in short story form in a long series of *Novellen* (*Tales*), which give an effect of artificiality by their very polish. More enduring is his novel *Kinder der Welt* (1873) in which the "Children of the World" are bewildered by the onslaught of materialism and the many conflicting forces of their era. Friedrich Spielhagen (1829–1911) championed "novels of purpose," which also grapple with the besetting social and personal problems of his age.

Karl Marx (1818–1883)

With the preeminence of philosophy in the German tradition it is not surprising that the most powerful social philosophy of our day should have come out of Germany. Karl Marx, the son of a Jewish lawyer, was educated at the Universities of Bonn and Berlin where he studied history, philosophy, and law. Inclined by disposition to favor the underprivileged, he became a journalist to earn a living as well as to use his lively writing talent for propaganda purposes. Meeting Friedrich Engels in 1844, he became closely associated with him in working out a theory which culminated in the joint publication in 1847 of the *Communist Manifesto* (*Das Kommunistiche Manifest*). Disappointed with the democratic revolution of 1848 in Germany, he evolved a social theory called "dialectical materialism," which is elaborated in his *Critique of Political Economy* (*Zur Kritik der politischen Ökonomie*) (1867) and *Capital* (*Das Kapital*) (1867, 1885, 1895).

Marx's "dialectical materialism" was the result of his application of the Hegelian system of thesis, antithesis, and synthesis to the theory that the history of any society revolves about the economic conflict between the rich and the poor. Hegel's concept, which was derived, in turn, from Fichte, was that ultimate reality is actually a fusion or unification of two contradictory aspects of reality, or of two apparently opposed principles working in the universe.

The original principle is that of unity, thesis (for example, the seed of a plant). But within this essential unity there operates the violently opposed principle of diversification or antithesis (the disintegration of the seed into its constituents). The final truth, synthesis, is the unity that results from these two contradictory principles (the individual plant growing from the seed as an organic unit).

Marx transferred this concept to his own vision of social evolution in which the opposing forces of the capitalist bourgeoisie and the impoverished proletariat would ultimately blend into an international classless brotherhood of mankind. In this ultimate synthesis the concept of "property" would be nonexistent, and government, which he believed existed only to protect property, would become extinct. Universal happiness would accrue from the stable satisfaction of working for the common good rather than from the momentary and petty pleasures of personal acquisitiveness.

The path to this ultimate utopia would follow the stages indicated by Hegel. The original thesis would be completed when the process of industrialization had created a powerful capitalist class. The inevitable antithesis would result in the growth of a working class, the proletariat, who would become sufficiently aware of their slavery and of their strength to rebel against their bourgeois masters. For a time, following a global revolution, a proletariat dictatorship would be established, during which force would be used to destroy private property and the taint of individualism. When the work of the dictatorship was completed, the final synthesis or union of mankind in a world devoid of antagonism would be achieved.

Whatever logic or pragmatic value may reside in Marx's dialectic, the vast influence of his writings is unquestionable. In the world of literature, he numbered and still numbers many distinguished converts, and by focusing attention on both the miserable plight and the inherent strength of the working class, he gave impetus to the creation of a literature that devoted itself variously to championship of the lower class, to examination of the tribulations of the poor, to castigation of bourgeois morality, and to outright propaganda for the world revolution that was to come.

Friedrich Nietzsche (1844–1900)

Another powerful influence on late nineteenth and twentieth century thought was the philosophical doctrine of Friedrich Nietzsche. Educated in the classics and philosophy at Bonn and Leipzig, he was a professor of Classics at Basel from 1869 to 1879 when he was forced to retire because of ill health. After another ten years of restless wandering, he became insane in 1889 and died at Weimar the following year. Author of several books on esthetic and philosophical questions, he gives the most complete expression of his dominant theory in *Beyond Good and Evil* (*Jenseits von Gut und Böse*) (1886), which is made up of a series of maxim-like observations, and in the poetic *Thus Spake Zarathustra* (*Also sprach Zarathustra*) (1883–1891), in which mystical symbolic utterances placed in the mouth of the Persian Zoroaster present the rise of the Superman in thinly veiled allegories, parables, and oracular statements.

Although he did not systematize or organize his theory, it is possible from these works to reconstruct a logical synthesis of his basic premise. Accepting Schopenhauer's Will as the elementary moving force, he rejects the previous philosopher's pessimism by seeing this Will as an evolutionary forward-moving power. As in Darwin's theory of Natural Selection (Survival of the Fittest), he sees evolutionary progress as the result of the Will to Power whereby the struggle for mastery develops the highest potentialities of each succeeding generation. But Christian morality is rapidly halting the evolutionary process by preaching meekness, morality, altruism, and social responsibility for preserving and even allowing reproduction of the unfit. Instead, the masses must become subordinate to the Superman who will emerge by ruthless disregard of good and evil, of pangs of conscience, and of similar sentimentalisms. Struggle comprises the glory of humanity and will eventuate in an ever healthier and more powerful race. During the First and Second World Wars, the German imperialists justified themselves with scant accuracy as disciples of Nietzsche.

Gerhard Hauptmann (1862–1946)

Germany's part in the late nineteenth century dramatic revival that was stimulated by the plays of the Scandinavian playwrights Ibsen and Strindberg may be said to begin with the dramas of Gerhard Hauptmann. The son of a Silesian innkeeper, he early showed the artistic and quizzical temperament that made him attempt to satisfy his wanderlust by extensive travels and led him to investigate such varied spheres as sociology, sculpture, and science. Interested in the new naturalism of Zola and the spirit of social revolt engendered by Marx, he turned to literature as a means of expressing his hatred of social injustice and his acceptance of the Naturalistic theory that human destiny is determined by heredity, environment, and the dark instinctive urgencies which lie beyond human control.

After publishing *Promethidenlos* (*The Lot of a Promethean*) in 1883, an epic poem of rebellion against the injustices of capitalism, he turned to the writing of plays concerning lower and middle class characters who speak their own crude and simple language against earthy backgrounds. His first play, *Vor Sonnenaufgang* (*Before Sunrise*) (1889), depicts the depravity of a family of Silesian peasants who have become suddenly rich by the discovery of coal on their land. The effect of wealth on an essentially degenerate family leads to drunkenness, general libidinousness, and incest. The picture is somewhat relieved by the return of Helene from a convent. She attempts to find escape through the love of Alfred Loth, a socialistic reformer. But when his discovery of the family background turns him from her, suicide is her only refuge.

His outstanding proletarian play is the extraordinary drama *The Weavers* (*Die Weber*) (1893), which depicts in a panoramic series of shifting scenes the revolt of the Silesian weavers in 1844. Instead of concentrating on individual characters, he makes a protagonist of the entire population. Requiring forty characters, the play shows a kaleidoscope of typical scenes of the workers' oppression and poverty. Then the revolutionary Jaeger appears to incite the masses to rebellion. The ironic conclusion shifts to the household of the religious Hilse, who refuses to engage in mortal combat and is accidentally shot while sitting at home.

The Sunken Bell: Hauptmann had meanwhile been experimenting with comedy, domestic drama, and fantasy. With a broadening imagination and an increasing grasp of the poetic, he created a beautiful, fanciful, and symbolic fairy tale in *The Sunken Bell* (*Die Versunkene Glocke*) (1896). Written in verse, this delicate work suggests the conflict between duty and desire, between social responsibility and individual yearning, in the figure of the bellmaker Heinrich. Having created a bell to ring out the glory of God, he loses it when it rolls down a mountain into a lake, propelled by a mischievous wood-sprite. In search of the bell Heinrich meets Rautendelein, a nymph who draws a magic circle around him to remove him from ordinary life. When he is restored to his wife and responsibility through the offices of a witch, Rautendelein sheds her first tear and draws Heinrich back to her and the freedom of irresponsible enjoyment.

Heinrich now makes bells for the worship of nature until he is warned by the village vicar that the sunken bell will toll again. Then he finds himself tormented by the sprites, by an attack on his pagan temple by the villagers, and by the appearance of his children carrying an urn filled with their mother's tears. Suddenly, he hears the tolling of the sunken bell, struck by the hand of his wife who has drowned herself.

Leaving Rautendelein he attempts to regain his former responsible life, but finds himself unable to adapt to the ordinary after his taste of freedom. An attempt to return to Rautendelein is equally unsatisfactory because she has taken up her abode in a well with a water-sprite. Unable to live in either world and unable to follow the witch's mandate to become a superman, beyond good and evil, he is given a chance to return to nature if he will also suffer the penalty of death. He gladly accepts the offer of the witch, is permitted to receive Rautendelein's farewell kiss, and hears the sound of his pagan bells as he dies.

Hauptmann as a Naturalist: In his succeeding plays, Hauptmann divided his talents between fantasy and Naturalism, interspersing these serious plays with a few comedies. Of these later plays, the Naturalistic dramas are the best in their depiction of primitive urgencies which direct and destroy the lives of the characters involved. *Teamster Henschel* (*Fuhrmann Henschel*) (1898) is destroyed by a woman's desire for him. The heroine of *Rose Bernd* (1903) strangles her child to save it from the horrors of lust. In *The Rats* (*Die Ratten*) (1911) maternal instinct is an unreasoning motivating force. Even in his least effective plays Hauptmann displays a keen sense of reality, able depiction of domestic complexities, and a poetic grasp of the tragic spirit of the Naturalistic movement, which enlists pity and fear in behalf of the blind struggles of the entire human race rather than for the tragic strivings of individuals.

Hermann Sudermann (1857–1928)

A rival of Hauptmann during his life but now regarded as a distinctly secondary figure, Hermann Sudermann wrote plays, stories, and novels that contributed to the Naturalist movement. The son of a brewer in East Prussia, he attended the gymnasium at Tilset and the University of Königsberg, where a lively intellectual curiosity led him to pursue especially studies in philosophy and history. In 1877 he went to Berlin to become a tutor in private families. With a decided leaning toward liberal views, he came to a writing career through an apprenticeship in journalism. After his extraordinary popular success in the theater had made him wealthy, he retired to a villa in a suburb of Berlin to enjoy the profits from his often overslick and overtheatrical pieces. Sudermann's many plays use timely themes and are undeniably good theater, but they usually lack the depth and honesty of great art.

In the year 1887 he made his first appearance as a writer of fiction with a volume of short stories and his most famous novel, *Dame Care* (*Frau Sorge*), a powerful, simply constructed Naturalistic account of the struggles of a young man who is harassed by poverty and misfortune. In 1889, year of the beginning of the Realist movement in the German theater, he competed with Hauptmann's first play with his *Die Ehre* (*Honor*), a rather glib bow to Naturalism and Nietzschean morality, with a happy ending. The upper-class hero yields to instinct and seduces a lower-class girl. The girl's outraged brother is taught to forget his bourgeois conception of honor and ends by marrying the seducer's sister.

Sudermann's most popular play, *Die Heimat* (*Home*) (1889), is usually known as *Magda*, the name of the heroine. Magda is the essence of the unconventional new woman in revolt against parental authority and middle class morality. Returning home from Berlin, where she achieved operatic success and a complete bohemian freedom that included giving birth to an illegitimate child, she mocks the provincial attempts to make her a respectable woman. A long series of plays on similar themes, together with social satires, romantic and historical plays, and one fantasy, culminated in a trilogy that attempted to describe the German tragedy of the First World War.

Arthur Schnitzler (1862–1931)

An outstanding Viennese author of novels, stories, and plays, Arthur Schnitzler repudiated his father's profession of medicine to become a rare connoisseur of the delicate variations and many-shaded emotions connected with love. Combining romanticism, cynicism, sensuality, and refinement, he produced highly sophisticated pieces that breathe a distinctly continental atmosphere. The best known of his plays, a collection of one-acters, *The Affairs of Anatol* (*Anatol*) (1893), relates the delicate intrigues of a worldly man-about-town, accompanied by the cynical commentary of an interested friend. Its faint trace of theme concerns the conflict between the romantic dream of love and the worldly realities.

Rainer Maria Rilke (1875–1926)

The best known German lyric poet after Heine is Rainer Maria Rilke. A life of wandering which led him from Prague through Germany, Italy, Sweden, and Denmark was the outward manifestation of a lonely, hypersensitive personality whose delicate physique imbued him with a constant fear of death. Love and death are prominent in his intense and deeply personal poems, but any experience or any sight calls for a poetic recreation of the outward world. Rilke is precise in his rendition of externals, deeply perceptive, and almost mystical in his instinctive need to externalize the essence of a world through which he passed so painfully.

Rilke asserted that his serious work began with the publication of a three-part cycle of poems written between 1899 and 1903, *Das Stunden-Buch* (*The Book of Hours*) (1905). The speaker in these poems is a young monk who heaps prayer-poems upon his god, the incarnation of life. After a commission from a German publisher to write a book on Rodin, Rilke became closely associated with the famous French sculptor. In part under Rodin's influence, Rilke developed a new style of lyric poetry, the "object poem" style in which the dynamic or plastic essence of physical objects is captured in poetic language. His first collection of such poems appeared in *Neue Gedichte* (*New Poems*) (1907–1908), with a later prose counterpart, *Die Aufzeichnungen des Malte Laurids Brigge* (*The Notebook of Malte Laurids Brigge*) (1910).

Thereafter, except for a single short story, Rilke published nothing for thirteen years. Rilke served in the Austrian army during the First World War and then moved to Switzerland, where he took up residence in a Rhone Valley castle as the guest of a Spanish patron. There he began to write again with a passion and completed two important cycles of poems, the *Duino Elegies* (1922) and *Sonnets to Orpheus* (1922). His health began to fail in 1923 due to an illness diagnosed later as leukemia. After a final visit to such old Parisian friends as Andre Gide and Paul Valery, Rilke died in a Swiss sanatorium in 1926.

REVIEW QUESTIONS

THE RISE OF REALISM AND NATURALISM

Multiple Choice

1. _____ Realists believe that true beauty lies in
   a. formal rules
   b. functional design
   c. the depiction of truth
   d. the perception of ideal reality

2. _____ Realist novels
   a. usually deal with the future
   b. focus on external nature rather than human nature
   c. focus on story more than character
   d. describe the bare facts of experience

3. _____ Common topics in Balzac's novels are
   a. studies of social behavior
   b. affairs of business
   c. autobiographical experiences
   d. all of the above

4. _____ Balzac's novel *La Cousine Bette* is
   a. a powerful indictment of vice
   b. one of his more romantic novels
   c. focuses on the life of a beautiful socialite
   d. set in Provençe

5. _____ Flaubert revealed his Romanticism in his love of
   a. nature and hatred of the city
   b. the past and the exotic
   c. color and the grotesque
   d. all of the above

6. _____ Naturalist writers tend to
   a. idealize their characters
   b. emphasize the more brutal aspects of human character
   c. weave complicated plots
   d. be optimistic about life

7. _____ Augier wrote
   a. Romantic poetry
   b. tragic dramas
   c. stories about respectability
   d. passionate plays

8. _____ Hauptmann's plays were
   a. an important part of Germany's dramatic revival
   b. expressions of his acceptance of social inequities
   c. expressions of his repudiation of heredity as a force in human destiny
   d. of little influence upon other German playwrights

9. _____ Daudet's Naturalist novels are best characterized as
   a. bleak and depressing
   b. tender and charming
   c. unemotional and uninspiring
   d. vicious and impersonal

10. _____ According to Taine, all human events are the product of
    a. time, environment, and race
    b. free will
    c. predestination
    d. a divine plan

True-False

11. _____ Realism, the depiction of life as it is lived, emerged in the eighteenth century.

12. _____ It is easier to classify particular novels into a style than it is to classify their authors.

13. _____ Realist authors take sides with their characters and treat the concerns of their novels subjectively.

14. _____ Realist writers usually write dramas and lyrical poetry.

15. _____ Stendahl experienced his greatest popularity during his own lifetime.

16. _____ Flaubert's novel *Madame Bovary* was in part a self-portrait.

17. _____ Zola intended to use a laboratory technique to produce novels to supplement Balzac's *Human Comedy.*

18. _____ Zola wanted to demonstrate the theory of heredity through his novels.

19. _____ Maupassant was influenced stylistically by Flaubert and Zola.

20. _____ Eugene Scribe was heavily influenced by the literary movements of his time.

Fill-in

21. Although _____ wrote one of the greatest Realistic novels, he was by nature a Romantic, as most of his novels reflect.

22. _____ had the ability to objectify his own experiences to produce more than one hundred novels, even though his own life was spent almost entirely in literary composition.

23. _____ reject the Romantic and Realist treatment of writing as an art and prefer instead the view of writing as a scientific method.

24. In Maupassant's novel _____ a despicable man has great success because of his good looks.

25. _____ wrote plays for the lowest common denominator of the post-Romantic theater audience.

26. _____ writers believe that the pleasure in reading comes from the excitement created by the author's revelation of the ultimate truth about human life.

27. _____ believed that the history of any society revolves about the economic conflict between the rich and poor.

28. In his poetic novel *Thus Spake Zarathustra,* _____ presents the rise of the Superman through utterances by the Persian Zoroaster.

29. *The Sunken Bell* by _____ is a fairy tale about a man torn between duty and desire.

30. _____ endeavors in an almost mystical way to externalize in his lyrical poetry the essence of a world that was painful to him.

Matching

31. _____ Stendhal	a.	short story
32. _____ Balzac	b.	"well-made play"
33. _____ Flaubert	c.	Lucile-Aurore Dupin
34. _____ George Sand	d.	*Human Comedy*
35. _____ Zola	e.	dialectical materialism
36. _____ Maupassant	f.	indifference to moral codes for the sake of love
37. _____ Scribe	g.	*Beyond Good and Evil*
38. _____ Duman *fils*	h.	"le bon mot" (the perfect word)
39. _____ Marx	i.	*Camille*
40. _____ Nietzsche	j.	leader of the Naturalists

Answers

1.	c	10.	a	19.	t
2.	d	11.	f	20.	f
3.	d	12.	t	21.	Flaubert
4.	a	13.	f	22.	Balzac
5.	d	14.	f	23.	Naturalists
6.	b	15.	f	24.	*Bel-Ami*
7.	c	16.	t	25.	Scribe
8.	d	17.	t	26.	Naturalist
9.	b	18.	t	27.	Marx

28. Nietzsche
29. Hauptmann
30. Rilke
31. f
32. d

33. h
34. c
35. j
36. a
37. b

38. i
39. e
40. g

Part 4

THE RISE OF RUSSIAN LITERATURE

WORKS AT A GLANCE

Alexander Pushkin

1820	*Ruslan and Lyudmila*	1824	*The Gypsies*
1822	*The Prisoner of the Caucasus; The Fountain of the Bakchissaraï*	1825	*Boris Godunov*
		1833	*Eugene Onyegin*

Nikolai Gogol

| 1835 | *Taras Bulba;* "The Cloak" | 1840 | *Dead Souls* |
| 1835 | *The Inspector-General* | | |

Ivan Turgenev

1847	*A Sportsman's Sketches*	1862	*Fathers and Sons*
1859	*A House of Gentlefolk*	1867	*Smoke*
1860	*On the Eve*	1877	*Virgin Soil*

Feodor Dostoevsky

1846	*Poor Folk*	1869	*The Idiot*
1861	*The House of the Dead*	1871	*The Possessed*
1866	*Crime and Punishment*	1877	*Journal of an Author*
1867	*The Insulted and the Injured*	1880	*The Brothers Karamazov*

Count Leo Tolstoy

1824	*Childhood*	1879–1882	*My Confession*
1853–1855	*Tales from Sebastopol*	1884	*What Are We To Do?*
1854	*The Landlord's Morning, Boyhood*	1885	*My Religion*
1855–1857	*Youth*	1886	*The Death of Ivan Ilyitch*
1863	*The Cossacks*	1890	*The Kreutzer Sonata*
1865–1868	*War and Peace*	1897	*What Is Art?*
1875–1878	*Anna Karenina*		

7
THE FOUNDERS OF RUSSIAN LITERATURE

Russia was the last of the great European nations to produce literature of more than merely national interest. The reasons for this condition are various. Russia was the last of those nations to feel the impress of the cultural influences that periodically swept through Western Europe after the Middle Ages. It was not until the time of Peter the Great (1672–1725) that Russia began to take its place in the affairs of Europe; it was the same monarch who made the first efforts to Westernize his vast country. Moreover, the Russian language, the very alphabet of which seems fantastic to the Western eye, is quite remote from the languages of Western Europe and from classic Latin and Greek. It was not, therefore, until relations with the Western world began to open up that the Russian language tempted European scholars to acquire a knowledge of it. It would seem that even to Russians the strange mixtures of races and temperaments connected with Russian history formed an obstacle to the creation of a literary language. A scholarly critic of Russian literature has said in the twentieth century about the language that as a literary instrument it "was made but yesterday." Nevertheless, in the later nineteenth and early twentieth centuries, Russian literature, despite its late awakening, became one of the most imposing bodies of literature of its time, eagerly read and profoundly admired (in translation) the world over.

Early Russian literature is of small interest, being largely of ecclesiastical import. With Peter the Great came the first significant attempts to create a language suitable for literary expression. In that era the outstanding writers were Feofane Procopovich (1681–1736), who turned to the West for inspiration, and Pososhkov (1673–1751).

The immediate effects of Peter's interest in Western Europe can be read in the satires of Antioch Kantemir (1708–1744), imitated from Boileau; he also translated some of Horace and Fontenelle. Vassili Trediakovski (1703–1769) translated Boileau's *Art of Poetry*, Fénelon's *Telemachus*, and Æsop. But it was Michael Lomonossov (1711–1765) who was the outstanding writer of this period, and was extravagantly compared by his compatriots to Cicero, Virgil, and Pindar. He traveled and studied in Germany, and there experienced the outcropping of his poetic talents. Pushkin, Russia's first international literary figure, described Lomonossov as "the first Russian university," but he denied that his predecessor was a true poet. Nevertheless, scholars are agreed that Lomonossov was largely responsible in shaping a literary language for Russia.

During the course of the eighteenth century, Russian letters made great strides. Alexander Sumarokov (1718–1777) wrote tragedies and comedies rhymed in the French manner; he was appointed director when the first theater was opened at St. Petersburg in 1756. This was the first time that the Russian public had an opportunity to see plays not dealing with religious subjects.

Under Catherine II (1762–1796), herself a writer, literature made further advances. As Prof. Morfill has said: "Everything in Russia was to be forced like plants in a hothouse; she was to have Homers, Pindars, Horaces, and Virgils." Hippolytus Bogdanovich (1743–1803) imitated La Fontaine; Michael Kheraskov (1733–1807) wrote two vast and little read epics; Ivan Khemnitzer (1744–1784) first translated fables from the German, and then wrote his own, beginning a tradition of fable writing that has been very popular in Russia. Denis von Visin (1744–1792) was a writer of some importance in helping to bring about a national comedy; *The Minor* and *The Brigadier* are satirical comedies ridiculing the brutality of Russian society in its manners and its treatment of serfs. Gabriel Derzhavin (1743–1816) was considered the great poet of the age. He was interested in German literature, and adapted some verses of Frederick the Great. His *Ode to Sovereigns* was later considered rather revolutionary; but his reputation was made by his versifying of a fairy story by Catherine herself, in which he pays her extravagant compliments. But poetry has never been, according to the critic Waliszewski, "the natural blossoming of the national life," satire being the most typical poetical tone. Hence, Derzhavin never wrote poetry that has seemed worth the translating into other languages. The fairy story referred to, *Félitsa*, is a mixture of ode and satire, and is humorous in tone. He versified Addison's *Vision of Mirzah*, using the same title; in his *Ode on the Capture of Warsaw* he imitates Macpherson. Pushkin insisted later that Derzhavin was a man of inferior talents.

Under Catherine a great deal of French classical literature was published in translation, including the *Encyclopedia*, various works of Voltaire, Rousseau, Helvétius, and La Fontaine—in some of which enterprises the Empress herself took a hand.

Alexander Radishchev (1749–1802) spent some time in Germany, studied Voltaire and Rousseau, came to admire Lawrence Sterne, and under the last-named's influence wrote his *Journey to St. Petersurg and Moscow* (1790); he declared for freeing the serfs and granting them the soil they were tilling. Catherine, infuriated at the book, sent him off to Siberia for ten years. There he wrote a treatise *On Man, on Death, and Immortality*, full of the opinions of Newton, Locke, and Rousseau. On his recall by Paul I, he formulated a plan for a reform of the judiciary, calling for trial by jury; when asked whether he was anxious for Siberia again, he went home and committed suicide.

Nicholas Novikov (1744–1818) fought against the inundation of native Russian traditions by Western culture. He gave the best of his talents to journalism, for the chief purpose of popularizing knowledge, as Addison and Steele had done in England. Later he was busy in the founding of schools and printing works and the opening of bookshops. But his advanced opinion met with disfavor at Court, and he was imprisoned.

Alexander I (1801–1825) came so much under the influence of revolutionary ideas that he was applauded in Mme. de Staël's salon for announcing that the serfs in Russia were about to be freed. The event, of course, never came to pass in his reign. But he trifled all his lifetime with liberal dreams, never troubling to realize them in fact, and for a long time encouraged bold thinking among his writers. At this time English literature became popular in Russia.

Nicholas Karamzin (1766–1826) was a poet, historian, essayist, and novelist, who visited Germany, Switzerland, France, and England. Under the influence of Richardson and Sterne, he wrote two sentimental novels, *Natalia* and *Poor Lisa* (both 1792); they were intended to prove that Russia's past afforded authentic literary material. His *History of the Russian Empire* is his most important historical work. He also translated Thomson's *The Seasons*. Ivan Dmitriev (1760–1837) wrote some pleasant lyrical poetry, under the influence of the English. Ladislas Ozierov (1769–1816) first wrote in French, later in Russian. He imitated the French in tragedy, adapted Macpherson's *Fingal*, and wrote a truly original work on a native theme in his tragedy *Dmitri Donskoï* (1807). Other classical tragedies by him include *Polyxena* and *Medea*. Vassili Zhukovski (1786–1852), when still very young, dramatized *Paul and Virginia* from the French and adapted Gray's *Elegy* in his *Thoughts on a Tomb*. Later he translated all of Kotzebue's plays, and works of Dryden and Schiller. His first celebrated poem was imitated from Gray's rather absurd *The Bard* with its sobbing winds and rushing cataracts in the early Romantic manner, and was called *The Bard in the Russian Camp*; the poem is said to have been immensely popular during the War of 1812. Later he translated the *Odyssey* and works of Goethe and Byron. Constantin Batiushkov (1787–1855) adapted Petrarch and Tibullus into Russian, and composed some good poetry before becoming insane fairly early in life. Ivan Krylov (1767–1844) imitated La Fontaine, Æsop and other writers of fables, but added a pungency and immediacy of his own. Ivan Kozlov (1774–1838), crippled and blind through accident, was a translator of Burns and other Englishmen. Alexander Griboyedov (1795–1829) has been compared to Beaumarchais because of his comedy, *The Misfortune of Being Too Clever*, written in 1823, but forbidden performance; it circulated, however, in thousands of manuscripts, for its withering sarcasm at the expense of the upper classes and their moral corruption pleased the *literati*. The work was much influenced by Molière's *The Misanthrope*.

In Pushkin, Russian literature at last has a figure of world stature.

ALEXANDER PUSHKIN (1799–1837)

IMPORTANCE

Alexander Pushkin in his brief lifetime managed to build a foundation for the development of a national literature. When he began to write, Russian letters, as we have seen, was a hodgepodge of foreign influences, most of it uninspired imitations of the French, the German, and the English. The classical tradition of skeptical wit and licentiousness from France, the humanitarian mysticism from Germany, and the sentimental or dashing Romanticism from England were all thriving side by side. Whatever was truly Russian was much more closely associated with ancient oral literature than with belles lettres. So beclouded was the literary scene that Pushkin's authentic genius was for a long time mistaken as merely imitative of the Western world. It is true that he did come under important Western influences, and even the appellation of "the Russian Byron" is not without point when applied to him; but his voice, once he found it, was genuinely his own. Had he written nothing but *Eugene Onyegin*, on which he spent nine years, he would have to be accounted as the man who began a truly Russian tradition in belles lettres.

Pushkin's education began largely in his father's library, stocked with French authors; he first wrote in French and had mastered that tongue long before he could write proficient Russian. After six years at the aristocratic College of Tsarskoïe Sielo (1811–1817), during which he wrote many verses in French, or in the French manner, or occasionally in imitation of British writers like Macpherson, he joined the Ministry of Foreign Affairs, and began his first major work, *Ruslan and Lyudmila*, a poem he completed in 1820. This effort has been labeled a "mere marqueterie" of Pushkin's favorite authors at this time of his life: Ariosto, Wieland, Herder, Molière, Chénier, Macpherson, and Béranger. The importance of the endeavor was that the young poet here was using a national legend, though he made the error of treating it ironically.

During this time Pushkin was leading the life of a man of fashion at St. Petersburg, and gave little hint of what was yet to come from him. Various of his poems were circulating in manuscript. One of them, an "Ode to Liberty" was very daring in its sentiments. It is not yet clear whether it was because of this poem or of some of the many ribald (and often obscene) verses that Pushkin learned to write from a study of the French authors in his father's library that he very nearly was sent to Siberia. He managed to escape that fate when he was persuaded to accept an official post in Bessarabia.

Now Pushkin's work took a new turn. Byron's influence gained complete ascendancy over him (1820–1824), and it somehow suited perfectly the stirring inspiration he felt while he was dwelling in the Caucasus. Playing the Byronic role himself, Pushkin created scandals everywhere by his eccentric behavior— his wild rides across the mountains, his duels, and his gambling. To this period belong the Byronic poems: *The Prisoner of the Caucasus*, the hero of which is another Childe Harold; *The Fountain of the Bakchissaraï*, in which a lover comes into conflict with the harem system; *The Gypsies*, dealing with a true Byronic hero who has fled from the hypocrisies of society; and the early portion of *Eugene Onyegin*.

At Odessa an Englishman introduced him to Shelley's work. Soon in a letter Pushkin was admitting atheism; the letter was intercepted and the poet was handed over to his father's keeping. The elder Pushkin behaved like a jailor until he was persuaded to wash his hands of his son completely, and the poet was left to the care of the local police at Mikhailovskoye.

Boris Godunov

In 1825 he published the tragedy *Boris Godunov*, an imitation of Shakespeare, in which the hero is a kind of synthesis of Henry IV, Macbeth, and Richard III; some scenes are right out of the English master. The play did the stage the service of ridding it of the French influence under which it had so long been thwarted of any possibility of developing a national drama. But *Boris Godunov*, probably because of the massive music which Moussorgski later wrote for it, has been much overpraised. It is a procession of historical scenes rather than a play, its material taken from the chronicle of Karamzin.

In 1598 the Czar Theodore died without an heir; Boris Godunov, although suspected of having ordered the assassination of the late czar's younger brother Dmitri, is urged by people and nobles alike to take over the crown in the troubled times facing them. In 1603 a young monk, Gregory Otrepiev, at the monastery of Chudov has had his head turned by the stories of Dmitri's death as related to him by an old monk.

Gregory, of the age that Dmitri would have been had he lived, is determined to pass himself off as the prince saved from death by a miracle. Escaping from the monastery, he eludes the guards sent after him and goes to Lithuania. There he proclaims himself to be Dmitri and succeeds in winning the support of the Polish king to help him gain the Russian throne. But Gregory, in love with the Polish girl, Marina, admits to her that he is an impostor, for he wishes her to know who he really is. At first she scorns him, but when he promises to wrest the Russian throne from Boris, she admires his ambition and promises to marry him if he can carry through his enterprise.

The drama now shows us several battle scenes and conferences of the leaders. The false Dmitri at first wins, then loses the fight. He retreats but begins to gather new forces. Czar Boris now dies, after giving his son advice right out of the mouth of Henry IV (when addressing words of warning to Prince Hal). But the people now rise up at the false Dmitri's bidding, kill the young prince and princess, and the false Dmitri wins.

Eugene Onyegin

Between the completion of *Boris Godunov* and the publication of *Eugene Onyegin* in 1833, Pushkin narrowly escaped being involved in the punishment meted out to members of the Decembrist conspiracy (1826), there being no question of his sympathy with them; but the Czar proved merciful. Pushkin immediately plunged into a life of extreme dissipation until his marriage in 1830 to Natalia Gontcharov. But during these years he was also turning out some of his best prose and poetry. In 1831 *Boris* was presented at last on the stage, but it created no stir. The next year his long labors on *Eugene Onyegin* were at last completed.

The story of this seven-thousand-line poem is very simple. Eugene Onyegin, soured with his dissipated life in the metropolis, comes to stay in the country at an estate that he has inherited. He is joined by his friend Lensky, newly returned from Germany and full of Schiller and Kant. Lensky introduces Eugene to the Larin family, whose two daughters are Tanya, shy but imaginative, and the pretty schoolgirl who is her sister. Lensky loves the younger; Onyegin is impressed with neither; Tanya falls madly in love with Eugene. Tanya, perceiving that Onyegin looks down upon her, writes him a letter declaring her passion.

He is too honorable to take advantage of her, and too sophisticated to be interested in an inexperienced girl; in an interview with her he urges her to forget him. Later, he has a duel with Lensky, kills him, and leaves the neighborhood. Tanya, pining away, is taken by her aunts to Moscow.

There she agrees to marry a wealthy man, who introduces her into a brilliant society, where she becomes the most brilliant of them all because of her beauty and elegance. Onyegin sees her again, recognizes her, and falls madly in love with her now. Her revenge comes at the expense of her own happiness. She still loves Onyegin, but she informs him that she will never betray her husband.

Tchaikovsky later used Pushkin's text for his beautiful opera.

The influences upon Pushkin in this poem are easy enough to trace: Byron's *Don Juan* in the many digressions the poet permits himself; Byron's *Beppo* in the story throughout; Rousseau's *La Nouvelle Héloïse* in the portrait of the heroine. Nevertheless, the work is thoroughly original and Russian—"an encyclopedia of Russian life," as Bielinski declared, though he might have said instead "of Russian aristocratic life."

IMPORTANCE

The importance of the portrait of Onyegin himself to Russian literature is immense; he became the typical Russian hero—the man who feels superfluous in the ranks into which he has been born, does not know how to escape from them, and consequently leads a life of good intentions during which nothing is ever accomplished. We meet this character again and again in Russian literature. Dostoevsky has said of him that he is the eternal vagabond whom Russian civilization has produced, separated by his culture from the mass of his own countrymen.

Pushkin as a Lyric Poet and Storyteller

Pushkin's marriage turned out to be a complete failure, and he soon returned to the corrupt society of the capital. The Baron d'Anthès, now his brother-in-law, aroused Pushkin's jealousy by the attentions paid the poet's wife, and they fought a duel in which Pushkin was mortally wounded. He died two days later in agony.

Despite his premature death, Pushkin left behind him an enormous legacy of poetry and prose. As a lyric poet he is the author of countless short poems remarkable for their perfection and clarity. His love poems are full of tenderness and sweet pathos. There are many poems too on his own profession; in them he disclaims any intention of bettering the lot of the masses or instructing readers to lead a better life; "we poets are born for enthusiasm, for sweet music, and for prayers." Among his more ambitious poems are an "Ode to the Sea" and "The Battle of Poltava."

He was also a spirited writer of prose tales. Among his best are a historical story, "The Captain's Daughter;" "The Undertaker," a horror story; "The Pistol Shot;" and the best known of them, "The Queen of Spades," which Tchaikovsky also made into an opera (*Pique Dame*).

Pushkin's Successors

Michael Lermontov (1811–1841) was Pushkin's most important successor in poetry. He too felt powerfully the influence of Byron, and cultivated the Englishman's pose of misanthropy. He was at his best in the lyric, which he composed with great delicacy.

Alexis Koltsov (1809–1842), the son of a merchant, was a truly national poet, a kind of Russian Burns, who died early from tuberculosis. He has left a number of lovely songs that are treasured by the Russian people.

Ivan Nikitin (1826–1861) was first a tavernkeeper, then a bookseller. He carried on the tradition of Koltsov. His most admired poem is *Kulak*, on the peasantry.

NIKOLAI GOGOL (1809–1852)

Nikolai Gogol was born in the province of Poltava, in southern Russia where the old traditions concerning the Cossacks were still strong. At the Niezhin Gymnasium he wrote for the school magazine a novel and a tragedy, *The Robbers*, imitated from German originals, which he publicly affected to despise. When he left school, full of the Romantic temper, he published a poem, *Italy* (1829), and another idyl that was bitterly ridiculed. He now decided to exploit the Cossack legendry which he knew so well.

In 1831 appeared his volume *Evenings at a Farm near Dikanka*, a collection of stories reflecting with vivacity and mirth the life of the Ukraine. It took the literary world by storm because of its novelty. He was soon offered a professorship at St. Petersburg, but he did not retain the position long. Planning a compendious history of the Middle Ages and another of Little Russia, he presently gave up these learned tasks and continued to issue more of his tales and sketches of Little Russian life instead. Some of these were collected under the title of *Arabesques*.

IMPORTANCE

Nikolai Gogol was the first important novelist in Russian literature. Before him there is little that can be described as of interest in the novel. In the Sir Walter Scott tradition, Mikhail Zagoskin (1789–1852) wrote *Yuri Miloslavski* (1829), and Thaddeus Bulgarin (1789–1859) was for a long time admired for his *The Russian Gil Blas* (1829).

But the Russians have proved since then that their genius takes most kindly to Realism, not to Romanticism, and it remained for Gogol not only to discover that fact but also to start the great tradition of the Russian novel, through the medium of which Russia was to take her place among the great literary peoples of the world. The truth about Gogol, however, is similar to the instance of Stendhal among the French: It is the manner rather than the subject matter of both these writers that is Realistic.

Taras Bulba

To this period of Gogol's composition, when he was still frankly a Romantic, belongs *Taras Bulba* (1835), a poem in prose of almost Homeric directness and simplicity. It is a kind of prose hymn to the barbaric Cossacks of the fifteenth century. The work itself has a kind of barbaric majesty.

Taras Bulba, a great Cossack leader, is pleased to have his sons Ostap and Andrii home from the Royal Seminary at Kiev. He ridicules the monkish clothes they wear, and in good Cossack tradition Taras and his son Ostap fall to blows. Taras is delighted to know his son has not been ruined by his education and is a good fighter; he takes his sons off to the Cossack camp, the Setch. There the lads prove their mettle by drinking with the best and showing their readiness for any deed of daring.

Kirdyaga is chosen the new leader of the camp and urges his fellows to engage on a raiding exploit. Learning of persecutions in Poland, they start to plunder that country. At Dubno they find the city well defended; they therefore surround it and cut off food supplies, enjoying themselves in riot and drink in the meantime.

One night Andrii is approached by a serving woman who tells him that an old flame of his student days has seen him from the walls, and begs him to bring food to her starving family. He steals some food, and meets his old love again, and finds her more beautiful than ever. For her sake he becomes a traitor to his father. Yankel, a Jew who has been within the city gates, reports to Taras his son's defection.

Some of the Cossacks now return to the Setch to fight the Tartars who have suddenly begun an invasion there. Taras and Ostap remain before Dubno, and later participate in a great battle. In the midst of it they see Andrii, richly clothed, fighting on the side of their enemies. Taras contrives to meet his son face to face and kills him.

The Cossacks suffer a severe defeat, and Ostap is captured. Taras is severely wounded, but manages to escape with his life. He is the only survivor of his Cossacks. He seeks out Yankel and persuades him to take him to Warsaw, which Taras enters, concealed under a load of bricks. At last he sees Ostap, but too late. It is the day the prisoners are being led to torture and death. Before dying, Ostap calls on his father, and Taras answers. He is pursued, but escapes. Back in the Ukraine, he becomes leader of the Cossacks, raises an army, and lays waste to Polish town after Polish town, sparing no one, crying, "This is a mass for Ostap's soul!"

In the end, when thirty men fall on him, he is captured, tied to a tree, and a fire is prepared at his feet. Observing that his Cossacks are about to fall into a trap, he calls to them in time. They dash over the cliff on horseback, ford the river, and escape. Taras is burned alive, but still lives in the memory of his fellows.

"The Cloak"

Among Gogol's stories none is more admired than "The Cloak" (1835). It exhibits his transition to the realistic manner, though the plot is fanciful enough to make it classed as a ghost story. "We have all," said a Russian critic, "come from Gogol's 'The Cloak.'" Russian Realism has been dated from it.

The hero of the story is a simple clerk, Akakii Akakievich, who has a genius for copying letters and who loves his work. For years he deprives himself of the smallest luxuries so that he can save enough to buy himself a fine new cloak. At last he buys it, and the first day he wears it, he loses it. Around this simple plot, Gogol contrives to paint a portrait that may rival Flaubert for its veracity and sharp observation, but which also sounds over-tones of pity such as Flaubert would have rigidly excluded. It also departs from Realism by concluding with a fantastic account of Akakii's return as a vengeful ghost.

The Inspector-General

A year later, Gogol wrote what has been called the first modern Russian play, *The Inspector-General* (*Revizor*) (1836). The manner of the play is, on the whole, French—the last scene bearing close resemblances, for instance, to *The Misanthrope* of Molière. But the idea, suggested to Gogol by Pushkin, is a very clever one, which enabled the author to pen a scathing denunciation of the corruption of Russian officialdom.

The plot of the piece is simple enough. Khlestakov, an impoverished young scamp from St. Petersburg, on his way to his family in the country for the holidays, can proceed no further on his journey because he is completely out of funds. He is about to be taken to the debtors' prison in a provincial town, when it suddenly occurs to the officials of the place that he must be the Inspector-General traveling incognito the better to observe their crimes. They have been awaiting that dread personage, and, convinced that they know their man, they load Khlestakov with attentions and bribes so that he may make a favorable report. Naturally, each of them is so anxious to preserve his own skin that he is willing to betray the others. Our young hero makes the most of his opportunities and leaves town just in time. The imposed-upon officials learn of their mistake only to hear that the true inspector is about to arrive.

Gogol's satire at the expense of petty officials and his exposure of bureaucracy were highly prized by the radicals, although he was a conservative himself.

Dead Souls

In 1836 Gogol left Russia to live chiefly at Rome, where much of his great novel, *Dead Souls* (*Mertvuiya Dushi*), was written. In 1840 he returned to Russia to oversee the publication of the first part of *Dead Souls*, and then returned to Italy. It is said that his residence in Italy was responsible for his developing into a fanatical mystic. In 1848 he made a pilgrimage to Jerusalem and then returned to Moscow, where he settled down. During his last days he destroyed the conclusion to *Dead Souls* because of his religious scruples. It was, therefore, never issued as a complete work. Zaharchenko attempted to issue a conclusion for it in 1857.

The "dead souls" of the title are dead serfs. The wealth of a Russian proprietor was computed for the taxes not according to the extent of his lands but according to the number of his male serfs, who were known as "souls" on the documents. The census, however, was taken so seldom that a landowner had to continue paying for dead serfs ("dead souls") until the next census. To a farmer oppressed by famine, these extra charges were serious. As De Vogüé puts it: "Chichikov, the hero of the book [*Dead Souls*], an ambitious and evil-minded rascal, made this proposition to himself, 'I will visit the most remote corners of Russia, and ask the good people to deduct from the number of their lists every serf who has died since the last census was taken. They will be only too glad, as it will be to their interest to yield up to me a fictitious property, and get rid of paying the tax upon it. I shall have my purchase registered in due form, and no tribunal will imagine that I require it to legalize a sale of dead men. When I have obtained the names of some thousands of serfs, I shall carry my deeds to some bank in St. Petersburg or Moscow, and raise a large sum on them. Then I shall be a rich man, and in condition to buy real peasants of flesh and blood.'"

The plot thus becomes only an excuse for Gogol's describing Chichikov's adventures as he drives around Russia in his troïka. The result is a picture of the whole of Russian provincial society. Gogol gives us every type of Russian and depicts the social suffering of the country. The author himself admitted that it was *Don Quixote*, to which he was introduced by Pushkin, that gave him his earliest ideas for the work. What is significant throughout the work is the great element of pity for even the worst wretches depicted. Here again we have a trait that becomes common to Russian literature. Nevertheless, Gogol's prevailing tone is comic, and the satire is irresistible.

The reader meets people from every rank of society during Chichikov's travels. At length the rascal comes to grief through forging a will, which he does too carelessly. His lawyer, however, wins him liberty by using some known scandal against every notable in town so that the issue becomes confused, and Chichikov is allowed to leave town.

Gogol's Successors

Ivan Goncharov (1814–1891) wrote his first novel, *A Common Story*, under the influence of George Sand; his best known work, a study of the inertia which is so deeply rooted in the character of the Russian peasant, is *Oblomov*.

Dmitri Grigorovich (1822–1900) also wrote under the inspiration of George Sand. His stories of popular life are forerunners of Turgeniev's. Among the best of these are the *Village, Antony the Unlucky*, and *The Valley of Smyedov*. In *The Fishers* and *The Colonists* he describes the poverty-stricken conditions of peasants and factory hands.

Alexander Ostrovski (1824–1886) is considered one of Russia's leading dramatists. He is a Realist, a student of the Muscovite merchants, from whose ranks he came. His best plays are *Between Ourselves We'll Settle It* (1850) and *Every One in His Own Place* (1853); his drama *The Storm*, with a theme similar to the one Tolstoy was later to employ in *Anna Karenina*, is considered his masterpiece. His plays are hard to classify as comedies or tragedies; there is nothing to laugh at, and nothing to weep over. They have been called, instead, "representations of life." They have always been popular in Russia.

Alexis Constantinovich Tolstoy (1817–1875), not to be confused with the great Leo Tolstoy, was the author of a trilogy highly esteemed in Russia, *The Death of Ivan the Terrible*, *The Czar Fiodor Ivanovich*, and *The Czar Boris*, historical novels based upon authentic historical knowledge. They evoke powerfully the atmosphere of gloomy superstition that hung over Russia's dark ages. Alexis Tolstoy is also admired for his lyrical and satirical poetry.

IVAN TURGENEV (1818–1883)

Ivan Turgenev has seemed to the Western world the finest artist among the great nineteenth century Russians. While producing a nationalist literature, he nevertheless approached closer than the others to a Western European style. That may indeed be owing to the fact that he spent so much of his life in Paris and Baden-Baden and came to know personally the leaders of the French Realist movement. He is a writer of great delicacy and keen perception, over whose work pessimism broods like a mist.

He was born of a noble family at Oriel, the son of a colonel in the cavalry, and was left, while still a youth, to the rearing of an arrogant wealthy mother, who spoke Russian only to the servants. He was much more at home, at first, in French and German than in his native tongue. Later in life his mother was deeply chagrined that a son of hers could have descended so low as to become a novelist. Ivan's first acquaintance with the literature of his country came to him through the offices of an old serf, deeply attached to the family.

The great critic Bielinski was early attracted to Turgenev's youthful productions and encouraged the boy, to his lasting gratitude. But Turgenev never wrote anything of importance until the first of his *A Sportsman's Sketches* appeared in 1847; all at once, everyone was talking about it. Nevertheless, disgusted with Russia politically and intellectually, Turgenev left for Paris the next year, intending to remain away. He continued to write the series of *A Sportsman's Sketches* in Paris. It was perhaps the first work ever written to see the Russian peasant as he actually was, "with a soul of his own," and his own way of looking at life. It has been said that this book started Russia on the road to revolution, and began the movement for the emancipation of the serfs. Oddly enough for such consequences, it was written by a man who was too much of an artist to be a propagandist. But as a delicate Realist, he was able to show how the serf system had degraded the native Russian character to brutality and stupidity. The series was collected in 1852.

The same year he made the mistake of taking a short trip to Russia. Because of an article he wrote on Gogol's death, he was sent to prison for a month, and released through the influence of Mme. Smirovna. He now settled in a villa at Baden-Baden and began to write an uninterrupted procession of novels, stories, and tales. His next important novel was *A House of Gentlefolk* (1859), a very moving work that received wide appreciation. The hero of the novel, Lavretski, belongs to the tradition of Eugene Onyegin, a man of great soul and healthy mind who cannot act or decide to act. In 1860 appeared *On the Eve*, and in 1862 came his most celebrated novel, *Fathers and Sons* (sometimes translated as *Fathers and Children*), a remarkable description of the Nihilism then pervading Russia.

Fathers and Sons

The title refers to the older and newer influences at work in the Russia of Turgenev's day. So influential has the novel been that it is now impossible to decide upon the truth of the allegation that Turgenev invented the word *nihilism*. The term applies in the novel to the philosophy of the hero, Bazarov, the first Nihilist on record, whose whole philosophy is one of rebellion against the status quo.

Bazarov has come to stay with his former fellow student Arkadi at the latter's home on the conclusion of their studies at St. Petersburg. Arkadi's father, Kirsanov, is worried about Bazarov's indifferent demeanor from the very beginning. Kirsanov has some qualms telling his son that he has installed his mistress, now that his wife is dead, in their home. Arkadi accepts the news quite cheerfully.

Kirsanov becomes more and more irritated at Arkadi's doctor friend, Bazarov, for his opposition to all authority, and dreads the influence the young scientist has over his son. Chiefly he dislikes Bazarov because the young man seems to know too much and to have a biting tongue. But his older brother, Pavel, who has come to live with Kirsanov after disappointment in his career and in love, a thorough aristocrat in prejudice, dislikes Bazarov even more violently. Kirsanov, out of love for Arkadi, would like to keep peace. On the whole, Bazarov is not too difficult a guest for he is forever occupied with collecting specimens. Kirsanov has his own worries. Friendly to the approaching emancipation of the serfs, he has already rented out his land in small plots to his men, but feeling independent, the peasants are cheating him.

Bazarov and Arkadi go to the capital of the province for a visit and are introduced to the governor. They meet a fellow Nihilist, Sitnikov, and through him a young widow, Mme. Odinzov, whose mother had been a friend of Mme. Kirsanov. The two youths visit her home; Arkadi falls in love with Mme. Odinzov's younger sister, Bazarov with the widow herself. Despite his contempt for all traditions, Bazarov does propose marriage to her, but he is rejected.

The two young men leave for Bazarov's home, where the latter's father Vasili lives in fear and admiration of his brilliant son. They quickly tire of the Bazarov home, though everything is done to please them. They stop at Mme. Odinzov's again, but are not warmly received. They return to Arkadi's home. But Arkadi secretly returns to the Odinzov home to see his beloved Katya. In the meantime, Bazarov has been giving medicines to Kirsanov's mistress, Fenichka, and her little baby, and becoming very friendly with her. One day he impulsively kisses her. Pavel sees the incident and is all the more incensed against Bazarov. He challenges him to a duel, and is wounded in the leg by the young Nihilist. Bazarov leaves the Kirsanov home.

Misunderstanding Arkadi as in love with Mme. Odinzov herself, Bazarov presses his friend's suit. He is greeted by the lady once more in a way to make him feel ridiculous. He decides to return to his father's home. Vasili, established as the country doctor, is glad to have his son's help. Bazarov finds some consolation in working for the health of the peasantry. However, he contracts an infection through carelessness and becomes mortally ill. He sends for Mme. Odinzov, who alleviates his last hours.

Kirsanov, on Pavel's advice, marries his mistress. Arkadi marries Katya, and is happy running his father's farm. Mme. Odinzov marries a prosperous lawyer. Fenichka is happy as a wife and mother, and Kirsanov is busy as a magistrate settling the disputes of the liberated serfs.

IMPORTANCE

Fathers and Sons is said to have divided Russia in half—those who sided with the old order and those who sided with the new. The authorities thenceforth used the word *Nihilist* to stigmatize their radical enemies. But in addition to furnishing a clear and unbiased picture of the times, Turgenev's great novel has universality, for it portrays the inevitable division in all times between the older and younger generations.

Smoke

Turgenev's last novels include *Smoke* (1867) and *Virgin Soil* (1877).

Smoke is laid in the period immediately following the emancipation of serfs against the background of the Nihilist movement in Russia, fostered by a group of intellectual radicals from the universities. They worshiped science, reason, and education and despised political autocracy and the Orthodox Church. Their version of Darwinism was a belief in the inevitable evolution of society from autocracy to democracy. At first the Nihilists were contented to discuss and publish, but the censorship imposed against them resulted in their forming secret societies that operated among the masses and in the army.

Although the backgrounds of *Fathers and Sons* and *Smoke* are similar, the latter novel is more unashamedly a love story into which the political issues of the time barely intrude. The plot centers around the attempts of Irene, a society beauty, to enkindle once more the passion of Grigory Litvinov, her former suitor, whom she has rejected; the fact that he is now engaged to marry another girl, Tanya Shestov, is what motivates her caprice.

Finding he still loves her, he has an affair with her but decides at last that he will not live in this clandestine way. She must go away with him, or he will renounce her. She agrees but at the last minute does not join him on the train. He returns to his father's estate in Russia, and after a few years meets Tanya again, is forgiven, and they marry.

The one idea permeating the book is that there is yet hope for Russia, if the Russians will only get down to serious work.

Virgin Soil

Virgin Soil is laid at a somewhat later date in the same period. It is brilliantly written and shows Turgenev a Realist at his best. Nezhdanov, a student of noble lineage though born out of wedlock and in poor financial circumstances, is an admirer of the Nihilists and has joined their secret organization. He accepts the offer of the post of tutor in the household of the aristocratic liberal Sipyagin. Marianna, an impoverished niece of the Sipyagins, lives with them and is secretly an admirer of the Nihilists too. The two young people meet privately at night to discuss politics but do not yield to their love for each other.

Nezhdanov is discharged and takes Marianna away with him. For a time they live as sister and brother, dress as peasants, and try to work for the revolution. But the peasants do not understand his speeches; when he tries to drink with them to show he is one of them, he only gets quite sick. Marianna becomes more and more convinced that Nezhdanov is a weakling and is drawn more and more to the strength of a fellow conspirator, Solomin, a machinist. When the authorities have found their hiding place and are ready to swoop down on them, Nezhdanov in a letter urges Marianna to marry Solomin and then kills himself in despair at his own weakness. Solomin and Marianna marry and escape in time.

Nezhdanov is, again, the traditional Russian intellectual who finds himself unable to realize in action his high ideals. Solomin, on the other hand, is a new kind of Russian hero—the realist-idealist, who doesn't talk elegant ideas but proves by his honorable and quiet dealings his ability and his sincerity; it is the dignity of labor, as shown in his career, that will bring about a free society for workingmen. The dilettante liberal, like Sipyagin, can be depended upon to become vicious when his own comfort becomes at all involved. These are the ideas that made *Virgin Soil* one of the most important books connected with the struggle against Russian autocracy.

Turgenev's Stories

The same artistic finish and brooding melancholy that distinguish his novels will be found in Turgenev's short stories. A number of them are equal to anything he wrote, and are often very subtle in their psychological analysis. The best are "Rudin," "The Diary of a Superfluous Man," "A Lear of the Steppes," and "First Love."

FEODOR DOSTOEVSKY (1822–1881)

In English-speaking literary circles it has been fashionable for generations to say of Dostoevsky that he is unquestionably the world's greatest novelist, and to disparage by contrast Thackeray and Dickens (the works of either of whom would be enough to give importance to the literature of any language). It would be foolish, from a sense of outraged justice, to diminish him in order to be grateful to them. For there is no denying that Dostoevsky is almost unique in his ability to create a world of his own within his best novels—a world so powerfully real that while one is reading him the tangible world about one is likely to seem comparatively pale and unreal. Whether or not it is accurate to number him among the Realists is another question. Although he satisfies all Realism's requirements with his discerning observation of everyday life, even at its seamiest, and is certainly one of the world's profoundest and subtlest psychologists in the field of the novel, the sum total of each of his masterpieces is something larger than life, wonderful but also undefinably mysterious—like a terribly vivid nightmare that is both true to experience and yet different from it. Despite Dostoevsky's great vogue in our time, his name was unknown to the English-speaking world until 1885, when *Crime and Punishment* was first translated.

Feodor Dostoevsky, son of a military surgeon, was born at Moscow, educated there, and later at the St. Petersburg School of Engineering, where, despite his periodic epileptic seizures and his general poor health, he was a brilliant student. He had, however, been devouring Pushkin, Gogol, Balzac, and George Sand. To her omnipresent humanitarianism he owed a great deal. When the elder Dostoevsky died in 1844, Feodor resigned his year-old commission of sublieutenant to take up the profession of letters.

Another youthful admirer of George Sand, Grigorovich, of whom we have already spoken, introduced him to the poet Nekrassov, who was at the time looking around for contributors to a periodical he was projecting. Uncomfortable in Nekrassov's presence, Dostoevsky thrust the manuscript of his first novel into the poet's hands, and fled without a word. To console himself he went to some friends with whom, characteristic of the times, he spent the night reading Gogol aloud. The next day Nekrassov and Grigorovich burst in upon Dostoevsky after a night devoted to reading his novel. They had been overwhelmed by it.

This book was called *Poor Folk* (1846). The story is of a pathetic man who loves an equally pathetic girl of the people; she marries a wealthy man, and he dies of a broken heart. *Poor Folk* has often been compared to the work of Dickens, and the hero described as another Tom Pinch. But the truth is that Dostoevsky was not familiar with the work of the great Englishman he so much resembles. Actually *Poor Folk* is a brilliant variation on the character portraiture of Gogol's "The Cloak"; Gogol emphasizes the external pathos of his hero, but Dostoevsky, not interested in comedy, penetrates to his hero's sensitive soul. The production was amazing for a youth of twenty. No wonder Bielinski, the great critic, exclaimed: "He owes a great deal to Gogol, just as Lermentov owes a great deal to Pushkin; but he is original. He begins as no author before him has ever begun."

Delighted with his sudden fame, Dostoevsky immediately began taxing his health, applying feverish energy to his writing as he did for the rest of his life. He wrote a series of tales for the magazine *Annals of the Country* but was paid wretchedly small sums. His physical sufferings and poverty increased the gloom that was natural to his temperament. In 1847 he joined a revolutionary group led by Petrachevski, whose meetings were given over to nothing more harmful than discussion of economic theory. Their favorite idea was the Slavophil doctrine that Russia had no need of Western models to advance in culture.

In April 1849 the club was arrested and confined in the fortress of St. Paul and St. Peter at St. Petersburg. There Dostoevsky wrote the tale called *A Little Hero*. After eight months' imprisonment he was conducted with other prisoners to a scaffold in Simonovski Square. In the bitter cold, they were stripped to the waist, and heard their sentence of death read. Coffins were on hand to receive their bodies, they were bound in threes to stakes, the priest offered them the crucifix to kiss, the soldiers snapped their swords over the condemned men's heads, and they were ready for execution. Dostoevsky was third in line. He made his farewells to his two neighbors, when suddenly the drums beat a tattoo, the prisoners were unbound, brought back to the scaffold, and informed that the Czar had spared their lives. The prisoners now put on convict uniforms, and prepared for exile in Siberia. One of them had lost his reason in the interim. But Dostoevsky always insisted that it was his four years' imprisonment in Siberia that saved him from the insanity that otherwise, he was sure, would have been his fate.

His four terrible years in Siberia "buried alive" have been powerfully recorded in *The House of the Dead* (1861). His release brought with it compulsory military service for the rest of his days. But the intervention of a friend raised him to the rank of a petty officer. When Alexander II came to the throne in 1859, Dostoevsky's exile was repealed, and he was allowed to leave Siberia. In 1858 he had married a widow, with whom he had an unhappy life, and they came to live at St. Petersburg.

For the next years he was in constant debt because of various journalistic ventures in the Slavophil cause and also because of his incorrigible passion for gambling. He was often forced to leave Russia to escape his creditors. At Baden-Baden he gambled away whatever he had with him. At Florence he was bored in a few minutes with the great art galleries, and spent his time talking at a café or reading the newly appearing *Les Misérables*.

In the meantime his novel, *The Insulted and the Injured* (1867) was not very well received, and his wife died. His reputation was very much alive in the public's mind, however, not only because of the profound impression made by *The House of the Dead*, but because in 1866 he had astounded the Russian world of letters (as he did the next year in Western Europe when the French translation appeared) with *Crime and Punishment*. For the rest of the nineteenth century *Crime and Punishment* was held to be the top of his achievement. Since then *The Brothers Karamazov* has been generally thought his masterwork.

Despite the harassment of debts, the attacks of epilepsy, and his failing health, Dostoevsky's last years were a little more pleasant. He returned to Russia in the early seventies, and managed *The Russian World*, and later (1876) a magazine called *Carnet d'un Écrivain* (*A Writer's Notebook*), for which he wrote a number of reflections and pieces of autobiography. He married a second time; his second wife, although not highly educated, took good care of him, and managed affairs so well that he was able at last to get clear of debt. His closing years were spent in comparative financial ease at St. Petersburg.

In addition to *Crime and Punishment* (1866), his best novels are *The Idiot* (1869), *The Possessed* (1871), and *The Brothers Karamazov* (1880). *The Journal of an Author* (1877) is full of biographical interest. Dostoevsky is also the author of some remarkable short stories, some of them unsurpassed in their kind: "The Double," "The Eternal Husband," "An Honest Thief," "The Gambler," "White Nights," and "The Friend of the Family" being among the best.

IMPORTANCE

It is not a simple task to describe Dostoevsky's art. It reminds us of Dickens in its all-pervading humanity, its sympathy for those the world neglects, its tender understanding of those who transgress against the moral law, as well as an impression left with the reader of vastness and a certain formlessness. But Dostoevsky is a Realist to a degree that is rarely true of Dickens.

On the other hand, he is like no other Realist we know; he seems, for instance, as infinitely removed from the objectivity of Flaubert or the documentary "science" of Zola's Naturalism as from the cold matter-of-factness of Maupassant. He has none of their ability to organize his material, to control his story, to differentiate the talk of various characters. His interest was exclusively in man's spiritual life. Prof. Brückner observes that in Dostoevsky's novels the exterior is always illuminated from within, and goes on to say, with much point,

> One may be unable to form any idea [as to how his heroes may have looked,] but in return, every impulse, every fibre of their psychical organization is very familiar to us—and they are very complicated organisms. . . . He places men face to face and speaks, analyzes, and argues for them with a passionateness and enthusiasm, with an endurance and keenness, a versatility and profundity, which are as yet unmatched.

Crime and Punishment

As in a novel by Dickens, there are always various plots loosely intertwined in a novel by Dostoevsky. In *Crime and Punishment*, however, the predominance of one story—Raskolnikov's—is clearer than in the later novels. The ruling idea of this great book is a fundamental teaching of Christianity; one may pay for one's crimes by suffering, and by suffering be regenerated. In every life, the author knows, no matter how fallen, there are moments of pure selflessness and goodness. So, he believes, by love and mutual kindness, the Russian people might some day evolve without the use of force into a happy nation.

Raskolnikov, a poor student living at St. Petersburg, is generous, warm-hearted, and highly idealistic—a bold thinker subjected to the same current of ideas as Turgeniev's hero, Bazarov (in *Fathers and Sons*). His body starved and his mind depressed by hunger, he decides to take the life of a disgusting old widow, a pawnbroker of greed and cruelty, who, he feels, has small claim to live. He plans what he intends shall be a perfect crime, kills her, and robs her lodgings of some jewelry.

When the police summon him, he is sure his guilt is known. As it turns out, he has been called on the complaint of his landlady for back rent. He faints from relief, and his conduct arouses suspicion. Safe in his room, he lapses into a fever.

His sister's fiancé, Luzhin, whom he dislikes, arrives in St. Petersburg and is treated rudely by Raskolnikov because the young man knows that Dounya is going to marry him only to rescue the family's finances. Raskolnikov now goes out to read the newspapers, and in his feverish state becomes greatly excited over the fact that no clues have developed in the murder case.

Unexpectedly witnessing an attempted suicide in the poverty-stricken vicinity, he is about to give himself up, but changes his mind when a friend of his is run over by a carriage and killed. He gives his friend's widow the money he has.

One day he finds his mother and sister waiting for him in his room. He cannot bear their presence in his state of mind, and asks his friend Razumihin to entertain them while they are in town. The latter finds himself drawn powerfully to Dounya.

Porphiry, the police inspector, seems fairly convinced that Raskolnikov is the murderer and, lacking any evidence, is systematically trying to break the young man down by his ironic questioning. Raskolnikov, made rash by danger and a victim of his belief in his own genius, declares to Porphiry that he considers men of genius exempt from moral restrictions. He also convinces his mother and sister that Luzhin is a pompous ass, and the latter is given his dismissal; this decision is all the easier for Dounya since she has met Razumihin. The new suitor suddenly comes into money and asks Dounya and her brother to join him in a publishing project. She accepts, but Raskolnikov begs off. Wishing them all happiness, he asks them to go their way and leave him to his.

He now seeks out Sonya, the daughter of the friend who had been killed in an accident. She has become a prostitute to save her family from starvation, her father having been a hopeless drunkard. Raskolnikov realizes that the girl, despite her way of life, is pure at heart. Together they read aloud the story of the raising of Lazarus from the dead from her copy of the Bible, and he notes the fervor of her faith. His own soul is so deeply affected that he promises to tell her the identity of the old pawnbroker's murderer.

He is drawn to the office of Porphiry, where the police inspector continues to plague him with his hints. Raskolnikov's life now is one endless spiritual ferment.

Sonya's mother gives a party for her late husband's acquaintance. At it Luzhin accuses Sonya of stealing money from his room, his purpose being to revenge himself upon Raskolnikov through Sonya. However, his plan is foiled because a neighbor has seen him slipping the money into Sonya's pocket.

At last Raskolnikov confesses his guilt to Sonya and admits that his crime has destroyed all that was worthwhile in himself. But this confession is overheard by Svidrigailov, in whose employ Dounya once had been a governess, and he informs the young man of what he has heard. Porphiry pushes Raskolnikov further by telling him outright that he is the murderer; he begs the young man to confess, plead temporary insanity, and thus mitigate the penalty. Raskolnikov temporizes.

Svidrigailov has always been attracted to Dounya. He now tells her the truth about her brother and promises to keep what he knows to himself if she will marry him. She tries to shoot him with a pistol in her possession. He knows now that she detests him. He leaves her a large gift of money and kills himself.

Comforted by the love of Sonya, Dounya, and his mother, Raskolnikov, whose regeneration has been effected by the example of the prostitute's innate goodness, surrenders to the police. He is tried and sentenced to exile in Siberia. During this time Sonya follows him to a village near his prison and becomes known throughout the prison for her kindness to the men there. Raskolnikov knows now that he can begin a new life of happiness with her when his term is over. Dounya and Razumihin, thriving in their publishing adventure, are now happily married.

Dostoevsky wonderfully recreates the sense of dirt and misery in the St. Petersburg slums throughout the novel. He also delivers, through Raskolnikov's mouth, some of his favorite opinions—his fury against Napoleon and other great heroes who ought to be accounted murderers for their acts against humanity.

The Idiot

The popularity of *The Idiot* among English-speaking readers is rather hard to explain, for surely this is the most difficult of all of its author's novels for a Western mind to comprehend. One understands that in the person of its hero, Prince Myshkin, Dostoevsky is embodying the idea that anyone who has the courage always to be saintly and truthful and compassionate will appear to be an idiot to members of society hardened by the process of daily living. That much one can conceive, and it is a noble concept. But unfortunately the Prince is made (autobiographically) an epileptic and a clumsy man, for no apparent reason; and sometimes, moreover, he does behave in a way so irrational that he must be thought not quite sane. Finally, at the end of the novel, when he is actually confined to an asylum, one becomes confused at the author's possible meaning in having such a hero.

Outside of this important restriction, the novel is powerful in its delineation of the other characters, particularly Natasya and Rogozhin, who are torn between the conflict of good and evil in their strong natures. The character of the Prince, moreover, if one excludes the confusing elements that the author has added, is very appealing in its sweetness. His unfailing sympathy for the wretched and the tortured in soul, his love of children, his constant kindness and humility, his total want of false pride—are all wonderfully depicted and very touching. Yet in the end he remains an enigma because he is touched with something like lunacy; Dostoevsky therefore seems to have defeated his own intentions of showing us a picture of the truly Christian life. Perhaps the Prince suffers from too much kinship with the traditionally ineffectual hero of Russian literature.

The plot of the novel is fairly complicated. The merchant Rogozhin is attracted, on a train going to St. Petersburg, to a shabbily dressed gentleman, Prince Myshkin, who has just left a sanatorium in Switzerland, where he has been under treatment for epilepsy. They become friends. At the capital, the Prince presents himself to the family of General Epanchin, distant relatives of his. They are all pleased with him, and the General helps him with the gift of some money. Because he is completely without guile, they begin to call him affectionately "The Idiot."

The General's secretary, Ganya, desires to marry the General's daughter Aglaya for her money. But he is also having an affair with a beautiful kept woman, Natasya. The Prince realizes the goodness underneath Natasya's mask of gaiety and asks her to marry him. Unwilling to be the cause of disaster to him, she refuses and goes off instead with Rogozhin, who has offered her a vast sum of money. Her purpose is to prove to him how worthless she is. The General's family express their disgust with her, but Myshkin remains unconvinced. Something about him causes others to confess their shortcomings, and Rogozhin and Ganya, each in turn, confess the sordidness of their lives to him and vow their love for him.

But Natasya abandons Rogozhin, and he, suspecting her love for Myshkin, threatens to kill him. Aglaya has fallen in love with Myshkin, but her pride will not allow her to treat him with less than contempt for his simple-mindedness. But Mme. Epanchin, seeing the true state of affairs, agrees to an engagement, and arranges a party to introduce him to society. To prevent his making his usual blunders, they advise him to keep silent all evening. But the General's lady forgets, encourages him to talk, and is appalled to hear him go off into one of his wild discourses. The guests are sufficiently stunned at his conduct, when suddenly he makes matters worse by knocking over a precious vase, staring stupidly at the wreckage, and falling into an epileptic seizure.

Aglaya has become friendly with Natasya, and Myshkin accompanies her to the latter's flat. A violent quarrel between the women ensues, during which it is clear that Aglaya is very much in love with the Prince. Natasya faints, Myshkin rushes over to help her, and Aglaya leaves in anger. The General and his wife feel that they have put up with enough from Myshkin, and inform him he is no longer welcome. Natasya now seems willing to give in to her love for Myshkin, and agrees to marry him. But on their wedding day, he waits for her in vain at the church. She has flitted off with Rogozhin because of her conviction that she and the merchant are each other's evil destiny.

Myshkin surprises everyone by accepting the situation without anger. He goes in search of Natasya to the city. After a futile inquiry among friends, he goes to Rogozhin's apartment and learns that Rogozhin has been there recently. The Prince understands that the other would willingly kill him, but he searches for him anyhow. They meet in the street, and go back to Rogozhin's apartment. There on the bed lies Natasya, slain by her lover. The Prince is overwhelmed with pity for Rogozhin, and spends the night there with him and the corpse. In the morning, Natasya's friends arrive with the police.

Rogozhin confesses, and the Prince is sent back to the sanatorium with no expectation of ever being normal.

The Possessed

The Possessed was Dostoevsky's answer to Turgenev's *Fathers and Sons.*

For the first ten years of his reign (1855–1865) Alexander II had pursued a policy of liberalism and reform. On March 3, 1861 he abolished all property rights of the nobles over their serfs and purchased land from the former to give to the emancipated serfs. In 1864 he established local assemblies (*zemstvo*), each with the right to decide on local taxes. He also reformed the judiciary, encouraged education, and diminished much of the censorship of the press. But by 1865 he suffered a change of heart. He began to tamper with the reforms he had instituted and restored the right of the national government to intervene in local matters and seize upon political offenders. He injected new life into the activities of the secret police instituted by his father (Nicholas I), and thousands of intellectuals became its victims.

Under this renewed oppression, the radical movements began to explode into active life, particularly the Nihilists, Anarchists, and Terrorists. The Terrorists were a group consisting of those Nihilists, Socialists, and Anarchists who could not accept the pacific intellectual approach of their fellows and believed in winning freedom by violence. As their activities increased, the Czar's measures stiffened. He was terrified—and, as it turned out, with good reason. On March 13, 1881, he was himself assassinated.

Dostoevsky could not, like Turgenev, look upon the Nihilists with the sympathetic eye of understanding; he felt they were a menace to Russia, with their dependence on Western science and knowledge. Turgeniev and his Occidentalism come in for much ridicule in the pages of *The Possessed.*

A more accurate translation of the title of the book would seem to be *The Devils.* It is derived from the passage in *Luke* viii dealing with the demons leaving the possessed man and passing into the swine. The patriot Stepan Verhovenski, in the novel, reflects on this scriptural anecdote:

> The demons that passed out of the possessed man and into the
> swine are all the plague-sores, all the uncleannesses, all the devils
> and devils' offspring that have gathered into our great beloved sick

man, our Russia, for centuries. But a great will may bless it yet from on high, and out will come all those unclean things, all the filth and foulness that have festered in us, and will cause them to pass into swine—they may indeed have already passed. And such are we [the old Liberals] and the Nihilists and [my son] Petrusha and his comrades . . . , we senseless and possessed ones will fall headlong from the cliff into the sea and all be drowned . . . ; but the sick man [Russia] will become whole, and place himself at Christ's feet, and all [the nations of the world] will be moved who behold it.

That is the central idea of the novel. As for the plot, it is extremely complicated, even for Dostoevsky. But its very complexity gives a powerful impression of the chaos of contemporary Russia that he was desirous of painting. The central story deals with the return of the materialistic Nikolai Stavrogin to the home of his wealthy widowed mother, Varvara Stavrogin, in a small provincial town. Nikolai had been tutored as a child by the liberal Stepan Verhovenski, has attended school in St. Petersburg, has been an army officer, has resigned his commission to live in the slums of the city, and has now come home at his mother's insistence. It develops that Nikolai, Verhovenski's son Pyotr, the former servant Shatov, and the engineer Kirillov are all members of a group of Terrorists, of which Pyotr is the leader. Pyotr begins to plan a campaign of terrorism in the vicinity. He succeeds in all kinds of mischief, inciting the workingmen to rebel, and causing a rift between his father (who has always been deeply tied to her) and Varvara. As a result of the endless trickery of Pyotr, Captain Lebyadkin, his idiot-sister Marya, and their sister are found murdered in their home, while a fire is devouring houses along the river. Lizavetta, daughter of a friend of Varvara, is beaten to death by the maddened townsfolk because of her closeness to Nikolai. Nikolai thereupon disappears from town.

Mistrust sets in among members of the terrorist group. Fedka, an exconvict, who had perpetrated the murders at Nikolai's suggestion, is soon found dead in the suburbs. Shatov is shot by Pyotr and his body thrown into a lake. Kirillov, out of fanatic devotion to the cause, signs a false confession to Shatov's murder and then shoots himself. Pyotr leaves town. Nikolai commits suicide too. In the end Varvara and Stepan are reconciled, just before the latter's death.

The violence of *The Possessed* gives it a melodramatic air not usual in Dostoevsky. Nevertheless, the history of the inner workings of the various totalitarian and terrorist groups of our own century give the novel new point today.

Actually, Dostoevsky was not much concerned with the political meanings of his novel. As is stated quite clearly in his *Journal*, he believed that the salvation of the Russian people lay in the Orthodox Church, for it alone had preserved "the Godlike image of Christ in all its purity." It may even be Russia's destiny, he thinks, to bring back that image to the rest of the world which has lost it. He says of his fellow countrymen that they will "realize that to become a real Russian simply means endeavoring to bring final peace among European complications, to show the malice of Europe a way of escape in the Russian soul." It is Shatov, the reformed Nihilist, who voices clearly the author's position when he cries: "I believe in Russia, I believe in its Orthodox doctrine, I believe in Christ's body, I believe that a Second Coming will take place in Russia."

It is in Nikolai, therefore, that Dostoevsky is most interested, for Dostoevsky is indeed, as he has been described, "the painter of abnormal men, of criminals and mad men, epileptics and neurasthenics, degenerates and mystics, dreamers, and skeptics, all the disinherited and the outcasts." Nikolai, a confusion of noble ideals and foolish acts, bored with life and with himself, is an old man at thirty, a source of misery and catastrophe to those who know him; full of potentialities for goodness, he is forever lost because he has broken his ties with Russia and the Orthodox Faith. This is Dostoevsky's version of what men who follow in the footsteps of Turgeniev's Bazarov must come to.

The Brothers Karamazov

The Brothers Karamazov is Dostoevsky's most ambitious novel. As it stands, it is only the first part of what he planned to write. The real story, which was to come, is only hinted at. Originally the book was to have consisted of five parts and to have been called *The Life of a Great Sinner*, and was to have followed the careers of several generations—possibly because of the recent appearance of Tolstoy's *War and Peace*. But Dostoevsky changed the plan by reducing it to two parts, of which the second was never written. It is perhaps for this reason that *The Brothers Karamazov* took longer than the other novels to establish itself as one of its author's greatest—most critics would now say its author's very greatest. It is perhaps the profoundest study in the field of the novel of the conflict between Good and Evil in man's soul.

Feodor Karamazov is a miserly, brutalized old sensualist who has three legitimate sons. Dmitri (Mitya), the eldest, a soldier by training, who inherits his father's sensuality and his mother's strength, has nothing in common with his father's sneaking obscenity; Dmitri is open and violent, and he plunges headlong into immorality. He symbolizes ancient Russia without culture or intellect. Ivan (Vanya), the middle brother, is well educated at the university, a product of the Nihilist movement, a student of philosophy and literature; he denies religion and immortality; his brilliance of intellect, as Dostoevsky sees it, is only a symptom of his mental illness. He symbolizes the nineteenth century Westernized Russia, the creation of skeptics and intellectuals. Alexei (Aloysha), the youngest, is religious, gentle, sweet-tempered, a lover of his kind, who seeks the monastic life not because he is at all fanatic but because he deems it the best way to live in the light of God's love. He symbolizes the Russia of the future, when the people will have cleansed themselves of the spiritual sickness represented by the other two.

The arguments between Ivan (about whom Dostoevsky is profoundly concerned) and Alexei occupy long sections in this very long novel. Those pages are among the profoundest ever written on the subjects of God and immortality. Ivan cannot understand his younger brother's saintliness. He himself states: "One can love men only from a distance, near at hand they are intolerable. . . . I demand retribution: the murderer and his victims must not sound a joint Hosannah to the Creator. Nothing must be forgiven, and without forgiveness there can be no harmony. Out of love for humanity I prefer to stick to . . . my tireless indignation."

What men have made of religion Ivan tries to illustrate in his famous allegory of "The Grand Inquisitor." The Spanish Inquisitor has just given orders for another *auto-da-fé* when Christ appears in the world again and is recognized and acclaimed by the crowd in the public square. The Inquisitor has Him arrested, and orders that He be burned the next morning. In the night the Inquisitor appears to justify himself before Christ:

> "Thy teaching is not suitable for mankind, only for a chosen few. It indeed makes man free . . . but Thou biddest him reject all that man needs—miracles, . . . authority, the earthly sword, earthly bread. Therefore with Satan's help we have rectified Thy teaching: we make men happy, let them work and feast, commit sins and obtain pardon, and give them the happiness of weak creatures such as they are. They will . . . beyond the grave find only eternal death. But we keep the secret and entice them, for their happiness, with . . . eternal rewards. . . . Thou hast claimed to govern men by love alone! Behold whither this has led them. . . . They scoff at love and cry for bread. We give them bread, and they accept our chains. Tomorrow I will have Thee burned!" The only answer Christ makes to this is to kiss the old man on his lips. The Inquisitor opens the dungeon door, and cries: "Go Thy way, and never come again, never!"

Feodor has an illegitimate son, Smerdyakov, whose mother, an idiot girl, died giving birth to him. Subject to epileptic seizures, Smerdyakov is reared in Feodor's home as a servant. Dmitri is Feodor's son by an early marriage, Ivan and Alexei by a second. During their childhood old Karamazov has completely neglected the boys. Dmitri has led a wild wasted life as a soldier; Ivan has been teaching, after going to college at Moscow, and is fairly well known for his literary articles; Alexei has become a pupil of the famous monk Zossima at the local monastery, much to his father's derision.

The three legitimate brothers meet in their provincial birthplace. Ivan is out of funds, and Dmitri has come to collect a legacy from his mother, which he believes his father is holding back from him. At the monastery, where they all gather, Feodor humiliates his sons by behaving like a clown before Father Zossima. The old man accuses Dmitri of wanting his money only to spend it on the loose-moraled Grushenka, whom Feodor desires for himself. Dmitri answers his father hotly, declaring the old man's sins are too well known for him to upbraid anyone. Father Zossima, feeling that Dmitri is destined to an evil fate, falls down before him. Later Zossima urges Alexei to quit the monastery when he himself dies; he fears too much the sensual nature inherited by all the Karamazovs and wishes the young man to go out in the world.

Dmitri is betrothed to Katerina, a colonel's daughter, but Ivan is in love with her. Something in Alexei makes Dmitri confess to him that he has spent thousands of roubles belonging to Katerina on a spree with Grushenka. He begs Alexei to ask Feodor for the sum so he can repay Katerina. Alexei visits his father, when suddenly Dmitri enters looking for Grushenka, and attacks Feodor. Alexei next comes upon Katerina in the act of trying vainly to bribe Grushenka to give up Dmitri. Ivan is anxious that Dmitri marry Grushenka so that he himself can wed Katerina, who returns his affection, but will not give in to it. Understanding that she feels it her duty in life to protect Dmitri, Ivan loves her all the more.

When Father Zossima dies, a miracle is looked for, but none occurs. His body decomposes in the normal way. This is taken by some skeptical monks as a sign that he has been a false teacher. Disheartened, Alexei decides to visit Grushenka, who has amused herself with the idea that it would be easy to seduce him. But she has had enough of the Karamazovs, she thinks, and is preparing to run away with an old lover. She responds to the saintliness in Alexei.

Dmitri, unable to raise the money owed to Katerina, is almost crazed. He becomes more distracted in losing track of Grushenka. He searches for her at his father's house, carrying a pestle with which he intends to kill his father. In his fury he wounds an old servant with it. Learning that Grushenka has left town, he goes off after her.

When he finds her at a tavern with two strangers, she welcomes him, swearing her love for him. The two embark upon another spree. In the midst of it, the police appear and arrest Dmitri for the murder of his father. Feodor has been robbed and found killed. There is blood on Dmitri's clothes, he has a large sum of money, and his threats against his father have been heard by everyone. Dmitri protests his innocence, and insists that the money is what is left of Katerina's money. But his case seems desperate.

Ivan and Katerina plan Dmitri's escape. Grushenka becomes very ill. Dmitri begins to look upon himself as a sacrifice for the sins of the world. Ivan persists in asking Smerdyakov questions, for Smerdyakov has established his innocence because of a seizure he was having at the time of the murder. In the end, Smerdyakov confirms Ivan's suspicions: He had feigned the seizure to cover up the fact that he was the murderer. But he hurls the guilt back in Ivan's face. Is it not Ivan who has been insisting that Feodor's death would be a blessing to everyone? Smerdyakov has chosen a moment that would implicate Dmitri and relies upon Ivan's protection hereafter. He hands over the stolen money to Ivan. The latter, in his room, becomes delirious and has a vision of the demon residing in his soul. Smerdyakov hangs himself the same night.

At the trial, things look black for Dmitri. Katerina, unable to forgive the slight of Dmitri's last orgy with Grushenka, shows a letter from him in which he declared his intention of murdering his father to procure the money owed her. Ivan, still very ill, recounts Smerdyakov's confession and produces the money. But his fever mastering him, he confuses the case by telling of the devil he has seen. The jury finds Dmitri guilty.

Katerina, conscience-stricken, goes to Dmitri and begs his forgiveness in the presence of Alexei and Grushenka. Alexei, counseling his friends to love men, is preparing to go to Siberia with Dmitri. He is ready to put into practice Father Zossima's injunctions on sending him into the world: "Be no man's judge. Humble affection is a terrible power which effects more than violence; only active Love can secure faith for us."

COUNT LEO TOLSTOY (1828–1910)

IMPORTANCE

It is the consensus of opinion that Leo Tolstoy is the greatest international figure that Russian literature has thus far produced. His life, hardly less than his work, has been a source of inspiration to many men and women who feel that the career of one such selfless man is worth more in leading humanity out of its sufferings than whole political movements. His life was one untiring search for truth. His "conversion" in his later years struck many people as a violent change; but anyone familiar with his most cherished views could have found nothing unusual in it, for there is an amazing, consistency in his story. It is true, however, that he was many years in finding the right course of action for himself.

Leo Tolstoy was born September 9 at Yasnaya Polyana, the ancestral home of the Tolstoys', in a large manor house. One of his ancestors, Count Petr Tolstoy, had been a celebrated statesman under Peter the Great. Tolstoy's father had married into a great fortune and was able to live the life of a country gentleman. Our author lost his mother when he was three, and his father six years later.

There are no writers in the world who have revealed themselves more completely and with more candor than Tolstoy. For many years he wrote of his life and his opinions under the name of various of his heroes: Irtenyev, Nekhludov, Olyenin, and Levin, for example; later he continued to record his life frankly in the first person. In *Childhood,* his earliest work, we learn that Tolstoy, when a boy, decided that it was one's duty to be happy in the present, and luckily for him his boyhood was a happy one, filled with sports and reading.

In 1840 the lad went to live with his aunt, Mme. Zhushkov, at Kazan, where he was exposed to the frivolous free-thinking life of upper-class society in that town. In 1843 he entered the university there and spent more of his time in the pursuit of pleasure than in study. After an endless succession of balls and parties, he began to weary, as he tells us in *Youth*, of the round of social excitement. He tried to concentrate first on Oriental languages, then on law, with small success, for very little learning went on at his university. He gave up interest in history. At this time he became an atheist. His attendance at lectures became more and more irregular, and he decided that he was wasting his time at college. In 1847 he left.

He returned to the family estate with the intention of seriously taking up his duties as a landlord and helping the peasants who were working his lands. Under the influence of his reading in Rousseau, he tried to share the problems of his serfs, but they were only suspicious of his good intentions, and he gave up the attempt for a while. He tried to continue his education at St. Petersburg but soon was back in the country again, this time dissipating his time and energies in gambling, hunting, and drinking, as we see in his *Landlord's Morning*. By 1851 he had accumulated enough debts to make it seem advisable to go off to the Caucasus to join his eldest brother, who was stationed there with a regiment of soldiers.

His brother persuaded him to join the army too, and Tolstoy enlisted in the artillery. Suddenly he began to write. His *Childhood* (1824) was accepted by the *Russian Contemporary*, in the pages of which the works of Russia's leading writers appeared. Tolstoy soon followed with *The Landlord's Morning*, *Boyhood* (1854), and *Youth* (1855–1857), all intensely autobiographic. In these pieces we find his conviction that communion with Nature is the only road to happiness.

The Crimean War then broke out, and in 1854 Tolstoy was with the army at the Danube. When hostilities ceased in that quarter, Tolstoy asked to be sent to Sebastopol. There he walked right into the midst of a terrific defensive battle; after experiencing all the rigors of war, Tolstoy went into retreat with the Russian army. Somehow or other, in the midst of the horror, he managed to write his *Tales from Sebastopol* (1853–1855), which won him instant literary fame. He terminated his war experiences by being sent with his report of the battle to St. Petersburg.

His observation of the courage and patience of the common soldier had reawakened his humanitarianism, and he had also acquired a disgust for the selfishness of the officers, who came of the nobility. On his return, Tolstoy was welcomed to the ranks of great authors by men like Turgenev; the leaders of society also began to fête the brilliant new author, and for a little while Tolstoy did not pursue his serious intentions because of the round of pleasure into which he once more threw himself.

It was not long, however, before he felt dissatisfied with such a life. Moreover, he became irritated with the cliques his literary friends had formed. The rational side of Tolstoy was ever the strongest part of his character; his common sense was boundless, and he was too much a dogged individualist ever to fall in with anyone else's creed or dogma. At this time of his life, if it is necessary to give him a political label, he was more a conservative than anything else. *War and Peace* and *Anna Karenina*, his two masterpieces, appeared in a magazine that was well known as "reactionary." His most intimate friend, the poet Fet, was of the same political complexion.

With the growth of the movement for the emancipation of the serfs, as we have seen, Russian literature took on a new life in dealing with current social problems. *Polikushka*, describing the evils of serfdom, was his contribution to the current excitement. He now felt that he ought to see something of the way the rest of Europe lived. Between 1857 and 1861 he made three trips to the continent—the only times he left Russia in his life; he visited Germany, Italy, Paris, Lucerne, and London.

In 1861 he was established again at Yasnaya Polyana. Even before the enactment of emancipation, Tolstoy had freed all the serfs on his estate. His travels had not afforded him much intellectual stimulation, though he did admire the educational system of Germany, and was much impressed with Fröbel's new kindergarten system. He himself opened a school for the peasants' children; he taught drawing, Bible history, and music there. For two years the school flourished, and was copied, and then closed because of the desertion of pupils and teachers. To recuperate he went for a trip to the steppes; later when with renewed courage he wished to reopen the school, the governmental authorities refused their permission.

During these two years of occupation with the welfare of his peasantry, Tolstoy completely neglected his literary talents. He also accepted the arduous post of Arbitrator, whose duties included supervising the new distribution of the land among the emancipated serfs, readjusting the taxes, and settling all matters connected with the purchasing of land in the vicinity. He enjoyed his task immensely, convinced that he was working in a profoundly valuable cause. As their champion, Tolstoy came to understand that the emancipation had not been sufficiently prepared: the peasantry was not ready for it. They were full of distrust for him. On the other hand, the nobility of the district considered Tolstoy their enemy because of his consideration of the peasants' rights as being of paramount importance in deciding any issue.

In 1863 he issued *The Cossacks*, which was actually written during the siege of Sebastopol; it is animated by the Rousseauistic notion that civilized values conduce to unhappiness. Discouraged once more in his efforts for the peasantry in his post of Arbitrator, Tolstoy went for a rest to the provinces in the southeast. En route he passed through Moscow, saw his old friends of the Behrs family, and became interested in the younger daughter, Sophia. Later in the year he returned to Yasnaya Polyana, and sold the old house to pay his gambling debts. Somewhat in the style of his hero Levin (in *Anna Karenina*) he was drawn to Sophia again, and ran off once more to Moscow to see her. The Behrs family soon returned the visit. After a little difficulty, he won Sophia's hand, and they were married on September 23, 1862. As he recorded later in the *Confession*, he found his whole life now revolving about his family.

Tolstoy and his wife remained on his lands for the next eighteen years; his wife bore him thirteen children. Tolstoy enjoyed directing his children's education and doing manual labor on his farm. He set to work writing again soon after his marriage, and began *War and Peace* (1865–1868) and *Anna Karenina* (1875–1878), his two greatest accomplishments in literature. They were liked by neither conservatives nor radicals at the time. Although espousing a completely different philosophy from Turgeniev's, during his literary labors he valued his criticism above anyone else's except possibly the poet Fet's. Unfortunately he quarreled with Turgeniev over a trifle in 1864, and they remained unfriendly until 1878, when, during a severe illness, Tolstoy believed himself to be dying and offered to end the misunderstanding; Turgeniev hastened to reassure him of his friendship.

The pressure of work, for literary composition was an arduous task for him, enervated him to such a degree that after *War and Peace* was published he went southeast again (1870) to live among the nomads. In the village of Karalieck where he settled for a while there was nearby a group of Molochans, a religious sect that recognizes no authority save that of the Bible and rejects the ministry of the church. Tolstoy observed them and their industrious ways with interest, and soon thereafter bought large acreage in the vicinity. A famine brought desolation in 1872–1873, and Tolstoy went from village to village distributing food. At this time of his life he was also enthusiastically studying Greek and the writings of Schopenhauer, which he came to admire profoundly.

But in 1873 two of his children died and he became restless. He began to study the Bible earnestly, and recurrent illness and his concern over the Russo-Turkish War made him recast his view of himself once more. As he later described it, he had reached his third stage; his first had been a pursuit of pleasure, his second an always frustrated pursuit of humanity's welfare. Now he found himself anxious to enter the service of God. He had been through all kinds of religious opinions from the atheism of his youth to an acceptance of the Orthodox Church. But now when he heard the priests praying for the destruction of the Turks, he was revolted by such sentiments and renounced that faith. Just as Gogol and Dostoevsky had ended by making religious fervor their last preoccupation, so did Tolstoy end. His admirers were sorrowed that he should surrender his great gifts as a literary artist and become an ardent propagandist.

All other religions having failed him, he forged a Christianity of his own. Convinced now from his study of the Gospels that physical toil was the only salvation, he gave up the kind of life which he might have been expected to live as Count Tolstoy, and in 1880 began to rise at dawn and work in the fields like a peasant, sowing, cultivating, ploughing, and reaping the grain, and helping the poor with their crops. He learned the craft of the shoemaker, and labored happily at that. He felt that he had found the cure at last for unhappiness. "Simplicity!" was his watchword.

But the world's affairs intruded on his peace. His sons were going to the university, his daughter was entitled to an introduction into society, and he and his wife had to be often in Moscow, much to his distaste. He had come to loathe money too as a source of much of the world's misery.

In 1880 he volunteered for the census taking, and he had an unexampled opportunity to see how the poor lived. Had his family and the government permitted, he was prepared to give up all he owned, he was so much sickened at the misery he witnessed. His *What Are We To Do?* (1884) is a graphic record of his experiences in the taking of the census.

In 1888, after many family misunderstandings, he felt he could not with peace of mind remain a landed proprietor; in that year he made everything over to his wife and children. He felt relieved of a vast burden, and now began to write a series of simple tales exposing the evils to which the peasants were subjected, such as their excessive drinking and the general brutality of their lives. His play *The Power of Darkness* is written in the same spirit.

Important works of his last period include *My Confession* (1879–1882), *My Religion* (1885), *The Death of Ivan Ilyitch* (1886), *The Kreutzer Sonata* (1890), and *What Is Art?* (1897).

There was a dreadful famine in 1891–1892, and he and his family served tirelessly in supplying food and clothing to the poor. In 1895 the Dowkhobors, a sect of pacifists that lived in a kind of communistic society based upon simple Christian teachings, were being persecuted by the government for their unwillingness to serve in the army. Tolstoy rushed to their defense and won sympathy for them all over the world, until they were at last permitted to emigrate. It was because of them that he wrote *Resurrection* (1900), containing an attack on the Orthodox Church; after its publication he was excommunicated by the Church. Tolstoy died on November 20, 1910.

The religion that Tolstoy had at last found was a product to a large degree of his fundamental rationalism. No phrase in his religious works is more common than "Reason, i.e., Good." He rejected all ritual and dogma of the Churches, and did not believe in an anthropomorphic deity. He felt, somewhat in the manner of Milton, that God would be found inside a man's own breast, an inner light that everyone could find if he would but search his heart.

One of the interesting aspects of his career is that although an enemy of violence and war, he was greatly admired by the revolutionaries. Though utterly condemning their methods, he agreed with them in their condemnation of private property and of the evils of Russian society generally. To Tolstoy the only method by which a Christian communism could be achieved would be a voluntary surrender by the landlords of their possessions. He had the right to hold such a view since he had practiced it. Indeed, Tolstoy was one of the few *practicing* socialists in the history of mankind.

War and Peace

War and Peace is one of the most remarkable historical novels ever written. It deals with the Napoleonic Era (1805–1813), and more particularly with Bonaparte's invasion of Russia. But while the French Emperor and Kutuzov, Commander of the Russian Armies, both appear in its voluminous pages, these military chiefs are only appendages to the plot; Tolstoy was primarily concerned with his intention of showing how the people, unknown to history, are affected by war and peace and how they also make their mark on them. The vast picture Tolstoy unfolds constitutes a kind of prose epic of Russian life during the years he selected for his story.

The very plan of the work meant that it must lack the kind of unity we are accustomed to look for in a novel. Important characters appear, disappear, die, or are forgotten. Indeed, it is the irresistible march of events that must make them do so—just as they do in life. The fullness of the pictures, the restless motion of the narrative, the endless variety of happenings—all of which make for a chaotic final impression—lend a sense of reality and of the continuity of life such as no other novel has succeeded in establishing.

Characters grow and change before our eyes as the men and women of the story react to the pressures about them. Though the picture is largely that of Russian aristocracy, the ordinary people are not excluded. But the narrative centers around four families high in Russian society: the Bezuhovs, the Rostovs, the Bolkonskis, and the Kuragins. The men of this class are all more or less divided between a thirst for making a reputation and an addiction to a life of pleasure; the women live for romance and gossip.

Of the men none is more interesting than Pierre Bezuhov, a masterful portrait of what is finest and worst in the Russian character. It is likely that once more Tolstoy was drawing himself; like his author Pierre is capable of the highest ideals and yet is prey to self-doubt and tortured puzzling over the meaning of life and death.

When the novel opens (in 1805), it is obvious that there can be no avoidance of war with Napoleon. After the defeat of the Austrians at Austerlitz, the intelligent know that conflict is coming, but Russian society pursues its pleasures as though peace might be expected to endure forever. What if Austria is a political ally? There can be no threat to Russians on their own soil.

Nikolai Rostov has joined the hussars partly because of his great devotion to the Czar, partly because he looks so dashing in a uniform, and partly because the army is the logical place for ambitious young men of rank to make themselves a career. He is the idol of his sister Natasha, and his cousin Sonya is deeply smitten with love for him.

A friend of the Rostovs, Pierre Bezuhov, is not at all the success Nikolai is. Returned from his studies in Paris, he cannot find a place for himself, idles away his time and income in gambling, and considers a military career as stupid. His demeanor at social gatherings has won him a reputation as a nuisance: He is fond of argument, during the course of which he is likely to start shouting in a manner shocking to good taste; at other times he will lapse, just as unreasonably, into sullen silence. But although Pierre is not liked in the circles in which he moves, his father's sudden death makes him the master of millions, and he at once becomes much sought after.

Unwilling to account for his new popularity in terms of his recent fortune, Pierre feels his personality expanding. He gives up his old sullenness and convinced that he is generally loved, loves everyone. Among his many new friends, none is more faithful than Prince Kuragin. The latter's daughter Ellen is highly regarded in society's drawing rooms, and the Prince deems Pierre and his millions eminently suitable for Ellen. Pierre is easily inveigled into a courtship, and a marriage ensues—a marriage in which Pierre never finds happiness.

Another intimate of Pierre's is André Bolkonski, a man of devouring ambition, overbearing and cynical. Lisa, André's wife, known to her friends as "the Little Princess," is about to bear a child, but her husband has no use either for her or for the conditions imposed by matrimony. Accepting a commission in the army, André has left Lisa in the care of his autocratic father, Prince Bolkonski, and his sister Marya, and has joined his regiment. Lisa in his absence bears a son, but dies in childbirth. After the defeat at Austerlitz, André returns a free man. But, as he confides to his good friend Pierre, freedom brings him no peace of mind, and he is beset by a feeling of emptiness and loneliness.

Because he is so wealthy, Pierre is welcomed by the society of Freemasons. For a time he seems to find consolation in their philosophy, and attempts to cheer up André in his despair. In an access of enthusiasm for freedom, Pierre frees the serfs in his employ, and turns his energies to managing his estates. He possesses, however, no administrative ability and is soon losing a vast amount of money. He is compelled to give up these plans and hand over the management to a deputy. It is with relief that he quits his estates and goes off with André.

Napoleon is now at Berlin, and Nikolai has seen plenty of danger in the service. When Napoleon and the Czar agree to the treaty of peace at Tilsit, Nikolai supposes that the war is ended. Napoleon, now busy with his campaign in Spain, seems to justify such a view. Nikolai enjoys the interval of peace, and André returns from battle again to live in the country. On a visit to the Rostovs, André falls in love with Natasha. He seeks the advice of Pierre, who is now separated from his own wife, and who has been stupid enough to become involved in a duel with a man he has wrongly suspected of having an affair with Ellen. Despite his personal unhappiness, Pierre rejoices at the possible union of André and Natasha; in the same glow of romantic feeling Pierre succeeds in effecting a reconciliation with Ellen. Natasha returns André's feelings, and the Rostovs favor the match; but old Prince Bolkonski insists that the lovers must wait a year because of Natasha's youth. The latter, although upset at the patriarch's decision, agrees to wait and to keep their engagement secret.

Natasha visits Ellen in Moscow. There she meets Ellen's brother Anatole, a reprobate, married to a peasant girl whom he had wronged. André joins the army once more, and Natasha is pressed with the attentions of Anatole, whom she finds far too attractive for her own peace of mind. Unable to resist the scamp, she consents to an elopement with Anatole and innocently is prepared to go through a marriage ceremony with him, ignorant of the fact that

Anatole is already married. But her mother discovers in time the plans for the elopement and locks her in her room. Crushed, Natasha writes to André a letter releasing him of all obligations to her.

Pierre, learning the story, goes to comfort Natasha, thus endearing himself to her. André, in the meantime, is deeply wounded by the affair, but finds himself distracted by the military situation. Napoleon is now frankly planning to march against Russia. By 1812 he has made his way to Smolensk, where he finds only the ruins of a city to conquer. The strategy of General Kutuzov seems futile. Only later will Russia understand that the only way to conquer the Little Emperor is to allow him to penetrate more and more deeply into the heart of Russia until his line of communications can be severed behind him. At Borodino the French and the Russians sustain heavy losses in battle; the weary Russians allow Napoleon to capture Moscow.

In the general exodus towards the East, the Rostovs are abandoning their home, when the wounded André is brought to town in one of the carts bearing the casualties of the late battle. Natasha undertakes to nurse him. Old Bolkonski is dead, and Natasha's brother Nikolai provides for the shelter of André's son and sister. Grievously ill, André is only too painfully aware that his love for Natasha is as great as ever. He dies of his wound. After that Marya, André's sister, and Natasha become fast friends because of their shared love for the dead André.

Pierre's mind is now filled with a desire to serve his country by a bold exploit: he will try to assassinate Napoleon. But before he can even formulate a plan, he is arrested as a prisoner of war.

Napoleon, having waited far too long for the Czar to offer his terms of peace, decides to head for France again. But his once mighty army is thoroughly demoralized and has degenerated into a group of ragged marauders. Traveling with them as a prisoner back to Smolensk, Pierre finds he can be happy enough now on the occasions when he can manage merely to satisfy his hunger and be warm enough during that bitter winter. For the first time in his life he learns to achieve a measure of objectivity and detachment towards life. He becomes a favorite of his French captors.

The French fare worse and worse. Bands of Cossacks attack the lines of the invaders and free the Russian prisoners while they seize valuable supplies. Pierre at last is freed too, and goes back to Orel. He now learns of the deaths of André and Ellen. The French soon are completely routed. After passing through a serious illness, Pierre recovers and becomes aware of a sense of joy in the mere fact of living.

He returns to Moscow. Seeing the Rostovs again, he renews his friendship with Natasha and finds that his feelings are those of love. He proposes and is accepted, and the pair are married. Natasha proves a good, though rather domineering wife, who manages her husband's affairs with great skill. Pierre is very happy. Nikolai proposes to Marya, André's sister, and they are married too, and adopt André's son. The union of these families brings happiness to all four, far in excess of any of their expectations.

Anna Karenina

Anna Karenina has often been called the greatest novel ever written on the subject of love. It would be fairer to say, however, that its subject matter is rather the destructive force of love. Anna, a beautiful, elegant, sensitive woman of the world, has, when we first meet her, little interest or respect for the passion, as a result of her marriage. Though essentially a woman of great honesty and candor, she has become too sophisticated in her acceptance of worldly values for her own good. When love unexpectedly overwhelms her, she has no ethical values to cling to, no principles to guide her. Lifted up in a whirlwind of passion, she gives herself to it, only to be destroyed by it. Her lover, Count Vronsky, for all his adoration of her, is motivated chiefly by his pursuit of pleasure; like her he is too worldly to be capable of any kind of self-sacrifice for the sake of her whom he loves, though he thinks otherwise of himself. These two who make passion the reason for their life bring only misery on their own heads.

On the other hand, we find a pair of lovers who, because they do not make themselves victims to their passions and have the courage to endure and to wait, eventually do find happiness and contentment. Levin, Tolstoy's most important self-portrait in fiction, chooses no easy path to inner peace; the record of his life and of his love for Kitty is the story of endless struggles with doubt and despair. But in those struggles he finds his belief in God and in the healing quality of goodness extended to others; above all, he discovers the all-important truth that in useful work there is always salvation. Kitty, too, could easily have followed the path that poor Anna took, for at first she is smitten with the dashing Vronsky, and she actually anticipates a proposal from him. But it is characteristic of both Levin and Kitty that they live by moral codes, and that neither would expect to find happiness outside of ethical conduct. Anna, on the other hand, though far more exciting as a woman and radiant as a human being, neglects the moral order and is willing to live by passion. She finds only death and disillusion. Levin and his Kitty, after long doubts and intellectual struggles, win fulfillment because they have been willing to submit their personal satisfactions to larger moral considerations. Levin finds that the good that resides within his bosom makes rightfully larger demands than self-seeking Reason ever can.

Anna Karenina is therefore a novel hymning the sacred doctrine of useful work, the self-rewarding principle of living for the good of others. That principle Anna fails to understand; Levin comes to live by it.

Stepan Oblonsky has broken his promises to reform his dissipating ways so often that his wife, Dolly, is determined on a separation from him. His love for his wife, despite his weakness, is genuine enough, and his sister Anna comes to their home in Moscow to make peace between them again. Anna is married to Alexei Karenin, a man of aloof and cold manners, and very ambitious. There is a foreboding of evil when a man commits suicide on the railroad the day of Anna's arrival.

At the time of Anna's visit to Moscow the dashing Count Vronsky is there too, and they meet. Although it is generally supposed that he is interested in Dolly's sister Kitty, he never makes the expected proposal, for he has fallen in love with Anna. Kitty has rejected the proposal of Constantine Levin, a high-principled descendant of an old family of Moscow who is deeply in love with her. Kitty is frankly astonished that Vronsky has remained merely cordial.

Smitten with Anna, Vronsky follows in Anna's footsteps when she returns to her husband and child in St. Petersburg. A woman as passionate as she is beautiful, Anna yields to her fascination for Vronsky, accompanies him to various homes on social calls, and goes with him to the theater. Karenin, who prefers to believe that this means nothing dangerous, is nevertheless highly annoyed at the gossip that will arise, and even more at the sorry figure he will seem to cut. He warns Anna in a very stiff manner that she must be more careful, and forbids her to receive Vronsky when he calls on her in the future. For the sake of her beloved little son, she promises to obey Karenin.

Her good intentions are blasted, however, when Vronsky is injured at the races, and her concern for him makes her reckless in public. Karenin is outraged and scolds her bitterly. He even meditates divorce or a duel, but recoils from either expedient because he knows that the deceived husband always cuts a ridiculous figure. He consoles himself with the reflection that his behavior is consonant with Christian conduct. Anna, unable to resist her passion any longer, is now meeting Vronsky secretly.

Levin, although hurt by Kitty's refusal of him, is too sane and balanced to destroy himself. He goes to his estate in the country and keeps himself usefully occupied with his farming projects and the problems of the peasants who work for him. He finds salvation in work. One day (just as Tolstoy himself is said to have done), he seizes a scythe from one of the serfs and works along with the others, exulting in the task. But hearing that Kitty is still free, he decides to try his luck again. He therefore goes to Moscow, full of hope that he can win her this time.

Anna now realizes that she is with child by Vronsky. Her lover, anxious to stand by her, begs her to ask her husband for a divorce. But Karenin, still concerned only about public opinion, is now less inclined to procure a divorce than ever. He assumes a false nobility, declaring he will acknowledge the child as his own; he, moreover, threatens to separate Anna and their little boy if she does not cease her folly at once. Anna is so utterly crushed, that she is resolved to do what he wishes.

But one night, believing her husband gone, she urges Vronsky to come to her. Unhappily, the two men meet. For once Karenin loses his hauteur, and in a rage threatens Anna with divorce. However, as he thinks it over, he finds his old objections still there, and he delays. When he soon thereafter gains a coveted post, he is less anxious than ever to begin proceedings, though Anna's time of confinement is fast approaching.

The child is born, Anna becomes quite ill, and Vronsky is so overwhelmed with remorse that he attempts to kill himself. Karenin, whose better qualities are aroused by Anna's sickness, agrees to anything she wishes, and allows her to see Vronsky.

She recovers and goes away with Vronsky. In Italy they live as happily as their reduced circumstances and sense of guilt permit. At this time, Levin has won Kitty's hand, and they are married.

After a while Anna comes back to Russia with Vronsky and accompanies him to his estate. Karenin has not instituted a divorce suit, and is everywhere regarded as a man of great nobility of character and forbearance. Every now and then, when she feels it safe to do so, Anna makes a fleeting visit to her son; but these experiences only sadden her. Without realizing it, she is becoming embittered, and Vronsky begins to be bored. She is soon convinced that he has another woman.

One day she wanders to the railroad station. She suddenly remembers that on the day she met Vronsky a man had been killed by the onrushing train at the station in Moscow. She now watches the approach of a train, hurls herself in front of it, and is killed. Vronsky, grief-stricken, and anxious for death himself, joins the army.

Levin and Kitty, in the meantime, have found in work mutually shared happiness and peace. He understands that there is much good he can do with his wealth, by aiding the peasants. Kitty shares his enthusiasm. He resigns himself to the fact that he cannot accomplish all that he would like to do, but he finds fulfillment in meeting each day's challenge.

Tolstoy's Later Works

Tolstoy's active pen never ceased producing work after work—all, whether attractive or repugnant, endowed with the same terrible sincerity and intellectual integrity. As his rationalized Christianity, discarding all tradition and all elements of mystical belief, developed, he became more and more the lecturer. Nevertheless, competent scholars assure one that from the standpoint of literary excellence his prose in Russian never suffered any artistic decline. There are those, indeed, who insist that his dogmatic autobiography, *My Confession* (1882, published because of censorship outside of Russia), is the finest of his artistic successes.

Three of these late works do demand our attention: *The Death of Ivan Ilyich* (1886), *The Kreutzer Sonata* (1890), and *What Is Art?* (1897).

The Death of Ivan Ilyich, one of his most powerful studies, is a novelette or long short story. Its hero is a commonplace man of the class of petty officials. He is struck down by a slow-working fatal disease, traced in its progress with great vividness by the author. As he gradually faces the fact that he is dying, Ivan reviews his whole life and is overwhelmed by its emptiness and vulgarity. His only wish at first is a bitter one—to be done with his miserable existence and those human beings who were presumably dear to him. All his friends and his family have no meaning to him now that he sees everything in the dim light of disillusionment. But by degrees he wins a measure of peace and even joy from the faithful ministrations of his peasant-servant Gerasim, whose simple and honest devotion to him is a light in his darkness. Before he dies, because of Gerasim Ilyich achieves faith and a belief in the power of love.

The Kreutzer Sonata is shocking enough to the prudish to have achieved a popularity quite beyond its deserts. It is a study of love, jealousy, and revenge—all the product of sexual attraction. The novel will not bear comparison on any level with Tolstoy's great productions. The general idea pervading the book might have resulted, in a more carefully considered work, in an excellent novel: the need for spirituality in all of life's activities. But Tolstoy pushes the idea too far. He indicts physical love as by its nature evil; it is to be condoned in the marriage relationship, according to him, only as a means of continuing the race. A modern mind is likely to revolt against Tolstoy's arbitrary departmentalizing of the affections into the spiritual and the "carnal." It is common experience that the spiritual and physical elements in love cannot so be divided from each other.

What Is Art? is a sweeping rejection of all esthetic values in art. Considering Tolstoy's own past achievements as an artist, his denunciations in this book are astounding: Shakespeare is an incompetent poet and thoroughly immoral; Homer is immoral because *The Iliad* and *The Odyssey* idealize cruelty and anger; Racine is worthless because he wrote exclusively for an aristocratic audience; Beethoven and Wagner wrote heartless music, and are therefore empty. Some few "inferior" artists and works of art he allows merit because they transmit a sense of common human feelings: *Don Quixote, David Copperfield,* some pieces by Molière, Gogol, Maupassant. The great works of art are few; those listed include *Les Misérables*, Schiller's *The Robbers, The Tale of Two Cities, The Christmas Carol, Adam Bede,* and *Uncle Tom's Cabin.* Tolstoy's criterion for admission to his small gallery of the great is excessively simple: an ability on the part of the creator to "infect" a reader's soul with "sympathetic feelings." On such grounds he finds a gypsy song superior to Beethoven, and the crude old play of *King Leir* better art than Shakespeare's. Everything that does not "infect" with "sympathetic feelings" is bad art. Tolstoy recognizes no need on the part of the audience to educate itself to a level that will enable it to understand Shakespeare, Racine, Homer, Beethoven, or Wagner. Apparently everyone equipped with a pair of eyes and a pair of ears is ready to set up as a critic. According to Tolstoy, any art that requires cultivation for comprehension is outside art. Tolstoy also excludes sexual love, patriotism, and religious exaltation from the province of worthwhile subjects. He does not leave much for art to deal with.

REVIEW QUESTIONS

THE RISE OF RUSSIAN LITERATURE

Multiple Choice

1. _____ Early Russian literature is
   a. mostly folklore
   b. ecclesiastical in nature
   c. primarily historical dramas
   d. primarily epic in type

2. _____ Alexander Sumarkov wrote
   a. tragedies
   b. comedies
   c. in a French manner
   d. all of the above

3. _____ Gabriel Derzhavin was noted primarily for
   a. poems
   b. dramas
   c. plays
   d. novels

4. _____ *Felitsa*
   a. is a fairy story
   b. is humorous in tone
   c. was written by Catherine the Great
   d. all of the above

5. _____ Pushkin was greatly influenced by
   a. Renaissance writers
   b. Michael Lermontov
   c. Byron
   d. John Locke

6. _____ Nikolai Gogol was known primarily as
   a. a dramatist
   b. an uneducated serf
   c. Russia's first important novelist
   d. a political prisoner for most of his life

7. _____ The Russian literary genius is most compatible with
   a. Romanticism
   b. Realism
   c. Expressionism
   d. Naturalism

8. _____ The title of Turgenev's *Fathers and Sons* refers to
   a. older and newer influences in nineteenth century Russia
   b. a patriarchical society
   c. the Russian aristocracy
   d. the Russian church

9. _____ Dotoevsky is renowned primarily for his
   a. novels
   b. dramas
   c. short stories
   d. poems

10. _____ Leo Tolstoy dedicated his life from early manhood to
   a. writing dozens of novels
   b. searching for truth
   c. sensual pleasures
   d. religious pursuits

True-False

11. _____ Satire is the most typical poetic tone in Russian literature.

12. _____ Gogol's religious fanaticism caused him to destroy the conclusion to his novel *Dead Souls*.

13. _____ Russia commonly imprisoned authors in the nineteenth century.

14. _____ *The Brothers Karamozov* was Dostoevsky's least ambitious novel.

15. _____ Throughout his life, Tolstoy never tired of seeking pleasure and socializing with the aristocracy of Russia.

16. _____ Tolstoy's novel *The Cossacks* was written during the seige of Sebastopol.

17. _____ Tolstoy's greatest novels, *Anna Karenina* and *War and Peace*, were applauded by both conservatives and radicals.

18. _____ Pushkin was immediately hailed as a uniquely authentic Russian genius.

19. _____ Nikolai Gogol started the tradition of the great Russian novel.

20. _____ Turgenev used a Western European style while writing nationalistic Russian novels.

Fill-in

21. _____ was largely responsible for shaping the Russian literary language.

22. Catherine the Great had much _____ literature published in translation.

23. Ivan Khemnitzer first translated and then wrote _____ that were very popular in Russia.

24. *The Minor* and *The Brigadier* by Denis von Visin are satirical _____ about the brutality of Russian society in manners and their treatment of serfs.

25. Derzhavin versified a fairy story called *Felitsa*, which was written by _____ .

26. Tolstoy stopped writing for several years while he worked to improve the lot of _____ .

27. Ivan Goncharov wrote his first novel, _____ , under the influence of George Sand.

28. Tolstoy's novel _____ is animated by the Rousseauistic notion that civilized values are conducive to unhappiness.

29. *Oblomov* is the best known work of _____ and treats the inertia so deeply rooted in the character of the Russian peasant.

30. After the publication of Turgenev's novel *Fathers and Sons*, authorities began using the word _____ to describe their politically radical enemies.

Matching

31. ____ *War and Peace*		a. *Eugene Onygin*
32. ____ Tolstoy		b. first important novelist
33. ____ Pushkin		c. historical novel
34. ____ *Boris Godunov*		d. lifelong charitable worker
35. ____ Novikov		e. *Crime and Punishment*
36. ____ *Anna Karenina*		f. talented journalist
37. ____ Dostoevsky		g. destructive force of love
38. ____ Turgeniev		h. leading dramatist
39. ____ Ostrovski		i. Shakespearean tragedy
40. ____ Gogol		j. pessimistic writer

Answers

1. b	11. t	21. Lomonossov	31. c
2. d	12. t	22. French	32. d
3. a	13. t	23. fables	33. a
4. d	14. f	24. comedies	34. i
5. c	15. f	25. Catherine the Great	35. f
6. c	16. t	26. serfs	36. g
7. b	17. f	27. *A Common Story*	37. e
8. a	18. f	28. *The Cossacks*	38. j
9. b	19. t	29. Goncharov	39. h
10. b	20. t	30. Nihilist	40. b

Part *5*

EXPERIMENTATION AND REVOLT

WORKS AT A GLANCE

Charles Leconte de Lisle

1852	*Antique Poems*	1862	*Barbarian Poems*

José-Maria de Heredia

1893	*The Trophies*

Sully Prudhomme

1865–1866	*Stanzas and Poems*	1872	*Vain Tenderness*
1869	*Poems of Solitude*		

Théodore de Banville

1842	*Caryatids*	1857	*Rope-Walking Odes*
1846	*Stalactites*		

Charles Baudelaire

1857	*Flowers of Evil*	1866	*The Waifs*
1861	*Richard Wagner and Tannhaüser in Paris*	1869	*Little Prose-Poems*

Paul Verlaine

1866	*Saturnine Poems*	1881	*Wisdom*
1869	*Gallant Fêtes*	1884	*Once Upon a Time and Not So Long Ago*
1870	*Happy Song*		
1874	*Romances Without Words*		

Arthur Rimbaud

1886	*Illuminations*
1873	*A Season In Hell*; "Drunken Boat"

Stéphane Mallarmé

1876	"The Afternoon of a Faun"	1893	*Verse and Prose*

Maurice Maeterlink

1889	*Princess Maleine*	1896	*Aglavaine and Sélysette*
1890	*The Blind*	1909	*The Blue Bird*
1892	*Pelléas and Mélisande*		

Henrik Ibsen

1855	*Lady Inger of Ostraat*	1879	*A Doll's House*
1856	*The Feast at Solhaug*	1881	*Ghosts*
1857	*Olaf Liljekrans*	1882	*An Enemy of the People*
1858	*The Vikings at Helgeland*	1884	*The Wild Duck*
1862	*Love's Comedy*	1886	*Rosmersholm*
1864	*The Pretenders*	1888	*The Lady from the Sea*
1866	*Brand*	1890	*Hedda Gabler*
1867	*Peer Gynt*	1892	*The Master Builder*
1869	*The League of Youth*	1895	*Little Eyolf*
1873	*Emperor and Galilean*	1896	*John Gabriel Borkman*
1877	*Pillars of Society*	1900	*When We Dead Awaken*

August Strindberg

1882	*The New Kingdom*	1890	*By the Open Sea*
1884	*Married I*	1899	*There Are Crimes and Crimes*
1886	*Married II*		
1887	*The Father*	1901	*The Dance of Death*
1888	*Miss Julia*	1902	*The Dream Play*

Anton Chekov

1896	*The Seagull*
1900	*Uncle Vanya*
1901	*The Three Sisters*
1904	*The Cherry Orchard*
1881–1900	"The Party"; "Ward Number Six"; "The Steppe"; "The Darling"; "Vanka"; "The Post"; "The Privy Councillor"; "The Bet"; "A Dreary Story"; "My Life"; "Happiness"

8
NEW DEPARTURES IN FRANCE AND SCANDINAVIA

Romanticism, Realism, and Naturalism were the leading literary movements of the nineteenth century; their history we have traced. There remain to be examined other literary schools that produced works of importance.

As the century advanced, national boundaries began to be less confining, as movements found adherents all over Europe. Together with this cosmopolitan trend we find another tendency. It becomes increasingly difficult, as we progress towards and into the twentieth century, to identify authors with the same certainty with which we can call Hugo a Romantic and Zola a Naturalist. Writers like Ibsen, Strindberg, and Hauptmann defy absolute departmentalization; they wrote sometimes in one school, sometimes in another. In many cases one must be content to observe the tendency of individual works without aligning the writer with one school or another.

New schools did, nonetheless, continue to appear (and continue to appear); of these the most important were the Parnassian movement and the Symbolist movement.

THE PARNASSIANS IN FRANCE

The Parnassian movement of the nineteenth century was to a degree the offspring of Gautier's insistence on the doctrine of "art for art's sake," and his stress on form as of paramount importance in literature. The nickname for this group of writers, "Le Parnasse," comes from a publication of the bookseller Lemaire in 1866. Parnasse, as he called it, contained verses by Leconte de Lisle, Sully Prudhomme, José-Maria de Hérédia, François Coppée, Villiers de L'Isle-Adam, Mallarmé, Verlaine, and others. Actually these gifted men were as remarkable for their mutual disagreements as for any common literary theory. Mallarmé and Verlaine, for instance, dissociated themselves from the movement and became the leaders of the Symbolist movement— and were, moreover, in complete disagreement with each other. But one thing can certainly be said about the Parnassians: They were writing in strong reaction against the effusiveness of Romanticism. They were also in reaction against the values of a middle-class society absorbed in industrial advancement.

The name "Parnassian" was meant to signify that these writers abandoning the subjectivism and storminess of the Romantic movement, were as objective and as calm in their reflections as the Olympian gods. These poets were indeed sometimes called "*les impassibles*" ("the poets who cannot be moved"). Leconte de Lisle, leader of the movement, in 1852 had already stated its ideals:

> There is vanity and even profanation in publicly expressing the anguish of the heart. . . . However powerful the political passions of the time may be, they belong to the world of action, not of thought. . . . We must find solace in the contemplative life, in learning, as a sanctuary of peace. . . . Art and science, too long separated . . . , must operate to unite closely.

It would be fair to say that the Parnassian movement also owes something, therefore, to the rise of Realism. Realism being unsuited to their poetic visions, the Parnassians' objection to Romantic excess took the shape of a new classical enthusiasm for form and objective observation.

Charles Leconte de Lisle (1818–1894)

Leconte de Lisle, born on Réunion Island, near Madagascar, commemorated the exotic scenery of the tropics in his early verses. He was sent to France to study law and settled in Paris. There he supported himself by making translations of Homer, Theocritus, and the Greek dramatists, and by teaching. In 1852 he published his *Poèmes Antiques* (*Antique Poems*) and in 1862 his *Poèmes Barbares* (*Barbarian Poems*).

Under the influence of the ancient Greeks his verse contains pieces on the "Venus de Milo," "Niobe," and "The Childhood of Hercules," as well as a three-act drama, "Les Erinnyes (The Furies)," imitated from the trilogy of Æschylus. His travels in the East and his interest in Buddhism were responsible for his exotic "La Fontaine aux Lianes" (The Liana Spring), "Les Éléphants" (The Elephants), "La Panthère Noire" (The Black Panther), and "La Bernica." His Buddhism united with his scientific interests to produce also some poems of philosophical pessimism, such as "Midi" (Afternoon), "Nox" (Night), and "Dies Irae" (Day of Wrath).

His style is austere and rhetorical, and remarkably successful in suggesting a sculpturesque quality. His love of formal beauty belongs so clearly to the ancient world that Gautier said of his work, in a humorous vein, "It would have been simpler to write in Greek."

José-Maria de Heredia (1842–1905)

Heredia was a Cuban aristocrat by birth. His place in French poetry was earned by a single volume, *Les Trophées* (*The Trophies*) (1893), a collection of poems, chiefly sonnets, which had appeared in the magazines. These short pieces are exquisitely turned, the product of a learned mind. They celebrate the "trophies" of civilization throughout the ages. Best known are: "Antoine et Cléopâtre" (Anthony and Cleopatra), "Soir de Bataille" (Night of the Battle), "Les Conquérants" (The Conquerors), and "Le Chevrier" (The Goatherd). Heredia's sonnets, because of their powerful compression of an epoch's history into a handful of lines, often possess a grandeur that is astounding for poems of such brevity.

Sully Prudhomme (1839–1908)

Prudhomme, a philosophical poet, was an assiduous student of science. His chief volumes are *Stances et Poèmes* (*Stanzas and Poems*) (1865–1866), *Les Solitudes* (*Poems of Solitudes*) (1869), and *Les Vaines Tendresses* (*Vain Tenderness*) (1872). He was one of the most representative poets of his age; in his sculptured lines we are impressed with the pessimism of the times, the emphasis on exquisite form, and the fine finish of the verse. He has proved especially interesting to English-speaking readers, for the clarity of his style and its air of simplicity make him readily apprehended.

Théodore de Banville (1823–1891)

Banville carried to its logical extremes Gautier's doctrine of "art for art's sake." His interest in and complete mastery of intricate verse forms have made him the victim of a somewhat unfair charge of superficiality. It is true that, like Swinburne, his brilliant manipulation of rhythm and rhyme has somewhat obscured the content of his lines. But, also like Swinburne, he was equally at home in the serious and the comic, and without discounting the perfection of his artistry, one will find him often genuinely inspired.

His many volumes include the following, which are particularly of interest: *Les Cariatides* (*Caryatids*) (1842), *Les Stalactites* (*Stalactites*) (1846), and *Odes Funambulesques* (*Rope-Walking Odes*) (1857).

CHARLES BAUDELAIRE (1821–1867)

Both the Parnassians and the Symbolists have claimed Baudelaire; yet, like many men of his century, this great genius escapes classification.

It is doubtful whether there would now be much dispute as to his title of great poet. It was not so long ago, however, that academic historians, because of the scandal attaching to his name, dismissed him as a writer of no consequence. Indeed, many of the mid-twentieth century anthologies of French literature in use in the schools either omitted him or passed over him with but a word or two.

Baudelaire's father, an amateur artist, died in 1827, and the poet's mother married Col. Aupick the next year. Baudelaire received a good education at Lyons and at the Collège Louis-le-Grand in Paris. Very early he was determined to become a man of letters; it is worthy of note that as a boy he was an enthusiast of English literature, particularly the writings of the Gothic novelists, like "Monk" Lewis.

Baudelaire's temperament was an unusual mixture of willfulness, a love of dissipation and debauchery, a cultivated singularity of conduct, and a strong religious bent. After taking his degree in 1839, he spent the next two years so fruitlessly that he was sent off to India (1841). He was back in Paris in less than a year, came of age, fell into a small inheritance, and lived as he chose thereafter.

By 1845 he was already on the tongues of the *literati* because of his unconventional ideas. In 1846 he discovered the great enthusiasm of his life, the writings of Edgar Allan Poe, in which he professed to find many dreams of his own imagination given shape by the genius of the American poet. Until 1865 he was largely concerned with his translation of Poe, which appeared in 1852, 1857, and 1865. Poe's literary credo, with its close affinity to Gautier's "art for art's sake," vastly impressed Baudelaire, and his French versions of Poe's tales are among the most remarkable translations ever made.

Baudelaire was a partisan of the revolutionaries in 1848, and for a few years he gave some attention to republican politics. But it was impossible for him to remain in that camp. His deep religious strain drew him to Catholicism, and by intellectual preference he was an aristocrat.

IMPORTANCE

In 1857 appeared the book on which Baudelaire's fame chiefly rests, his first volume of original poetry, *Fleurs du Mal* (*Flowers of Evil*). The brilliant poems in this volume had been written with the utmost skill and painstaking artistry; unlike the verses of Banville, these were cast in essentially simple forms. It is the chiseled perfection of Baudelaire's poetry that allies him to the Parnassians.

The book by its very nature was calculated to appeal to few people, but the morbidity of the subject matter of the poems made it notorious. Soon *Fleurs du Mal* became synonymous, in the minds of the critics and the general public, with indecency and moral corruption. The quality of the grotesque hovering over the volume bespeaks the influence of Poe. But there are dimensions in Baudelaire quite beyond the reach of the American author. A strange fusion of delight in the senses and a "mystical analysis of passion," such as we find in the poetry of John Donne, gives the poetry of Baudelaire its unique tone.

Unfortunately, it was the more obviously unconventional nature of the topics Baudelaire chose that for many years drew attention to the volume. Hugo wrote to him: "*Vous dotez le ciel de l'art d'un rayon macabre; vous créez un frisson nouveau.*" ("You endow the heaven of art with a macabre light; you create a new shudder.") One critic has found in Baudelaire all the symptoms of what has come to be known in literature as "Decadence": debauchery, perversity, "profound introspection, deliberate eccentricity of conduct, violent and extreme moods, and a strong addiction to the mysticism and ritual of the Roman Catholic religion." Some of these traits, in any event, so much offended the authorities that Baudelaire and his publisher were prosecuted for offending public morals.

The poems that had caused the greatest scandal were removed from the 1861 edition, and a number of new poems were added. In 1866 the poet issued all the suppressed verses at Brussels in a volume called *Les Épaves* (*The Waifs*).

There was also much notoriety given to the fact that Baudelaire's mistress was a black woman; what the public did not know was his endless kindness to her, despite her outrageous conduct, until the end of his days. It was well known, too, that he took opium and drank heavily. Nevertheless, his life was actually an uneventful one, and its devotion to literary tasks was patient, untiring, and profound.

As a matter of fact, although some of Baudelaire's poems are concerned with such macabre subjects as corpses, opiates, vile odors, and vampires, these are by no means entirely representative. There is nothing macabre about many of his best pieces: "L'Albatros" (The Albatross), "Le Chat" (The Cat), "La Vie Antérieure" (The Previous Life), "La Beauté" (Beauty), "Hymne à la Beauté" (Hymn to Beauty), and "Les Litanies de Satan" (Satan's Litanies). Somehow or other, Baudelaire the artist was able to stand aloof from the depravities of Baudelaire the man, a detached student of the latter's sensations, and an objective recorder in sharply etched lines of what he there observed. The peculiar quality of Baudelaire's genius is, thus, an unusual union of extreme Romanticism and the severest classicism. His content is voluptuousness; his form is all restraint.

Baudelaire was also the author of a volume of brilliant *Petits Poèmes en Prose* (*Little Prose-Poems*), and some valuable literary criticism. It is worthy of note that he was perhaps the first man to appreciate the true importance of Flaubert's *Madame Bovary*, which appeared the same year as *Fleurs du Mal*.

Towards the close of his brief life Baudelaire became paralyzed from the excesses of his dissipations. His last two years were spent in hospitals at Brussels and Paris.

His influence on later nineteenth century and twentieth century poetry has been considerable. The quality of his images has been held responsible for the Symbolist movement. Also, he was the first Frenchman to understand the greatness of Wagner's music. In 1861 appeared his *Richard Wagner et Tannhaüser à Paris* (*Richard Wagner and Tannhaüser in Paris*). The Symbolists were devotees of Wagner's music dramas, in which they seemed to find their own theories incarnated.

THE SYMBOLIST MOVEMENT IN FRANCE

Although Verlaine began as a Parnassian, he became the leading poet of a Romantic reaction against that group, the Symbolist movement. To the newer poets the Parnassians were too unfeelingly objective and placed too much emphasis on form. They accused Leconte de Lisle, Gautier, and Hérédia of being materialistic; for the same reason they objected to the Realist novel. They charged Parnassians like Sully Prudhomme with exiling thought by emphasizing the perfection of their chiseled lines.

Above all, the Symbolists wished their lines to suggest, rather than to state, a meaning. They were interested in what the poem could evoke, not in what it could expressly state. They were highly subjective and sought to evoke mystery and magic by the music of their verse and its imagery. Their chief predecessor was Baudelaire because of his innovations in exploring varied sensations. The meaning of their poems is always to be found between, not in, the lines.

The Symbolists claimed affinities to the art of music, and indeed were enthusiastic Wagnerians. They often remind us of their contemporaries, the English Pre-Raphaelites. As a matter of fact, the whole tendency of the Symbolist movement is more akin to the traditions of English poetry, in which the power to suggest associated ideas is not uncommon. The genius of the French language and temperament has always been towards precision and pointedness. The Symbolists, characteristically, included many poets who were not native to France—Vielé-Griffin, Moréas, Rodenbach, Verhaeren, Maeterlinck, and Stuart Merrill.

At the beginning their movement was stigmatized with the appellation *Decadent*, a term they were willing enough to accept, and by which they are often still designated.

Paul Verlaine (1844–1896)

Verlaine's biography reads unattractively like an account of the kind of Bohemian irresponsibility that people think characteristic of all poets—and which is true of very few of them. It is a tale of alcoholism, disease, prisons, hospitals—and wasted abilities. Though he loved his wife sincerely and expressed that love in some exquisite verse, he later fell under the spell of the wild, gifted boy-poet Arthur Rimbaud, who turned his muse in a new and significant direction, and with whom he had a brief homosexual love affair that terminated in a break with Mme. Verlaine and in the longest of Verlaine's imprisonments.

His earliest publications were in the first issue of the *Parnasse* (1866), where he is to be found an extreme disciple of Gautier in the precision of his lines. His first volume, *Poèmes Saturniens* (*Saturnine Poems*) (1866), also exhibits his indebtedness to Baudelaire, for though the attitude is objective in the Parnassian style, the poet exhibits an interest in morbid subjects. The next volume, *Fêtes Galantes* (*Gallant Fêtes*) (1869) was inspired by the paintings of the eighteenth century painter Watteau, and with exquisite elegance recreates eighteenth century charm and artifice. In *La Bonne Chanson* (*Happy Song*) (1870) the poet leaves Parnassian objectivity to write of his love for his betrothed; the volume contains much lyric sweetness.

Verlaine's new manner, developed during the period of his greatest personal confusions, appeared in *Romances sans Paroles* (*Romances Without*

Words) (1874), a title that emphasizes the fact that the meaning of these poems was to be delivered chiefly through the music of the lines. Here at last, as a product of his theorizing about poetry with Rimbaud, Verlaine reveals the true Symbolist manner. "Music above everything" is the banner of the school; "we want nuance, not color."

Verlaine's manner from this time on is simple in the extreme, with a genius for recording evanescent and wayward impressions and moods. The music of the verse itself is full of variety and freshness. At this time, too, Verlaine had been converted to Catholicism, in which he expressed fervent faith even though his acts were at considerable variance from his beliefs. There is keen poignancy in his confessions of error, and these make *Sagesse* (*Wisdom*) of 1881 particularly touching. His sincerity is plain to feel, and is almost childlike in its simplicity and self-abasement.

Jadis et Naguère (*Once Upon a Time and Not So Long Ago*) (1884) is his last significant volume. After that, in the intervals between confinements to charity hospitals and addiction to absinthe, Verlaine's genius rapidly deteriorated into scarcely coherent effusions of eroticism.

At his best he was certainly the finest poet of the Symbolist movement, and the only peer of Baudelaire in his generation. He excels the latter in his power to touch the heart, in his sweetness, and in his fluidity of music. Luckily for English readers, his contemporary Ernest Dowson has made several excellent renditions of Verlaine. The following will give a good idea of Verlaine at his most characteristic:

> *Tears fall within mine heart,*
> *As rain upon the town:*
> *Whence does this languor start*
> *Possessing all mine heart?*
> *O sweet fall of the rain*
> *Upon the earth and roofs!*
> *Unto an heart in pain,*
> *O music of the rain!*
> *Tears that have no reason*
> *Fall in my sorry heart:*
> *What! was there no treason?*
> *This grief hath no reason.*
> *Nay! the more desolate,*
> *Because, I know not why,*
> *(Neither for love nor hate)*
> *Mine heart is desolate.*

Arthur Rimbaud (1854–1891)

Rimbaud was a madcap genius, who had a catastrophic influence upon Verlaine's private life but a beneficent influence on his poetic career. Before he was out of his teens, Rimbaud was through with literature forever; suffering some revulsion of feeling at his mode of life, he went off to Africa, where he devoted himself to trade. During his few years on the literary horizon he was highly successful in shocking even Paris with his scandalous conduct and manners.

His eruption into the world of letters began when he sent Verlaine a sheaf of his poems. The older man was deeply impressed with the youth's genius. Soon they became inseparable. Verlaine deserted his wife and the two men went off to England and Belgium and spent a year wandering about. In a quarrel Verlaine wounded Rimbaud with a revolver and was sent to prison.

Rimbaud's output was, naturally, small: a collection of his poems and prose-poems, issued by Verlaine under the misapprehension that Rimbaud was already dead, *Illuminations* (1886); and the one volume Rimbaud issued himself, a prose-poem psychological autobiography, *Une Saison en Enfer* (*A Season in Hell*) (1873). The former contains the poem that first attracted Verlaine's, notice, "Bateau Ivre" (Drunken Boat), written in 1871. His most famous poem, "Sonnet des Voyelles" (Sonnet of Vowels), in which he professed to find definite colors attaching to each vowel, states:

> *A is black, E white, I red, U green, O blue.*

(It should be remembered that the vowels in French have all entirely different values from English). The "Bateau Ivre," a poem evoking the moods of an aimlessly drifting boat, has also been vastly admired.

Rimbaud's work is remarkable for its music, its "tone color," and its strange combination of simplicity and fantasy. He used words in unfamiliar ways, was very free in his versification, and employed imagery pushed to the limits of sensibility. He has recently been described as the forerunner of the Surrealistic movement.

Stéphane Mallarmé (1842–1898)

Mallarmé was, with Verlaine, a leader of the Symbolists. He was a teacher of English and translated Edgar Allan Poe; during a stay in England he became personally acquainted with the Pre-Raphaelite poets there. A man of charm and interesting conversation, he attracted to himself many of the younger Symbolists. His life was otherwise uneventful. His work was published chiefly in periodicals, is small in bulk, and was collected in 1893 as *Vers et Prose* (*Verse and Prose*). His most celebrated work is "L'Après-Midi d'un Faune" (The Afternoon of a Faun), issued in 1876 but unnoted until the composer Debussy composed his beautiful symphonic poem around it.

Mallarmé's conception of Symbolism was at considerable variance from Verlaine's. Verlaine communicated the emotion itself; Mallarmé wished to convey the idea of the emotion. Like Verlaine, however, he relied as a poet on the associative value of the music of his lines. Whereas Verlaine is simple in the extreme, Mallarmé is obscure; where Verlaine's lines are fluid, Mallarmé's are crowded. In consequence Mallarmé's lot has been to be either deified or damned. His worshippers approve his contention that a poem ought to be meaningless to the uninitiated; his critics pronounce him utterly incomprehensible—at best, they say, his verse is but "rhythmic sound." It is true that the images in Mallarmé huddle upon one another so much that one must find one's way through his mists of lovely sound without hoping for aid from syntax or dictionary.

Other Symbolist Poets in France

At the end of the century the Symbolist movement became the rallying ground of much able and talented creativeness in poetry—though no poet of Verlaine's stature emerged.

There were many reactions and counterreactions to Symbolism, the Parnassians, and the issues of Realism and Romanticism—too numerous to disentangle in so brief a survey as this. Suffice it to say that the following, making due allowances for shifts in many of their careers, have been associated with the Symbolist movement: Francis Jammes (1868–1938), a follower of Rimbaud, a poet of simplicity and intuition, best known for his pictures of the South of France in *De l'Angélus de l'Aube à l'Angélus du Soir* (*From Dawn to Eventide*) (1898) and *Les Géorgiques Chrétiennes* (*Christian Georgics*) (1911–1912); Albert Samain (1858–1900), of Flemish origin, a follower of Verlaine's *Fêtes Galantes* manner in his eighteenth century sketches, *Au Jardin de l'Infante* (*In the Garden of the Infanta*) (1893); Georges Rodenbach (1855–1898), a Belgian who wrote in prose of his homeland in *Bruges la Mort* (*Dead Bruges*) (1892), and whose delicate poems appeared in various volumes such as *Les Tristesses* (*Sorrows*); Gustave Kahn (1859–1936), who sponsored the use of free verse in *Les Palais Nomades* (*Nomad Palaces*) (1887) and *Le Livre d'Images* (*The Book of Images*) (1897); Vielé-Griffin (1864–1937), an American by birth, who pushed further the use of free verse in volumes celebrating the pageantry of life, such as *Cueille d'Avril* (*April Gathering*) (1886); Stuart Merrill (1863–1915), also an American, who espoused the cause of socialism, and mingled his political views with a pantheistic religion in *Les Quatres Saisons* (*The Four Seasons*) (1900); Henri de Régnier (1864–1936), an aristocratic poet who celebrated Versailles in *La Cité des Eaux* (*The City of Fountains*); Jean Moréas (1856–1910), a Greek, *né* Papadiamantopoulos, who is said to have given the movement its name, but who ended in *Les Stances* (*Stanzas*) (1905) by writing with almost classical polish; and Emile Verhaeren (1855–1916), a Belgian, who hymned the realities of modern life in *Les Forces Tumultueuses* (*Tumultuous Forces*) (1902) and *La Multiple Splendeur* (*Multiple Splendor*) (1910), after having earlier been an enthusiast for Wagner and Ibsen.

Of all the Symbolists, none is better known than the dramatist Maeterlinck.

Maurice Maeterlinck (1862–1947)

Maeterlinck was born in Ghent and lived most of his life in Belgium. Early a Symbolist, he won the rather elaborate title of "the Belgian Shakespeare" with his first play *La Princesse Maleine* (*Princess Maleine*) (1889). Already the tendency of his work is to be seen here: mysticism, gloomy atmosphere attenuated speeches, significant silences. *Les Aveugles* (*The Blind*) (1890) is full of vague terror. Maeterlinck's best-known play is *Pelléas et Mélisande*, a delicate love story, which is likely to be long remembered only because of the exquisite music Debussy wrote for it; the plot deals with the old triangle familiar to us in the story of Francesca da Rimini, but here the emphasis is not on passion but on imminent and impalpable terror. In *Aglavaine et Sélysette* (1896) two sides of the love-triangle are represented this time by women. In *L'Oiseau Bleu* (*The Blue Bird*) (1909), which has long been popular with children, Maeterlinck gave up for the moment his love of vague terror in behalf of a bright allegory on the idea that happiness is to be found at home.

This is but a partial list of a long succession of plays authored by Maeterlinck. Most of them are characterized by a gloomy, oversensitive, mystical atmosphere which is at first strangely moving, but can easily become fairly boring on further acquaintance. The extreme simplicity of his dialogue is artificial to the last degree, largely because of purposeful repetition and understatement. Indeed, the understatement sometimes does not escape the ridiculous. When Mélisande's husband, suspicious of her fidelity, drags her about the stage by her long beautiful hair, she only cries: "I am not happy! I am not happy!" It is hard to imagine understatement going further.

Maeterlinck is also the author of a number of volumes of essays. The essay on "Silence" in *Le Trésor des Humbles* may be particularly recommended for the depth of its mystical vision.

THE INTERNATIONAL EMERGENCE OF SCANDINAVIAN LITERATURE

It will be remembered that Scandinavian sources were the inspiration for a considerable bulk of medieval literature. Not since the Middle Ages, however, did Scandinavia make its mark on the world of European letters. When in the nineteenth century literary influences tended to criss-cross national boundaries, that part of Europe began to be heard from again to good effect: in the novel, and particularly in the drama through the pens of Ibsen and Strindberg.

Henrik Ibsen (1828–1906)

The most influential of nineteenth century European dramatists was born at Skien, Norway, on March 20, 1828, the son of a merchant of Danish, German, and Scottish ancestry. When Ibsen was still a child, his father lost all his money, and so the boy was given only the briefest of formal educations. In 1834 he was apprenticed to an apothecary at Grimstad, where for seven years he pursued his unloved tasks. From boyhood on, Ibsen struck people with the highly unsociable quality of his temperament; but the discerning also respected him for his dauntless integrity of spirit. These were traits that were dominant in his nature for the rest of his life.

He was writing verse by his nineteenth year. Educating himself, he was preparing to enter the university at Christiania; in 1850 he enrolled there. Inspired by a reading of Cicero, he wrote his first play the same year, *Cataline*, a tragedy in verse, published through the assistance of friends. Later the same year *The Viking's Tomb* (*Kaempehojen*) was acted without success. For the ensuing year Ibsen earned a scanty living by journalism.

Then came a golden opportunity. Ole Bull, the celebrated violinist, founded a theater at Bergen and asked Ibsen to take on the responsibilities of poet and stage manager, at a modest competence. For the five years of his connection with the theater at Bergen, Ibsen not only had the assurance of having his plays presented, but he also profited by the experience of staging the plays of European dramatists; of these the plays of Scribe in particular taught him much of dramatic technique. In addition, Ibsen was allowed a sum for the purposes of traveling abroad to study drama. In 1852, for example, he went to Copenhagen and Dresden.

His earlier plays are interesting only as part of the history of his development. The first of these to show any signs of genius is *Lady Inger of Ostraat* (*Fru Inger til Ostraat*) (1855), a romantic drama laid in sixteenth century Norway. *The Feast at Solhaug* (*Gildet paa Solhaug*) (1856) a romantic tragedy, was written in imitation of the Danish dramatist Herz. Ibsen's last play at Bergen was *Olaf Liljekrans* (1857), another nationalistic play, which, however, was not a success.

Ibsen took a long time to discover his true bent. Although he was thirty, he still had years of uncertain experimentation ahead of him, years of discouragement and disillusionment. In 1858 occurred one happy event, nonetheless, his marriage to a woman with whom he spent a life of mutual devotion. The same year he was working on a fine drama, with materials taken from the ancient Icelandic sources, *The Vikings at Helgeland* (*Hermaendene paa Helgeland*) (1858); here Ibsen attempted to free himself of contemporary Danish influences. The play was rejected by the managers at both Christiania and Copenhagen; in the meantime Ibsen had been appointed to the unlucrative post of director of the small Norwegian Theater. Though neglected for a time, this play has since proved its merits on stages all over the world.

Love's Comedy (*Kjaerlighedens Komedie*) (1862), a brilliant comedy in rhymed verse, showing how middle-class values are murderous to romantic love, enraged the public when it appeared. The idea of having a clergyman as a character in the drama itself seemed scandalous. This clever play, the first of Ibsen's to be laid in contemporary times, has withstood the ravages of time, and has been very popular in Norway during our own century.

In his next play, *The Pretenders* (*Kongsemnerne*) (1864), showing a great advance in craftsmanship, Ibsen returned (this time in prose) to historic drama. The story is laid in the civil wars of thirteenth century Norway.

Ibsen's most gifted contemporary in Norway, Björnson, had been able to obtain a subsidy from the government, and Ibsen's own lack of success in procuring one angered him so much that he determined to leave Scandinavia. He began to travel in 1864 through Denmark, Germany, and Italy with his family, with the intention of establishing himself at Rome. The move was a lucky one for the literature of the drama, for his next two plays, *Brand* and *Peer Gynt*, not only inaugurate the period of his true greatness but also contain the quintessence of Ibsen's attack on society: in the first, the man of uncompromising principle and insufficient humanity is pilloried; in the second, the man of no principle and complete egotism is shown up in all the mediocrity of his moral shabbiness. These characters continue to reappear in most of Ibsen's masterworks.

Brand: From Italy Ibsen sent to Copenhagen *Brand* (1866), a poetic tragedy exposing the meanness of Norwegian values, but at the same time showing the failure of a too-superhuman hero who cannot compromise with life. Ibsen, who could be as unmercifully critical of himself as of everyone else, said of Brand that he was "myself in my best moments."

Brand is a minister who believes that all compromise is the work of Satan. He is loyal to an idea of perfect goodness beyond the reach of anyone he knows. He refuses to leave the icy regions where he feels the call to serve his parish, which he feels needs him, and hence bears the responsibility for his own son's eventual death in that northern winter.

Nothing daunts him. He urges a peasant to cross the ice in dangerous weather to visit the man's dying daughter; the peasant will not go and endeavors to restrain Brand from going. Brand scornfully knocks the man down.

Again, the priest sallies forth in a storm to bring consolation to a dying murderer; he requires someone to help him sail the boat across the fjord, but the fishermen will not venture out in that weather on such a mission. A woman, deeply stirred by his high idealism, agrees to hold the rudder of the boat for him. This is the beginning of an attachment that ends in marriage between them and the birth of a child whom they both dearly love. The child dies, and Brand makes his wife give the dead baby's clothes to a needy gypsy. His wife, deprived of everything that held her to life, dies of a broken heart.

The people at last recognize him for a saint. Ambitious for yet greater spiritual heights, he calls upon them to leave the church and worship God in the mountains, God's own church. Soon the people tire of his uncompromising attitude, and stone him. He goes forth, and meets his own death in an avalanche. Symbolically Ibsen shows Nature itself stoning this fanatic. At the end Brand hears a celestial voice telling him the truth he has missed: "God is Love."

Peer Gynt: *Peer Gynt* (1867), also written in verse, returns to the attack on middle-class society by having as its hero a man who represents the moral cowardice of the Norwegian national character, as Ibsen saw it. Whatever Ibsen's castigating purposes may have been, the play is so brilliantly written that its muddle-headed, blundering hero emerges as a highly likable rascal, for all his ethical mediocrity. From the purely literary point of view *Peer Gynt* has often been called Ibsen's greatest work. Despite its quality, however, Ibsen soon came to feel that poetry is "injurious to the dramatic art," and soon gave verse up altogether as a vehicle for dramatic expression.

The hero of *Peer Gynt* is an egocentric, self-seeking, unscrupulous rascal, a true picaresque hero, whose roots nevertheless are deep in Norwegian folklore. He is a ne'er-do-well who succeeds for most of his life in escaping from reality and in convincing himself, in the process, that he is a great fellow. When we first meet him, his mother, Ase, is upbraiding him for his worthlessness. He tells her that he plans to run off with Hegstad's daughter tonight, right in the middle of the girl's wedding feast. When Ase protests, Peer picks her up and sets her on the roof of their little house.

At the wedding, only a girl he has never seen before, Solveig, pays any attention to Peer. Peer drinks too much, and begins to give a fantastic account of his adventures. In the meantime, the bride has locked herself up and refuses to come out; the groom appeals to Peer for help. Peer not only frees the bride; he also runs off with her.

Peer soon tires of the girl, abandons her, and penetrates into the forest. There he comes upon the Trolds, repulsive semihuman elves; pretending to himself that the Trold King's hideous daughter is a beauteous princess and that the grim ravine in which the Trolds dwell is a gorgeous palace, Peer agrees to live among them. When, however, the Trolds undertake to make his self-deception complete by slitting his eyes, he objects. Soon he is deserting the Trold King's daughter too.

Peer has been declared an outlaw for his elopement with Hegstad's daughter. He goes to live in the forest; Solveig comes to join him there. For a while Peer is happy with her; but one day he meets the Trold King's daughter in company with a horrid little Trold, his son by her; his Trold family have come to claim their rights. Peer is forced to run away again. Before leaving, he asks Solveig to wait for his return. He also goes for a last visit with Ase, and finds her dying.

Now he goes on his adventures all over the world: in America he becomes prosperous in the slave trade; in Asia he sells idols. In some lands he sells Bibles, in others rum. At last we find him in the African desert down on his luck again. Finding a white horse, he is acclaimed a prophet by an Arabian tribe, and once more a life of luxury is open to him. He falls in love with Anitra, a dancing-girl, who robs him of all his worldly goods as well as the white horse and leaves him stranded once more. Wandering about again, he comes upon the Sphinx and a German who is pondering the meaning of the Sphinx. Peer explains to him that the Sphinx is itself. The answer strikes the German as so profound that he urges Peer to accompany him to Cairo to lecture on his idea to a club of learned gentlemen there. At Cairo Peer discovers that the learned club is an insane asylum; here in the madhouse Peer is crowned Emperor of Himself.

We find him old now, and tired of wandering. On his return to Norway he meets the Button Moulder (Death), who informs Peer that he is destined to be melted down, like other mediocrities, in the Button Moulder's ladle: Peer, though unworthy of Heaven, has been too much of a nonentity to be worthy of Hell. Outraged at the prospect of losing his identity in this undignified way, Peer boasts of his misdeeds. But the Button Moulder's verdict is that they were all too petty to be punished in Hell. While disputing, the two come upon Solveig, an old woman still waiting for Peer's return. She still believes in Peer, and now that he is back, nothing else matters to her. She cannot serve, as Peer hoped, as testimony to his wickedness, for her happiness at having him by her side is now complete. The Button Moulder leaves, promising to see Peer again. Peer takes refuge in Solveig's arms and in her faith in him.

The League of Youth: Ibsen's next play, *The League of Youth* (*De Unges Forbund*) (1869) is his first political play, and is written entirely in prose. It is a brilliant comedy that has been strangely neglected, for its dialogue is bitingly satirical, and it is more full of point today than ever.

Here the hero, an ambitious young lawyer, temperamentally akin to Peer Gynt, becomes a violent Radical overnight because he is wounded by an insult from a landlord in his community, and is hailed as the idol of the liberals. The landlord, however, misinformed as to the object of the lawyer's attack, invites the latter to a party to meet the local aristocracy. His head turned by the friendship of the "upper crust," our lawyer is soon spinning out a new political theory: the need for an aristocracy to teach a life of culture and grace to the rest of society. Like most "idealists" in professional politics, our hero proves that he can be bought at not too high a price.

The play, satirizing conservative and liberal alike, was received with rage when presented. However, Ibsen was now becoming successful at last. *Brand* was selling well, the government had granted him a pension, and his days of want were over.

In 1868 he left Italy for Dresden, where he remained until 1874.

Emperor and Galilean: In 1873 appeared a two-part poetic drama, the last of his poetic plays, on which he had been working for several years, *Emperor and Galilean* (*Kejser og Galilaeer*)—study of the attempt of the Emperor Julian to stem the growing tide of Christianity. The play has generally been thought to be Ibsen's weakest, but it is said to have been his own favorite.

The clash between "the old beauty (of paganism) that is no longer beautiful and the new truth (Christianity) that is no longer true" is the battle that the Apostate Emperor must wage within himself. The "first empire" of pagan living in the flesh is dead; the "second empire" of Christian asceticism is already decayed. What Julian (and Ibsen) look forward to is the "third empire," when man will look upon himself is a piece of godhead, and learn to bridge the abyss between flesh and spirit.

Pillars of Society: *Pillars of Society* (*Samfundets Stötter*) (1877) was written after Ibsen had made a brief return to Norway in 1874. He came back to Germany, and did not settle in Christiania until 1891.

With this play, he definitely set the writing of poetic drama behind him. Moreover, he abandoned any attempt to write pure tragedy or pure comedy thereafter; the element of satire is ever present in his work. Persuaded that radicals, liberals, and conservatives alike would never do anything for the improvement of society, Ibsen became thoroughly disenchanted with the whole world of politics, and looked for better things only in terms of individual development. For this reason he undertook to diagnose the ills of society with the purpose of teaching each man and woman to be his own moral physician.

Pillars of Society, though effective, is not on a par with the series of great plays that it inaugurates. A vivid picture of the corruption in the life of small towns, the play centers around the person of Consul Karsten Bernick, inheritor of a famous shipbuilding concern. Bernick has allowed another man to bear the disgrace for his own love affair as well as the guilt of a theft that was never committed. His excuse is that being a pillar of society, he cannot let society down by admitting his culpability and thus inviting a total lack of respect for the structure he helps to maintain.

A Doll's House: Ibsen's next play, *A Doll's House* (*Et Dukkehjem*) (1879) created a scandal that took years to subside. Because of this play Ibsen was depicted as a man who had attacked the sanctity of both home and marriage. The boldness of his championship of women's right to be respected as human beings with minds, souls, destinies of their own, apart from their role as wives, struck Ibsen's contemporaries as shocking and irreligious. Nevertheless, the reverberation of the door Nora slams at the end of the play, echoed all over the civilized world for decades thereafter. Probably no single work did more to speed the political and economic emancipation of women than *A Doll's House.*

Actually, however, to read in the play no more than a tract on women's rights is to underestimate both it and Ibsen's largeness of purpose. Nora does come to understand that her marriage has been built on sand; but her husband also is forced to face the fact of his own inadequacy. In a way, the play is as much his as it is Nora's, for his need to reexamine himself is as great as hers. Both of them need to confront the facts at last—a message that Ibsen was never tired of delivering in all his plays. From this time on he became the inveterate enemy of all pretense, sham idealism, self-delusion; for him man's only hope is in relentless acknowledgment of all the facts of his life.

A Doll's House opens with a touch of the Symbolism that became increasingly strong in Ibsen's work, despite his importance as a Realist in drama. The crucial matter in the story of this play is money, and as the curtain goes up we find Nora over-tipping a porter who has helped her carry home her Christmas purchases. It is Christmas Eve and Nora Helmer has been shopping. Her husband Torvald enters from his study, a little put out by the fact that she has been spending money a little recklessly. She reminds him that this is the first Christmas in many years in which they do not have to watch their pennies. He has just been made manager of a bank, and after the New Year their financial troubles will be over. When she seems a little discouraged by his sermon, he relents, but urges his "little lark" to try not to be too careless in the future.

We find Nora unconsciously enacting the role of the sweet spoiled darling that her husband expects of her. As Torvald goes back to his room, Christine Linde, an old schoolfriend of Nora's, arrives. It is ten years since the women last saw each other. Mrs. Linde is now a childless widow and has come to town in the hopes of finding some employment to engage her interest. Nora assures her that she will wheedle Torvald into getting Christine a position at the bank.

When Christine speaks proudly of her having married without love in order to help her mother and brothers, Nora boasts that she too has something to be proud of, though everyone thinks her such a brainless, irresponsible creature. Some years ago Torvald's life depended upon his going to Italy for his health; they had no money then for the trip, and her father was not able to help them. It was Nora at that time who borrowed the money for the trip. At first she had tried to get Torvald to raise the sum on the pretense that it was she who wanted to travel; but Torvald had refused to give in to what he deemed mere feminine caprice. So, to spare Torvald the knowledge that he owed her his life, she pretended to him that she had borrowed the money from her father just before the latter's death. Torvald has never learned the truth. She has had a very difficult time scraping the sums together to meet her payments by buying for herself only the cheapest clothes and secretly doing work at home to earn extra money. All this time Torvald has been thinking of her as charmingly but incorrigibly self-indulgent. Now that Torvald has a wonderful new post at the bank, she feels her strain will be ended.

Nils Krogstad, a lawyer employed at the bank, enters. He has come to see Torvald on urgent business. It develops that Krogstad, a shady character, was an old suitor of Christine's; she had in fact jilted him to marry for money. After Torvald has gotten rid of Krogstad, Nora easily persuades Torvald to give Christine a position at the bank; he is the more eager to do this as it will give him an excuse to discharge Krogstad, whom he has always disliked.

The others leave, and Nora is busy with her children for a while. Krogstad comes back. He is the man who has loaned her the money, and has been as difficult as all usurers are. He has guessed that Christine is to take his place. He now threatens Nora: she must persuade Torvald to retain him or he will tell her husband the facts. At first Nora is defiant, thinking that if her husband does learn the truth he will pay up the sum, and she will be rid of Krogstad. But the lawyer makes it plain that his hold over her involves more than money. Nora gave her father as surety for the loan; but Krogstad has discovered that the bond is dated three days after the old man's death, and that the signature was forged—obviously by Nora herself. To Nora this is a matter of small consequence inasmuch as she has been making her payments regularly enough. Krogstad assures her that his reputation as a blackguard rests on a crime no more serious than hers; the position at the bank is important to his self-respect. If he loses that, he will see to it that she is ruined too. Krogstad leaves. When Torvald comes back, Nora's first hints in Krogstad's behalf are clearly futile; Torvald cannot bear that hypocrite. Torvald indeed shudders at the idea of any home's being poisoned by the presence of a liar and cheat.

In Act Two, on Christmas Day, Christine tells Nora that she fears that her friend may have borrowed the money from Dr. Rank, a constant visitor at the Helmer home, and that she may thus have put herself under too great obligation to the physician. Nora dispels Christine's fears; Rank is a man of honor. He is a very ill man, dying of an incurable disease inherited from a dissipated father.

Christine goes to the children, and Nora now begs Torvald to retain Krogstad as a favor to her. Her excuse is that she fears Krogstad will write scurrilous articles against Torvald in revenge. But Torvald is adamant. Even though Krogstad is a good worker, he will not have him, if only because Krogstad presumes on their boyhood acquaintance and can be depended upon to be far too familiar with him at the bank. He then and there, to put an end to Nora's childishness, sends off a letter to Krogstad to notify him that he is discharged. Torvald assures her that she need not worry about anything Krogstad can do; whatever is to happen, Torvald can shoulder the troubles for her and himself. Torvald goes into his study.

Dr. Rank comes in. Nora coquets with him charmingly because he is in a grim humor at the thought of his approaching death. She is even thinking of trying to get the needed money from him, so she can pay off Krogstad. But Rank makes the request impossible by revealing his deep but hitherto unconfessed love for Nora. She is deeply touched, and admits that she has always found it easier to talk to him than to either her father or husband—for both have always treated her like a charming child. "Being with Torvald is a little like being with papa," she says. When Krogstad is announced, she asks Rank to join her husband.

Now that he has been fired, Krogstad is determined not only to get his job back, but to use Nora's bond to advance himself. He expects to have Torvald so much under his thumb that it will be he who will run the bank. He takes out a letter that he has written to tell Torvald the truth, and with a warning to Nora that even her suicide would not help matters, he drops the letter outside the door in their letter box.

Nora wildly confides in Christine now. Above all she is terrified that Torvald will do a "wonderful thing" which must not happen—shouldering the responsibility for her act. Christine comforts Nora with the promise that she can get Krogstad to ask for the return of his letter; her old suitor will do that much for love of her. Nora's problem is only to keep Torvald from the letter box until Krogstad returns. Christine goes out in search of the lawyer, and Torvald enters. To keep him busy Nora begs him to watch her practice the tarantella, a dance that she is to give tomorrow night at the costume ball. He agrees, and she dances like a woman possessed until Christine returns. As they all go into dinner, Christine whispers to Nora that Krogstad has left town for the day, and will not be back until tomorrow night.

In Act Three we hear the sound of music coming from above. Christine is waiting. Krogstad comes in; he admits to Christine that when he lost her, he lost all incentive to decency. She explains why she had felt compelled to marry without love. Christine is still in love with him, and suggests that they mend their broken lives together. Greatly moved, Krogstad determines to ask Torvald for the letter before it is read. But now it is Christine who forbids that: she has seen that Nora's happiness is built upon a lie, and feels that it is high time the Helmers face the facts about themselves. Torvald must read the letter. Krogstad leaves in joy at the great happiness in store for him.

Torvald, who has had a little too much champagne at the party, enters with Nora, whom he boasts to have been the queen of the ball. Christine leaves, and Torvald expresses his passion and desire for Nora; he feels as though they were newlyweds. They are interrupted by Rank on his way home—for the last time. Nora understands that they will not see him again; he is going home to die like a wounded animal. The thought of death sobers Nora. She realizes that she cannot prevent the great sacrifice Torvald is to make. He must read the letter now. Torvald takes all the mail from the box and goes to his study. Soon he is rushing out in a fury.

To Nora's horror, so far from assuming responsibility, Torvald at once puts an abyss between them. He accuses her of being a liar and cheat. They will live together hereafter for appearance's sake, but she is to have nothing more to do with her children. He has been ruined by a criminal wife. Nora coldly listens to his vituperation.

The maid brings in a letter from Krogstad returning the bond. Krogstad, who has found happiness in the return of Christine, will release Nora from further responsibility. Torvald is overwhelmed with relief. Noting for the first time that Nora is subdued, he tells her to forget his words, that he forgives her. She ironically thanks him. She changes from her fancy dress to everyday clothes, and announces that she is leaving. But first there must be "a settling of accounts."

Quietly she shows him a picture of the lie on which their marriage has been built. Like her father, Torvald has always treated her as though she never owned a mind or a soul, but were just a pleasant plaything. And now she understands that after eight years of marriage Torvald and she are total strangers to each other. When he realizes how serious is the breach between them, he even promises to try to be different. Perhaps he can, Nora says, if his doll is taken away from him.

She now puts on her things for outdoors. He need not fear to be bothered by any financial obligations to her. She gives him back his ring, and demands hers from him. From now on they are both to be free. She does not want to hear from him again. He need not expect to see her again, despite his pleading, unless "the most wonderful thing of all" could happen. That is, both of them would have to be so much changed that their life together "would be a real wedlock." She leaves. As the sound of the door closing behind her is heard, Torvald is left only with the hope that "the most wonderful thing of all" might yet occur.

When society is purged of its lies and pretenses, there could be hope of dignity in the relation of men and women. That is Ibsen's final thought.

Ghosts: In his next play, *Ghosts* (*Gengangere*) (1881), Ibsen elaborated on the theme of venereal disease hinted at in the person of Dr. Rank (in *A Doll's House*). The work was greeted with howls of execration by the critics; it was called "positively abominable," "disgusting," "a loathsome sore unbandaged," "gross, almost putrid."

Now that venereal diseases may be discussed without evoking general horror, *Ghosts* still holds its own as a powerful drama. The reason for its continued success is that the fundamental issue goes beyond disease of the body, just as the fundamental issue of *A Doll's House* goes beyond the question of women's rights. Both plays are an examination of moral disease inherited from the past, and of which the present is dying because of its inability to shake off its ghostly inheritance. The very title of this play is symbolic.

Among the ghosts with which this play deals is the inherited idea that a woman's place is beside her husband no matter what he is. The heroine of this play has not left her home, although she was as much prepared to do so as Nora finally becomes at the end of *A Doll's House*. But she was counseled by the man she loved to remain for the sake of duty. It is this warped sense of duty that is under indictment here by Ibsen. Mrs. Alving has brought evil on herself and everyone connected with her just because she was persuaded not to leave her husband.

There are only five characters in *Ghosts*: Mrs. Alving, a high-minded, modern-thinking widow of means; Oswald, her son, just returned from Paris where he has been painting; Manders, a cautious, principled, but narrow-minded clergyman of the parish; Engstrand, a sly, coarse, hypocritical carpenter; and Regina, his daughter, who has been raised by Mrs. Alving, and given a good education, and with whom she lives as a privileged domestic.

Act One opens with Engstrand trying to force his way into the house to speak with Regina, who is by no means pleased to see him. Now that his work on the Orphanage has been completed, he pretends that in order to avoid the temptation of drink at the opening ceremonies tomorrow, he is going to take the night boat back to town. He wants Regina to come with him. His plans are to open a "restaurant" for sailors, where he thinks Regina's good looks will be of use. He tells her she might even make a good catch, with or without matrimony. In pretended indignation, she pushes him out. She has other hopes.

Manders comes in. It is his opinion that her place is with her father. Manders, who is perpetually duped by Engstrand's parade of humbleness, has no idea of the kind of place this Sailors' Home is to be! Regina cannot agree to help her father. The catch phrases in French she is always using imply that she aspires higher. She goes out when Mrs. Alving comes in. Manders has come to talk over legal matters connected with the Orphanage that Mrs. Alving has had erected in memory of her husband, who died ten years ago. She is bored with the details.

When he counsels not taking out fire insurance on the Orphanage because to do so would show insufficient faith in God, she accepts the idea, but warns she would spend nothing to replace the building once it is erected.

He is disturbed to find, by the books lying about, that she is reading too many "modern" books, and is even more upset to learn that she agrees with them. When he suggests that Regina should go to help her father, she strongly objects.

Oswald comes in. His mother is obviously overjoyed to have him home again. He is smoking his father's pipe, and speaks with admiration of him, though his recollection of the time his father urged him to smoke is connected with unpleasantness. Manders questions him about Paris, and is shocked to find that the young man not only loves that city but greatly admires the freedom from convention with which the artists live there; Oswald is disgusted only with the respectable men who cut up in Paris when they go there for a vacation.

He goes out, and Mrs. Alving tells Manders she completely agrees with her son's values. Manders then delivers a sermon to her on her ideas. He reminds her how when she had been married only a year he had saved her from a ruined life by sending her back to her husband when she had come to Manders to offer the clergyman her love. He reminds her, too, that everything eventually turned out for the best. Then Mrs. Alving tells him the truth at last: though the world never knew, Alving remained a corrupt, dissipated man to his dying day. He died of his excesses. The worst of her memories was the time when she discovered him making love to their servant, Regina's mother. The truth is that Alving was Regina's father. They gave the servant some money, she trumped up a story about an affair with a wealthy foreigner, and got Engstrand to marry her for the money. These are the reasons Mrs. Alving has raised Regina. And the Orphanage has been built to dispose of the last of Alving's money; she wants no part of it, having made enough, as the business head of the family's fortunes all these years, to live on her own. She was forced to keep her son away at school lest he be corrupted by his father.

Oswald comes back, and goes into the dining room to help Regina with the wines. Through the open door, they hear her begging him to behave. Mrs. Alving is petrified. It is like the ghost of his father reenacting the same scene with Regina's mother.

Act Two begins after dinner. Mrs. Alving is resolved that Regina must go away before something tragic occurs. Manders is still annoyed to think that Engstrand has lied to him all these years about Regina's parentage. Now Mrs. Alving regrets having put up a front to mask her husband's life. She has mistakenly lived, as has Manders, according to notions of duty. If Oswald wants to marry Regina or have her as his mistress, even though they are brother and sister, she is willing—so long as there be no more deceit. Manders is outraged at such ideas. He is determined that Regina not stay in the house.

Engstrand comes in to ask Manders to conduct an evening service at the Orphanage among the workmen before its opening. But Manders wants him to face the music. Engstrand does not know, of course, that Alving was Regina's father, but he at last admits as much as he does know. He hypocritically convinces Manders that his silence on the subject has been born of a desire to shield his wife's good name. He pretends outrage at the suggestion that he ever saw a penny of the money. Manders is convinced, and begs his pardon for the ill thoughts he had briefly entertained of him. He agrees to come over to the Orphanage.

When Engstrand goes out, Mrs. Alving realizes that Manders is incurably childlike. Manders goes. Mrs. Alving finds to her surprise that Oswald is still sitting at the table in the next room drinking. He asks her for something to drink, because he has something difficult to say. Fearfully, she sends for champagne, which Regina brings in.

He informs his mother, when Regina leaves, that he has come home because his life's work is over. He has been terribly ill, and at first the doctor was convinced that he was a victim of congenital venereal disease, until Mrs. Alving's letters proved what a fine man his father had been. In any event, the diagnosis is that Oswald faces total mental collapse. He cannot live at home, despite his mother's love, because he wants joy in his life—joy that he knows Regina can give him. She is beautiful and full of life. Besides, he has more or less committed himself to taking her to Paris, and is willing to marry her, if that is what she wants. Their relationship is still innocent, but he needs her, and at once. He asks for more champagne, and when Regina comes in with more, he asks her to stay.

Mrs. Alving is willing. She feels the moment has come to tell them the truth about their relationship. She is just about to speak, when a fire breaks out in the Orphanage, and they all rush out.

Act Three takes place just before dawn. Engstrand follows Manders in, assuring him that the minister is responsible (innocently) for starting the fire, which has razed the Orphanage to the ground. It is clear that Engstrand has done the job himself, and now expects, quite correctly, to make Manders forever indebted to him by pretending that he will never let anyone else know the facts. Manders promises to help him with his Sailors' Home. The building was not insured and so the project is ended.

Oswald comes in and now Mrs. Alving tells the truth to Oswald and Regina, and assures her son he need no longer reproach himself for his illness. After a rest, he will be cured. But Regina, impudently, rejects the idea of being anything to an invalid—she had no idea he was ill—and leaves determined to do something for herself, if necessary, in the way her mother managed it.

Left alone with his mother, Oswald tells her that his next attack will be his last. He cannot face the possibility of years of imbecility, and has provided himself with morphine. Had his mother not deprived him of Regina as she just has done, he knows Regina would have poisoned him if only to get rid of a sick man. Now his mother must promise him that she will do this for him. She owes it to him. After a terrible struggle, she agrees.

The sun begins to rise, and she has hopes that all will yet be well. She is prepared to dedicate the rest of her life to saving her son. But then, after all the excitement of the day, Oswald's mind snaps, and he cries to his mother, "Mother, give me the sun!" When she realizes that all is over, she forces herself to take the powder from his coat, and as the curtain falls she stands transfixed with horror at what she now must do.

An Enemy of the People: In rage at the reception accorded *Ghosts*, Ibsen wrote *An Enemy of the People* (*En Foldfiende*) (1882) at white heat. The comedy suffers somewhat from the air of personal exasperation with which it was written, but it has managed to hold its own on the boards. The conviction achieved by the hero that "a minority may be right—a majority is always wrong," was not calculated to win new friends for the dramatist.

The play is set in a little town that makes its living from the tourists who come to take its famous baths. Dr. Stockmann discovers that the waters have been contaminated by the local sewage system. He insists that the facts must be revealed, and expects that the city authorities will be grateful for his discovery. To his astonishment he finds that he has become an enemy of the people because he insists that the truth be known and the evil corrected. Doggedly he decides to fight on for truth even though the whole community is against him.

The Wild Duck: The play that followed is considered by some to be Ibsen's masterpiece. *The Wild Duck* (*Vildanden*) (1884) was probably conceived, as a reaction to *An Enemy of the People*, in a self-critical mood. Ibsen could be as merciless on himself as on his fellow men. Brand showed the futility of abstract, dehumanized idealism. *The Wild Duck* is a picture of the wholesale damage a reformer can do in the world when he takes no measure of the potentialities of those he would rescue.

The Symbolistic trend, which had become stronger over the years in Ibsen's work, is remarkably and powerfully in evidence here. From this time on it becomes idle to try to decide whether Ibsen is a Symbolist or a Realist. He is a great artist who manages to fuse both elements into a wonderful unity.

The portraits in the play are remarkable throughout: the soul-sick Gregers, a caricature of Ibsen himself, going about to save souls with the truth, and unable to see through the shallowness of his idol; the sham Hialmar, hypocrite even to himself, living like a parasite on the goodness of others, mouthing noble principles and self-centered to the core; the tragic failure, Old Ekdal, living in a world of his own fantasy; the uneducated but straight-thinking Gina, capable of enduring almost any amount of sacrifice, whose prosiness is like a healthy breeze in the midst of the fetid air in which Gregers and Hialmar choose to live; the touching Hedvig, all goodness and love, whose affection Hialmar never merits. In this pitiless exposure of sham idealism, even an old sinner like Werle seems noble by comparison, for he at least is capable of a decent relationship with his housekeeper, because their attachment is founded on honesty.

The Wild Duck opens in the study of the home of Werle, a wealthy industrialist. Werle and his housekeeper, Mrs. Sörby, who acts as his hostess, have been giving a dinner party on the homecoming of his son Gregers. There were thirteen at table because Gregers had invited his best friend and old schoolmate, Hialmar Ekdal. Werle makes reference to the unlucky number on his way into the music room with his own guests.

Left alone, Hialmar and Gregers, who haven't met in some sixteen years, talk over their lives since. Gregers, after his mother's death, had gone up to the Werle works in the forest-country of Höidal, and stayed there. Soon after that, as Hialmar reveals, the company had got into trouble for some illegal cutting of timber at Höidal; Hialmar's father, Old Ekdal, a partner in the concern, had been found guilty, and was ruined and publicly disgraced; Gregers' father had been exonerated of any complicity in the swindle. Hialmar had been forced to leave college. Through the beneficence of Werle he had been able to study photography, set up a studio, and marry. His wife is Gina, once housemaid in the Werle home during the last year of Gregers' mother's life.

All this is news to Gregers, who, hating his father intensely, is glad to hear that he can respect him for some kind acts. But he begins to be suspicious when he hears that Gina, at the time she met Hialmar, knew something about photography, and that their meeting had been more or less engineered by Werle. Hialmar, a self-deceiving sentimentalist, talks dramatically of being his old father's only support.

The guests return, and Mrs. Sörby is seen to be a capable and sophisticated hostess; Hialmar is almost tongue-tied. Just then, Old Ekdal, who has been calling for some copy work that he does these days for the Werle firm, is conducted out of the house through the study by the servants. Hialmar, embarrassed at seeing his father, turns his back so as not to have to acknowledge him. The old man scrapes his way out, and Hialmar, humiliated, soon leaves too. Gregers and Werle are left alone for the moment.

Gregers makes it clear from his talk that he knows his father was the guilty party in the shady business for which Old Ekdal has paid the price. Werle declares that having been found not guilty, he is virtually innocent. Werle and his son are soon accusing each other bitterly. Gregers' mother, who had finally suffered a mental collapse, had trained her son to believe it was all his father's fault. Although he knows of his son's hatred, Werle asks him to go into partnership with him since his eyesight is beginning to fail him. They need not live even in the same town. He intends to retire up to the works, after he has married Mrs. Sörby. Declaring his indifference as to whether his father marries or not, Gregers accuses his father of summoning him to put a good face on things. But he warns Werle that he will do nothing to kill the rumors about the sufferings that his mother endured at Werle's hands. He also lets his father know that his mother had told him Werle was having an affair with Gina at that time, and accuses him point-blank of marrying off his old mistress to innocent Hialmar. Gregers declares that he is leaving Werle's home forever—that his mission in life must be to undo the wrong that his father has done to the Ekdal family.

The rest of the play takes place in Hialmar's studio. Gina, his wife, a capable but uneducated woman, and their daughter, Hedvig, a fourteen-year-old, sensitive girl, are waiting for Hialmar's return from the party. Hialmar has promised to bring the child some goodies from the dinner. They are living very closely, and hope that they can rent the vacant room to someone. They already have as lodgers Relling, a broken-down doctor, and Molvik, an unfrocked clergyman, both drunkards.

Old Ekdal comes home, and, soon after, Hialmar too. The latter is very sentimental over his father, whom he pretends not to have seen at the Werle's, and goes through the farce of depicting himself as a brilliant conversationalist at the party by mimicking things he heard said there. His family admire him very much. Hedvig is very much disappointed to find her father has forgotten to bring her anything; he consoles her by giving her the menu of the dinner. Hialmar is annoyed that Gina hasn't found a lodger yet. To placate him, Hedvig brings him his flute and he plays a sentimental melody.

Then Gregers comes in. Gina is not happy to see him, and Hialmar is embarrassed to have him meet her. Dramatizing his responsibilities, Hialmar confides to Gregers that Hedvig is doomed to eventual blindness. Struck by the remark, Gregers questions Gina and Hialmar about the length of their marriage. Old Ekdal comes out, and when Gregers tries to pity him for having to live this shut-in life, Old Ekdal, once a great hunter, announces that the family must show Gregers its secret.

They open the sliding-doors at the back, and there is revealed a garret-room with a skylight. In the moonlight Gregers sees they have a miniature forest planted there: a few Christmas trees, some rabbits, hens, pigeons, and—the pride of the collection—a wild duck. The wild duck "belongs" to Hedvig. It was shot, some time ago, by Werle on a hunting-trip; the dog had dived into the seaweed where wild ducks dive to die, when wounded, and brought it up; when Werle found it did not thrive on his place, a servant of the Werle house, Pettersen, had given it to Old Ekdal.

Gregers announces that he wishes to rent the vacant room. Gina tries to dissuade him, but he is firm. Hialmar is delighted at the new income. Now he can have a freer mind to work on his invention—to which he has consecrated his life.

In Act Three it is morning. Gina has found that Gregers has already made a mess of his room. Hialmar has invited him and Relling and Molvik to lunch. Hialmar makes a pretense of working at some photograph retouching, but he cannot resist going with his father into the "forest" room, and working on a new contraption they have planned for it: a new path to the water trough.

Gregers comes in and has a chance to talk to Hedvig alone. Despite her bad eyes, over which Hialmar is so sorrowful, her father has asked her to work on the photographs while he is tinkering around inside. She is an avid reader, and loves the garret-room, and especially her wild duck. To her the room is like what she imagines the depths of the sea to be. A shot is heard from the garret-room. Hialmar and Old Ekdal are having fun pretending to hunt with an old double-barreled pistol. Hialmar comes in, and speaks glowingly of the great invention he is working on, the details of which he is not yet prepared to discuss. He is going to accomplish his great feat only to restore the honor of the family and to provide for Hedvig's future: he expects to die (for no apparent reason) at the conclusion of the work. But Gregers assures him that he is like the wild duck: he has dived down among the seaweed and is waiting in the dark to die. Hialmar considers all this nonsense.

Lunch is ready, and Relling and Molvik come in. The latter is, as always, incoherently drunk. Relling, a sardonic man, has known Gregers up at Höidal, and despises him as a meddler who goes around peddling "the claims of the ideal." Old Ekdal comes through the room with a rabbit he has just shot. Hialmar, carried away at being host, makes a dramatic speech to Hedvig about safeguarding her future with his invention. She thanks him with tears in her eyes.

In the midst of the festivities, Werle appears. He asks for a few minutes alone with his son. His worst fears are only too true: Gregers is determined to rescue Hialmar from the "falseness and deception" in the midst of which the latter lives. Werle doubts that Hialmar is the man to want the truth. He announces that he is about to get married, and leave for the works. He offers Gregers his rightful share of the property. Gregers refuses to take a penny from his father. Werle prophesies that Hialmar will not prove equal to the heroism Gregers expects of him. He goes.

Angered at his father's challenge, Gregers asks Hialmar to take a walk with him: there is something vital to be discussed. Gina and Relling try to prevent it, for they fear the worst. But Hialmar insists on going.

When Act Four opens Hedvig and Gina are waiting for Hialmar to return. Gina expects trouble. When he arrives he is sullen. Obviously Gregers has told him that Werle had married off his old mistress to Hialmar. He talks gloomily of being through with any help from Gina (who has managed the entire business up to this). He is so disillusioned that he would like to wring the wild duck's neck. Hedvig is sent out, and Gina decides to face the music. She tells Hialmar the truth—which was not quite as Gregers thought it. Werle had tried to seduce her when she was working for him. Mrs. Werle falsely suspected her, so she left the Werle household.

But Werle followed her to her mother's. Her mother was anxious enough to throw Gina in his arms. Finally, weary, she gave in.

Then Hialmar came along, Gina fell in love with him, and agreed to marry him. If Werle's plan was to have easy access to Gina after that, he found out otherwise. She has been a true and faithful wife. Why didn't she tell him the truth at the beginning? Hialmar demands. Would you have married me if I had? she counters. He tells her indignantly that of course he would never have married such a woman! When she reminds him of all their years of happiness together, he speaks of them as years of deceit. She asks him bluntly what would ever have become of him without a wife like her?

When Gregers comes in, instead of the scene of shining reconciliation that he had envisaged, he finds Gina miserable and Hialmar gloomy. Relling comes in, and upbraids Gregers for being a busybody. He warns him to deal gently with Hedvig, for she is at the dangerous age. Hialmar feels that he has only Hedvig to live for now.

Mrs. Sörby comes in. It is clear that Relling has been her lover, but that she gave him up because of his dissipated life. When Gregers asks her how she would like to have her husband-to-be know of it, she laughingly assures him that they both know everything about each other. She by no means blames him entirely for his past misdeeds, for Gregers' mother was a nagging, moralizing woman who did all she could to kill the joy of living in Werle. She admits that she's entering a bargain with Werle, but adds that she expects to give as much as she takes. Werle, the truth is, is going blind, and she will have to nurse him soon.

Hialmar announces that he wishes a full statement of all the money Werle has advanced the Ekdal family: he will pay it back—eventually—at five percent interest. Hialmar is angry to think that Werle and Mrs. Sörby have managed to contract a decent marriage, while his has been a lie.

Hedvig comes in with a letter that Mrs. Sörby gave her in the street, a present for Hedvig's birthday tomorrow. Hialmar insists on opening it then and there. It turns out to be a bequest of a regular income for Old Ekdal until his death; thereupon the income, a large one, is to revert to Hedvig for the rest of her life. Gregers sees in this the trap his father has set to prove that Hialmar can be bought. This gift in addition to the news of Werle's impending blindness convinces Hialmar that Hedvig is not his own child. He demands the facts from Gina. She tells him, honestly, that she doesn't know whether the child is his or Werle's. He thrusts Hedvig from him, and cries, "Gregers, I have no child!" He dashes out. Hedvig is utterly wretched.

As Gina goes out to find Hialmar, Gregers suggests to Hedvig that she can win her father back by an act of self-sacrifice. Since Hialmar has expressed a wish to kill the wild duck, why does she not get her grandfather to tell her how to kill her most treasured possession herself to please her father? He convinces her that she must do this.

Act Five opens in the cold light of early morning. Relling appears to explain that after a night of debauchery with him and Molvik, Hialmar is snoring away on Relling's couch. Left alone with Gregers, he tells him off, and sneers at his hero-worship of Hialmar. Relling knows that Hialmar is a cheap humbug, and assures Gregers that this meddling is only a product of Gregers' own weakness. What everyone needs in the world is illusion, not truth, Relling says, to make life bearable.

Hedvig, intent on her sacrifice, asks her grandfather how a wild duck is to be shot to die instantaneously. He tells her. She goes off into the garret-room and closes the doors. Hialmar comes in disheveled. He goes through the motions of preparing to leave the house with his old father, but is easily coaxed by Gina to remain "for a while" until he can decide what to do. He is also careful to paste together the document of Hedvig's legacy, which he had torn—in case it might be needed. When Gregers urges him to work on his great experiment, he answers crossly that there are inventions enough in the world. Obviously, he has as yet had no idea for one.

They hear a shot from the next room. At first they think it is Old Ekdal, but he appears. Then Gregers tells Hialmar joyfully that Hedvig has just sacrificed her dearest possession—the wild duck—to prove her love. In a burst of sentimental forgiveness, Hialmar tears open the door. Hedvig has killed herself—has indeed committed suicide. Relling comes up. It is too late. Hialmar pleads that she live "only just till I can tell her how unspeakably I loved her all the time." As Hedvig is carried out, Relling says bitterly that life would be quite tolerable if it weren't for confounded dunces like Gregers who "keep on pestering us in our poverty with the claim of the ideal."

Rosmersholm: *Rosmersholm* (1886) is a powerful and gloomy play continuing the attack of *The Wild Duck*.

Rosmer, a country clergyman is a kind of weaker Brand, who feels called upon to save the world. He is a man of fine perceptions but is married to a woman who, though she loves him passionately, does not feel him appointed to reform mankind. Into their sedate lives comes Rebecca West, an emancipated woman, a freethinker and radical. Mrs. Rosmer becomes attached to Rebecca, and knowing the young woman has no home, insists that she come to live with them. Rebecca, an ambitious woman, is only too glad to accept, for she feels that she can use Rosmer to further her desire to become a leader in his cultivated circle.

But Mrs. Rosmer's complacency about the world as it is becomes an impediment. Rebecca, who has fallen in love with Rosmer, feels that she and Rosmer can never rise to the heights that destiny intends for them with Mrs. Rosmer in the way. Mrs. Rosmer, aware that the two are enamored of each other, is utterly wretched, and having fallen under Rebecca's sway, comes to think of herself as standing in the path of their self-development.

To force the issue, Rebecca threatens to leave Rosmersholm to avoid a possible catastrophe. Mrs. Rosmer thereupon removes herself from their way by throwing herself into the stream that runs through the garden.

Rosmer seems to be the only one who believes that his wife was mentally deranged, for he has been himself unaware of his love for Rebecca. After a period of mourning, Rosmer is invited to edit a Conservative paper his friends are starting. Rebecca urges him to decline and announce to the world that he is a freethinker and radical too. His friends now turn against him. And a Radical editor refuses to accept him for his freethinking, for the Radical editor has hopes that some respectability will carry his own purposes further. They are all determined to prove that Mrs. Rosmer was a suicide because of an affair between Rosmer and Rebecca.

Rosmer now feels that he is not pure enough to save the world. To rescue him from despair, Rebecca publicly admits that she drove Mrs. Rosmer to suicide for the sake of her ambition, but she suppresses the fact of her love for Rosmer. Rebecca is about to leave Rosmersholm, when Rosmer asks her the reason for her confession. She assures him that his right to save the world is still uncorrupted, for it was he who has changed her from an adventuress to a self-sacrificing woman. Her argument fails to convince him, for he remembers that she has already duped him on the grounds of his ideals. Moreover, he realizes that no one can be saved by external forces. He proposes the only test by which he can now believe in her. Dare she commit the act of suicide his wife has committed? Then only will he believe in his power to ennoble others.

"You shall have your faith again," she says. She is ready to go to her death, and he realizes he must join her too. "We must do justice upon ourselves," he declares. He solemnly declares her his wife, and they die together. But she goes transfigured by victory, for she dies to expiate her crime. He goes to death as a failure.

The Lady from the Sea: The Lady from the Sea (*Fruen fra Havet*) (1888) is a highly symbolic drama, full of poetic overtones though written in prose.

Its central idea is that only when we are free to act as we please can we act with integrity. Ellida Wangel, who was raised on the seacoast, is living a useless life of ease with her husband, Doctor Wangel, a physician. Having nothing to occupy her life except her husband's love, she lives in a state of endless restlessness and longs almost desperately for the sea again.

Into her life comes again an old lover, a sailor, who claims her as his own. Once they had plighted their love by each throwing a ring into the sea. He had been forced to run away because he killed the captain of his ship. Now that he comes for her, Ellida believes that he is a symbol of the sea that has been calling for her and that she must go with him.

She tells her husband of her decision. In his love for her he naturally forbids her to go. She tells him sadly that all he can do is to keep her under lock and key. And what pleasure can he take in a wife kept by force? He offers to help defend her against herself only until the sailor leaves town. But she assures him that that will be futile. When the seaman comes to take her, she will have to go.

The sailor is sure of his triumph, and boasts to the husband that he does not want her unless she comes of her own free will. Ellida demands that her husband release her from her oaths of marriage. At the end of his resources, Wangel, in humiliation, tells her she is free to go. Finding herself at last a free agent, Ellida suddenly understands that she does not need to go with her old lover after all. She is free to choose, and she chooses to stay with her husband and at last take on the responsibilities of being truly his wife. The sailor has lost his hold on her and goes off without her.

Hedda Gabbler: *Hedda Gabbler* (1890) remains one of the greatest triumphs in Ibsen's career. He never wrote a play better designed for theatrical representation, and it is no wonder that the role of the heroine has attracted many leading actresses ever since the drama first appeared.

Hedda is a not-so-distant relative of Emma Bovary. She is high-strung, sensitive, utterly restless, and without any way to channel her energies except mischief. She is married to a complete mediocrity who knows of her only that she is a beauty and an aristocrat. She despises him and his dullness, and feels a strong attraction for the brilliant but unstable Lovborg. Despite her fascination with Lovborg, however, Hedda had been unwilling to risk an alliance with him, for at heart she is a coward, afraid of the dangers attendant upon being either wife or mistress to a rake. Lovborg had indeed made improper advances to her, and she had driven him away with one of her father's pistols. But the interest in him remains. After her father's death, finding herself out of funds, she has accepted Tesman's offer of marriage, despite her contempt for that blundering pedant.

Living far beyond her husband's means, Hedda is enraged at the prospect of bearing him a child, for she loathes his middle-class family and their intended kindness to her. In the midst of circumstances she scorns, she finds some comfort in the visits of Judge Brack in her husband's absence. Judge Brack would like to become her lover, but she will not yield to him, though she enjoys his sophisticated conversation. Brack, on the other hand, seizes the opportunity to place Tesman under obligation to him so that he can be free to come and go in their home as he wishes.

At first Lovborg had continued downhill rapidly. He lost his post at the university, and was forced to take employment as a tutor to the children of Sheriff Elvsted. But the second Mrs. Elvsted, a timid ex-governess, has welcomed Lovborg in the Elvsted home, and become a good friend of his. To her he has confided his literary ambitions, and she has encouraged them. Whereas Hedda, in the old days, had listened attentively to Lovborg's account of his dissipations, Mrs. Elvsted is so shocked at his drinking that he has given it up. Indeed, her help has seen Lovborg through the publication of a book, which has made him talked about; and she has acted as his secretary in preparing the manuscript of a second. From this work he expects the opportunity to rehabilitate himself.

Lovborg has given up his position as the Elvsteds' tutor and has come to town with some money from his first book. Mrs. Elvsted, worried about him, does not choose outward respectability as had Hedda, but leaves her husband, and follows Lovborg. Knowing that Tesman was an old rival and schoolmate of Lovborg's, and because of a girlhood friendship with Hedda, Mrs. Elvsted has the courage to ask about Lovborg at the Tesman home. She pleads with the Tesmans to accept Lovborg in their circle, for his salvation depends on the company he keeps. Tesman and Hedda agree, Hedda for her private reasons.

Lovborg wastes no time trying to win Hedda's interest in him. When he accuses her of cowardice, she agrees, and within herself feels that behaving unethically calls for a courage she lacks. She therefore sees the Lovborg who tried to seduce her once as a heroic character, and Mrs. Elvsted as the woman who in trying to make him a solid citizen is depriving him of his courage. She jeers at Lovborg's subjection to Mrs. Elvsted, and taunts him into going to a party from which he ought to absent himself and drinking himself into intoxication. During the night's revels he loses his precious manuscript. At a house of prostitution, where he ends his debauch, the police take him in charge for the night when he makes a scene over his lost manuscript. He does not know that Tesman has picked it up during the evening for safety's sake.

Hedda succeeds in procuring the manuscript on the pretense she will keep it safe. Since Lovborg has spoken of the book as his and Mrs. Elvsted's child, Hedda looks upon the manuscript as a symbol of his love for Mrs. Elvsted. Thinking the work lost, Lovborg pretends to the two women that he has destroyed the manuscript himself because of his fall from grace. To Hedda alone he tells what he believes the truth: he lost it at a house of prostitution. Hedda, seeing a heroic deed in the offing, gives him one of her pistols and asks him to kill himself "beautifully." Hedda, alone, burns the manuscript in the stove, crying out in imagination to Mrs. Elvsted: "I am burning your child."

But Lovborg is not equal to the heroics Hedda has expected of him. He returns to the house of prostitution, and threatens the madame there with Hedda's pistol unless his manuscript is returned. In the scuffle he shoots himself in the abdomen. The police pick up the pistol.

Brack arrives at Hedda's with the true account of Lovborg's end; since he is able to identify the pistol as Hedda's, he gives her to understand she is now in his power, unless she is prepared to face a public scandal. Mrs. Elvsted's reaction to Lovborg's death is to procure the help of Tesman in the rewriting of the book from Lovborg's notes.

Hedda, alone with her would-be lover, the elderly Judge Brack, seeing before her only a life of boredom and slavery to Brack's whims, shoots herself with the other pistol that was once her father's.

This play is more completely a character study of the central figure than any other play of Ibsen's. Among many other things, it shows the viciousness into which the talents of someone without work to do in the world is likely to degenerate. It also shows the intimate relationship between cowardice and wickedness. The timid Mrs. Elvsted was strong enough to put better things first, and so the story of her life is an account of usefulness even in the teeth of adversity and unkind chance.

The Master Builder: The Master Builder (*Bygmester Solness*) (1892) is generally accounted Ibsen's last great play. When Ibsen wrote it, he had returned to live permanently in Christiania.

It is a highly symbolic work in which the two leading characters are a great architect, Solness, and a young woman, Hilda, who urges him to tasks beyond his powers. Under her influence he builds a great tower from which he falls to his death. One may read in this play the eternal dissatisfaction of the younger generation with the accomplishments of the past.

Ibsen's Last Works: Ibsen's last plays show an increasing loss of control over an art of which he had been long undisputed master. *Little Eyolf* (1895) and *John Gabriel Borkman* (1896) have wonderful flashes, but cannot be compared with Ibsen's great work. *When We Dead Awaken* (1900) is more confusing than convincing. All three plays suffer from too heavy a mysticism and an obscurity in outline in the drama.

In 1901 Ibsen fell prey to severe ill-health that made all mental exertion impossible. Soon he had lost his reason, and had only intermittent periods of intellectual clarity. His last six years, indeed, were spent largely in complete mental collapse. It was a terrible end for so powerful a mind.

AUGUST STRINDBERG (1849–1912)

IMPORTANCE

Out of a stormy and turbulent personal life, August Strindberg carved a series of dramas that, although not so widely performed as the plays of Ibsen, have been very nearly as influential in determining the tone and some of the techniques of contemporary drama. Although he wrote historical plays as well as naturalistic tragedies and poetic fantasies, his uniqueness lies in the latter two genres. His pessimistic broodings and violent expressions of the uncontrollable forces of nature struck a sympathetic note among audiences newly interested in the dark powers of the unconscious and in the naturalistic credo of man's domination by emotion, instinct, and desire.

Strindberg's restless career of tensions, hatreds, and dreams began with his birth in Stockholm in 1849, the son of an exbarmaid and an impoverished aristocrat. In a crowded household, half-starved, frightened by his father, and oppressed by a maniacal religiosity, he became morbidly nervous and subject to uncontrollable rages. Intending to become a Lutheran minister, he attended the University of Upsala to prepare himself for a religious vocation. When he decided that he was really an atheist, he turned to the study of medicine but found himself unsuited for scientific training.

There followed a period of great uncertainty, during which he tried his hand at tutoring, teaching, telegraphy, journalism, and acting, until a position in the Royal Library at Stockholm, which he held from 1874 to 1882, provided him a minimum of security. In 1877 he married his first wife, Siri von Essen, who divorced her husband to marry him after an ardent courtship. During the early years of their stormy marriage Strindberg won renown through the publication of *The Red Room,* a cynical, bitter novel depicting bohemian life in Stockholm. A series of cheerful historical plays on Sweden's past was followed in 1882 by *The New Kingdom,* an attack on modern Sweden. In 1883 he journeyed to Switzerland where he associated with Russian revolutionaries, acquired a growing social consciousness, and adopted the Rousseauistic theory that the future of civilization resides in the natural strength of the peasant. He became a Deist, a pacifist, and a believer in the socialist doctrine of utilitarian literature. His succeeding novelettes are generally optimistic but reflect the antagonisms of his domestic life in their attacks on women and opposition to feminism. A series of stories, *Married I* (1884) and *Married II* (1886) describe woman as a tyrant and a remorseless exploiter of man while assuming for the author a kind of Nietzschean superman position. His plays written during this period are blatantly naturalistic and in total revolt against social formalities.

After a divorce in 1887 he married a Viennese journalist Frida Uhl, but a single year of violent domestic wrangling, which made it clear that his attitude toward marriage was pathological, resulted in another divorce. In a novel, *By the Open Sea,* published in 1890, he renounced socialism as a degenerate form of Christianity and preached absolute individualism. After a nervous breakdown, he took as his third wife a young actress, Harriet Bosse.

Removing to Paris, he became interested in botany, astronomy, chemistry, and occultism. He was reconverted to Christianity through the inspiration of Swedenborg and continued to write plays in which an undercurrent of cynicism is colored by religious Romanticism. During the last years of his life his writings display a curious revival of nearly all the motifs of his previous work. He died of cancer in 1912 and was accorded an international funeral.

IMPORTANCE

Strindberg's plays, which are largely autobiographical and generally pathological, reveal a strange naïveté submerged beneath their passionate force. Possessed of a bizarre imagination that moves from melodramatic naturalistic bitterness to the symbolism of dreams, he gave fanatical expression to his ideas, opinions, hatreds, and undulating moods. Believing, like Ibsen, that drama should be serious adult entertainment, he presented the raw volcanic passions of life in adherence to the Naturalist tenet that pleasure in literature should proceed from the learning and understanding of the violent and cruel basic structure of the universe.

In dramatic technique he espoused natural dialogue, striking and stark rather than luxurious scenery, and the use of symbol, pantomime, and any other special devices that would add to the drive of the basic theme of the play. He also favored the abolition of acts and scenes or any other diversions from the mood established on the stage.

Most distinctive of his innovations is the idea that characters should be characterless in the usual sense of sharply typed stage characters. Since human beings are propelled by instinctual drives rather than by deliberate control of the ego, sudden changes and apparent reversals of "character" reveal human beings in their true light as being merely repositories of the forces behind life. As in many other Naturalist writings, the female is the Nietzschean symbol of the Dionysian power of Mother Nature, which attempts to stifle the freedom-loving intellectualism and spirituality of the Apollonian male.

The Father: Published in 1887, *The Father* is Strindberg's most notable contribution to the literature on the battle of the sexes. Holding that life is a war in which the individual is at the mercy of a malicious environment, that life is "appallingly monotonous" in its repetition of basic patterns, he here objectifies his views on the nature of love, which he sees as an "embattled opposition of two spirits destined to destroy each other in the ineffectual endeavor to be one." The male is usually in the right because he has more of a conscience. The female, because of her lack of conscience, is not only usually wrong but is almost inevitably triumphant. Release from the hatreds engendered by love comes only in death.

The "father" in this play is a distinguished mineralogist who is thwarted in his studies and continually harassed by his wife Laura. Their antagonism comes to a head in a conflict concerning the education of their daughter Bertha. He wants her removed from the bad influence of too many women, while she insists that the child be kept at home. In order to make certain of having her own way, Laura tells their doctor that her husband is mad and all but succeeds in making him so by suggestions concerning the paternity of Bertha. When in a stormy scene he is provoked into throwing a lamp at his wife, the doctor declares him insane, the nurse tricks him into a straitjacket, and even the pastor who knows Laura to be wrong ultimately sides with her, victimized by the overwhelming power of woman.

Miss Julia: From the point of view of naturalism, *Miss Julia* (1888) is an excellent study of the power of the natural man, rising from nonmoral peasant and proletarian stock, over the effete, conventional, and anemic aristocracy.

Miss Julia is the victim of the same kind of upbringing to which Bertha in *The Father* was subjected. Inheriting her mother's passionate nature and anti-masculine feelings, she has been brought up by her father as if she were a man. Having been jilted by her fiancé when she attempted to dominate him, she drifts into the kitchen of the Manor House during the earthy festivities of May Eve. Deliberately arousing the passions of the valet Jean, she dances with him, forces him to lose his self-control, and seduces him. Then attempting to face the question of her honor and unable to confront her father, she suggests to Jean that they flee together. Jean, cold-blooded, sensible, and practical, suggests that they run a hotel together, setting up the establishment on her capital. When she confesses that she has no money in her own right, he suggests and then urges suicide as her only escape. She kills herself, demonstrating the Naturalists' belief in the spinelessness and conventionality of the upper classes in contrast to the rugged nerves and direct thought and action of the lower classes.

There Are Crimes and Crimes: A product of Strindberg's later religious period, *There Are Crimes and Crimes* (1899) is built on crimes "not mentioned in the criminal code," crimes against the spirit and punished by the spirit. In keeping with its theme, the spirit rather than the action of this play is paramount; disregard of probability, lapses of time, and sudden outwardly unmotivated changes within the characters are frequent.

The scene is laid in Paris, where Maurice, a hopeful young playwright, is a frequenter of the *cremerie* or restaurant of Mme. Catherine, a befriender of young artists. He is in love with Marion, who has borne him the child Jeanne and whom he intends to marry as soon as he becomes a success. Wrapped up in his own devotion to the theater and worldly success, Maurice commits his first crime when he forgets an appointment and keeps her waiting two hours for him at their rendezvous in a graveyard. She refuses to go to the opening night of his play, believing that her presence would be out of place among his worldly friends, but makes him a present of a tie to wear for the occasion. Maurice then sees his friend Adolph, a struggling artist, seated at a table in the *cremerie* with the beautiful Henriette. Maurice joins them, fascinates Henriette, and offers her the ticket to the play that had been intended for Marion, with the understanding that Adolph will join them after the performance. Throwing Marion's tie into the fireplace, he takes Henriette to the play and then waits for two hours in a cafe with Henriette for Adolph. Although his play has apparently been a success, he commits another crime by not returning to Mme. Catherine and to the *cremerie* where his friends are waiting for him. Instead, he spends the night with Henriette, caught up in a passion that has been encouraged by their mutual confessions of their past misdeeds.

In the morning, Adolph comes to announce the news of the success of the play and to assure Maurice that no one at the *cremerie* is angry because of his failure to put in an appearance on the preceding night. Adolph has also been generous in his acceptance of Henriette's transfer of her affections to his friend. Maurice is preoccupied with plans for his future with Henriette, commits another crime by wishing his child were dead, and thinks to have a child by Henriette to kill his love for Jeanne.

The news that Marion had died fifteen minutes after Maurice had last seen her follows hard upon the announcement that Adolph's art has been rewarded by a medal. Through the gossip of waiters, Maurice and Henriette are involved in a scandal concerned with Marion's death and are taken to the police station. When Henriette rails about Maurice's behavior, Adolph explains to her the true significance of Maurice's crimes. Maurice is legally cleared of the murder charge, but the play closes because of the scandal. After a quarrel in a cafe, Maurice leaves the table for a moment. When he returns, he finds that Henriette has been thrown out as a street walker and that he is refused further service. Maurice and Henriette indulge in mutual recriminations but feel tied to each other by their past, and decide they must marry.

After each has individually accused the other to Adolph, Maurice becomes morally rejuvenated. He writes to Jeanne for pardon and makes an appointment with the abbé. When a package from Jeanne arrives containing the discarded necktie and news comes that his play is reopening, he wavers between going to church or to the theater. The abbé advises church today and theater tomorrow, and, when Maurice groans about the hardship of his punishment, the abbé reads him a brief concluding lecture on the triviality of his suffering compared to the enormity of his crimes.

The Dance of Death: The theme of *The Father* is elaborated in the two plays, undivided into acts and scenes, that bear the macabre title *The Dance of Death*. Part I (1901) presents the dominant male figure of the Captain who is a proud and hated officer of Coast Artillery stationed on an island. His wife Alice, a former actress, is embittered by their isolation and the memories of her former triumphs. They have a mutual friend in Curt, the master of quarantine, who had originally introduced them to each other. The Captain has isolated their daughter Judith from her mother by sending her to the city whence he receives secret messages by telegraph. When Alice discovers his use of the telegraph, their basic mutual antagonism flares up to a higher intensity, and both appeal to Curt to act as an arbitrator. Lured by passion for Alice, Curt becomes dominated by her will, but when her behavior sends the Captain into an uncontrollable paroxysm Curt nurses and soothes him.

After a subsequent trip to the city for medical attention, the Captain returns with Curt's son whom, against Curt's will, he intends to train as a cadet, having procured guardianship over the boy from his mother. When he states that he has also filed papers for a divorce, Alice threatens to reveal his defalcations with military funds. The doctor announces that the Captain had lied about instituting divorce proceedings and that he had been told that his death was imminent. A bitter quarrel breaks out, at the end of which the Captain falls into a swoon after threatening Alice with a sabre.

Alice turns to Curt, but is repulsed. The Captain begs Curt not to leave him. Husband and wife are reconciled when Alice confesses that she did not reveal the Captain's defalcations after all. Asking only for peace, the Captain finds Alice willing to continue with him in the capacity of nurse, an agreement that concludes the play.

In the Captain one sees Strindberg's concept of the paternal tyrant determined to be superior to the natural forces of life represented by Alice. Curt is the average man, drawn both ways at once and doomed therefore to be an ultimate victim. The sea is the source of life and the end of life, an all-encompassing natural force. The island symbolizes momentary human life thrown up by the eternal force. It is full of seaweed, monstrosities, and corruption. The price of individuality is too high, and the individual finally finds peace in the all-encompassing quietude of death.

Part II of *The Dance of Death* is a repetition and intensification of the same pattern. Judith has returned home and is being courted by Curt's son Allan. Quarreling has broken out again between Alice and the Captain who has now retired. Out of a virulent hatred of Curt, the Captain does everything in his power to destroy him personally, socially, militarily, and financially. He meanwhile plans a marriage for Judith with an elderly colonel. When he is notified by a vicious telegram from Judith that her love for Allan has triumphed over his schemes, he falls into his final paroxysm and dies.

As a postlude Alice says that she is inclined to think well of him because all of life seemed a hoax to him. Allan calls him "a noble man." Curt points out that he had fought for his own and his family's welfare. Alice sums up by revealing that she had both loved and hated him, and gives him her benediction.

The Dream Play: Among Strindberg's symbolic fantasies, *The Dream Play* (1902) is the best example of his melancholy vision of life. Using all the illogic of a dream, the author is free to mingle poetry, fantasy, and absurdity in a vision in which the observer's mind is the only integrating factor. In a prologue the daughter of the Hindu god Indra asks her father about the world. She says that she sees beauty in life but hears an undercurrent of wailing. She is told to observe for herself and report back.

In the variegated tapestry of life that is then unfolded, there are several prominent threads. There is the Officer who waits eternally for Victoria to come out of the opera while the Portress at the opera knits the fabric of life. There is the Lawyer enmired in man's misery and meanness. The Lawyer's wife, the Daughter, lives with her children in poverty and squalor. There is the Door that the Daughter wishes to open. The savants quarrel about their beliefs in what the opened door will reveal. When it is opened, it reveals nothing. There is, finally, the Poet who gives meaning to life by translating what the Daughter tells him.

At the end, after the Door has been opened, Strindberg's conclusions are revealed through the Daughter of Indra, who believes that all are to be pitied, especially the rightminded. When the rightminded demand that she be stoned, she says she will die and ascend. Creation was the meeting of the Divine with earthly matter. The fall into sin was caused by the spirit's mingling with earth. The world is a dream, an image of this impure commingling. Man craves to suffer as Divinity suffered, but he also craves enjoyment. From this conflict within man arise suffering, injustice, and universal misery.

ANTON CHEKOV (1860–1904)

Anton Chekov, the greatest Russian writer after Tolstoy, was the grandson of a serf who had acquired enough wealth to buy his own freedom. Chekov's father was a prosperous merchant at Taganrog, on the Sea of Azov, at which town the writer was born on January 17, 1860.

His parents were both simple but very religious people, and the family circle was very close. The children were all given a good education. Unhappily while Anton, next to the youngest, was still at gymnasium (high-school), the business world of Taganrog was fairly ruined by the building of a railroad through a neighboring town, and the Chekovs had to close up their business. After completing his studies at Taganrog, Anton went after his family to Moscow in 1879, entered the university at the capital as a student of medicine, and took his medical degree in 1884. Thereafter Chekov never left his parents or his sister until his father's death. Since he earned a good income with his pen, he also became their chief support.

When Chekov was still a medical student, he was already a frequent contributor to the humorous periodicals of Moscow. In 1886 some of his pieces were collected in book form with such success that the author soon followed with another volume. The latter attracted the notice of Suvorin, the editor of *Novoe Vremya*, the largest newspaper of the time; and he began a weekly literary supplement expressly for Chekov's contributions. There resulted a close friendship between the two men, and Chekov's letters to Suvorin form the most interesting part of his thoroughly interesting correspondence. Chekov, who never got around to practicing medicine was now established as an important writer, gave up his merely humorous writings, and began (1886) to write in the vein that the world now associates with him.

At about this time he wrote his first play, *Ivanov*, which was produced in Moscow at the end of 1887. The story of his life remained thereafter without event, and is merely the account of close intimacy with his family and fruitful literary production. The only significant traveling he did was through Siberia in 1890, with its consequent study of life among the convicts, *Saghalien*

Island (1891). The humanitarianism of this work was characteristic of a man remarkable for his warmth of heart and the generosity with which he gave away most of his earnings.

In 1891 Chekov was able to buy some land fifty miles out of Moscow at Melikhovo, where he lived for six years with his parents, sister, and younger brother, participated in local civic affairs, and wrote many of his best stories. But Chekov's health began to fail. He became afflicted with tuberculosis, and he began to frequent health resorts, and at last settled in 1900 at Yalta.

His connection with the Moscow Art Theater in his later years did much to alter the course of his life; he also became more and more identified with the liberals in politics. This latter tendency ended in a break with Suvorin, and his new friendship with the most important of the younger writers, Maxim Gorky. When the Academy elected Chekov to membership and almost immediately after disqualified Gorky as a member, Chekov resigned. But his political progress to the left occasioned no important change in his work as a writer of short-stories.

The most important change in his later life, as has been said, was owing to his intimate relation with the Moscow Art Theater. After composing several light pieces subsequent to *Ivanov*, Chekov saw his first important play, *The Seagull* produced at St. Petersburg in 1896. Because of a poor performance the work was hissed, and Chekov vowed never to write another play. But the new directors of the Moscow Art Theater, Stanislowski and Danchenko, procured *The Seagull* for one of their early productions, and in 1898 it became a great success.

Chekov, encouraged again by the brilliant company at the Moscow Art Theater, wrote *Uncle Vanya*, which the troupe produced in 1900. This was followed by his two dramatic masterpieces, *The Three Sisters* (1901) and *The Cherry Orchard* (1904). All were greeted with acclaim. In 1901, a few years before his early death, Chekov married an actress of the Moscow Theater company, Olga Knipper. But he was not to enjoy much happiness from his fame, because of his increasing ill-health. He died on July 2, 1904.

Chekov's Short Stories

Although Chekov's stories run into many copious volumes in their English translation, some of the tales that are best known in Russia have never been translated. These are chiefly the comic stories in which the author frankly plays the clown, and jests in ways that would be comprehensible only to a Russian. Curiously enough, this part of his output lacks the humanity and the higher comedy of the stories by which Chekov is justly acclaimed by non-Russians as the world's greatest writer of short stories. He himself never wished them reprinted from the newspapers in which they first appeared.

It is as a great realist that Chekov is preeminent in this form (though occasionally, as in the masterful story "The Black Monk," he makes an excursion into fantasy). The stories are remarkable for their pathos and irony. Perhaps no one has exceeded Chekov in depicting the void which stands between every human being and every other, no matter how intimately related.

The only serious contender for Chekov's position as the world's leading writer of the realistic short story is Maupassant. It is the glory of Chekov's creations, however, that they lack the cold clinical air of the Frenchman's, and that though they are written with perfect objectivity, they are infused with warmth and compassion.

Among so many excellent stories it is almost idle to single out individuals. But the following may be safely classed with Chekov's best productions: "The Party," "Ward Number Six," "The Steppe," "The Darling," "Vanka," "The Post," "The Privy Councillor," "The Bet," "A Dreary Story," "My Life," and "Happiness."

IMPORTANCE

One of the remarkable aspects of Chekov's stories is the fact that when his characters speak, he makes no attempt to individualize them. It is as though he were deliberately trying to show their common humanity by depriving them of personality. Chekov's unending theme is the loneliness of the human soul, and he was a delicate observer of the infinitesimal forces which operate upon human lives and often destroy them. He is a master of mood. Hence in many of stories, as in his two greatest plays, the poetic overtone is achieved through touches of symbolism.

Chekov's Plays

The emphasis on small detail everywhere to be found in the stories, is the foundation of his practice as a dramatist. *The Sea Gull, Uncle Vanya, The Three Sisters*, and *The Cherry Orchard* have no plot in the usual sense of the word, only an aggregation of significant detail. They are deliberately static.

The characters constantly speak to one another without any surface interchange of ideas in their remarks, as though each were exclusively occupied with his own reflections. This method, highly poetic in his hands, emphasizes his favorite idea of the incommunicability of human beings with one another.

From one point of view, of course, this realistic drama is not so real. For no one in Chekov's plays talks like a real human being. In life we do respond to one another. But this artistic convention of his is highly effective in evoking the sense of human loneliness with which he was preoccupied. It is a method that has greatly influenced twentieth century drama.

It would be very shallow, however, to conclude that Chekov's plays lack direction. They have an inner unity which pushes them to a conclusion of irrefutably logical consistency.

The Three Sisters: *The Three Sisters* (1901) has less surface action than any great play ever written. The story, such as it is, concerns the ambition of three sisters living in the provinces to leave the pettiness of their surroundings, and go to live in Moscow. Moscow to them is a shining ideal, a symbol of all that they have missed in life. But they are trapped by the details of daily living, and never are able to go there.

They rely on their brother Andrei to be the means of their liberation, for he expects a professorship in the capital. But he marries a stupid, pretentious woman, who soon deceives him. He degenerates into a commonplace provincial. One of the girls gives up her life to schoolteaching, another to being the wife of an uninspired schoolteacher. Up to the end there is some hope that the youngest, Irina, will not give up her dream; but her suitor is killed in a duel, and her hopes die with him.

These three vital women live wasted lives in an atmosphere charged with coming change, but which brings no change for them.

The Cherry Orchard: The same dramatic characteristics are to be found in *The Cherry Orchard* (1904), although there is more semblance of a plot. The play is a powerful study of the collapse of the old aristocratic order in Russia; Chekov's sympathies are all with a better newer life, but he is too much the artist to record the passing of the old ways without compassion for the victims of the change.

Madame Ranevski returns after an absence of five years in Paris to her estate. The affairs of the property are in sad confusion, and it is about to be put up for sale. Her brother, raised to be a charming gentleman of leisure, is unable to be of any assistance; he and she are trapped by the associations of sentiment they have with their old life on the estate.

A wealthy merchant, Lopakhin, whose grandfather had been a serf on the estate, out of sympathy for her, urges her to have her celebrated cherry orchard cut down, and the land divided up into building lots, which are sure to be bought. But such an act seems like an outrage to their lovely past, and neither Madame Ranevski nor her brother will hear of it. Instead, they think of one impractical idea after another to salvage their fortunes; what they are actually doing is refusing to contemplate the disaster inevitably facing them.

Incapable of any decisive move, they find the day of the auction upon them before they have done anything to rescue themselves. Lopakhin, having tried every possible expedient to shake them into doing something for themselves, buys the estate.

As the play ends we hear the stroke of the axes cutting down the cherry trees, even before the old owners have departed. Lopakhin, representative of the new Russia and its progress, is making room for the small homes that are to be built on the ground where the beautiful old cherry trees grew.

The universality of Chekov was amply demonstrated during the theatrical season of 1949 in New York, when Joshua Logan by a simple transposition laid the scene of the play in Louisiana, in his deeply moving adaptation of this work, *The Wisteria Trees*. With few changes, everything Chekov had said about Russia became true of the old aristocratic South in the United States.

REVIEW QUESTIONS

EXPERIMENTATION AND REVOLT

Multiple Choice

1. _____ The Parnassian movement was named on the basis of
   a. a region in Paris
   b. its leader's name
   c. a publication
   d. a famous opera

2. _____ The Parnassian school reacted against
   a. middle-class industrial values
   b. the importance of form in literature
   c. too little emotion in poetry
   d. French philosophy

3. _____ The poets of the Parnassian school were nicknamed
   a. those who can't be found
   b. those who can't be moved
   c. the writers of paradise
   d. the Paris ten

4. _____ The leader of the Parnassian movement was
   a. Condillac
   b. Volney
   c. Leconte de Lisle
   d. Victor Hugo

5. _____ Baudelaire's temperament reflected
   a. his love for debauchery and dissipation
   b. his strong religious bent
   c. his interest in the grotesque
   d. all of the above

6. _____ Symbolist poets wanted to write poems that would
   a. expressly state a fact
   b. communicate a moral lesson
   c. evoke a suggested feeling
   d. remain objective

7. _____ Mallarmé believed that his poems should be
   a. accessible to any audience
   b. simple in diction and structure
   c. meaningless to the uninitiated
   d. traditional in subject matter

8. _____ Henrik Ibsen is known primarily for his
   a. poems
   b. dramas
   c. novels
   d. short stories

9. _____ Strindberg's dramas are characterized by
   a. pessimistic broodings
   b. optimistic declarations
   c. simple characters
   d. pastoral settings

10. _____ Strindberg believed that the future of civilization lay in
   a. ardent religiosity
   b. the natural strength of the peasant
   c. return to nature
   d. Enlightenment ideals

True-False

11. _____ As the nineteenth century progressed, national literary boundaries became more and more distinct.

12. _____ Gautier stressed that form was of paramount importance in literature.

13. _____ The Parnassian school reacted against the effusiveness of Romanticism.

14. _____ Baudelaire's book of poems *Fleurs du Mal* became synonymous soon after its publication with love and romance.

15. _____ Writers of the Parnassian movement were united in their view of aesthetic and poetic theory.

16. _____ Symbolist poets imitated the objectivity they valued in Realist novels.

17. _____ The meaning of a Symbolist poem is usually expressly stated.

18. _____ *Peer Gynt* is a drama written in verse.

19. _____ *The Wild Duck* is a poem by Baudelaire.

20. _____ Plays by Strindberg influenced the subjects, themes, and staging of contemporary drama.

Fill-in

21. The Parnassian school abandoned the subjectivity and storminess of the _____ movement.

22. Mallarmé and Verlaine eventually dissociated themselves from the _____ movement.

23. _____ was a poet whose love of formal beauty reflected his knowledge of Greek classical literature.

24. _____ is a poet whose life and work have been labeled decadent because of the debauchery and perversity contained in some of his poems.

25. Poets of the Symbolist movement accused Parnassian poets of being _____ because of their emphasis on form and objectivity.

26. The Parnassians sought solace in a _____ life rather than a life of action.

27. The poets who wished to evoke mystery and magic in their poems belonged to the _____ movement.

28. The Symbolist manner of expressing the meaning of the poem through-out the music of the lines is most apparent in the poetry of _____ .

29. While Verlaine wanted to communicate an emotion itself, _____ wanted to communicate the idea of the emotion.

30. The title character of Ibsen's play _____ is an uncompromising minister.

Matching

31.	_____ Leconte de Lisle	a. grand sonnets
32.	_____ Hérédia	b. leader of the Symbolists
33.	_____ Baudelaire	c. pessimistic Swedish dramatist
34.	_____ Verlaine	d. "God is Love"
35.	_____ Rimbaud	e. father of Parnassian movement
36.	_____ Mallarmé	f. Bohemian lifestyle
37.	_____ *Brand*	g. drama about the battle of the sexes
38.	_____ Chekov	h. grotesque and morbid poems
39.	_____ Strindberg	i. Russian writer
40.	_____ *The Father*	j. "Sonnet of Vowels"

Answers

1.	c	15.	f	28.	Verlaine
2.	a	16.	f	29.	Mallarmé
3.	b	17.	f	30.	*Brand*
4.	c	18.	t	31.	e
5.	d	19.	f	32.	a
6.	c	20.	t	33.	h
7.	c	21.	Romantic	34.	f
8.	b	22.	Parnassian	35.	j
9.	a	23.	Leconte	36.	b
10.	b		de Lisle	37.	d
11.	f	24.	Baudelaire	38.	i
12.	t	25.	materialistic	39.	c
13.	t	26.	contemplative	40.	g
14.	f	27.	Symbolist		

Part 6

RECENT DIRECTIONS FOR MAJOR WORLD LITERATURES

*Perhaps more than that of any other century, the world litera-
ture of our own time can be said to belong to us all, not merely to
the country or region of its origin. Most renowned literary figures
of our day, including Samuel Beckett, Thomas Mann, and
Heinrich Böll, perceived themselves as writers with an international, not exclusively national, audience. The general regional
and national groupings in this Part, therefore, should not be
understood in a restrictive way. It is often the case in the twentieth century that writers share more with their international peers
than with fellow writers from their own country.*

WORKS AT A GLANCE

Thomas Mann

1898	*Little Herr Friedemann*	1943	*Joseph in Egypt; Joseph the*
1900	*Buddenbrooks*		*Provider*
1912	*Death in Venice*	1949	*Doctor Faustus*
1918	*Reflections of an Unpolitical*	1951	*The Holy Sinner*
	Man	1953	*The Black Swan*
1924	*The Magic Mountain*	1954	*The Confessions of Felix*
1933	*The Tales of Jacob*		*Krull, Confidence Man*
1935	*The Young Joseph*		
1939	*Lotte in Weimar (The*		
	Beloved Returns)		

Heinrich Böll

1959	*Billiards at Half-Past Nine*	1977	*Missing Persons*
1963	*The Clown*	1979	*The Safety Net*
1964	*Absent without Leave*		
1974	*The Lost Honor of*		
	Katharina Blum		

Günter Grass

1959	*The Tin Drum*	1972	*From the Diary of a Snail*
1961	*Cat and Mouse*		

Fernando Pessoa

1917	"Maritime Ode"	1928	*The Book of Disquiet*

Juan Ramón Jiménez

1914	*Platero and I*	1954	*Naked Music: Poems of Juan*
1953	*Three Hundred Poems,*		*Ramón Jiménez*
	1903–1953		

Federico García Lorca

1918	*Impressions and Landscapes*	1935	*Lament for Ignacio Mejias*
1920	*The Butterfly's Evil Spell*	1936	*First Songs*
1921	*Book of Poems*	1937	*Poem of the Conte Jondo*
1927	*Songs; The Gypsy Ballads;*	1940	*Poet in New York*
	Mariana Pineda		

Jean-Paul Sartre

1938	*Nausea*	1943	*Being and Nothingness; No*
1939	"The Wall"; "Childhood of a		*Exit*
	Leader"		

Simone de Beauvoir

1948	*The Blood of Others*	1969	*The Woman Destroyed*
1949	*Second Sex*	1972	*The Coming of Age*
1955	*All Men are Mortal*		

Albert Camus

1942	*The Myth of Sisyphus; The Stranger*	1945	*Caligula*

Jean Genêt

1948	*The Maids*	1956	*The Balcony*
1949	*Thief's Journal*		

Marguerite Duras

1958	*Moderato Cantabile*	1984	*The Lover*
1964	*The Ravishing of Lol V. Stein*	1986	*Blue Eyes Black Hair*
1969	*Destroy, She Said*		

Andre Gide

1887	*The Fruits of the Earth*	1911	*Isabelle*
1899	*Philocetes*	1914	*The Vatican Swindle*
1901	*King Candaule*	1919	*The Pastoral Symphony*
1901	*Strait Is the Gate*	1926	*Counterfeiters*
1902	*The Immoralist*	1946	*Theseus*
1903	*Prometheus Misbound*		

François Mauriac

1909	*Clasped Hands*	1925	*The Desert of Love*
1913	*Young Man in Chains*	1927	*Thérèse Desqueyroux*
1914	*The Stuff of Youth*	1932	*The Viper's Knot*
1922	*The Kiss to the Leper*		

Maxim Gorky

1899	*Sketches and Stories*	1908	*The Last*
1901	*The Petty Bourgeois*	1911	*The Life of Matvei Kozhemyakim*
1902	*The Lower Depths*		
1905	*Children of the Sun, Summer People*	1916	*Through Old Russia*
		1925	*The Artamonov Business*
1906	*The Barbarians, The Enemies, Mother*	1931	*Yegor Bulychov*

Boris Pasternak

1914	*The Twin in the Clouds*	1931	"The Year 1905," "Spektorsky," *Safe Conduct*
1917	*Over the Barriers*		
1922	*My Sister Life*	1945	*The Terrestrial Expanse*
1923	*Themes and Variations*	1957	*Dr. Zhivago*

Aleksandr Isayavich Solzhenitsyn

1962	*One Day in the Life of Ivan Denisovich*	1972	*August 1914*
1966	*The Cancer Ward*	1974–1976	*The Gulag Archipelago*
1967	*The First Circle*		

Bertolt Brecht

1926	*The Threepenny Opera*	1943	*Buckower Elegies, Galileo, The Good Woman of Setzuan*
1927	*The Rise and Fall of the City of Mahogonny*		
1939	*Svendborger Poems*	1948	*The Caucasian Chalk Circle*
1941	*Mother Courage and Her Children, The Purchase of Brass*	1955	*The ABC of War*

Samuel Beckett

1931	*Proust*	1952	*Waiting for Godot*
1938	*Murphy*	1961	*Happy Days*

Milan Kundera

1967	*The Joke*	1973	*Life is Elsewhere*

Franz Kafka

1914	"In the Penal Colony"	1925	*The Trial*
1915	"The Metamorphosis"	1926	*The Castle*
1920	"The Burrow"	1927	*Amerika*
1921	"Josephine the Singer"		

George Lukacs

1955	*The Historical Novel*	1980	*The Meaning of Contemporary Realism*
1968	*Goethe and His Age*		

Witold Gombrowicz

1937	*Eerdydurke, Yvonne: Princess of Burgundia*	1947	*The Marriage*

Czeslaw Milosz

1936	*Three Winters*	1953	*The Captive Mind*

Amos T'utuola

1952	The Palm-Wine Drinkard and His Dead Palm-Wine Tapster in the Dead's Town	1958	The Brave African Huntress
1954	My Life in the Bush of Ghosts	1962	The Feather Woman of the Jungle
1955	Simbu and the Satyr of the Dark Jungle	1967	Ajaiyi and His Inherited Poverty
		1981	The Witch-Herbalist of the Remote Town

Chinua Achebe

1958	Things Fall Apart	1966	A Man of the People
1960	No Longer at Ease	1988	Anthills of the Savannah
1964	Arrow of God		

Ezekiel Mphahlele

1961	The Living and the Dead	1971	The Wanderers
1962	The African Image	1984	Father Come Home
1965	The Role of Education and Culture in Developing African Countries	1985	Down Second Avenue

Jorge Luis Borges

| 1944 | Ficciones | 1960 | Dreamtigers |
| 1949 | The Aleph | | |

Manuel Puig

| 1971 | Betrayed by Rita Hayworth | 1979 | The Kiss of the Spider Woman |
| 1976 | Heartbreak Tango; The Buenos Aires Affair | | |

Mario Vargas Llosa

1952	The Escape of the Inca	1973	Captain Pantoja and the Special Service
1963	The City and the Dogs	1982	The War of the End of the World
1966	The Green House		
1968	The Cubs and Other Stories		
1969	Conversation in the Cathedral		

Gabriel García Márquez

1955	Leaf Storm and Other Stories	1972	Eyes of a Blue Dog
1962	In Evil Hour	1976	The Autumn of the Patriarch
1967	One Hundred Years of Solitude	1978	Innocent Erendira and Other Stories
1968	No One Writes to the Colonel and Other Stories; The Novel in Latin America	1983	Chronicle of a Death Foretold

9
EUROPEAN LITERATURE OF THE TWENTIETH CENTURY

As the close of this century approaches, the general form of its literary history becomes more apparent, and scholars are able to trace with some confidence the development of modern literature. Still, there are undoubtedly numerous works and authors as yet undiscovered or unrecognized, just as there are those which, though they merit our attention, are all too often overlooked when a broad picture of literature must be drawn. It is this picture that is presented here for the student who, while working with a specific literary period or on the literature of a specific country in all its fine textual detail, wishes to establish points of reference across the vast cultural and linguistic spectrum of the literature of our century.

GERMANY

Thomas Mann (1875–1955)

Born in a German village, Thomas Mann in his mid-teens lost his father and relocated with his mother to Munich, the center of German art and culture in that period. After two brief and dissatisfying attempts at insurance work and editing, he devoted himself completely to writing. A first collection of tales, *Der kleine Herr Friedemann* (*Little Herr Friedemann*) appeared in 1898. In these tales, mistfit artists struggle simultaneously with the meaninglessness of existence and the profundities of philosophy, especially that of Nietzsche and Schopenhauer. This general thematic interest is extended in *Buddenbrooks,* a novel that traces the story of a business family over three generations, showing how the artistic bents of its younger members cripple them for careers in commerce.

Mann's happy marriage in 1905 to Katja Pringsheim and the subsequent arrival of six children did not dissuade him from somber themes. In 1912 he published *Death in Venice* (*Der Tod in Venedig*), a novel about an overstressed writer vacationing in Venice just as a mortal disease sweeps across the city. With the outbreak of the First World War, Mann struggled to reconcile his artistic and intellectual beliefs with world developments. His solutions appeared in *Reflections of an Unpolitical Man* (*Betrachtungen eines Unpolitischen*) (1918);

using quite untraditional arguments, Mann supports the forces of authoritarianism against what he then saw as the excesses of democracy. Later he would repudiate these ideas.

Mann's new views on democracy appear particularly in *The Magic Mountain* (1924), his best-known work. In this novel, Hans Castorp, a young engineer, temporarily leaves the freedom of his city life to visit an ill cousin, a soldier, who lives in the seductively secure, controlled environment of a sanatorium. Hans gradually succumbs to the seemingly timeless, purposeless environment of the sanatorium. He begins checking his pulse and temperature obsessively. When his cousin leaves the sanatorium to rejoin his regiment, Hans remains behind. The three weeks he had originally intended to spend at the sanatorium have stretched to more than seven years. The sudden news of the outbreak of the First World War, however, stuns Hans out of his reveries and malaise. As the novel closes, he bids farewell to the other patients he has come to know well and sets out for the trenches of war.

Between the world wars, Mann occupied himself with the writing of essays (particularly on Freud, Goethe, Wagner, and Nietzsche) and public lectures opposing the rise of the Nazi regime. After Hitler's rise to power in 1933, Mann and his wife settled first in Switzerland and then, in 1938, in the United States. He returned to Zurich in 1952, where he died in 1955. His novels include *The Tales of Jacob* (1933), *The Young Joseph* (1935), *Joseph in Egypt* (1943), *Joseph the Provider* (tetralogy title, *Joseph und Seine Brüder*) (1943), *Lotte in Weimar* (*The Beloved Returns*) (1939), *Doctor Faustus* (1949), *The Holy Sinner* (*Der Erwählte*) (1951), *The Black Swan* (*Die Betrogene*) (1953), and *The Confessions of Felix Krull, Confidence Man* (1954).

IMPORTANCE

The overriding theme of Mann's fiction, early and late, was the dilemma of the artist and artistic values in a mercantile, bourgeois world. Even within his or her own being, the artist experiences the dichotomy between the intellectual/imaginative world and the physical priorities and necessities of mundane existence. Thus, the artist often experiences existence as a state of illness or emotional imbalance. Something is not right, and the effort to express that "something" is for Mann both the genesis and the end of art.

Heinrich Böll (1917–1985)

The son of a struggling German sculptor, Böll was raised in Cologne. Upon graduation from state schools, he was drafted in 1938 and served in the German infantry throughout the war. Böll achieved early fame thereafter with *Billiards at Half-Past Nine* (*Billiard um halb zehn*) and *The Clown* (*Ansichten eines Clowns*), both works all the more rueful and cynical for their apparent light-heartedness. Böll then turned in earnest to his major theme, the interpretation of the postwar German spirit and ethos, with *Absent without Leave* (*Entfernung von der Truppe*) (1964). At the same time, he became a familiar figure in the German peace movement; Böll wrote and spoke widely against the presence of U.S. nuclear devices in West Germany.

As decades distanced him and his country from the war years, Böll broadened his concerns to the potential corruption, alienation, and cruelty lying near the heart of an increasingly prosperous and self-contented nation. *The Lost Honor of Katharina Blum* (1974), *Missing Persons* (1977), and *The Safety Net* (1979) all explore in different ways the precarious balance between stability and collapse, both personal and societal.

Günter Grass (1927–   )

Born the son of a grocer in Danzig, Grass was drafted into the German army during the Second World War at the age of sixteen and taken prisoner soon after. He worked as a farm laborer and stonecutter after his release to support his interest in stage design and sculpture. His world-wide fame came in his early thirties with the publication of *The Tin Drum* (*Die Blechtrommel*) (1959), a scathing satire of Nazi Germany presented in the allegorical tale of a prescient three-year-old boy who communicates simply by banging his drum. Two years later, Grass published *Cat and Mouse* (*Katz und Maus*) (1961), in which another outsider, this time a teenager with a prominent Adam's apple, shrewdly directs attention to the attitudes and images of the New Germany versus the Reich.

Grass, always the visual artist, wrote *From the Diary of a Snail* in 1972, the central image communicating his more recent vision of steady, committed progress rather than revolutionary change. As president of the former West Germany's Academy of Art in Berlin, Grass remains one of his country's most influential cultural forces.

SPAIN AND PORTUGAL

Fernando Pessoa (1888–1935)

The Portuguese poet Fernando Pessoa is today recognized as one of the most extraordinary writers of the twentieth century, and he holds a position as yet unequaled, except perhaps by the baroque poet Luis de Camoens, in the history of Portuguese letters. Born in Lisbon in 1888, Pessoa spent ten years of his adolescence living with his mother and step-father, a Portuguese diplomat, in South Africa. He became fluent in English, and even won the Queen Victoria prize for his entrance examination at the University of Cape Town. Pessoa composed some poetry in English, erudite and somewhat archaic in style, but still proclaiming his poetic genius. The cultural shock and isolation he endured living in South Africa, combined with the premature death of both his father and brother, certainly contributed to his creative genius. Fiction became for Pessoa the sole respite from what he considered vapid reality.

Having returned from South Africa in 1905, Pessoa enrolled in the University of Lisbon, only to drop out shortly thereafter due to political upheavals of the time (the Portuguese overthrew their last monarch and founded the republic in 1910). He was interested in writing and publishing, but his efforts to start a publishing house also failed, and at the age of twenty he found himself alone and penniless in his native Lisbon. Pessoa began working as an office clerk, not unlike the young Kafka, and it is the huge disparity between their banal lives and their marvelous literary achievements that prompts a comparison.

As Pessoa drifted further into the solitude of an obscure life, his creative instincts returned to his boyhood, when he had created characters (the Chevalier de Pas is the earliest known) through whom he could express the multiplicities of his own personality, and also escape from the self he often loathed. Over the course of his life, Pessoa created some seventy of these pseudonyms, or *heteronyms* as he called them, each one a mirror of himself, a kind of creative mask that allowed him to be other(s) than himself through poetic fictions. The three most famous of these heteronyms, through whom the vast majority of Pessoa's poetry was written, are Alvaro de Campos, Alberto Caeiro, and Ricardo Reis. Pessoa lived vicariously through these heteronyms, even imagining dates of their births and deaths, their family histories and social class, and, of course, their education and poetic influences. So distinct are the poetic styles and themes, the aesthetic and philosophical outlooks of these three, that critics often speak of the poetry of Caeiro or Reis rather than that of Pessoa.

The most prolific and most widely read of the three major heteronyms is Alvaro de Campos, a civil engineer of middle-class origins. According to Pesoa, de Campos, though not a great literary craftsman, writes tolerably well. De Campos took inspiration from the Italian futurist movement, but found the true grounding and guiding light for his *sensationalist* ideals in the poetry of Walt Whitman. De Campos' lengthy "Maritime Ode" (Ode Marítima) is as much a tribute to the howling individualism of Whitman as to the glorification of Portugal in Camoes' epic Os Lusíadas.

Alberto Caeiro, whom de Campos called his greatest mentor, is Pessoa's sensationalist par excellence. A shepherd with a simple, unaffected writing style, Caeiro composed mostly short descriptive poems of nature, which often doubled as expositions of his highly realistic philosophy. Uneducated but far from ignorant, Caeiro claims no allegiance to any school of poetry or philosophy. His poems are pure, inspired only by the natural world that surrounds him, and constitute his complete vision of reality. In some ways Pessoa clearly modeled Caeiro after one of his own poetic influences, Césario Verde (1855–1886), whose writings extoll the virtues of life far from the city.

Finally, Ricardo Reis was Pessoa's token Neoclassical monarchist, his poetry the antithesis to that of Caeiro. Highly educated, Reis was a doctor and traveled widely, especially in Asia. His style is exaggerated and erudite, and many of his themes are based loosely on classical mythology, thus the designation Neoclassical. Reis coldly refutes Caeiro's ideals of purity through nature, and sees the key to happiness in the acceptance of the never-ending game of ruse and deception played by both gods and men.

Aside from his own poetry and that of his heteronymns, Pessoa also wrote a substantial prose work under the pseudonym Bernardo Soares. In essence a journal composed by the poet over the last two decades of his life, *O Livro do desassossego* has been newly translated and compiled in an edition entitled *The Book of Disquiet*. Pessoa's other literary activity during his relatively short life consisted of his association, with the poet Camilo Pessanha, with the *Orpheus* literary journal. Though it only produced two volumes, this modernist literary and artistic review was a playground for the Portuguese futurists, including the painter and poet Santa Rita Pintor, and Pessoa's close friend the poet Mario de Sá-Carneiro, who later commited suicide in Paris. Sá-Carneiro's poetry, like that of Pessoa, questions identity as a concept and expresses a good deal of existential doubt. Although Pessoa lived with and greatly contributed to the literary movements of his time, we see today that he is much less a part of a style or movement than he is one of the most original voices in twentieth century poetry. Fernando Pessoa died of apparent liver failure in Lisbon in November of 1935.

Juan Ramón Jiménez (1881–1958)

The Spanish poets Juan Ramón Jiménez and Federico García Lorca, separated in age by nearly two generations, are the two quintessential figures of tewentieth century poetry in Spain. Jiménez, who won the Nobel Prize for Literature in 1956, began his poetic career as one of the founders of Spanish modernism. Although brief, his modernist period had a great influence on the movement, both in Spain and in Spanish Latin America. Much of his early work is marked by a return to more basic forms; like Blake in *Songs of Innocence and Experience*, he wrote in simple yet lyrical verse. His prose-poem of 1914, *Platero and I, (Platero y Yo)* tells the story of a mule called Platero. This work appears to the reader at first as a child's tale, but one quickly realizes that the work merely speaks to the child in each of us. His work is at the same time a highly subjective and individual expression and pure and universal in its poetic form. Jiménez's later work reveals his spiritual nature, and again like Blake, he sought by increasing isolation from the world to find an essence or absolute through his poetry. The poems of Jiménez appear in many anthologies of Spanish literature, and have been finely translated in several editions, including *Three Hundred Poems, 1903–1953*, and *Naked Music: Poems of Juan Ramón Jiménez*.

Federico García Lorca (1899–1936)

García Lorca grew up in rural Spain, the son of a farmer. At an early age, his obvious musical skills prompted his mother to give him piano lessons and enroll him in a Jesuit school. In spite of his father's pressure upon him to study law, García Lorca pursued classes in literature, music, and painting. His first publication, *Impressions and Landscapes* (1918), was a travel narrative of his trip to the Castile region. Lorca took up residence the next year as a scholar at the University of Madrid. There he had daily opportunity to associate with both established and emerging artists and writers, including Salvador Dali, Rofael Alberti, and Juan Ramón Jiménez. Within that circle, Lorca "published" his first poems through recitations. This began a life-long commitment on Lorca's part that poetry, as in troubadour days, should be performed as a living art.

Many of his experimental poems written during this period were published in *Book of Poems* (*Libro de poemas*) (1921) and *Songs (Canciones)* (1927). His first play, *The Butterfly's Evil Spell* (*El maleficio de la mariposa*), opened in Madrid in 1920, but closed after the first night. Shortly thereafter, Lorca found much greater success in the writing of folk lyrics, in collaboration with Manuel de Falla. *The Gypsy Ballads* (*Romancero gitano*) (1927) and *Poem of the Cante Jondo* (*Poema del cante jonda*) (1937) gather many of Lorca's folk poems, ballads, and lyrics from this period. Lorca's trademark in such poetry is the refreshing mixture of contemporary imagery with traditional literary forms.

After the success of *The Gypsy Ballads*, Lorca turned his hand again to drama, this time successfully in *Mariana Pineda* (1927). Lorca then made a spiritual journey in 1929 to Cuba and the United States in search of new beginnings and themes. His experiences are imaginatively rendered in *Poet in New York* (*Poeta en Nueva York*), published posthumously in 1940.

In 1931 Lorca was again in Spain, now as an internationally recognized poet and playwright. His dramatic trilogy *Blood Wedding* (*Bodas de sangre*), staged in 1933, deals with a love triangle and the conflicts between passion and honor. In 1934, one of the Lorca's close friends, a bullfighter, was gored to death. Lorca wrote an elegy, *Lament for Ignazio Mejias* (*Llanto por Ignazio Mejias*) (1935) that has since become his most famous poem and a Spanish classic.

In July 1936 came the Civil War. Lorca left Madrid for Grenada but, upon arriving there at night, was shot and killed by Nationalist forces.

ITALY

Three exceptional Italian writers of prose stand out as influential in the development of the Italian novel, and must be mentioned in the context of European literature. It is noteworthy that all three of these writers experienced the Fascist dictatorship of Mussolini, and their work was profoundly affected. Working under the watchful eyes of censors, Italian writers and artists were forced to seek secondary, often highly metaphoric forms of expression that under other circumstances they might have passed over for simplicity's sake.

Thus much of the writing of this time took on an almost allegorical nature that, coupled with the advent of modernism and its penchant for stark and sometimes surreal representations, created a stunning effect.

Novelists

The best example of this metaphorical writing comes in Elio Vittorini's *Conversation in Sicily* (1944), which subtly but systematically derides the Fascist regime while speaking to the reader on a very personal level. As a successful publisher during the year of Fascism in Italy, Vittorini (1908–1966) helped a score of younger Italian writers to publish their works. His last novel, *Women of Messina* (*Le donne di Messina*), (1949, trans. 1972), shows his disaffectation with Communism, which he later espoused in reaction to years of tyranny. Above all, Vittorini illustrates the irony that many of Italy's finest literary works were written at a time when suppression and censure were the rules.

One of the numerous writers sponsored by Vittorini and another author and publishing executive, Cesare Pavese, was Italo Calvino (1923–1985). Calvino also worked in the publishing industry. He was a member of the Communist resistance to Mussolini and, after the latter's fall, stayed a member of the party until the unpopular invasion of Hungary forced him out. Calvino was truly the master of the allegorical style described above, as evidenced in his triptych *The Cloven Viscount* (1952), *The Nonexistent Knight* (1959), and *The Baron in the Trees* (1956) (trilogy title, *I nostri 'antenati*). As the main writer in the postwar genre of Neorealism, Calvino's work often takes on the fantastic or magical proportions associated with the fable. At the same time his style remains well-crafted realism, an effect at which readers and critics alike marvel.

Yet another novelist of this same circle was Natalia Levi Ginzburg, who met Vittorini and Pavese while writing, along with Eugenio Montale, for the *Solaria* literary journal in Florence. A militant radical, Ginzburg lived in exile along with her husband Leone in a small Italian village. She described his painful experience in *The Road to the City*, her first novel. Her work can be justly compared to that of Marguerite Duras, for although Duras uses a much sparser minimalist style, they both have written novels centered around a family unit (be it "complete" or not), and tend to draw on their own experiences as inspiration for their clearly autobiographical novels.

Poets

Two Italian poets won the recognition of the Nobel committee this century. The first, Eugenio Montale (1896–1981), awarded the Nobel Prize in 1975, was another writer who produced some of his best verse during the years of Fascism. Montale was well-educated and even more well-read, and he spent his professional life working in publishing and library science and was subsequently employed as a literary and music critic for a popular Italian newspaper. In opposition to the Neobaroque, highly affected, and ornamental style of his day, Montale's poetry appears, like that of Blake, void of ruse or artifice, transparent to the connotative weight of the most simple and stripped vocabulary. Montale is known to scores of Italian readers not only for his poetry but for his many translations of English and American writers including T. S. Eliot, William Faulkner, Eugene O'Neill, and Herman Melville. Fluent in several languages, Montale was influenced by Spanish and French modernist and symbolist poets, and especially by the Italian poet Salvatore Quasimodo. Among the best English translations of Montale's work are *Bones of the Cuttlefish: Selected Poems in Translation* (1925) and *Otherwise: Last and First Poems of Eugenio Montale.*

The brother-in-law of Elio Vittorini, Salvatore Quasimodo (1901–1968) is best known for the sense of tragedy in modern like that he conveys in his poetry. Quasimodo, although educated in the sciences, soon came to the realization that his life was to be devoted to the study (he was a professor of literature at the University of Milan) and production of literature. The isolation of the first years of his professional life stands in sharp contrast to his humanistic and philanthropic later period, when he abandoned the idealized image he had created of Sicily and looked with more cynicism at the world around him. The volumes of poetry in this later period include *Day After Day* (1947) and *The Incomparable Land* (1966). Quasimodo contributed extensively, as did Ginzburg and Montale, to the *Solaria* journal. Translating attracted Quasimodo's interest, and he translated into Italian such greats as Molière, e. e. cummings, and Ezra Pound. He was awarded the Nobel Prize for Literature in 1959.

FRANCE

Often viewed as the cultural center of Western Europe, France is the origin of many of the most important literary tests and movements of the twentieth century. Just as the French dramatists of the seventeenth century—Molière, Racine, and Corneille—looked to the commedia dell'arte of Italy and the classical theater of ancient Greece and Rome, many of the early modernist writers throughout Europe and Latin America looked to the Parnassian and Symbolist poets of France for inspiration. This helped to establish France, and especially Paris, as a sort of creative leader in literature—a fact at least partially evidenced by the large number of American expatriate writers who migrated to Paris in the first decades of the twentieth century, including Hemingway, Gertrude Stein, and Henry Miller.

Surrealism

Surrealism, though it had roots all through Europe, developed into a movement of great literary and artistic import in the Paris of the 1920s. The origins of Surrealism are essentially threefold. First, the advance of industrialism had reached a point of critical mass in which utilitarian society, as viewed by the Surrealists, was turning humankind away from its creative and spontaneous nature. Secondly, the First World War, fought in large part on French soil, had brought a mass destruction the likes of which the world has never seen. The horrific events of this war were beyond the grasp of most people, appearing in themselves beyond reality. Finally, coupled with these first two factors was a relative lack of new means of artistic expression, especially ones that could unleash the inner workings of what Freud had recently named as the subconscious mind. It is important to be aware of the etymology of the word *surreal*: from the French *sur* or beyond and *réel* or reality, the term designates that which lies beyond our habitual conceptions and perceptions of reality.

The Surrealist movement took some of its inspiration from Dadaism, an artistic revolt against the First World War and the conventions of modern society. Dadaism, named completely at random, was more an artistic than a literary movement, and included such figures as the painter and sculptor Marcel Duchamp (famous for his "ready-made objects"), Man Ray, Max Ernst, and Raoul Hausmann. More than a simple prolongation of Dada, Surrealism encompassed both the graphic and the literary arts. In 1924, André Breton (1896–1966) published his *First Surrealist Manifesto*, outlining the basic precepts of Surrealism and the techniques by which one can create Surrealist art. Essentially the Surrealists sought to liberate subconscious, repressed instincts or emotions through a constant effort towards the unique, the original, and the unexpected. Surrealism was in fact an antiliterary movement in the sense that it played with the rigid set of conventions that society had established to delineate *art* and *literature*.

Surrealist writers and artists stood in opposition to conventional forms of order and logic. Through dreams, humor, and random exploration of the first thoughts that came to their minds, Surrealists created a whole body of work that seemed to function according to a different set of codes and that possessed an incontestable poetic originality. Breton, in addition to his several *Manifestos* (1924, 1930, 1936), also published a large number of poems and at least one surrealist novel, *Nadja* (1928), in which he used a technique called automatic writing and, based on a character he imagined, put down any and every thought that passed through his mind. He was also active in the graphic arts, and the Centre Georges Pompidou in Paris presented a retrospective of his work in 1991.

Surrealism lent itself well to other forms of artistic expression, including the theater and film. Salvador Dali is undoubtedly the quintessential Surrealist painter, whose work also stretches far beyond the limits of the movement he helped to create. Dali also directed and produced several short Surrealist films, including the famous *Chien andalou* (1929), which is an ideal and quite disturbing example of Surrealist techniques. Other Surrealist painters include Miró, Brunel, Masson, and the Italian sculptor Giacometti. In the theater, Alfred Jarry's *Ubu Roi* (1907), which he wrote while in his teens, became a representative Surrealist piece as well as an inspiration for later absurdists. Finally, the painter, playwright, and film maker Jean Cocteau popularized what was a somewhat obscure intellectual movement, first through his theater (*La machine infernale*, 1934) then in such film classics as *La belle et la bête* (1949) and *Orphée* (1953). One of the great theorists of the theater, Antonin Artaud, presented many of the ideas that Surrealism had espoused in *The Theater and Its Double* (1939).

Jean-Paul Sartre (1905–1980) and Existentialism

Jean-Paul Sartre, dramatist, novelist, philosopher, and political activist, stands as one of France's most important literary figures. Born in Paris to a middle-class family and educated at the prestigious *Ecole Normale Supérieure*, Sartre taught in various French high schools in the early thirties before being enlisted in the ambulance corps in the Second World War. Returning from Germany, where he had been taken prisoner, Sartre resumed his teaching career and also became a vocal force for socialism, a political ideology that he would hold, though sometimes tenuously, throughout his life. In the late sixties Sartre became more militant in his views and partici-pated actively in the Parisian student uprising of May 1968. Sartre's life-long partner Simone de Beauvoir is among his finest biographers. Her philosophi-cal works are also of utmost importance to the advance of feminism, espe-cially her ground-breaking *The Second Sex,* in which she systematically examines the repression of women in the Western world.

IMPORTANCE

As an existentialist philosopher, Sartre valued the tangible aspects of human existence (responsibility, commitment, authenticity in action) over any preconceived essence (religion, God, a self separate and unique from one's actions). His most formidable philosophical work is *Being and Nothingness* (1943), in which Sartre establishes his concep-tion of existentialism: that human beings are confronted, in a universe void of divine meaning, with mortality and the ultimate responsibility for their own actions. The work of the German philosopher Edmund Husserl, whose phenomenology examined the workings of the con-scious mind in an effort to comprehend what constitutes existence, greatly influenced Sartre's philosophy.

Yet Sartre was not interested in philosophy, literature, or art as existing in and for themselves. Nearly the entirety of his career as an intellectual was spent expounding his view that a writer must be committed to, or engaged (engagé(e)) in, his or her ideology. As Sartre shows so succinctly in his play of 1943 entitled *No Exit* (*Huis clos*), a human's image of *self* is perceived pri-marily through his or her interaction with other people (what both Sartre and Jacques Lacan see in a more collective sense as the Other). A human being's actions are all that the Other sees, and these actions therefore take on great importance in establishing a person's essence. The only possible Hell is experienced by a human being when constantly under the judging eye of the Other, labeled and objectified (as a coward, a lesbian, a criminal) and unable to create a new and changing essence of self. This is the scenario with which Sartre works in *No Exit*.

In dividing the self into two distinct essences, the being *in-itself* and the being *for-itself*, Sartre seems to follow the pattern of many philosophers who sought to explain existence through dualities. The *being in-itself* is a kind of static object-self, which exists *in* the world yet has no obligation to act *on* the world. The *being for-itself* is fluid, in constant motion, and conscious of its freedom and transitory nature. A human being's desire to be free of responsibility and choices coincides with *being in-itself*, which views the solid, unchanging state of an object as ultimately fulfilling. Organized religion, society, government and family structures are all forms of authority that, in making choices for us, respond to this primal human desire to exist outside or beyond the sphere of *being for-itself*. As living and conscious beings, we should, according to Sartre, recognize our own liberty in our decisions and make choices based on our own authentic beliefs.

Most of Sartre's fiction deals explicitly with existentialist themes. In the short story entitled "The Wall" (1939), the author depicts the crisis of three men as they await execution during the Spanish Civil War. In a story that appears in the same volume *(The Wall)*, "Childhood of a Leader," Sartre traces the formation of an anti-Semitic xenophobe from his innocent childhood through a troubled adolescence and finally on to the violent hate crimes that plagued prewar Germany and France. Lucien, the protagonist of his story, seeks clarity and simplicity in his existence, but through an act of self-deception and inauthenticity (what Sartre terms "bad faith") he finds it in a fascist ideology of hate and exclusion.

Satre's first novel, *Nausea* (1938), is also his masterpiece of psychological insight and narrative craftsmanship. The novel is presented as the "recently discovered" autobiographical journal of one Antoine Roquentin, with Sartre in the role of editor. In it, the reader follows Roquentin through an existential crisis that causes him to place his whole life and value system into question. Roquentin, resident of Bouville (literally "Mudtown"), is hard at work on research for a biography of a minor French nobleman, Monsieur de Rollebon, who lived in the eighteenth century. Roquentin's long solitary walks through this gloomy bourgeois port town, which Sartre modeled after Le Havre, finally lead him to the public garden. There, while observing rather dazedly the root of a chestnut tree, Roquentin suddenly disassociates the tree as an object from the word or concept (the sign) "tree." It is through this philosophical contemplation of an object that Roquentin becomes conscious of his own existence, of his nature as a living being, capable of action, and fundamentally distinct from the objects that surround him. Only by crossing the viscous and unstable space that lies between being and nothingness can

Roquentin finally realize his authentic nature, his existence. At the end of the novel Roquentin wonders paradoxically if he could write something, not a research paper but perhaps a work of literature. The reader then realizes that he already has.

Simone de Beauvoir (1908–1986)

Simone de Beauvoir, French writer and philosopher, was a close friend and professional associate of Jean Paul Sartre since they met at the Sorbonne in the 1920s. In the 1940s, she and Sartre played influential roles in establishing the principles of modern existentialism, a philosophical doctrine in which moral decisions and responsibility are determined and accepted by individuals acting in the absence of generally accepted theological or ethical tenets.

Beauvoir graduated from the Sorbonne in 1929 and went on to teach philosophy at several women's colleges before beginning her writing career in earnest in 1943. Beauvoir's central themes are among the most prominent in cultural and political discussion in the modern age: the inferior roles assigned to women by a male dominated society, in *The Second Sex* (*Le Deuxième Sexe*) (1949); the neglect of the elderly, in *The Coming of Age* (*La Vieillesse*) (1972); and the importance of individual responsibility, in *The Blood of Others* (*Le Sang des autres*) (1944; transl, 1948), *All Men Are Mortal* (*Tous les hommes sont mortels*) (1946; transl, 1955), and *The Woman Destroyed* (La Femme Rompue) (1949). Beauvoir also wrote four volumes of autobiography, which provide a richly detailed history not only of her own years but also of her relationship with Sartre. She died in Paris on April 14, 1986.

Albert Camus (1913–1960)

Born in Algeria in 1913, Albert Camus is associated with Sartre and the existentialisxt movement in post-Second World War France. In addition to his novels, Camus also wrote several philosophical essays. The most notable of these is *The Myth of Sisyphus* (*Le Mythe de Sisyphe*) (1942). In Greek mythology, Sisyphus was eternally damned to push a rock up a hill only to have it roll down the other side. Camus uses this myth as a point of departure for a discussion of the absurdity of human destiny and an explication of his existentialist position. Camus' writing for the theater includes *Caligula* (1945). Although he died tragically in an automobile accident in 1960, it is interesting to note that most of Camus' great works date from the time of the Second World War and the German occupation of France. Despite, or perhaps because of, the censorship and repression of the German Nazi regime and the Vichy government in France, Camus and many other wartime writers were inspired to new artistic heights.

It is for his first novel, *The Stranger* (*L'Etranger*) (1942), that Camus gained the most notoriety outside of France. In this work the protagonist, a *pied noir* (French person born in Algeria), Mersault, murders an Algerian man on the beach. The text presents Mersault as a sort of bohemian, a man of few feelings and even fewer words, who, in his search for simplicity and immediate physical contact with his world, stumbles unwittingly into murder. Camus creates in Mersault a character that at one moment appears a sociopath, and at the next a simple, even kind man living his life as immediately as possible.

Divided very neatly into two halves, the novel opens with the death of Mersault's mother. This event troubles Mersault so little that the other characters of the novel begin to question his sanity. Mersault meets a young woman whom he begins dating and whom he accompanies to the Algerian beach with another couple on the day of the murder. Camus' style is often called journalistic, and his penchant for the clear, concise, and short sentence is obvious throughout the novel. In fact, this writing style in some ways reflects the manner in which Mersault perceives his own existence—as a series of factual events without, necessarily, links or consequences. The murder is presented as having almost no motivation. Mersault's friend Raymond (truly only an acquaintance) exchanges words with an Algerian and a challenge ensues; the two men return home to get a pistol and, as Mersault and Raymond confront the two Algerian men, Mersault suggests that he will hold the gun on one man while Raymond has a "decent" hand-to-hand fight with the other. However, the Algerian pulls a knife and, the sun blinding his eyes, Mersault shoots him once, then again four times.

The second half of the novel shows Mersault's imprisonment and trial, and ends as he is taken off to be executed. A slight change in Camus' style, which appears at once more lyrical and more psychological, accompanies Mersault's inner searchings as he sits in his prison cell awaiting death. Not dissimilar in theme to Sartre's "The Wall," *The Stranger* is by no means an apology for a murderer, nor a plea for simplicity. The few words that pass Mersault's lips reveal, in Camus' world, the inner workings of a highly complex and human nature.

Jean Genêt (1910–1986)

If his work cannot be directly associated with that of the existentialist writers, the novels and theater of Jean Genêt did gain their attention and their respect; to such an extent in fact that Sartre, author of a study of Genêt's work entitled *Saint Genêt, Dramatist and Martyr*, championed a group of intellectuals who petitioned for Genêt's pardon from life in prison. Genêt was born in 1910, abandoned by his parents and adopted by a poor provincial family. At the age of ten he began his long career behind bars, having been imprisoned for stealing. A brief stint with the Foreign Legion ended in desertion, at which point Genêt voyaged through Europe, committing petty crimes and being imprisoned quite often along the way. Much of Genêt's fiction was written while in prison, and, after receiving a life sentence in France, he was pardoned by Auriol, president of the Republic, in 1948.

Genêt's major themes include prostitution, homosexuality, crime, and alienation from society. His *Thief's Journal* (*Le Journal du voleur*) (1949) gives an autobiographical accounting of Genêt's own life as a homosexual man and a criminal. Perversity pervades the work, but still its artistic merit and literary beauty are undeniable. Genêt is best-known, however, for his theater. The stage, in all of its illusion and artifice, seems the perfect place in which Genêt's literary world can take form. Sartre shows that Genêt's dramas function through a constant mirroring effect, an image that in turn reproduces an image. This "dédoublement" (re-doubling) of Genêt's already fictional characters moves them one step further from the possibility of representing perceived reality. "In Genêt's plays," says Sartre, "each character must play the role of a character who plays a role." This concept has its most overt treatment in *The Balcony* (*La Galère*) (1956). This highly expressionistic piece of theater represents life inside a bordello to which clients come to act out their fantasies in a specific role. The opening scene shows an archbishop, dressed in full papal attire, supplicating a prostitute.

In *The Maids* (*Les Bonnes*) (1948) Solange and Claire, two sisters employed as servants in the bourgeois French tradition, plot to murder their mistress. The incestuous relationship between the two, at least on a psychological level, is immediately apparent. Disdainful of their mistress in her absence, the maids are fawning, even obsequious, when she is near. When left to their own devices, the servants enact intricate imaginary scenes in which they alternately play the role of Madame. Invariably this playacting ends with the image of Madame being insulted and abused by one of the servants. The dream world of their scheme to kill Madame is shattered when Madame does not return home at the planned hour, and Solange, taking the role of Madame, forces her younger sister to drink the poisoned tea. In her final soliloquy, Solange, having metaphorically if not actually killed Madame, assumes a double personality and proclaims the two sisters free.

The New Novel

In his essays, compiled under the title *For a New Novel* (1963), Alain Robbe-Grillet (1922–   ) states that "the new novel is simply following in a constant evolution of the novel as a genre." The new novel (*nouveau roman*) was born not out of literary theory but out of the desire of several writers, including Robbe-Grillet, Claude Simon (1913–1984) (Nobel Prize, 1985), and Nathalie Sarraute (1902–   ), to break radically with the traditions of Realism and Naturalism and to present a novel that could, through its style and form, put into question the readers preestablished ideas as to what language can do, as to what constitutes literature. As Nathalie Sarraute illustrates in her essay "The Age of Suspicion" (1956), Realism no longer corresponds to the formal or thematic needs of the modern author. The rigid structure and the insistence on the believability of characters are no longer important criteria, says Sarraute, for the new novel. Instead, the new novelists seek forms that coincide with modern experience. Themes of the new novel include the relative autonomy of objects over people (subjects) and, as a result, the subtle yet inescapable objectification (reification) of the character.

Reading a new novel can thus be a very disorienting experience. The novels of Robbe-Grillet, for example, are both precise and well-crafted, yet they truly do not conform to any of our Western conceptions of what a novel *should* be. In *Jealousy* (1957), the reader is introduced to a lovers' triangle through the highly subjective eyes of the husband. This seems a relatively banal theme, yet the structure of the novel renders it both unique and fascinating to read. The novel never employs the first person, nor is the name of the husband or the word "husband" ever mentioned. The only two explicit characters are the wife, known only as A . . . , and her suspected lover, Franck. Thus, simply to arrive at the understanding that there are actually *three* characters is a feat of interpretive skill.

The husband owns a banana plantation, and a good part of the text consists simply of his observations of day-to-day life, complete with the specific terminology associated with growing tropical fruit. The reader, sensing this effect of constant repetition, is given the impression of having already read certain parts. Robbe-Grillet's fictional device allows the reader to enter into the husband's psychology beyond the level of pure description. In fact, the novel presents his every thought, from the most revealing about the affair to the most obscure and seemingly unimportant. Thus this work takes on the air of a detective novel, each of the husband's thoughts revealing or hiding his suspicions. The novel's title has a double meaning in French, *la jalousie* also being the word for "venetian blind," through which the inquisitive eyes of the husband peer at his wife.

Robbe-Grillet's other fiction includes *The Voyeur* (1958), *In the Labyrinth* (1959), and *Project for a Revolution in New York* (1968). Robbe-Grillet has also worked with the new wave film maker Alain Resnais on the marvelously complex film *Last Year in Marianbad* (1960). Other important novels in this genre are Claude Simon's *The Flanders Road* (1960) and Nathalie Sarraute's *The Golden Fruits* (1963) and *The Planetarium* (1959).

Marguerite Duras (1914–   )

Although she is often grouped with the new novelists, the work of Marguerite Duras transcends genre definition, and appears broader in its scope and, perhaps, more personal it its narration. Duras was born in Indochina, at the time a French colony, in 1914. She spent her early childhood and adolescence with a destitute and abusive mother and two brothers, constantly defending the younger brother from the physical and emotional abuse of her older sibling. She was clearly marked by her experiences in Indochina, and a good number of her novels are autobiographical, depicting these years of her life. A prolific writer, Duras has published over twenty-five novels and written for the theater and film. She too collaborated with Alain Resnais to make her first film, *Hiroshima mon amour* (1959), which is without a doubt one of the finest French films of its time. Her best early novel, and one that, because of its minimalist and rather dissonant style, is associated with the new novel, is *Moderato Cantabile* (1958). Other fine works by Duras include *The Ravishing of Lol V. Stein* (1964), *Destroy, She Said* (1969), and *Blue Eyes Black Hair* (1986). In 1984, Duras published *The Lover*, which won the prestigious Prix

Goncourt and became an international success. It tells the story of a young woman of fifteen who, living in Indochina, has her first romantic encounter with a young, rich Chinese man. The text itself is deceptively simple, but the reader soon uncovers layer upon layer of hidden beauty and tragedy in the voice of the narrator, who looks back on her experiences as a young girl. Along with a handful of other novels from Europe, *The Lover* stands as one of the great literary works of our century.

Andre Gide (1869–1951)

Gide was born to a well-to-do and intellectual Protestant family. His father, a law professor, died when Gide was eleven years old, leaving the young boy to be raised by a harsh and inflexible mother. The pressure to obey her many rules affected Gide's emotional and physical health. He sought refuge in books and in occasional periods of religious fervor.

A sea voyage to North America in 1893 proved momentous for the young man's development. In alien cultures he glimpsed lifestyles uninfluenced by Victorian prudery. At the same time, he allowed himself to confront his own homosexual impulses without self-loathing. Not long after this trip, Gide married his cousin Madeleine Rondeaux, a union that was not consummated. Incredibly, the couple remained together until 1918 when, in a fury of frustration over Gide's homosexual involvements, Madeleine burned all his letters to her.

The North African trip also prompted a flurry of literary activity for Gide. A lyric prose poem, *The Fruits of the Earth (Les Nourritures terrestres)* (1897), was followed by three plays: *Philoctetes (Philoctète)* (1899), *King Candaule (La Roi Candaule)* (1901), and *Saul (Saül)* (1903). Even more important for his growing reputation and future course were two satires, *Marshlands (Paludes)* (1899) and *Prometheus Misbound (Le Promethee mal enchaine)* (1899), and a first-person narrative, *The Immoralist (L'Immoralist)* (1902). In these works, Gide aims to act as what he called a "disturber" of settled moralities and patterns of conduct. That imperative necessitated radical changes not merely in the thematic materials of literary art but in its structures as well. This latter interest is best explored by Gide in *The Vatican Swindle (Les Caves du Vatican)* (1914; transl. 1925; also as *Lafcadio's Adventures,* 1927; *The Vatican Cellars,* 1952), an insightful parody of the process of the generating fiction, and in *Counterfeiters (Les Faux-Monnayeurs)* (1926), a novel that contains its own revolution in novelistic conventions. Other memorable works include *Strait Is the Gate (La Porte étroite)* (1909), *Isabelle* (1911), *The Pastoral Symphony (La Symphonie Pastorale)* (1919), and *Theseus (Thesee)* (1946). Gide died in Paris on February 19, 1951.

François Mauriac (1885–1970)

In an era of writers opposed to or oblivious of formal religions, Mauriac stands in relatively small company as a writer deeply committed to Roman Catholicism. Mauriac was born in 1885 to a devout Catholic family in Bordeaux. After attending the University of Bordeaux, he published in 1909 a first book of poems, *Les Mains jointes (Clasped Hands)*. The slight attention earned by this work persuaded Mauriac to make his reputation in another literary mode. Two early novels appeared in 1913 and 1914 respectively: *L'Enfant charge de chaines* (*Young Man in Chains*) and *La Robe pretext* (*The Stuff of Youth*). Both novels deal with a theme central to Mauriac's art and religion—the struggle between the spirit and the flesh.

Mauriac achieved his first real success as a novelist with *Le Baiser au lepreux* (*The Kiss to the Leper*, 1922). In this work, a wealthy but ugly man is married to a beautiful young peasant girl who is revulsed by him. To repay her in kind, he leaves her upon his death his entire fortune, provided that she never remarries. His next novel, *Le Desert de l'amour* (*The Desert of Love*, 1925), won for Mauriac the Grand Prix du Roman. This novel, too, deals with marital discord, as does *Thérèse Desqueyroux* (1927). Mauriac's most famous novel, however, is *Le Noeud de viperes* (*The Viper's Knot*, 1932), in which an attorney tries to explain his feelings of bitterness toward his family.

Mauriac was elected to the French Academy in 1933 and was a member of the French Resistance during the Second World War. An ardent political observer and critic, he published a well-received biography of General Charles de Gaulle in 1964.

RUSSIA

Maxim Gorky (1868–1936)

Gorky, a pen name for Aleksei Maksimovich Peshkov, worked on Volga River steamers to support himself as a boy after the early death of his father. After a failed attempt to enter Kazan University in 1884, he became more and more deeply involved in revolutionary activities, for which he was arrested in 1889 and then placed under police surveillance. His early literary notice came primarily from the sketches he wrote for Moscow and St. Petersburg journals. In 1899, he published *Sketches and Stories*, a three-volume collection of his works. Recognition swiftly followed, as did literary friendships with Chekhov and Tolstoy.

Perhaps because of his literary notoriety, however, Gorky was even more intensely politically persecuted. In 1901 he was exiled to a rural village. His election to membership in the prestigeous Academy of Sciences was set aside by Czar Nicholas II, who feared the end result of Gorky's radical social ideas. Gorky eventually spent several months in prison in 1905 for his political ideas. Only a spirited protest by European and Russian intellectuals convinced the government to release him.

In 1906, Gorky traveled to the United States to raise funds for the Russian revolutionary movement. The disclosure that he was not married to his female traveling companion outraged American audiences and Gorky retreated to a mountain lodge to complete essays on bourgeois corruption. Thereafter, he moved to Capri, where, together with the literary critics Bogdanov and Lunacharsky, formed a movement called "Forward" that advanced Bolshevik doctrines.

In 1913 Gorky was granted amnesty and returned to Russia. After Lenin's rise to power in 1918, Gorky founded the Workers' and Peasants' University, the World Literature Publishing House, and the Petrograd Theater. Health problems associated with tuberculosis forced Gorky to a warmer, Italian climate in 1924. He returned to visit Russia in 1928 and 1929, and settled there permanently in 1931. Gorky was widely acknowledged thereafter as the dominant writer of the Soviet period.

Gorky's novels deal powerfully, if somewhat simply, with social injustices as he perceived them. *Mother* (1906) traces the beginnings of the revolutionary movement among factory workers. A more profound economic and social anatomy can be found in his next work, *The Artamonov Business* (1925), which tells the story of three generations of a Volga merchant family. His unfinished epic, *Kim Samghin,* was also begun in that year and relates the political, literary, and social events for the four decades preceding the 1917 revolution. Gorky's short stories in such collections as *The Life of Matvei Kozhemyakim* (1911) and *Through Old Russia* (1916) reveal Gorky's unflagging faith in the courage and essential goodness of the Russian peasant and working class.

Gorky also wrote more than a dozen plays, including his best-known, *The Lower Depths* (1902), which deals with the frustrations of people labeled "useless" by their culture. Other plays include *The Petty Bourgeois* (1901), *Summer People* (1905), *Children of the Sun* (1905), *The Barbarians* (1906), *The Enemies* (1906), *The Last* (1908), and *Yegor Bulychov* (1931).

Boris Pasternak (1890–1960)

Pasternak, a Russian novelist and poet, was awarded, but refused, the Nobel Prize for Literature. Although his poetry is well-known in the states of the former U.S.S.R., his fame in the West rests primarily upon his crowning novel, *Dr. Zhivago* (1957, first English translation 1958).

Pasternak was born in 1890 to artistic parents—his father a painter, his mother a pianist. He studied music for several years before shifting to law, then philosophy. He attended both the University of Moscow and the University of Marburg. Even while in college, however, Pasternak had begun writing poetry. Three volumes appeared spanning the war years: *The Twin in the Clouds* (1914); *Over the Barriers* (1917); and *My Sister Life* (1922). By the time his next volume appeared, *Themes and Variations* (1923), he had achieved widespread recognition as an important postrevolutionary Russian poet.

Powerful Communist critics, however, joined their voices against his supposed failure to promote political themes and social values in his works. In two long poems, "The Year 1905" and "Spektorsky" (1931), Pasternak apparently tried to constrain his art to more politically correct themes, characters, and images, a difficult artistic transition he describes in an autobiographical work, *Safe Conduct* (1931).

His movement away from the Party-approved artistic path was aided in the later 1930s by his ambitious translations of Polish, German, French, and English poets. In poetry published after these translations, including *On Early*

Trains (1943) and *The Terrestrial Expanse* (1945), a freer, more elemental and natural style once more emerges. Pasternak met Olga Ivinskaya shortly after the war, and their romantic relationship lasted to the time of his death in 1960. Ivinskaya's *A Captive of Time* (1978) tells the story of their relationship.

Pasternak had completed *Doctor Zhivago* by 1955, but could not have it printed in full in the U.S.S.R. An Italian translation appeared in 1957 and the English translation in 1958. In that year, Pasternak was awarded the Nobel Prize for Literature. At first, he gratefully accepted the award. A few days later, however, he withdrew his acceptance after having been expelled from the Soviet Writers' Union. In *Doctor Zhivago*, Pasternak treats the revolutions of 1905 and 1917 and their aftermath much as he experienced those dangerous and tumultuous times.

Aleksandr Isayavich Solzhenitsyn (1918 –   )

Solzhenitsyn's tumultuous life is inseparable from his fiction. After graduation from the University of Rostov in 1941, he served as an artillery captain in the Second World War. A casual remark critical of Stalin was found in one of his letters and led to his arrest and imprisonment for treason in 1945. From his cell in a Kazakhstan labor camp, he focused his attention on the dehumanizing details of the Soviet prison system, and he began to write. After his release in 1953, Solzhenitsyn taught physics and mathematics while pursuing his other life as a writer in secret. In 1962 Premier Khrushchev indicated his willingness to publish anti-Stalinist works. Solzhenitsyn's *One Day in the Life of Ivan Denisovich* (1962), an account of Stalin's prison camps, appeared in the U.S.S.R. with official approval.

That brief hiatus of censorship soon ended, however, with the removal from office of Krushchev in 1964. Thereafter, Solzhenitsyn's novels *The Cancer Ward* (1966) and *The First Circle* (1967) had to be smuggled out of Russia for publication in the West. In 1968, Solzhenitsyn won the Nobel Prize for Literature, but could not claim it for fear he could not regain admittance to the Soviet Union. A series of historical novels, also published in the West, followed the Nobel Prize: *August 1914* (1972), which deals with the events leading to the First World War; and *The Gulag Archipelago* (1974–1976), a three-part study of the network of Soviet prisons.

With the publication of the first two volumes of *The Gulag Archipelago* came the end of Solzhenitsyn's welcome in the Soviet Union. In February 1974 his citizenship was revoked and he was exiled to the West. Later that year he traveled to Stockholm to claim the Nobel Prize he had been unable to accept earlier. Settling at first in Zurich, Switzerland, Solzhenitsyn moved in 1975 to an isolated farm in southern Vermont. He was able to return to Russia in May 1994.

EXPERIMENTATION IN THE THEATER

Realism in drama reached the United States in the mid-1920s in the plays of Eugene O'Neill (1888–1953). As a rather experimental author, O'Neill still did not push his dramatic creations to the extremes encouraged by the French director and theorist Antonin Artaud. Artaud worked first as an actor, producer, and director before turning his attention to theory, and his treatise on the subject, *The Theater and its Double* (1929), had a profound effect on modernist drama. O'Neill's work may appear subdued next to Artaud's theory, but in fact his plays are both intense and disturbing. Among his most important works are *The Hairy Ape, The Iceman Cometh, Long Day's Journey into Night* and *Desire Under the Elms*. Other American Realist writers for the stage include Tennessee Williams (*The Glass Menagerie, A Streetcar Named Desire*), Lorraine Hansberry, and Arthur Miller (*All My Sons, Death of a Salesman*).

Clearly, Realism is not the only movement one finds in twentieth century drama. Although perhaps more feasible and certainly more practical when applied to poetry or fiction, Surrealism found its place in drama as well. The influence of the playwright, actor, and director Antonin Artaud (1896–1948) cannot be underestimated in the development of Surrealism and the Theater of the Absurd. His important manifestos of 1932 and 1933, both called *The Theatre of Cruelty*, decried the corruption of language itself as a medium to faithfully convey the playwright's vision. Artaud argued against safe, cerebral theater and for a more confrontative, mythically violent dramatic experience that would release the audience from the restraints of rationality and habitual perception. Both actors and audiences, Artaud wrote, should be "victims burnt at the stake, signalling through the flames." Although his own plays, such as *The Cenci* (1935), do not fulfill this vision, Artaud's essays and correspondence proved a profound influence on such playwrights as Harold Pinter, Rober Vitrac, and Rene Daumal. The French writer Andre Breton, whose *Manifest of Surrealism* began the movement, also inspired other Surrealist authors, discussed earlier, such as Jean Cocteau. Active in the theater as well as film, Cocteau was a very experimental author, and his plays often rely as much on staging as they do on the text. Another French playwright, Jean Genêt, merges a brutal realism with a certain surreal atmosphere, again often created in the staging. His dialogue is rich and often shocking, as are his themes, and Genêt is known for the strong antiestablishment and antibourgeois sentiment of his work. Among his finest plays are *The Maids* and *The Balcony*.

Bertolt Brecht (1898–1956)

Like the English poet Keats, Brecht studied medicine in college and worked as a medical orderly. Influenced by the human suffering he observed, Brecht began his career as a writer by opposing war and the nationalistic attitudes that precipitated it. In the mid-1920s he worked under Max Reinhardt at the Deutsches Theater in Berlin, where he studied the dialectical materialism of Marx and the political theater of Piscator. These influences appear prominently in the two operas he wrote with Kurt Weill, *Die Dreigroshenoper* (*The Threepenny Opera*) (1926) and *Aufstieg un Fall der Stadt Mahagonny* (*The Rise and Fall of the City of Mahagonny*) (1927).

When the Nazis came to power in Germany in 1933, Brecht moved to Switzerland, then Denmark, Finland, and Russia, as the German occupation proceeded. From 1941 to 1949 he lived in California, where he worked with Charles Chaplin. He returned in 1949 to East Berlin to form a company of actors known as the Berliner Ensemble theatre.

Brecht considered the theater the most effective means of communicating his vision of a liberated working class. At the same time, Brecht rejected a narrowly didactic view of drama. He did not consider any of his plays completed until they had been performed several times, with accompanying adjustments and alterations by the author based on input from both audiences and actors. Among his greatest plays are *Mutter Courage und ihre Kinder* (*Mother Courage and her Children*) (1941), *Der gute Mensch von Sezuan* (*The Good Woman of Setzuan*) (1943), *Leben des Galilei* (*Galileo*) (1943), and *Der Kaukasische Kreidekreis* (*The Caucasian Chalk Circle*) (1948).

Brecht also wrote more than 80 stories and a lengthy treatise on the theater and literary arts generally, *Der Messingkauf* (*The Purchase of Brass*) (1941). Brecht's poetry is concerned primarily with the potential for change within individuals, classes, and societies. His best known volumes of poetry are *Svendborger Gedichte* (*Svendborg Poems*) (1939), *Buckower Elegien* (*Buckow Elegies*) (1943), and *Die Kriegsfibel* (*The ABC of War*) (1955).

Samuel Beckett (1906–1989)

The Irish-born novelist, poet, and playwright Samuel Beckett deserves a special place in our discussion of modern drama. Beckett was born in Dublin and educated at Trinity College. He was a lecturer in Paris at the *Ecole Normale*, and he completed work on his master's thesis at Dublin University on Racine's *Britannicus*. After settling in Paris in 1937, where he worked occasionally as a translator for James Joyce, he turned to writing in French as his first literary tongue.

According to the author, this decision came in part as a conscious effort to find a more neutral medium for his artistic expression, a language in which he would not tend towards imitation of a certain style or fall in with a certain movement (such as the Irish renaissance). Thus, after having written one critical work, *Proust* (1931), and his first novel, *Murphy* (1938) in English, Beckett wrote nearly the entirety of his vast body of work in French. Clearly feeling the need to have his writings appear in his native tongue, Beckett also translated the majority of his work.

Often labeled difficult or obscure, Beckett's style is actually simple, even stripped. His themes center around solitude, despair, the paralysis of will, and, finally, nonexistence and nothingness. But despite the pervasive darkness of Beckett's themes, his works nearly always possess a certain grotesque irony, often in the form of surprising humor. The contingencies and absurdities of life, represented with such a serious tone in the existentialist literature of Sartre and Camus, turn into biting irony in Beckett's work.

His portrayal of seemingly absurd situations, which often contain a strong element of social criticism, led the structuralist critic Martin Esslin to adopt the somewhat overused term for the theater of Beckett and others: the Theater of the Absurd. Yet the world of Beckett's theater and fiction does represent humankind, often in its darkest, most ignorant and ignoble hour. His characters wage battles against nothingness with verbal games and vapid dialectics. One frequently sees more of a brutal realism, always tinged with humor, than of a pure effort at the absurd in his work. Beckett won the Nobel Prize for Literature in 1969, and his prolific career in the theater, film, radio, and the novel continued into his old age.

Clearly, the traditional plot summary cannot be used for the work of Beckett, for the simple reason that quite often nothing tangible, no action in the classical sense, takes place. In his two-act play *Happy Days* (1961), the heroine Winnie appears buried waist-high in dirt, able to move only her head and arms. She is awakened each morning by a piercing bell, which rings again if she tries to close her eyes before nightfall. Her husband Willie, unable to stand, grovels behind her small hill of dirt, occasionally responding to Winnie's meandering monologue. The objects that surround her, the "capacious black bag, shopping variety" and the "collapsible collapsed parasol" serve to underscore her virtual paralysis. The bag in fact contains a revolver, which is often the focus of her attention, though it remains out of reach. Act II presents a significant change in Winnie's situation. She is now "imbedded up to neck, hat on head, eyes closed." Her head is immobile, and only her eyes and her smile suggest the elaborate body language of Act I. Willie at last appears near the end of the act, "dressed to kill," but crawling to Winnie on all fours, unable to gather the strength, despite Winnie's encouraging words, to climb the small mound to her. "There was a time when I could have given you a hand," says Winnie, "and then a time before that again when I did give you a hand." The play ends with a happy song, inspired perhaps by Willie, who finally speaks to his wife, or at least calls her by her name. Here is the final irony of the play, that Winnie, in the arms of desperation and death, can and does find reason to sing, reason to declare this "another happy day."

One of Beckett's most critically acclaimed works, and certainly his most popular, is the two-act *Waiting for Godot* (1952). The simplicity of the play cannot be overstated. The entirety of the drama consists in a dialogue between two homeless and slightly crazed men, Vladimir and Estragon, as they wait in a sort of no man's land for the arrival of Godot. Of course, Godot never arrives, which allows the playwright to examine the possibilities of a play with no action, no development, no resolution. The result is one of the masterpieces of theater in the twentieth century, at times hilarious and also unexpectly profound and despairing.

Other Dramatists

Dramatists in the second half of the twentieth century continued to product exciting and experimental work. Two notable British playwrights, Harold Pinter and Tom Stoppard, write in the absurdist tradition while also reaching in new directions. Pinter's play *The Dumb Waiter* (1960), although written in a highly minimalist style, also conveys meaning on several levels through its silences and double entendres. In Stoppard's *Rosencrantz and Guildenstern are Dead* (1966), these two Shakespearian characters step onto a modern stage and proceed to revel in their own despair. The prolific American playwright Sam Shepard's *True West* (1980) has become a modern classic, presenting American pop culture and the subtle interplay of illusion and reality.

The performance theater of the 1960s and 1970s, which often had a strong political or social message and sought truly to collapse the boundaries between play and audience, has been somewhat eclipsed by a more personal and frequently violent and expressive performance art. While Grotowski experimented in the 1970s with a "poor theater," which went against the conventions of the costly theater performance, new stage innovations were underway as playwrights explored the possibilities of the theater in the round (Peter Weiss's *Marat/Sade*, 1964). There are an ever-increasing number of female dramatists, including Caryl Churchill, Marsha Norman, and Ntsoka Shange, whose work treats both traditional and experimental themes and forms. As it always has, theater will continue to evolve and grow to meet the artistic needs of both authors and audiences.

EASTERN EUROPEAN LITERATURE

In general, Eastern European writers have survived and developed as artists through the same horrors of war experienced by German and French authors. In the case of Eastern Europe, however, the Second World War was followed not by a Marshall Plan and prosperity, but by decades of oppression and poverty. The works of Eastern European writers, not surprisingly, are marked by an even more vitriolic and satiric tone than that of their French and German counterparts.

Milan Kundera (1929 –   )

In his first novel, *The Joke* (1967), Milan Kundera launches a blistering attack on the corruption and duplicity of Czechoslovak politics. The story focuses on what could have been no more than a tempest in a teapot, were it not for the tragic ramifications of the event: on a postcard, a young Communist teasingly mocks his girlfriend's political pretentions. The wrath of the establishment comes down on his head, ruining his life and career. This novel was translated into a dozen languages and, under Kundera's direction, made into a film. The Prix de Medicis was awarded to Kundera for his 1973 novel, *Life is Elsewhere*. Kundera now lives in Paris.

Franz Kafka (1883–1924)

Because of the social ambitions of his father, Franz Kafka found himself after his graduation from Charles University in Prague a German-speaking Jew in a Czech-speaking Christian world. He was further isolated intellectually and emotionally by his occupation in the civil service from 1908 to 1917. Shortly after, Kafka developed tuberculosis and could no longer work. He died on June 3, 1924, in a sanatorium near Vienna.

Kafka's fiction, from the great short stories such as "The Metamorphosis" and "In the Penal Colony" to his posthumously published, unfinished novels *The Trial (Der Prozess,* 1925), *The Castle (Dos Schloss,* 1926) and *Amerika* (1927) share a common quality: they resist binding interpretation in favor of a more elusive, provocative approach to literature. Peter Foulkes, author of *The Reluctant Pessimist: A Study of Franz Kafka* (New York, 1982), detects a significant trend in Kafka's early to late fiction:

> When his works are read in chronological order they reveal a growing tendency on Kafka's part to rid his prose of stylistic fashion and to create a fictional world devoid of local color, with no precise references to time or place of action. For instance, in his final novel, *The Castle,* society is reduced to the barest essentials. Some of the later short stories ("The Borrow" and "Josephine the Singer") carry the technique still further, portraying a world in which only the voice of the narrator provides a point of access for the reader's understanding.

George Lukacs (1885–1971)

Hungary's most famous and prolific modern literary critic is George Lukacs. In the years following the First World War, Lukacs became active in the Hungarian Communist party. With its defeat, he was exiled and spent years as an itinerant professor and student in Berlin and Moscow. Eventually becoming a professor of aesthetics in Budapest, he was removed from that position after the suppression of the 1956 uprising for his approving attitudes toward and interest in non-Marxist literatures. Lukacs continued to write, however, and is now widely viewed as the preeminent Marxist critic of our era, particularly for his work with eighteenth and nineteenth century French, German, and Russian literatures. His best-known critical works are *The Historical Novel* (1955), *Goethe and His Age* (1968), and *The Meaning of Contemporary Realism* (1980).

Witold Gombrowicz (1904–1969)

Setting out to become a lawyer at Warsaw University and ending up as Poland's most famous novelist, Witold Gombrowicz's startling use of Surrealistic images and techniques in *Eerdydurke,* (1937) his first novel, took Warsaw by storm. Two plays, *Yvonne: Princess of Burgundia* (1937) and *The Marriage* (1947), bolstered his reputation and, in translation, brought him a wide international audience. Gombrowicz escaped to Argentina during the Second World War and saw his works banned in Poland first by the Nazis and then by the Communists. The ban, briefly lifted in the 1950s, was reimposed in 1958. Gombrowicz spent his last years as a writer in exile in France.

Czeslaw Milosz (1911–   )

Czeslaw Milosz is among the most noted poets and intellectual interpreters of Eastern European literature. His first volume of poetry appeared in 1933, followed three years later by the poems of *Three Winters.* These strong politically pregnant poems are generally classed with the "catastrophic" poetry common to a number of Polish writers in that period. Milosz continued to write in hiding throughout the Second World War. He left Poland in 1951, and now lives and teaches in the United States. His best-known critical work remains *The Captive Mind* (1953), which assesses the relationship between Eastern European intellectualism and Stalinism. In 1980 he won the Nobel Prize for Literature.

10
THE LITERATURES OF OTHER CULTURES

AFRICAN LITERATURE

The story of the emergence of African literatures is a rich and complex one. We must consider not only written literature but oral traditions as well, and those of many cultures. Much African literature has been written in Western languages—French, Portuguese, English—and some in native languages. Recently, African theater has come into its own for its dazzling use of poetic and musical techniques to support dramatic development.

Poetic Forms

Like *Beowulf* and other folk epics, the traditional tales and poetry of African tribes are based on myths. The most involved of these myths is that of the Dogon of Mali; their retelling of the creation myth takes a week in recitation. Similar genesis myths in other African cultures portray God as a victim of human cruelty (the Lozi of Zambia); the world as a creation of ants (the Pangwa of Tanzania); and the universe as evolving from a huge drop of milk (the Fulani of Mali).

Shorter poetic forms common to many African cultures are praise names, oracle verse, incantations, magic formulas, and hunters' songs. The praise name is a poetic tribute to one's gods or especially valued friends, animals, or places. Once composed, the praise name (a rhythmic collection of laudatory sentiments, generally without fixed form) is retained by the recipient of the praise name poem much as a living epitaph. Oracle verse are a combination of mythic lore and practical law. Again without fixed form, these verses are collected and recited (usually by the tribal priest) as an education for listeners about the basis for legal and moral decisions made by the priest or chief. In some tribes, oracle verse has grown to substantial length; the Ifa oracle of the Yoruba exceeds any one priest's ability to memorize it completely, and the telling of major portions often consumes a day. Incantations and magic formulas, the first reserved primarily for healing and the latter for placing curses, involves the ritualistic repetition of key words, many from obscure origins. These phrases hold power insofar as they are repeated accurately and faithfully. Finally, hunters' songs recount memorable hunting events and urge the participants to be strong and brave. Like virtually all African poetry, hunters' songs are accompanied by and inseparable from music and rhythm.

Prose Sources

African prose has evolved from folktales, particularly the animal-trickster tale, the escape story, and dilemma tales. Like Chaucer's *Nun's Priest's Tale* involving Chanticleer and Pertelot, the animal-trickster tale usually involves an animal—a rabbit, turtle, fox, or chicken—who, by deception, gains a surprising advantage over other animals or humans. The attributes of animals, such as a bird's long beak, are often explained in the course of animal-trickster tales. The escape story involves the same cast of characters or, often, human figures who manage by cleverness and courage to extricate themselves from apparently disastrous situations. The dilemma tale recounts a morally challenging scenario usually involving one's duties to family, tribe, or the gods. Just when the tale reaches its climax, the audience is asked to supply a suitable ending. The effect is not unlike that of the American short story "The Lady or the Tiger."

A portion of such oral tradition was collected by J. G. Cristaller in 1879 and, more recently, by Amos Tutuola in *The Palm-Wine Drinkard* (1952) and *My Life in the Bush of Ghosts* (1954). These latter works retell the central folkloric traditions of the Yoruba tribe.

African Languages

African literature written in African languages is a rather late development. The earliest written African language, Ge'ez, is now dead. Usually as part of the process of colonization or trade, Latin and Arabic alphabets have been used to establish a graphic equivalent for spoken African languages. Like Welsh writers, African authors have faced a dilemma regarding the use of their tribe's or country's native written languages. On the one hand, the native language may be a more expressive and authentic medium for cultural materials. On the other hand, the writer's own interests might be furthered by the use of English, French, or another widely read language. Some writers, however, such as Ngugi wa Thiong'o, have led the way toward a productive compromise, with the original of a literary work written in the native language, followed by translations into major trading languages such as French or Swahili.

In addition, the high rate of illiteracy in many African countries inhibits the development of indigenous publishing houses. The hunger of the populace for imaginative verbal art cannot be doubted, as evidenced by the huge popularity of radio, television, and film dramas throughout Africa. Nevertheless, written literatures in native languages are making progress. The writing system of the Yoruba tribe, for example, was standardized in 1875, with the first book of Yoruba poetry (*Iwe Ekini Sobo*) appearing in 1905. Since then many novels have been published in the Yoruba language, including Daniel Olorunfemis Fagunwa's *The Forest of a Thousand Demons* (1950) and Afolabi Olabimtan's *Leopard Cub* (1967).

The Hausa language went through a conversion from Arabic to Roman characters at the beginning of this century. Its poetry and prose is primarily oriented toward scripts to be recited, often over radio or television. An early poetic work in Hausa was Alhaji Umaru's *Zuwan Nasara* (1903), which told of the coming of Christianity to Hausaland and its devastating effects on native customs. Even to the present, many Hausa poems contain strong appeals to religious or moral behavior. Blind beggars throughout Hausaland memorize these texts and receive alms for reciting them to the public.

The official language of Ethiopia is Amharic, and that country's most famous novelist Arawarq Gabra Iyasus, who wrote the first Ethiopian novel, *Imaginative Story* (1908). Many Ethiopian works such as Hawaryat's *Araya* (1949) focus on the well-intentioned but doomed efforts of Western-educated Ethiopians to apply their newly learned skills to native problems and personalities.

Swahili originally was written in Arabic script, but now Roman characters are standard. As a widely spoken trading language, Swahili commands a broad readership. The oldest written document in Swahili is *Hamziya* (1749), a court poem by Sayyid Aidarusi. Later didactic verse was published in Swahili by Mwana Kupona binti Msham and Muyaka bin Haji al-Ghassany, both of Kenya. In the twentieth century, the most prominent author in Swahili has been Shaaban Robert of Tanganyika. In 1960 he published the highly regarded volume of poems, *African Diamonds*, and thereafter a number of novels and essay collections.

Prominent African writers using French, Portuguese, and English, respectively, include Leopold Senghor, first president of Senegal and author of *Anthology of the New Negro and Madagascan Poetry* (1948); Mario de Andrade of Angola, author of a number of highly militant poetry collections; and Wole Soyinka of Nigeria, Africa's most famous playwright. Among the most-read African works in English are autobiographies such as Bloke Modisane's *Blame Me on History* (1963) and Mphahlele's *Down Second Avenue* (1959). Leading African poets writing in English are K. A. Noortje, Mazisi Kunene, and Dennis Brutus.

Amos T'utuola (1920–)

T'utuola, a Nigerian author with only six years of formal schooling, has won a large British, American, and African audience for his several novel-like prose epics and tales, the great majority of which are based on Yoruba folktales. Drawing upon his Salvation Army school literary education in such works as *The Thousand and One Nights* and *Pilgrim's Progress*, T'utuola embues the materials of Yoruba folktales with rich fantasy elements, often involving a quest of some kind.

In *My Life in the Bush of Ghosts* (1954), for example, T'utuola traces the fanciful experiences of a boy who, in trying to escape slave traders, finds himself, literally and figuratively, in a weird, fantasy-laden region of the jungle. A similar quest motif is present in T'utuola's best-known work, *The Palm-Wine Drinkard and His Dead Palm-Wine Tapster in the Dead's Town* (1952). In *Simbu and the Satyr of the Dark Jungle* (1955), a rich, attractive young girl leaves home for the first time and experiences hunger and poverty. Later works include *The Brave African Huntress* (1958), *The Feather Woman of the Jungle* (1962), *Ajaiyi and His Inherited Poverty* (1967), and *The Witch-Herbalist of the Remote Town* (1981). *The Palm-Wine Drinkard* has now been rewritten as a stage play and as a folk opera.

Chinua Achebe (1930 –   )

Chinua Achebe, one of Nigeria's foremost writers, was born in Ogidi, Nigeria, to a lay Christian minister and his wife. He attended Nigerian government schools and eventually earned his B.A. at London University (1953). In 1956 he studied broadcasting at the British Broadcasting Corporation.

Achebe's career has been unusually varied and rich. He has served as controller of the Eastern Region of Nigeria (1958–1961), founder of the Voice of Nigeria (1961–1966), professor of English at several Nigerian and American universities, director of a Nigerian publishing house, and deputy national president of one of Nigeria's political parties (1983).

Although best known as a novelist, Achebe has distanced himself from the conventions of the English-language novel, particularly the principles of "art for art's sake." For Achebe, literature must have a strong, easily perceived message of contemporary social importance. At the same time, Achebe has endeavored to flavor the English language used in his works with the rhythms, idioms, and nuances of the Ibo dialect.

Things Fall Apart (1958) and *Arrow of God* (1964) trace Nigerians' relations with the British from early colonial days onward. The first of these novels focuses on Okonkwo, an Ibo village leader in the late 1800s. The stability and pleasure of his life as a respected elder in the community is suddenly disrupted by the intrusion of white culture. In the end, Okonwo's stature and sense of self fall to nothing as his world, in the words of the title, falls apart. The second novel also deals with the British presence in Nigeria, this time in the 1920s. Ezeulu, a chief priest of the god Ulu, pits his power within his culture against the British Christian missionaries and their proselytizing.

Three later novels, *No Longer at Ease* (1960), *A Man of the People* (1966), and *Anthills of the Savannah* (1988), treat personal and societal struggles in various stages of African independence. In 1987, Achebe was nominated for the Booker Prize for *Anthills of the Savannah*. *Things Fall Apart* has been widely broadcast as a radio play in Africa and recently as a television play produced by the Nigerian Television Authority.

Ezekiel Mphahlele (1919 –   )

Ezekiel Mphahlele, who has also written under the pseudonym Bruno Eseki, was born in Pretoria, South Africa, to a messenger and a domestic maid. After attending a teachers' college in Natal (1939–1940), he took a position as a clerk in an institute for the blind for four years. In 1945 he married Rebecca Mochadibane, a social worker, and began teaching English and Afrikaans in a Johannesburg high school. Thereafter, he edited a literary magazine, lectured in English literature on the university level in Nigeria, directed African programs for an intercultural association in Paris, and, from 1974 to 1977, taught at the University of Pennsylvania. He returned to South Africa in 1978 as a senior university professor and inspector of education.

Mphahlele was banned from the classroom in 1952 by the South African government in response to his public criticism of the segregationist Bantu Education Act. For more than a decade threafter he was in virtual exile, during which time he worked to explain and recreate African issues and themes in English-language fiction (*The Living and the Dead* [1961]), essays (*The African Image* [1962]), and social commentaries (*The Role of Education and Culture in Developing African Countries* [1965]). He has written works for juveniles, including *Father Come Home* (1984), several writing textbooks, and his autobiographical novels *Down Second Avenue* (1985) and *The Wanderers* (1971).

CHINESE LITERATURE

After the first Opium War (1839–1842), China was opened forever to Western influence, including the appearance of many Western works of literature in translation. Early translators of note were Yen Fu and Lin Shu. The excellence of these translations and the popularity of "exotic" Western themes for a Chinese audience led quickly to the marked influence of Western literary structures on native Chinese forms. In this regard, Liu E's *The Travels of Lao Ts'an* (1907) should be compared to the English picaresque novel, such as Smollett's *Expedition of Humphrey Clinker*.

The Westernization of Poetry and Prose

Under similar influence from Western poetry, the highly stylized and ritualistic forms of traditional Chinese verse underwent dramatic change toward the experimental, expressive, and personal. In the first decades of the twentieth century, Huang Tsunhsien and Lian Chi-chao led a virtual revolution in Chinese poetry and prose, culminating in a new, flexible style of writing that could accommodate foreign phrases, and the frank expression of emotion.

China, like France, considered it possible to overhaul language itself. That bold enterprise, undertaken after the fall of the Manchu Dynasty and establishment of the Republic in 1912, resulted in the beginnings of a new literature written in the vernacular and promulgated through several literary societies and "small press" publications. Early works in this movement were written by Chou Shu-jen, including "Diary of a Madman" (1918) and "Medicine" (1919). Later literary leaders were Lu Hsun, a noted critic, and Kuo Mo-Jo, who surprised his peers by converting to Marxism in 1924.

During the period between the world wars, China was in the throes of almost continual military clashes among Communist, Nationalist, and warlord forces. In response, Chinese writers banded together in the "League of Leftist Writers." This group included not only the essayist Lu Hsun but also talented novelists such as Lao She, Pa Chin, and Mao Tun. From a different quarter came novels from writers driven out of Manchuria by the Japanese annexation of that region. The novels of Hsiao Hung and Hsiao Chun were particularly influential in galvanizing Chinese youth against the Japanese.

Postwar Proletarian Literature

Since the Second World War, the winds of literary change have been driven by political and economic storms. In 1942, Mao Zedong delivered his famous "Talks at the Yenan Forum on Literature and Art." It was Mao's vision that literature, rightly understood, should be both popular and supportive of the politic agenda. All aspects of past and present Chinese writing came under the microscope of revaluation; in 1949, the First National Congress of Writers and Artists convened to define more clearly the new proletarian literature. Novels during this period focused on the virtues of land reform, the value of hard work, and the honor attached to political purity.

The Cultural Revolution of 1966–1976 took this approach to its extreme, limiting "correct literature" to a few works by Lu Hsun, the novels of Hao Jan, and a few propagandistic Peking plays. After the death of Mao, the pent-up energies of China's writers flowed freely and vigorously once again, most recently in the short stories of Wang Meng, the poetry of Pei Tao, and the nonfiction and journalism of Piu Pin-yen.

A relatively separate chapter in the development of recent Chinese literature is the literary activity of Taiwan. For the first several years after their exile from continental China in 1949, Taiwanese writers produced what now appears to be an insubstantial body of propagandistic anti-Communist literature. The few works to stand out in this period are Chang Ai-ling's *The Rice-Sprout Song* (1954), a story about the lives of peasants under Communist rule, and Chiang Kuei's *Hsuan-feng* (1959), about power struggles in the Communist regime. Beginning in the 1960s, however, a group of Taiwan University students led the way toward modern fiction in their stories and novels crafted on the models of Joyce, Hemingway, Woolf, and Kafka. Particularly notable from this group is Pai Hsien-yung, whose novel *Wandering in the Garden, Waking from a Dream* (1982) attracted international notice.

Taiwanese poetry during this period has been dominated by the nativist movement led by Huang Ch'un-ming (*The Drowning of an Old Cat* [1980]). The subject manner and setting used by this poetic school is the Taiwan countryside, especially those locales in transition from a rural to an industrialized urban culture.

JAPANESE LITERATURE

Much as the Opium Wars opened China to Western influence in the 1840s, so the arrival of Commander Perry's fleet in Japanese waters in 1855 could have inaugurated a sudden shift in Japanese literature toward Western themes and forms. That such a shift did not take place, or took place exceedingly gradually, was due largely to the limited intellectual and artistic prestige of the writers of *gesaku* works—the relatively trivial "hack" stories and verse common in Japan for centuries. There literally was no other hand to clap to mark the intrusion of new cultural elements and personalities from the West. When the capital was moved in 1868 to Tokyo (formerly Edo), the *gesaku* writers were turned out of national life almost altogether, accused by their Confucian opponents of promulgating immoral works.

The Influence of Translations

At about the same period translations of British and other European works began to appear, including Bulwer-Lytton's *Ernest Maltravers* (translated in 1879). Translators felt free to leave out difficult passages and to interpolate commentary regarding the motives of characters. Young Japanese writers glimpsed in such imperfect translations, however, a form of literature free from the necessity for moral or political propaganda. This insigh was formalized in 1885 by Tsubouchi Shoyo's *The Essence of the Novel*, a declaration of independence on behalf of literary art, including the novel.

The Modern Novel

Futabatei Shimei's *Ukigumo* (1887–1889) was Japan's first modern novel. Shimei employed the colloquial language, a revolutionary departure from the literary language used by the great majority of his contemporaries. An equally revolutionary collection of colloquial verse appeared in *Shintaishisho* (1882). The more expansive Western forms found in this collection showed Japanese readers how much human experience lay beyond the limits of such traditional forms as the tanka and haiku.

Two outstanding novelists in the first decades of the twentieth century were Natsume Soseki and Mori Ogai. Soseki's comic novel, *Botchan* (1906) and Ogai's autobiographical works remain classics in the eyes of most Japanese. Ogai and Soseki share the recurring theme of painful transition— the transition of a Japanese Everyman from the calm world of the past to the fast-paced, confused world of the present. Also of note in this period was Tanizaki Jun-ichiro, whose novels *Some Prefer Nettle* (1929) and, later, *The Key* (1956), reveal the self-division of the Japanese soul in its struggles with Western influence.

As in China some decades later, Japan underwent a period of proletarian literary revolt in the 1920s, led by Kobayashi Taki-ji. The movement was short-lived, however, and left few literary works worthy of note. In reaction, a group of writers formed the "Neosensualist" school, with poems, short stories, and novels that clearly eschewed any propagandistic purpose. Kawabata Yasunari, a leader in the movement, won the Nobel Prize in 1968.

Another school was that of the "I Novel," particularly as written by Shiga Naoya. He raised first-person narration from the level of diaries to that of first-rate fiction.

At the conclusion of the Second World War, the horrific events surrounding the dropping of the atom bomb led to many works of poetry and prose, including Ibuse Masuji's *Black Rain* (1965).

New Voices

Postwar Japan witnessed the rise of the first Japanese writer to find a wide international audience: Mishima Yukio. A playwright and novelist, Mishima is known primarily for *The Temple of the Golden Pavilion* (1956) and *The Sea of Fertility*, completed just before his death in 1970. Other writers whose fame has not spread so far as Mishima's are Abe Kobo (*The Woman in the Dunes*, 1962), Endo Shusaku (*Silence*), and Kita Morio (*The House of Nire*).

INDIAN LITERATURE

By the early 1800s, Indian literature had began to borrow Western forms such as the novel. In the Bengal region, for example, Bankim Chandra Chatterji (1838–1894) wrote a series of romantic novels that contributed in no small measure to the rising sense of national identity within India during the period. Rabindranath Tagore (1861–1941), India's most famous poet, wrote the anthem of the independence movement ("Jana Gana Mana") and won the Nobel Prize for Literature in 1911. In the Urdu region, Muhammad Iqbal (1876–1938) wrote poems important in the cultural development of Indian Muslims. Vivid descriptions of village life in central India can be found in the Hindi novels of Premchand (1880–1936).

In 1954 the government of India established the National Academy of Letters to provide support for the translation and publication of regional works of literature. The Academy also works to promote Anglo-Indian literature, works about Indian life written in English. Of particular importance in this tradition in the mid-twentieth century are the novels of Mulk Raj Anand dealing with India's poor and the middle-class novels of R. K. Narayan. Other notable Indian writers working primarily in English are V. S. Naipaul, Dom Moraes, Ved Mehta, Santha Rama Rau, Ruth Prawer Jhabvala, and Kamala Markandeya.

LATIN AMERICAN LITERATURE

The transition from Neoclassicism to Romanticism came relatively late to Latin America. Among the first Romantic poets was Esteban Echeverría, whose "The Captive" (1837) used experimental verse forms and native (though somewhat Byronic) themes. In a work that Rousseau would have approved because of its paean to the natural man, Domingo Faustino Sarmiento wrote *Civilization and Barbarism: Life of Juan Facundo Quiroga* (1845), an admiring study of the Pampas cowboy. His work, in fact, gave birth to a unique Latin American subgenre of "gaucho" tales and ballads.

High Romantic Period

The period of high Romanticism in Latin America was reached with *Tabaré* (1886) by Juan Zorrilla de San Martín of Uruguay. This epic poem tells the tragic but heroic tale of the Charruas Indians, slaughtered at the hands of the Spanish invaders. In Brazil, Romantics turned more to pleasant natural scenes than to nostalgic tales of the past. Domingo José Goncalves de Magalhaes set the early standard for such poetry with *Poetic Sighs and Longings* (1836), a work far surpassed in quality and now in fame by the poems of Antônio Gonçalves Dias.

The line between Romantic interest in rural customs and the Realist's or Naturalist's interest in "life as it is lived" became tenuous indeed after midcentury. The Chilean novelist Alberto Blest Gana wrote a series of novels focusing on local customs; the best of these is *Martin Rivas* (1862). Brazilian novelists included Joaquim Manuel de Macedo (*The Little Brunette*, 1844) and José de Alencar, whose novels on the lives and plight of Brazilian Indians continue to be avidly read to this day. By the mid-1870s, the spirit of such works was clearly Realist or Naturalist in temperament rather than Romantic. Aluizio Azevedo's *O Mulato* (1881) exposed the maladjustments and inequities of Brazilian social and economic life. More interior in their scope of examination were the psychological novels of Joaquim Maria Machado de Assis, the most famous of which remains *Philosopher or Dog?* (1891).

The Birth of Modernism

Just as Latin American authors had mined the vein of local custom topics to the point of formulaic, sentimental fiction, a new generation of writers— many educated in the art and philosophy of Europe—broke with the past, preferring "art for art's sake." Modernism was thus born. In Mexico, this loose movement was led by Manuel Najera; in Colombia, by José Silva; and in Cuba, by Julian del Casal and José Martí. The Shakespeare of Modernism in Latin America, however, was Rubén Darío of Nicaragua. His gathering of poems and prose in *Azul* (1888) showed a generation of writers how to combine formal experimentation with passionate expression of feeling.

Mexico experienced its bloody revolution in the years 1910 to 1917 as the rest of the world edged closer to its own conflagration. The Revolution deeply affected Latin American writers by instilling a new sense of urgency, even desperation, in their work. Social protest themes were common during this period. Existing side by side with such literature, however, was a body of love poetry written by such women as Delmire Agustini of Uruguay and Gabriela Mistral of Chile (Mistral won the Nobel Prize in 1945).

Since the Second World War, Modernism has pursued the same general course it followed in Europe—through Avant-gardism and Surrealism to Postmodernism. Pablo Neruda of Chile won the Nobel Prize for Literature in 1971 for his enormously rich hymn to the suffering of Latin America, *Canto General*. Journals such as *Contemporaneos* in Mexico and *Colonida* in Peru are the cornucopiae from which flow the poetry and short prose of Latin American writers of the last decade.

Jorge Luis Borges (1899–1986)

Borges was born and lived most of his life in Buenos Aires, Argentina. As a child he read widely not only in Spanish literature but also in the literatures of England, France, and Germany, having learned English from his British grandmother and French and German when his family lived in Geneva for four years. Returning to Argentina in his twenties, Borges set himself the challenge of becoming the foremost poet of Buenos Aires. That dream faded, however, with the rise of fascism after 1930, a movement in which Borges saw the dark side of nationalist zeal. Supporting himself as a library clerk, he turned to the writing of fiction. Bedridden for a prolonged period after a freak accident, Borges wrote some of his best-known stories, collected in *Ficciones* (1944) and *The Aleph* (1949). Out of favor with the Perón regime for his outspoken antifascism, Borges took a number of teaching positions until his eyesight failed almost completely by 1955.

His fortunes changed dramatically, however, with the fall of Perón. Borges was appointed director of the National Library and, in 1960, published his collection of parables, *Dreamtigers*. His international reputation soared after 1961, the year in which he shared with Samuel Beckett the International Publishers' Prize. For the remaining two decades of his life, he figured prominently as a literary experimentalist and critic, political commentator, and international celebrity of the humanities. He died in Geneva in 1986.

IMPORTANCE

Although he wrote no novels, Borges' short stories have played a shaping role for many twentieth century novelists interested in the possibilities of the surreal and the fantastic. Donald Barthelme, Robert Coover, Thomas Pynchon, John Barth, John Bardner and other writers have acknowledged his influence. In Borges' fiction, materials from daily life are transformed by dream imagery and fantasy to yield an imaginative world of seemingly endless possibility. The experience of reading Borges is for many readers an antidote to the depressive spirit of much existentialist writing. In Borges, a spirit of mischief, play, and magic presides, even over subjects that in themselves are deeply tragic.

Manuel Puig (1832–   )

Born in Argentina, Puig learned English as a child by watching American films. In 1957 he left Argentina to study film-making in Rome, a pursuit that eventually took him to Stockholm and London. He returned to Buenos Aires with several completed film scripts in hand, only to be disappointed by repeated rejections from the struggling Argentine film industry. His interests then turned to fiction. *Betrayed by Rita Hayworth* (1971) uses Joycean language games, flashbacks, and shifting points of view to depict the empty, routine life of a middle-class Argentine family whose only outlet for emotion comes through films.

Heartbreak Tango (1976) and *The Buenos Aires Affair* (1976) were modestly well received. His best known work to date, *The Kiss of the Spider Woman* (1979), captures the human and political dilemmas shared by a young revolutionary and middle-aged homosexual detained in the same prison. The story reached an even wider international audience when it was transformed into a vastly successful film starring William Hurt.

Mario Vargas Llosa (1936–)

Vargas Llosa is a Peruvian writer of novels, plays, and essays, most of them involved with aspects of social change. His early years were spent in Bolivia, where his grandfather was Peruvian consul. Later he attended schools in Peru, including a military academy. In 1952 began a steady stream of publications, beginning with *The Escape of the Inca*, a three-act play, and many short stories. His first novel, *The City and the Dogs* (1963), received extremely positive reviews and within a short time had been translated into more than a dozen languages. Using a substantial number of autobiographical details, the novel recounts the struggles of adolescents in a brutal, corrupt military school.

The Green House followed in 1966, the title referring to the dense Peruvian jungle that simultaneously embraces and strangles the central characters. *The Cubs and Other Stories* focuses primarily on the fate and symbolic importance of a teenager who has accidentally been castrated. Thereafter Vargas Llosa's work took a decidedly more political turn; *Conversation in the Cathedral* is a critique of Manuel Odria's regime, a period of political upheaval and deceit in Peru. The next target of his pen was the military and religious establishment, both satirized in *Captain Pantoja and the Special Service* (1973).

From 1969 to 1974 Vargas Llosa lived abroad, first in London for three years, then in Washington state, and eventually in Barcelona. During these years he concentrated on literary criticism, writing studies on Marquez, Flaubert, Sartre, and Camus. His collection of essays, *The War of the End of the World* (1982), dealing with political struggles in Brazil, was a best seller throughout Latin America.

Gabriel José García Márquez (1928–)

Born into poverty in Colombia, García Márquez nevertheless managed to attend universities in Bogotá and Cartagena, where he studied law and journalism. For two decades, beginning in 1948, he worked in various positions and locales (principally Bogotá, Rome, Paris, Havana, and Mexico City) as a journalist, foreign correspondent, publicist, and screenwriter. In 1955 García Márquez published the Spanish version of a collection of short stories that would later, in 1972, appear as *Leaf Storm and Other Stories*. In these stories he establishes the fictional setting used in many of his later works—the Colombian village of Macondo. He also unveils here his style of magical realism, a Latin American literary movement he helped to found. This style combines realistic description with vivid flights of fantasy and imagination.

Later stories appeared in *No One Writes to the Colonel and Other Stories* (1968), in which García Márquez examines the tragedy and irony implicit in his country's failure to recognize the heroism of an aged war veteran. A more explicit treatment of political ignorance and repression, set in Macondo, is the story *La mala hora* (1962), translated as *The Evil Hour* (1979).

García Márquez wrote his most admired novel, *One Hundred Years of Solitude* (1967), in Mexico in the mid-1960s. Again set in his fictional world of Macondo, it operates on several levels to tell the history of Macondo, the cultural evolution of Colombia, and in the broadest sense the myth of human experience generally. Stylistically, the novel is allusive, complex, and densely textured. (In his acceptance speech for the Nobel Prize for Literature in 1982, García Márquez acknowledged his stylistic debt to William Faulkner.)

In 1968 García Márquez co-authored with Mario Vargas Llosa one of the most important works of Latin America literary criticism, *La novela en America Latina* (1968). Collections of his short stories appeared regularly through the 1970s, including *Eyes of a Blue Dog* (1972) and *Innocent Erendira and Other Stories* (1978). *The Autumn of the Patriarch* (1976) is an Orwellian satire on the excesses, shallowness, and egotism of Latin American military dictators. *Chronicle of a Death Foretold* (1983), explores the motives, personalities, and traditions involved in a murder for honor that takes place in a Latin American village.

REVIEW QUESTIONS

RECENT DIRECTIONS FOR MAJOR WORLD LITERATURES

Multiple Choice

1. _____When compared to the literature of previous centuries, modern world literature is
   a. more nationalistic
   b. less nationalistic
   c. more uniform in character
   d. less experimental

2. _____The poet Fernando Pessoa is most closely linked with
   a. Argentina
   b. Portugal
   c. Mexico
   d. Chile

3. _____ Vittorini achieved success as a writer and
   a. a university administrator
   b. a professional athlete
   c. a publisher
   d. a stock broker

4. _____As in the eighteenth and nineteenth centuries, the cultural center of Europe remains
   a. Spain
   b. Germany
   c. Italy
   d. France

5. _____Surrealism was inspired most directly by
   a. Romanticism
   b. Hedonism
   c. Neoclassicism
   d. Dadaism

6. _____Sartre's life-long partner, Simone de Beauvoir, was also his
   a. cousin
   b. biographer
   c. physician
   d. first professor

7. _____Camus' most productive period as a writer came during
   a. his retirement in Provence
   b. the Second World War
   c. his teenage years
   d. his final two years

8. _____Jean Genêt distinguished himself both as a novelist and
   a. a playwright
   b. a poet
   c. an illustrator
   d. a musician

9. _____The new novel tends to make
   a. plot more important than theme
   b. believability of character more important than plot
   c. structure more important than description
   d. modern experience more important than novelistic traditions

10. _____Milan Kundera and George Lukacs are most famous, respectively, as
   a. a novelist and a critic
   b. a critic and a poet
   c. a playwright and a novelist
   d. a novelist and a playwright

True-False

11. _____ As a general rule, the modern literature of Eastern Europe is less agry or biting in tone that that of Germany and France.

12. _____ In poetry, African literature uses essentially the same line and stanza forms as European literature.

13. _____ The praise name in African literature is seldom more than three words in length.

14. _____ One important source of prose material for African literature is animal stories.

15. _____ Several African languages underwent a transition in alphabet from Roman to Arabic at the beginning of this century.

16. _____ Contact with the West brought more immediate changes to Chinese literature than to Japanese literature.

17. _____ For many centuries, most Chinese literature had been written in the vernacular.

18. _____ Mao's "Talks at the Yenan Forum" asserted that literature should be free to criticize state policies and politics.

19. _____ Throughout the nineteenth century, Japan refused to allow the sale or distribution of English works in translation among its people.

20. _____ The Nicaraguan writer Rubén Darío was known primarily for his "gaucho" tales.

Fill-in

21. In the years from 1910 to 1917, Mexico experienced a _____ .

22. Calvino was a master of the _____ style.

23. Sartre establishes his concept of existentialism in the 1943 work, _____ .

24. The genre of *Nausea* (1938) is that of a _____ .

25. Some of Camus' works feature characters from the land of his birth, _____ .

26. Saurraute and Robbe-Grillet are both important figures in the development of the _____ .

27. Marguerite Duras often writes autobiographically of her difficult early years in _____ .

28. *The Captive Mind* is a critical interpretation of _____ intellectualism.

29. Most African literatures feature one or more myths comparable to Genesis in Western literatures.

30. The ending to a dilemma tale is provided by the _____ .

Matching

31. Hausa   a. 1966–1976

32. *Travels of Lao Ts'an*   b. *Goethe and His Age*

33. Cultural Revolution   c. Japanese hack writers

34. *The Essence of the Novel*   d. Liu E

35. *gesaku*   e. poetry explaining laws

36. José de Alencar   f. a literary journal

37. *Contemporaneos*   g. an African language group

38. oracle verse   h. wrote about Indians

39. escape story   i. similar to trickster tales

40. George Lukacs   j. Tsubouchi Shoyo

Answers

1. b	15. f	28. Eastern European
2. b	16. t	29. creation
3. c	17. f	30. audience
4. d	18. f	31. g
5. d	19. f	32. d
6. b	20. f	33. a
7. b	21. revolution	34. j
8. a	22. allegorical	35. c
9. d	23. *Being and*	36. h
10. a	*Nothingness*	37. f
11. f	24. novel	38. e
12. f	25. Algeria	39. i
13. f	26. new novel	40. b
14. t	27. Indochina	

WINNERS OF THE NOBEL PRIZE FOR LITERATURE

1901	René F. A. Sully-Prudhomme (France)
1902	Theodor Mommsen (Germany)
1903	Bjørnstjerne Bjørnson (Norway)
1904	Frédéric Mistral (France) and José Echegaray y Eizaguirre (Spain)
1905	Henryk Sienkiewicz (Poland)
1906	Giosuè Carducci (Italy)
1907	Rudyard Kipling (Great Britain)
1908	Rudolf C. Eucken (Germany)
1909	Selma Lagerlöf (Sweden)
1910	Paul von Heyse (Germany)
1911	Maurice Maeterlinck (Belgium)
1912	Gerhart Hauptmann (Germany)
1913	Sir Rabindranath Tagore (India)
1914	(none)
1915	Romain Rolland (France)
1916	Verner von Heidenstam (Sweden)
1917	Karl A. Gjellerup (Denmark) and Henrik Pontoppidan (Denmark)
1918	(none)
1919	Carl F. G. Spitteler (Switzerland)
1920	Knut Hamsun (Norway)
1921	Anatole France (France)
1922	Jacinto Benavente (Spain)
1923	William Butler Yeats (Ireland)
1924	Wladyslaw S. Reymont (Poland)
1925	George Bernard Shaw (Great Britain)
1926	Grazia Deledda (Italy)
1927	Henri Bergson (France)
1928	Sigrid Undset (Norway)
1929	Thomas Mann (Germany)
1930	Sinclair Lewis (United States)
1931	Erik A. Karlfeldt (Sweden)
1932	John Galsworthy (Great Britain)
1933	Ivan A. Bunin (France)
1934	Luigi Pirandello (Italy)
1935	(none)
1936	Eugene O'Neill (United States)
1937	Robert Martin du Gard (France)
1938	Pearl S. Buck (United States)
1939	Frans Eemil Sillanpää (Finland)
1940–43	(none)
1944	Johannes V. Jensen (Denmark)
1945	Gabriela Mistral (Chile)
1946	Hermann Hesse (Switzerland)
1947	André Gide (France)
1948	T. S. Eliot (Great Britain)
1949	William Faulkner (United States)
1950	Bertrand Russell (Great Britain)
1951	Pär F. Lagerkvist (Sweden)

1952	François Mauriac (France)
1953	Sir Winston Churchill (Great Britain)
1954	Ernest Hemingway (United States)
1955	Halldór K. Laxness (Iceland)
1956	Juan Ramón Jiménez (Spain)
1957	Albert Camus (France)
1958	Boris L. Pasternak (Russia—prize declined)
1959	Salvatore Quasimodo (Italy)
1960	Saint-John Perse (France)
1961	Ivo Andrió (Yugoslavia)
1962	John Steinbeck (United States)
1963	Giorgos Seferis (Greece)
1964	Jean-Paul Sartre (France—prize declined)
1965	Mikhail Sholokhov (Russia)
1966	Shmuel Yosef Agnon (Israel) and Nelly Sachs (Sweden)
1967	Miguel Angel Asturias (Guatemala)
1968	Yasunari Kawabata (Japan)
1969	Samuel Beckett (Ireland)
1970	Aleksandr I. Solzhenitsyn (Russia)
1971	Pablo Neruda (Chile)
1972	Heinrich Böll (Germany)
1973	Patrick White (Australia)
1974	Eyvind Johnson (Sweden) and Harry Edmund Martinson (Sweden)
1975	Eugenio Montale (Italy)
1976	Saul Bellow (United States)
1977	Vicente Aleixandre (Spain)
1978	Isaac Bashevis Singer (United States)
1979	Odysseus Elytis (Greece)
1980	Czeslaw Milosz (Poland)
1981	Elias Canetti (Bulgaria)
1982	Gabriel García Márquez (Colombia)
1983	Sir William Golding (Great Britain)
1984	Jaroslav Siefert (Czechoslovakia)
1985	Claude Simon (France)
1986	Wole Soyinka (Nigeria)
1987	Joseph Brodsky (United States)
1988	Naguib Mahfouz (Egypt)
1989	Camilo José Cela (Spain)
1990	Octavio Paz (Mexico)
1991	Nadine Gortimer (South Africa)
1992	Derek Walcott (West India)

GLOSSARY

Allegory: A literary device, in prose or poetry, in which a literal character, event, or object also possesses a symbolic meaning. Thus an allegory may illustrate a philosophical idea or a moral or religious principle. A work of literature is said to be allegorical if it has more than one level of meaning. (Examples: the *Romance of the Rose*, La Fontaine's *Fables*, Kafka's *The Penal Colony*, Orwell's *Animal Farm*.)

Alliteration: The repetition of a sound, especially an initial consonant, in a line of poetry or prose. (Example: "Walking in a Winter Wonderland")

Allusion: An indirect or explicit reference to a well-known place, event, or person. Allusion in literature often takes the form of a figure of speech. (Example: In his "Ode to a Nightingale," "and Lethe-wards [I] had sunk," the poet alludes to Hades, the underworld.)

Antihero: Term used to designate the protagonist of many modern plays and novels. The antihero does not posses the classic heroic virtues of power, dignity, and bravery; rather, this character is weak, often ineffectual and passive. (Example: Roquentin, the protagonist of Sartre's *Nausea*.)

Aphorism: The brief statement of a principle, maxim, or opinion. La Rochefoucauld's *Maxims* are often aphoristic.

Archetype: In literature, archetypal criticism examines types of narrative, character, and image that occur in a large variety of texts. Literary archetypes, like the Jungian archetypes of the collective unconscious, are said to reflect a group of elemental and universal patterns that trigger an immediate and profound response from the reader.

Assonance: The repetition, in a line of prose or poetry, of similar or identical vowel sounds.

Bildungsroman: The German term for "novel of formation," a type of novel tht describes the development of the mind and character of its protagonist, usually from childhood, through some difficult period and on to higher knowledge or maturity. Included in the genre would be Goethe's *Wilhelm Meister's Apprenticeship*, George Eliot's *The Mill on the Floss*, and Hermann Hesse's *The Glass Bead Game*.

Catharsis: The purging or purification that occurs, according to Aristotle, through the representation of a dramatic tragedy. It is said to affect the audience, assuaging their guilt and freeing them from fear. Some critics also see it as an integral element of tragedy, attached to the tragic flaw of the hero.

Consonance: The repetition of consonant sounds, with a change in the vowel between the consonants. (Example: give-gave)

Denouement: Used for both tragedy and comedy as well as the novel, this French term, meaning literally "unknotting," describes the moment when the intrigue or action ends, when the misunderstanding has been explained or the mystery solved.

Genre: A French word meaning type, kind, or form; in literature the term is used to designate different literary forms, such as *tragedy, satire, epic* and more recently *novel, biography,* etc.

Irony: A figure in which the implicit meaning of a statement or action differs drastically from its explicit meaning. Types of irony include dramatic irony, verbal irony, and structural irony.

Lyric: A short poem, usually nonnarrative, in which the text expresses the speaker's emotional or mental state. A lyric is written in the first person and is often associated with songs and other musical forms.

Meter: Designates the recognizable and repeated rhythms and stresses created by verse form. Iambic pentameter is the most common meter of English poetry.

Metonomy: A figure of speech in which a literal term or attribute of one thing comes to represent another to which it has a contiguous relation. (Example: the use of "crown" to mean king)

Mimesis: A Greek word meaning "imitation," mimesis is the active or dynamic copying or representation of a literal (sensual) or metaphysical (spiritual) reality in a work of art or literature.

Motif: A thematic or structural element used and repeated in a single text, or in the whole of literature. A motif may be a literary device, an incident, a formula or a reference. (Also "leitmotif" or guiding motif)

Ode: A lyrical poem of high and formal style, usually rhymed, which often addresses itself to a praised person, object, or quality. (Example: Wordsworth's "Ode: Intimations of Immortality")

Personification: A figure of speech or rhetoric in which inanimate objects or abstractions are given human qualities or represented as having human form. (Example: "that lazy old sun")

Satire: A work of literature that attacks society's vice and folly through irony and wit.

Scansion: The analysis of verse or poetry to uncover its meter and rhythmic patterns.

Synecdoche: A figure in which a part of something is taken to represent the whole. (Example: "ten sails on the horizon," meaning ten ships.)

Theme: An idea presented and expanded upon in a literary work. A theme can be explicit or implicit, and is usually suggested by the narrative action.

SUGGESTED READINGS

General Studies—European

Allen, J. S. *Popular French Romanticism.* Syracuse, NY, 1981.

Alter, Robert. *Necessary Angels: Tradition and Modernity in Kafka, Benjamin and Scholem.* Cambridge, MA, 1991.

Arico, S. L., ed. *Contemporary Women Writers in Italy.* Amherst, MA, 1990.

Benedkt, Michael. *The Poetry of Surrealism.* Boston, 1974.

Berndt, C. A. *German Poetic Realism.* Boston, 1980.

Brombert, V. H. *The Hidden Reader: Stendhal, Balzac, Hugo, Baudelaire, and Flaubert.* Cambridge, MA, 1988.

Bullivant, Keith. *After the "Death of Literature": Western German Writing of the 1970s.* New York, 1989.

Burdick, Charles, ed. *Contemporary Germany: Politics and Culture.* Boulder, CO, 1984.

Caesar, Michael, ed. *Writers and Society in Contemporary Italy.* New York, 1984.

Champagne, R. A. *French Structuralism.* Boston, 1990.

Chapple, Gerald, ed. *The Turn of the Century: German Literature and Art, 1890–1915.* Bonn, 1983.

Charvet, P. E. *The Nineteenth Century.* New York, 1967.

Evans, M. N. *Masks of Tradition: Women and the Politics of Writing in Twentieth Century France.* Ithaca, NY, 1987.

Fairlie, Alison. *Imagination and Language.* Cambridge, 1981.

Field, G. W. *The Nineteenth Century, 1830–1890.* London, 1975.

Fowlie, Wallace. *Poem and Symbol: A Brief History of French Symbolism.* University Park, PA, 1990.

Furst, L. R. *Counterparts: the Dynamics of Franco-German Literary Relationships.* Detroit, 1977.

Glaser, Hermann, ed. *The German Mind of the Nineteenth Century.* New York, 1981.

Grana, Cesar. *Bohemian versus Bourgeois.* New York, 1964.

Greenfield, K. R. *Economics and Liberalism in the Risorgimento.* Baltimore, MD, 1954.

Hardin, James, ed. *German Writers in the Age of Goethe.* Detroit, 1989.

Harris, F. J. *Encounters with Darkness: French and German Writers on World War II.* New York, 1983.

Hatfield, H. C. *Clashing Myths in German Literature from Heine to Rilke.* Cambridge, MA, 1974.

Heller, Erich. *The Disinherited Mind: Essays in Modern German Literature and Thought.* New York, 1971.

Levi, Anthony. *Guide to French Literature: 1789 to the Present.* Chicago, 1992.

Lloyd, Rosemary. *The Land of Lost Content.* Oxford, 1992.

Matthews, J. H. *Toward a Poetics of Surrealism.* Syracuse, NY, 1976.

Menhennet, Alan. *Order and Freedom: Literature and Society in Germany from 1720 to 1805.* New York, 1973.

Mews, Siegfried, ed. *Studies in German Literature of the Nineteenth Century.* Chapel Hill, NC, 1972.

O'Brien, Justin. *Contemporary French Literature.* New Brunswick, NJ, 1971.

Orr, Linda. *Headless History: Nineteenth Century French Historiography of the Revolution.* Ithaca, NY, 1990.

Pascal, Roy. *From Naturalism to Expressionism: German Literature and Society 1800–1918.* New York, 1973.

Picon, Gaetan. *Contemporary French Literature, 1945 and After.* New York, 1974.

Pierrot, Jean. *Imaginaire Decadent, 1880–1900.* Chicago, 1981.

Porter, L. M. *The Literary Dream in French Romanticism.* Detroit, 1979.

Prendergast, Christopher. *The Order of Mimesis.* New York, 1986.

Rossel, S. H. *Scandinavian Literature, 1870–1970.* Minneapolis, MN, 1982.

Sabin, Margery, *English Romanticism and the French Tradition.* Cambridge, MA, 1976.

Seyhan, Azade. *Representation and its Discontents: The Critical Legacy of German Romanticism.* Berkeley, 1992.

Spalek, J. M., ed. *Exile: the Writer's Experience.* Chapel Hill, NC, 1982.

Terdiman, Richard. *Discourse/Counterdiscourse: The Theory and Practice of Symbolic Resistance in Nineteenth Century France.* Ithaca, NY, 1985.

Weightman, John. *The Concept of the Avant-Garde: Explorations in Modernism*. LaSalle, IL, 1973.

Whitridge, Arnold. *Critical Ventures in Modern French Literature*. New York, 1967.

Ziolkowski, Theodore. *German Romanticism and Its Institutions*. Princeton, NJ, 1990.

Russia

Brown, E. J. *Major Soviet Writers: Essays in Criticism*. Oxford, 1973.

Fennell, J. L. *Nineteenth Century Russian Literature*. Berkeley, CA, 1973.

Hayward, Max. *Literature and Revolution in Soviet Russia, 1917–62*. London, 1963.

Roberts, S. E. *Essay in Russian Literature*. Athens, OH, 1968.

Latin America

Bassnett, Susan, ed. *Knives and Angels: Women Writers of Latin America*. New York, 1990.

Bosa, M. C. *Nosotras: Latina Literature Today*. Binghamton, NY, 1986.

Castillo, D. A. *Talking Back: Toward a Latin American Feminist Theory*. Ithaca, NY, 1992.

Forster, M. H. *Vanguardism in Latin American Literature*. New York, 1990.

Gazarian-Gautier, M.L. *Interviews with Latin American Writers*. Elmwood Park, IL, 1989.

Gracia, J. E., ed. *Philosophy and Literature in Latin America*. Albany, NY, 1989.

Kaminsky, A. K. *Reading the Body Politic: Feminist Criticism and Latin American Women Writers*. Minneapolis, MN, 1993.

Meyer, Doris. *Contemporary Women Authors of Latin America*. Brooklyn, NY, 1983.

Asia

An Anthology of Contemporary Chinese Literature. Taiwan, 1974.

Birch, Cyril. *Anthology of Chinese Literature*. New York, 1972.

――― *Chinese Communist Literature*. New York, 1963.

Chai, Ch'u, ed. *A Treasury of Chinese Literature*. New York, 1965.

Dunlop, Lane. *A Late Chrysanthemum: Twenty-one Stories from the Japanese*. San Francisco, 1986.

Keene, Donald. *Anthology of Japanese Literature*. New York, 1988.

――― *Modern Japanese Literature*. New York, 1956.

――― *The Pleasures of Japanese Literature*. New York, 1988.

Nieh, Hualing, ed. *Literature of the Hundred Flowers*. New York, 1991.

Rimer, J. T. *A Reader's Guide to Japanese Literature*. New York, 1988.

Rubin, Jay. *Injurious to Public Morals: Writers and the Meiji State*. Seattle, WA, 1984.

Selden, Kyoto, ed. *The Atomic Bomb: Voices from Hiroshima and Nagasaki*. Armonk, NY 1989.

Siu, H. F., ed. *Mao's Harvest: Voices from China's New Generation*. Oxford, 1983.

Soong, S. C. *Trees on the Mountain: An Anthology of New Chinese Writing*. Seattle, WA, 1984.

Africa

Abraham, W. E. *The Mind of Africa*. Chicago, 1962.

Beier, Ulli. *Introduction to African Literature*. Evanston, IL, 1967.

Killam, G. D. *African Writers on African Writing*. Evanston, IL, 1973.

Shelton, A. J. *The African Assertion*. New York, 1968.

Moore, Gerald, and Ulli Beier, eds. *Modern Poetry of Africa*. New York, 1982.

Rousseau

Bloom, Allan, ed. *Emile: or, On Education*. New York, 1979.

Grimsley, Ronald. *Jean-Jacques Rousseau*. Brighton, 1983.

Melzer, Arthur M. *The Natural Goodness of Man*. Chicago, 1990.

Condillac

Knight, I.F. *The Geometric Spirit: The Abbé de Condillac and the French Enlightenment*. New Haven, 1968.

Helvétius

Smith, D. W. *Helvétius: a Study in Persecution*. Oxford, 1965.

D'Holbach

Kors, A. C. *D'Holbach's Coterie*. Princeton, NJ, 1976.

La Mettrie
Wellman, K. A. *La Mettrie: Medicine, Philosophy, and Enlightenment.* Durham, NC, 1992.

Turgot
Lodge, E. C. *Sully, Colbert, and Turgot.* Port Washington, NY, 1970.

Condorcet
Schapiro, J. S. *Condorcet and the Rise of Liberalism.* New York, 1978.

Chénier
Smernoff, R. A. *André Chénier.* Boston, 1977.

Saint-Pierre
Maury, F. J. *Studies in the Life and Work of Bernardin de Saint-Pierre.* Geneva, 1971.

Chateaubriand
Call, M. J. *Back to the Garden: Chateaubriand, Senancour, and Constant.* Saratoga, CA, 1988.
Paitner, G. D. *Chateaubriand: A Biography.* London, 1977.

de Staël
Gutwirth, Madelyn. *Madame de Staël, Novelist.* Urbana, IL, 1978.
West, Anthony. *Mortal Wounds.* New York, 1973.

Constant
Call, M. J. *Back to the Garden: Chateaubriand, Senancour, and Constant.* Saratoga, CA, 1988.

de Maistre
Lebrun, Richard. *Joseph de Maistre: An Intellectual Militant.* Kingston, Ontario, 1988.

Senancour
Call, M. J. *Back to the Garden: Chateaubriand, Senancour, and Constant.* Saratoga, CA, 1988.

Lamartine
Lombard, C. M. *Lamartine.* New York, 1973.

Hugo
Gerson, N. B. *Victor Hugo: A Tumultuous Life.* New York, 1971.

Musset
Gochberg, H. S. *Stage of Dreams: The Dramatic Art of Alfred de Mussett.* Geneva, 1967.

Castex, P. G. *Vigny.* Paris, 1969.

Dumas père
Maurois, André. *Alexandre Dumas: A Great Life in Brief.* New York, 1966.

Gautier
Grant, R. B. *Théophile Gautier.* Boston, 1975.

Sainte-Beuve
Lehmann, A. G. *Sainte-Beauve: A Portrait of the Critic.* Oxford, 1962.

Nodier
Nelson, Hilda. *Charles Nodier.* New York, 1972.

de Nerval
Knapp, B. L. *Gerard de Nerval: The Mystic's Dilemma.* New York, 1980.

Alfieri
Betti, Franco. *Vittorio Alfieri.* Boston, 1984.

Manzoni
Chandler, S. B. *Alessandro Manzoni: The Story of a Spiritual Quest.* Edinburgh, 1974.

Leopardi
Sigh, G. *Leopardi and the Theory of Poetry.* Lexington, KY, 1964.

Kleist
Burckhardt, Sigurd. *The Drama of Language: Essays on Goethe and Kleist.* Baltimore, MD, 1970.

Klopstock
Tombo, Rudolf. *Ossian in Germany.* New York, 1966.

Wieland
Craig, Charlotte. *Christoph Martin Wieland as the Originator of the Modern Travesty in German Literature.* Chapel Hill, NC, 1970.

Herder
Barnard, F. M. *Herder's Social and Political Thought.* Oxford, 1965.

Goethe
Fink, K. J. *Goethe's History of Science.* Cambridge, 1991.
Funke, M. R. *From Saint to Psychotic.* New York, 1983.
Geary, John. *Goethe's Faust: The Making of Part I.* New Haven, CT, 1981.

Muenzer, C. S. *Figures of Identity: Goethe's Novels and the Enigmatic Self.* University Park, PA, 1984.

Schiller
Miller, R. D. *Schiller and the Ideal of Freedom.* Oxford, 1970.

Kant
Booth, W. J. *Interpreting the World: Kant's Philosophy of History and Politics.* Buffalo, NY, 1986.
Forster, Eckhart. *Kant's Trancendental Deductions.* Stanford, CA, 1989.
Guyer, Paul, ed. *The Cambridge Companion to Kant.* Cambridge, 1992.

Wagner
Aberbach, A. D. *The Ideas of Richard Wagner.* Lanham, MD, 1988.

Richter
Berber, Dorothea. *Jean Paul Friedrich Richter.* New York, 1972.

Novalis
Hiebel, Friedrich. *Novalis: German Poet, European Thinker, Christian Mystic.* Chapel Hill, NC, 1954.

F. Schlegel
Eichner, Hans. *Friedrich Schlegel.* New York, 1970.

A. Schlegel
Ewton, R. W. *The Literary Theories of August Wilhelm Schlegel.* London, 1972.

Schelling
Brown, R. F. *The Later Philosophy of Schelling.* Lewisburg, PA, 1977.

Tieck
Trainer, James. *Ludwig Tieck: From Gothic to Romantic.* London, 1964.

Hoffmann
Daemmrich, H. S. *The Shattered Self: E.T.A. Hoffmann's Tragic Vision.* Detroit, MI, 1973.

Arnim
Liedke, H. R. *Literary Criticism and Romantic Theory in the Work of Achim von Arnim.* New York, 1966.

Brothers Grimm
Zipes, J. D. *The Brothers Grimm.* New York, 1988.

Eichendorff
Schwarz, Egon. *Joseph von Eichendorff.* New York, 1972.

Mörike
Slessarev, Helga. *Eduard Mörike.* New York, 1970.

Immermann
Porterfield, A. W. *Karl Lebrecht Immermann,* New York, 1966.

Kleist
Silz, Walter. *Heinrich von Kleist.* Philadelphia, PA, 1962.

Grillparzer
Yates, W. E. *Grillparzer: A Critical Introduction.* Cambridge, 1972.

Schopenhauer
Hamlyn, D. W. *Schopenhauer.* London, 1980.

Heine
Sammons, J. L. *Heinrich Heine: The Elusive Poet.* New Haven, CT, 1969.

Hebbel
Flygt, S. G. *Friedrich Hebbel.* New York, 1968.

Stendhal
Alter, Robert. *A Lion for Love: A Critical Biography of Stendhal.* New York, 1979.

Balzac
Schilling, B. N. *The Hero as Failure.* Chicago, 1968.

Flaubert
Lottman, H. R. *Flaubert: A Biography.* Boston, 1989.

Sand
Cate, Curtis. *George Sand: A Biography.* Boston, 1975.

Mérimée
Dale, R. C. *The Poetics of Prosper Mérimée.* The Hague, 1966.

Zola
Schom, Alan. *Emile Zola: A Biography.* New York, 1988.

Maupassant
Lerner, M. G. *Maupassant.* New York, 1975.

Goncourt Brothers
Grant, R. A. *The Goncourt Brothers.* New York, 1972.

Daudet
Roche, A. V. *Alphonse Daudet*. Boston, 1976.

Taine
Weinstein, Leo. *Hippolyte Taine*. New York, 1972.

Scribe
Arvin, N. C. *Eugene Scribe and the French Theatre*. New York, 1967.

Marx
Carver, Terrell, ed. *The Cambridge Companion to Marx*. Cambridge, 1991.

Nietzsche
Hollingdale, R. J. *Nietzsche: The Man and His Philosophy*. Baton Rouge, LA, 1965.

Hauptmann
Garten, H. F. *Gerhart Hauptmann*. New Haven, CT, 1954.

Schnitzler
Swales, Martin. *Arthur Schnitzler: A Critical Study*. Oxford, 1971.

Rilke
Prater, D. A. *A Ringing Glass: The Life of Rainer Maria Rilke*. Oxford, 1986.

Pushkin
Magarshack, David. *Pushkin: A Biography*. New York, 1968.

Gogol
Troyat, Henri. *Divided Soul: The Life of Gogol*. New York, 1973.

Turgeniev
Zhitova, V. N. *The Turgeniev Family*. London, 1947.

Dostoevsky
Frank. Joseph. *Dostoevsky: The Stir of Liberation*. Princeton, NJ, 1986.
Grossman, L. P. *Dostoevsky: A Biography*. Indianapolis, IN, 1975.

Tolstoy
Crankshaw, Edward. *Tolstoy: The Making of a Novelist*. New York, 1974.

Lisle
Denomme, R. T. *Leconte de Lisle*. New York, 1973.

Hérédia
Harms, Alvin. *José-Maria de Hérédia*. Boston, 1975.

Baudelaire
Hemmings, F. W. *Baudelaire the Damned: A Biography*. New York, 1982.

Verlaine
Stephan, Philip. *Paul Verlaine and the Decadence, 1882–90*. Manchester, 1975.

Rimbaud
Houston, J. P. *The Design of Rimbaud's Poetry*. New Haven, CT, 1963.

Mallarmé
Cooperman, Hasye. *The Aesthetics of Stephane Mallarmé*. New York, 1971.

Maeterlinck
Halls, W. D. *Maurice Maeterlinck: A Study of His Life and Thought*. Oxford, 1960.

Proust
Shattuck, Roger. *Marcel Proust*. Princeton, NJ, 1982.

Ibsen
Beyer, Edvard, ed. *Contemporary Approaches to Ibsen*. Oslo, 1971.

Strindberg
Meyer, M. L. *Strindberg*, New York, 1985.

Chekhov
Hingley, Ronald. *A New Life of Anton Chekhov*. New York, 1976.

Kafka
Hayman, Ronald. *Kafka: A Biography*. Oxford, 1982.

Mann
McWilliams, J. R. *Brother Artist: A Psychological Study of Thomas Mann's Fiction*. New York, 1983.

Gide
Juan, E. S. *Transcending the Hero*. New York, 1988.

Gorky
Levin, Dan. *Stormy Petrel: The Life and Works of Maxim Gorky*. New York, 1986.

Pasternak
Gifford, Henry. *Boris Pasternak*. New York, 1977.

Solzhenitsyn
Ericson, E. E. *Solzhenitsyn: The Moral Vision*. New York, 1982.

INDEX